D1564708

Russia Enters
the Twentieth Century

1894–1917

Edited by
ERWIN OBERLÄNDER (Executive Editor)
GEORGE KATKOV
NIKOLAUS POPPE and
GEORG VON RAUCH

SCHOCKEN BOOKS · NEW YORK

The chapters by Lothar Schultz, Erwin Oberländer,
Karl C. Thalheim, Nikolaus Poppe, Hans Bräker,
Gerhard Simon, Helmut Dahm and Oskar Anweiler
were translated from the German by Gerald Onn.

Contents

Introduction   *page* 7

Russian foreign policy 1880–1914   9
GEORGE KATKOV and MICHAEL FUTRELL

Constitutional law in Russia   34
LOTHAR SCHULTZ

The role of the political parties   60
ERWIN OBERLÄNDER

Russia's economic development   85
KARL C. THALHEIM

The agrarian problem   111
HARRY T. WILLETTS

The economic and cultural development of Siberia   138
NIKOLAUS POPPE

The 'nationalities question' in the last phase of
tsardom   152
VIOLET CONOLLY

The Muslim revival in Russia   182
HANS BRÄKER

Church, state and society   199
GERHARD SIMON

The outlook for philosophy and the fate of the
Slavophil Utopia   236
HELMUT DAHM

Russian literature from 1890 to 1917   *page* 263
ELISABETH STENBOCK-FERMOR

Russian schools   287
OSKAR ANWEILER

Notes   314
Select bibliography   333
The authors   339
Index   340

The dates in this book are based on the Julian calendar, which was used in Russia up to 1 February 1918. The corresponding Gregorian values can be obtained by adding twelve days to the nineteenth and thirteen days to the twentieth century Julian dates.

In the chapter on 'Church, state and society' the office described as that of 'Director General' of the 'Holy Synod' is the one commonly translated as 'Chief Procurator'.

Introduction

The history of victorious revolutions is written by the victors. This axiom applies not only to the revolution itself but also to the period immediately preceding it, which is made to appear in historical retrospect as a predisposing factor. Without exception, Soviet historians have treated the reign of Nicholas II (1894–1917) in this way.

This is not to say that Soviet historians have not made a significant contribution to our understanding of different aspects of this period. We are particularly indebted to them for the discovery and publication of previously unknown source material relating to various specific spheres, such as foreign policy and social history. But all Soviet research into Russian history prior to 1917 is based on the assumption that 'the victorious October revolution' was 'the inevitable outcome of the whole socio-economic and political development of the country, the inevitable outcome of the tireless work and the struggle of the Communist Party that was created and led by Lenin'. This is how the authors of the recent twelve-volume *History of the USSR* summed up the development of Russian history immediately prior to the October revolution. And if we take a look at the innumerable Soviet publications which appeared on the hundredth anniversary of Lenin's birth (22 April 1970) we find that he has been represented, not only as the great leader of the international proletariat, but also as the only man capable of saving Russia.

This kind of approach to history has two principal characteristics. On the one hand, it disregards or distorts anything that does not fit in with the Soviet conception of the inevitability of the October revolution; while on the other hand it vastly overrates anything that confirms, or appears to confirm, this thesis. Inevitably, this has led to the creation of a legend centred on Lenin and the Bolsheviks, whose party is shown proceeding step by step to its preordained victory. Consequently, all other Russian parties—several of which, including some left-wing groups, were more important than the Bolsheviks prior to the election of the Constituent Assembly at the end of 1917—are blandly dismissed as petit-bourgeois or reactionary. Moreover, new and important developments in the philosophical, pedagogical and literary spheres, which were alien or in some cases diametrically opposed to the Marxist-Leninist creed, are described as morbid symptoms of a decadent society, while pre-revolutionary reforms in the economic sphere, such as P. A. Stolypin's agrarian reform, appear to the Soviet historian as anachronisms that were doomed to failure from the outset.

Although this one-sided interpretation of pre-revolutionary Russia was intended primarily for home consumption, it has undoubtedly influenced the popular view of the period held in other countries as well. It would be quite wrong, of course, to replace this one-sided negative assessment by an equally one-sided positive assessment. Whether Russia passed through a 'silver age' between 1900 and 1914 and whether, but for the war, this would have justified the great promise which it seemed to hold out, are questions that have often been discussed. But, although the proposition is by no means unattractive, enquiries conducted along these lines are essentially hypothetical.

The contributors to this present volume are not primarily concerned either with the detailed ramifications of the Soviet legend or with the varying perspectives of the 'silver age'. Their object has been to provide the reader with an accurate account of this important period of Russian history which, although greatly prejudiced by the government's failure to introduce adequate and timely reforms, was by no means predisposed to a Bolshevist future. If they have succeeded in conveying an impression of the complex nature of this transitional phase, they will be well satisfied. It would, of course, also be highly desirable if this volume were to lead to further research into this period. The findings of such enquiries might then provide the material for a further volume.

Russian foreign policy 1880—1914*

GEORGE KATKOV AND MICHAEL FUTRELL

In the five centuries of Russian history leading to the period under consideration (1880–1914) two basic tendencies stand out: a strengthening of the central power in home affairs, and a steady expansion—both territorial and diplomatic—in foreign affairs. By the end of the nineteenth century, these tendencies were becoming less pronounced. The emergence of institutions of local government and the increasing demand for constitutional limitation on autocratic centralism were rapidly changing the political scene at home. In foreign politics, expansion had reached the shores of the Pacific Ocean, the edges of the Chinese empire and of the British sphere of interest in Central Asia and Transcaspia.

These two basic tendencies (centralisation and expansion) profoundly affected the ideas Russian statesmen had of their tasks and duties to their country. However, such teleological concepts as the 'destiny' of a nation or state and its fulfilment, or even the 'vital interests' of a country, are of a different type than purely descriptive characteristics, such as size, frontiers, population and so on. What the destiny of a nation is cannot be ascertained by any objective procedure, and depends fundamentally on what the people believing in it desire or fear it to be.

In the last resort, the question of what the vital interests of the country were, and what was to be regarded as the fulfilment of its destiny, lay entirely with the monarch who, at least in theory, was completely free to decide what course of action should be taken in any particular case. In this sense, it would be no oversimplification to say that the vital interests of Russia and its

---

* In this essay the authors have limited their task to one aspect of Russian foreign relations—the character and mechanism of political decision, and political initiative in the specific frame of an autocratic bureaucracy such as existed in Russia at that time.

destiny were what they appeared to be in the eyes of the Tsar. He was, however, neither an ideological high priest nor an oracle of historiosophic divination. He believed, as most people did then, that he should serve the interests of his country, which, according to the naïve conception of the time, could be determined objectively, and that he should lead the country along the path of its historical fulfilment. In order to find out what these vital interests were, he appointed advisers and consulted people of different opinions, among them his ministers. The advice of these ministers, however, had no particular status: they were appointed to carry out the Tsar's will, not to mould it. Should his decision go against the advice of the minister, this was no reason for him to resign. Even when a minister would claim that he could not carry on because he felt that he had lost the confidence of the monarch, a simple statement that this was not the case, sometimes reinforced by a public utterance, or the award of a distinction, would make it practically impossible for the minister to insist on his retirement. This was the practice in all branches of Russian administration. For the Ministry of Foreign Affairs it was of particular significance. Furthermore, the appointment of ambassadors always remained a prerogative of the Tsar, although their work was coordinated and their instructions drafted by the Minister of Foreign Affairs.

Again, the Tsar, though using his ministers and diplomats in relations with other countries, also maintained direct communications with the heads of other states, especially those with whom family relations existed. At times, such private communications could be helpful to the respective ministers of foreign affairs; but they could also become an extremely confusing factor, especially when the minister was not consulted, or even not informed about such private negotiations.

A further difficulty lay in the lack of coordination between the policies of various ministries, which often encroached on each other. Russia did not have a system of cabinet ministers under an imperial chancellor, as did Germany, or under a prime minister, as did parliamentary states. There was a coordinating body known as the Committee of Ministers, but it was of very minor importance. The real coordination and the resolution of conflicts between ministries rested with the Tsar. As far as the Ministry of

Foreign Affairs was concerned, the other ministries with which it could easily get into conflict were naturally the service ministries, that is War and Navy, and also the Ministry of Finance, which under Vyshnegradsky and Witte, assumed ever-increasing importance.

At a time when major wars represent such incalculable risks that almost any other solution appears better and more justifiable, we might easily forget that, in the last quarter of the nineteenth and at the beginning of our century, war, and even unprovoked aggressive war, was considered a legitimate means for a civilised state to achieve its political ends. This principle, sometimes referred to as the principle of freedom of action, would have led in a short time to the elimination of the sovereignty of small states and to the establishment of an incontestable hegemony by one of the large ones, had it not been restricted by alliances and treaties which gave to the smaller states some guarantee of quasi-independence, and prevented too frequent clashes between the large ones. Strange as it may now seem, such treaties were held by all parties to be really binding, and violations of treaties were, on the whole, rare. Accordingly, treaties concluded in this period were usually short-term agreements, promising the neutrality or assistance of one power to the other in specified circumstances, and not general agreements of friendship and non-aggression. Such treaties could be kept secret by mutual agreement, or could be widely publicised, depending on the effect they were intended to have on third parties. A unilateral repudiation of such an agreement was a grave matter, harmful to the political credit of the offending state. As far as Russia was concerned, the continuity of the régime and the dynasty was the main guarantee of their inviolability.

From the Dreikaiserbund *to the Franco-Russian Alliance*

The greatest strategist on the chessboard of contractual diplomacy was beyond any doubt Bismarck. Having wielded the weapon of war three times in his career, after exact and accurate calculations of the risks involved, Bismarck spent the rest of his activity as a statesman in securing, through the conclusion of appropriate treaties, an order in Europe which would make war unnecessary for Germany, and undesirable for the other larger states. This task was the more formidable because Bismarck had himself contributed to the creation of two centres of unrest in Europe, by the brutal annexation of Alsace-Lorraine, and by the frustration of the Russian empire at the Congress of Berlin after its victory over Turkey, achieved through enormous sacrifices. He had imposed his will in 1871 by military action, in 1878 by cunning diplomacy, and he was naturally apprehensive that France and Russia might join their efforts in seeking to reverse the situation. In France, the strength of the *revanchiste* feeling was such that it threatened the German empire with a new war. The only means to meet this eventuality was to increase the defence potential of Germany, and finally, if the constant pressure from France would not abate, to inflict on France a new defeat which would eliminate it as a great power. But such a course was only possible, without unreasonable risk, if Russian neutrality could be secured.

In the Balkans, the danger of an armed conflict lay in the rivalry between the Russian and the Austro-Hungarian empires for influence and preponderance. Austria had proved an unreliable and timorous ally of Russia both in the 1856–7 war and in 1877–8. It was competing with Russia for the spoils of the decomposing Ottoman empire, and therein lay the possibility of major conflict.

The method followed by Bismarck in dealing with these two main problems in the course of the 1870s was the maintenance of the so-called *Dreikaiserbund*. This was not based on a formal treaty, although a protocol embodying its principles was signed by the representatives of the three powers in 1879. It was rather a tacit agreement to follow a certain course of action in certain circumstances. The main point was the engagement of each of the three powers to maintain a benevolent neutrality if one of the others should get involved in a conflict with another great power, and to exert influence to reduce and liquidate such a conflict. The principle was that the three emperors had such strong common interests in maintaining the monarchic principle and in supporting their dynastic stability that conflicts which might lead to war between them could practically be disregarded.

The tragic death of Alexander II on 2 March 1881 brought a new Tsar who felt no compulsion to carry on the political traditions initiated by his predecessors. Even so, Alexander III was not a man to break with tradition abruptly. He took over the ministers of his father, including Giers, head of the Asian department of the Ministry of Foreign Affairs, who was in charge of the ministry during the absence of Gorchakov, and did not prevent him carrying on the complicated negotiations for the formalisation of the *Dreikaiserbund*. At the same time, he tried to impress on his ministers his own ideas about the part Russia should play in the world, ideas which were the result of his education under K. P. Pobedonostsev, of his reading the works of and his personal acquaintance with Dostoyevsky, and of the constant influence of Pobedonostsev's friend, M. N. Katkov, whose leading articles in the *Moskovskiye vedomosti* were the daily comment on current affairs which he regularly read.

The draft on which Giers and the Russian ambassador in Berlin, Saburov, had been working, gave the new Tsar no cause for disagreement. It asserted the principle of the closure of the Black Sea Straits to foreign warships by the Turks, under the threat that if the Turks were to open the Straits they would be regarded as being in a state of war with Russia and the guarantee of the *status quo* of their empire provided in the Treaty of Berlin would be withdrawn. On the other hand, the principle of benevolent neutrality in any conflict of one of the three contracting powers with a fourth great power was maintained, thus leaving Germany a free hand in its dealings with France. This Giers considered a proper *quid pro quo*, balancing the advantages provided in the treaty to Russia and to Germany.

As regards Austria, finalising the treaty was more difficult. Saburov drafted an annexe to the treaty about the demarcation of spheres of influence in the Balkans between Russia and Austria; but Austria had far-reaching plans to which Russia was not ready to agree, and in the end the protocol listing the specific problems connected with Russian and Austrian influences in the Balkans was dropped. The treaty was concluded on 18 June 1881, in the form prepared before the accession of Alexander III, with a relatively harmless annex providing for Russian toleration of the annexation of Bosnia and Herzegovina, and for the unification of Bulgaria which had been split in two by the Treaty of Berlin.

This was the first major document worked out by Giers as acting Foreign Minister. Giers was a very different type of bureaucrat from his predecessors, Gorchakov and Nesselrode. He came from a comparatively poor noble family of Swedish extraction, and could never assert himself in court and aristocratic circles. In his policy, he was extremely cautious and conservative. The *Dreikaiserbund* was and remained for him, until almost the end of his activity, the cornerstone of his diplomatic constructions. He refused to see that the principle had outlived itself, even when Bismarck was ready to give it up. As a second best he accepted, and made Alexander III accept, the conception embodied in the so-called Reinsurance Treaty, which was a bipartite agreement between Russia and Germany. In order to maintain this agreement, he was always ready to make concessions to the partners in the *Dreikaiserbund*, and this exasperated those in Russia who thought that an active and even aggressive foreign policy should go hand in hand with the rapid economic and social development of the country.

The treaty of 18 June 1881 remained secret for several years. But the constant complications arising in the Balkans acted as a testing-ground of Russian foreign policy, and revealed to the public the general principles which guided the policy of Giers.

We cannot here follow the winding course of Balkan affairs in 1881–7. Throughout these years it was Giers who always maintained the importance of the *Dreikaiserbund* and who renewed it in 1884. At that time the friction between Russia and Austria had not yet reached a critical state. In 1886, however, a crisis emerged. A short war had taken place between Serbia and Bulgaria in 1885, when Austria clearly showed its sympathies for the régime which it supported in Serbia, and prevented the Bulgarian ruler, Prince Alexander of Battenberg, from exploiting the initial victory he had won over the Serbian army. Battenberg himself had been kidnapped and removed by a pro-Russian faction of his officers, but made an attempt to return to Bulgaria from Austrian territory.

It was then that informed public opinion in Russia began to suspect that something was amiss with the foreign policy of the country; bound by treaties and agreements, the enormous realm had lost its 'freedom of action' and could not bring the weight of all its power behind the decisions which appeared to many as necessary and vital. The spokesman of these people and their inspired propagandist was the publicist, M. N. Katkov, whose interference in Russian state affairs in the years 1885–7 was totally unprecedented. The power which he exerted was not so much the result of an impetuous but lucid criticism of the country's foreign affairs, but rather the fact that it was read with interest and sympathy by the Tsar himself.

Giers, who disliked Alexander III for his bouts of temper and his intellectual slowness, was too meek and too unsure of himself to use his position in favour of a policy which was contrary to the desires of the Tsar. Other people, with a stronger position in Russian society than Giers, undertook with his knowledge, to force Russian policy on to a course which Alexander III disliked. The Russian ambassador in Berlin, Count Pavel Shuvalov, had a brother, Pyotr Shuvalov, who, after having been ambassador in London, lived in semi-retirement in St Petersburg. Pyotr Shuvalov enjoyed the confidence of the Grand Duke Vladimir, the Tsar's brother and was, like his brother (the ambassador in Berlin), a strong supporter of German–Russian friendship. Ostensibly, Giers asked Count Pyotr Shuvalov to sound the ground in Berlin, as to whether a letter from Alexander III to the two other emperors, expressing his disapproval of an eventual return of Battenberg to Bulgaria, would be received favourably in Berlin and Vienna. In fact, Pyotr Shuvalov went much farther than that in his contacts with the German Secretary of Foreign Affairs, Herbert Bismarck, son of the Chancellor. He produced a memorandum proposing the conclusion of a treaty between Russia and Germany.

In spite of the success of the Shuvalov mission, as far as Battenberg was concerned, the buccaneering diplomacy of Count Pyotr Shuvalov alarmed Giers considerably, and not without reason. When, on 17 January 1887, Giers presented his routine report, the Tsar rejected all plans of alliance, either one between the three emperors or a bipartite one with Germany. Doubtless this resistance was due to the pressure of public opinion, led and expressed by Katkov, as well as to the direct impact of the latter's views on Alexander III.

It soon became clear that Katkov was advocating not only a personal change in the Ministry of Foreign Affairs, but a total change in the orientation of Russian foreign policy. His attacks on the Ministry of Foreign Affairs culminated in his article on 20 March 1887 in which he divulged the existence of the *Dreikaiserbund*, and demanded its abrogation:

In order to see clearly the actual situation, one should consider that this March will expire the Triple Alliance [i.e., the *Dreikaiserbund*], which has been so detrimental to Russia, which was forced upon her at the time of her humiliation for a period of three years, and which was secretly renewed in 1884 for a further three years. The very fact of the existence of a written treaty was not known for sure. Only recently has one begun to realise its content, and to understand why the authority of Russia has fallen so low, why it is losing more and more the character of an independent power, and why it has been increasingly eliminated from the East.[1]

Russia, Katkov concluded, should recover her freedom of action, and be free to enter into alliance with any other power of her choice. Everybody in Russia understood what this meant. For the past two years, Katkov's pro-French attitude had been known and it had also been known that it found an echo in France itself. On the publication of Katkov's article of 20 March, Giers immediately called the Tsar's attention to the fact that a private person, without any position in the state hierarchy, had divulged to the public the existence of a secret treaty. Alexander III was furious, and wanted to give an official forewarning to Katkov's paper; under Russian laws on the press this was a severe penalty, and threatened the paper with closure. It is significant, however, that after intercession by Pobedonostsev, the Tsar withdrew his threat, and gave only a private warning to Katkov. He even received him in audience. He explained to Katkov that he depended on Giers because of his quiet and persistent nature, without trying to justify the basis of Giers' policy. What he said was tantamount to claiming that he fully realised that a better policy could be evolved but that the technical ability and reliability of his minister made him tolerate a course which he would prefer to be corrected. Giers, however, was not prepared to make any concessions. He refused to see Katkov, told the Emperor so, and redoubled his efforts to get the *Dreikaiserbund* renewed in the immediate future.

But Giers did not know of all the difficulties which he was to encounter and which finally forced him to accept as a second best the bipartite agreement with Germany, the so-called

Reinsurance Treaty. The main difficulty consisted in the fact that Russia and its monarch had never been properly informed of the character of the German–Austrian Alliance signed in 1879. According to this treaty, Germany was to go to the assistance of Austria in the event of a conflict with Russia.

No wonder that Bismarck was embarrassed at disclosing the existence of the Austro-German Treaty to Pavel Shuvalov when the latter pressed him to give a guarantee of German neutrality in case of a Russian–Austrian conflict. And when he did so, the impression produced on Pavel Shuvalov was disastrous, for he immediately understood what the reaction of the Emperor to these disclosures would be, and how the position of Katkov and the opponents of the Russo-German alliance would be reinforced. It was at that precise moment that the Russian ambassador in Paris, Mohrenheim, reported that a letter was in circulation in Paris which showed that Katkov had intervened in favour of the replacement of the French Foreign Minister, Freycinet, by Floquet. Although Katkov managed to bring conclusive evidence that there never had been such a letter and that it was a forgery, the spell of Katkov's personality on the Tsar was broken, and the Tsar was now open to persuasion by his Minister of Foreign Affairs. An amended clause to the Bipartite Treaty was worked out by Giers and Pavel Shuvalov, and finally, on 18 June 1887, the treaty with Germany with a 'very secret' additional protocol was signed, for a period of three years.

For Bismarck, the treaty securing Russian neutrality in case of war with France (unless France was attacked) was of considerable advantage. Germany promised neutrality in case of war between Russia and third powers, except if it resulted from a Russian attack on Austria. The value of this latter clause was somewhat dubious because of the difficulty of assessing who the aggressor was. In addition, Germany recognised Russian interests in the Balkans and especially in Bulgaria, agreed to oppose the restoration of Battenberg, and went as far as to promise diplomatic support if Russia should find it necessary to secure the Black Sea Straits—'the key to its empire'. The latter addendum was made on the initiative of Shuvalov and was readily agreed to by Bismarck who always wanted Russian expansionist tendencies channelled towards geographical points where they would alarm the British.

Katkov died on 1 August 1887. Giers lived on, but only to see the total futility of his diplomatic efforts. After Bismarck had resigned, negotiations on the extension of the Reinsurance Treaty (1890) were suspended, and Wilhelm's new advisers prevailed upon him to go back upon his previous decision to renew the treaty. And so Giers found himself in possession of that freedom of action which he feared so much and which Katkov had been trying for a time to press on him. It is one of the ironies of history that it fell to Giers to use this freedom of action in exactly the way his enemy had advised him some five years before, namely in order to enter into a cordial understanding and then a far-reaching military agreement with France. Characteristically, and in sharp contrast to Giers' disappointment, Alexander III learned of the demise of the Reinsurance Treaty with complete equanimity.[2]

We have surveyed some of the diplomatic developments of the reign of Alexander III from a point of view which makes the crisis of 1887 outstanding among all other crises of that period. This is because, at that time, there was the possibility of a choice between two different courses of Russian foreign policy which did not exist either before or after. One would have expected that, in an autocratic régime, the decision would have depended on the character and the convictions of the monarch. What we saw was something very different. At the critical moment, the forces which were acting in opposing ways on the will of the Tsar, began working against each other on other battlefields, no longer in the mind of the Tsar. Those who were insisting on the resumption of 'liberty of action' in Russian foreign affairs appealed to the weak and unorganised but nevertheless vocal public opinion in Russia; those who were against it worked underground, using the secrecy of diplomatic démarches for their private initiatives (for instance, Count Pyotr Shuvalov's mission in Berlin, December 1886). In this struggle the decisive factor was not the irresistible pressure of demographic and economic determinants, but the persistence and the skill of those manipulating political intrigue. Under a less authoritarian régime, the struggle between the factions, which crystallised around the decision on the course of Russian foreign policy, might easily have developed into a long-drawn-out internal strife which could well have sapped the energies of the nation at a time when it was undergoing very considerable changes in its internal structure, and had embarked on a course of rapid economic and subsequently political development. Owing to the autocratic régime, the struggle was cut short. The Tsar upheld the policy of his Foreign Minister, but only outwardly; he never believed in the antiquated concept after which Giers was so pathetically groping.

On the other hand, he made no rapid moves in the opposite direction. He probably believed that the Bipartite Treaty had been promoted by Bismarck (there is no evidence of his knowledge of the Shuvalov démarche) so that its rejection would be understood as an inimical gesture against his venerable uncle, the old Kaiser Wilhelm. He seems also to have believed that Bismarck would not rashly have recourse to open warfare in order to consolidate and increase the empire which he had created, unless he was tempted to do so by an opportunity which promised almost certain success. The Tsar of Russia could therefore bide his time, until he learned, in 1890, that the odium of repudiating the old monarchic friendship had fallen onto the young and unbalanced German, Wilhelm II. None the less, he was worried that this change presaged a less cautious, more adventurous, more irresponsible German policy than that pursued under Bismarck. We can therefore conclude that although the crisis of 1887 had shown how dangerous private initiative in state affairs could become for such a political structure as the Russian autocracy, the danger was on the whole overcome and neutralised by the phlegmatic, slow, and basically unexcitable character of Alexander III.

New initiatives

The conclusion of the Franco–Russian Alliance (1894) and the signing of the military agreement between the two countries coincided with the end of the collaboration between Tsar Alexander III and his only Minister of Foreign Affairs, Giers. The latter survived his august master by only a few months. The new international situation created by the abandonment of the Reinsurance Treaty with Germany led to what had been called 'freedom of action' for Russia and answered, on the whole, the aspirations of the educated classes in Russia. If right-wing public opinion as represented by Katkov had found it unbearable to see Russian foreign policy controlled by Bismarck, it would have been even less tolerant of the interference of the jumpy and jerky politics of Wilhelm II and those who chose to serve him. All shades of progressive and even radical public opinion could only welcome a closer contact with a republican France, commonly held to be the cradle of progressive radicalism.[3]

As the new trend of Russian foreign policy continued under Nicholas II (1894–1917) and his advisers, it was deeply affected by the emergence of three new factors. One was the rapid development of railway communications on as yet virgin soil, and the ensuing economic changes. This concerned the building of railways, not only inside the empire but also in bordering countries. Much of the rivalry with Austria–Hungary stemmed from the problem of railway building in the Balkans and beyond. Even graver were the consequences of building a railway system in the Far East. In these operations the Russian system had to deal with private capital, and only gradually learned the principles on which a sound financial basis for railway enterprises should be based. Railway building was one of the most attractive ways of getting quick and high returns on invested capital, and no wonder that these operations attracted hot money and often led to abuses and corruption. Moreover, it was not always clear where the interests of the state lay: conflicting points of view, frequently represented by various government departments, led to different conclusions as to the desirability of a railway project. There were the economic considerations: the opening-up of new natural resources to meet the rapidly increasing industrial and commercial needs and the intensification of foreign trade. On the other hand, there were strategic considerations, considerations of security, and colonial policy. Solving such problems required considerable technical knowledge and strength of character, especially as those persons with whom decisions rested were under pressure from powerful economic interests and, to put it simply, unlimited human greed.

The second factor was also of a technological character. The end of the nineteenth century was marked by a rapid development of the destructive power of the instruments of war. Although for us this is dwarfed by what happened in the following decades, the invention at the turn of the century of new explosives like dynamite and smokeless powder, the construction of new types of rifles and of quick-firing guns and the advent of heavy artillery on land, required a new approach to the problem of war. An alternative to decision by force of arms, threatening ever-increasing suffering and destruction, seemed desirable to many.

The third factor was itself of a political kind. The rapid Europeanisation of Japan, its tendency to expand and seek a foothold on the continent and the ensuing wars with China and Korea, and finally the Boxer Uprising, created an entirely new situation and fixed the attention of Russian foreign policy on the Far East.

Nicholas II, although conscious of these three factors, was not always able to handle the situation. The interplay of conflicting commercial interests and the complicated financial manipulations connected with railway building were often beyond his understanding. The new forms of corruption and predatory acquisitiveness manifested in ways not always illegal, escaped him as well as many of the economists of his day. The emergence of new possessors of enormous fortunes, who were able to press the defence of their economic interests on official circles, was a relatively new phenomenon in Russia. After the reforms of the sixties, Russia could pride itself on having got rid of bribery in its judicial system completely, and in its administrative apparatus to a large extent. But dishonest acquisitiveness emerged in big business, in deliveries to service departments and to the state in general, in concessions for the exploitation of mineral wealth and in the building of railways. The only way the new Tsar could ward off these dangers was to limit the choice of his personal advisers to the narrow circle of aristocratic families known to him and his father, of whom it was believed that their sense of personal honour, of devotion to the interests of the state and to the monarch, as well as their financial independence, would be a sort of guarantee against their succumbing to new and unheard-of temptations. Intellectual accomplishment, cleverness, even standards of education, seemed in these circumstances to be of relatively lesser importance.

The new Tsar was soon faced with a problem posed by Russia's regaining freedom of action. As soon as the young Tsar had completed his official European tour, pressure was put on him to try to solve the problem of the Black Sea Straits. On a visit home, the Russian ambassador in Constantinople, Nelidov, pointed out that he could easily provoke some disturbance in Constantinople which would justify the landing of Russian troops and the seizure of the northern banks of the Bosphorus. Plans for such an amphibious operation had been worked out by the Russian General Staff some time before. The Russo-German Reinsurance Treaty had contained the so-called double-bottomed clause, according to which Germany would support the neutral-isation of the Straits, but in case Russia should find it necessary to seize 'the key of its home' Germany would maintain a benevolent neutrality. So Nelidov's project had a certain historical back-ground. It was discussed between the Tsar, the Chief of the General Staff (General Obruchev), the acting Minister of Foreign Affairs (Shishkin), Count Witte, and both service ministers (1896). The general opinion was in favour of Nelidov's project. Witte was the only one to raise objections and he insisted that they be attached to the minutes of the discussion. He foresaw possible international complications, such as the simultaneous seizure of the Dardanelles by Britain and Italy. Furthermore he doubted France's sympathetic attitude, for as one of the principal creditors of Turkey she would dislike infringements on Turkish sovereignty. Although the Tsar agreed with the majority opinion, Nelidov's project never materialised and no order was issued to move troops to Constantinople. Witte in his memoirs tends to ascribe the young Tsar's change of mind to the influence of Pobedonostsev, to whom Witte had denounced the Nelidov plan.

The discussions concerning the possible consequences of a Russian seizure of the Bosphorus, the rather childish though patronising letters of Kaiser Wilhelm containing all sorts of proposals for grand alliances of great powers, and the impression produced by the Spanish–American War must have brought to the mind of the Tsar the possibility of a large military conflict on a world scale with incalculable consequences and unprecedented suffering for humanity. By March 1898 his Minister of Foreign Affairs, Count M. N. Muravyev, began to work out the project which resulted in the note to the great powers of 12 August 1898, in which the Emperor of Russia asked all countries represented in

St Petersburg to take part in a conference for the purpose of discussing the possibility of arms limitation.

Various theories have been put forward to explain this surprising initiative of the young Tsar. Among those who might have influenced Nicholas II's decision are mentioned his Minister of War, Kuropatkin, who was concerned over the introduction of quick-firing guns in the Austro-Hungarian armed forces. Others connect it with the six-volume work on the war of the future by the banker and railway promoter, Bliokh, which was published about that time and was known to the Tsar.

However, not only the content but the very wording of the two notes with which the Russian Foreign Minister invited the other powers to join in the discussion concerning the limitation of arms, reminds us of something which must have been familiar to Nicholas II and especially to his mentor and tutor, K. P. Pobedonostsev. Comparing the diplomatic notes with the apparently casual aside in an article by Dostoyevsky of 1873, entitled 'Day-Dreams and Reflections' and included in his *Diary of a Writer*, one will easily find the source for Nicholas' conception. In the same article by Dostoyevsky one finds the argument that the cost of military security, as well as the cost of railway systems, are incommensurably heavier in such a widely spread country as Russia than in any of its potential military rivals.

The initiative of Nicholas II was both premature and possibly even naïve. It met with the scorn and indignation of those on whom the success of the conference depended, and with the enthusiasm and meddlesome support of pacifists of all shades, who were incapable of breaking the resistance of institutionalised authority.[4] However, the simple logic of the initial documents, and the fear of letting the initiative of new forms of international relations slip out of their hands, induced the participants in the Hague Conference of 1899 and its successor, the Conference of 1907, to work out certain codes and conventions which might still become the prototype of a future organisation of international relations. In any case, Nicholas II's initiative was directly responsible for the establishment of the first all-embracing international permanent legal institution—the Hague International Court of Justice.

Russia and the Far East

For the first ten or twelve years of his reign, Nicholas II seems to have been more or less his own Minister for Foreign Affairs. The nominal holders of this office, Prince Lobanov-Rostovsky and M. N. Muravyev, stayed for relatively short times in the post, and complied with the tradition of being the mere executors of the instructions of the monarch. The main decisions which were to be taken were concerned with the direction of the Far Eastern policy in the troubled nineties. Japan's increasing pressure on China made it necessary to give support to the quiescent and archaic Chinese empire. The threat of an Anglo-Japanese agreement intensified the desire to counterbalance it by new engagements with European powers having an interest in the Far East. The pro-Chinese attitude of Russia in the early nineties was abandoned after the outbreak of the Boxer Uprising, when Russia aligned herself with other European powers and joined the expeditionary force sent to relieve the siege of the Peking diplomatic compounds. This resulted in a number of seizures or leases of Chinese territory and concessions to European powers, each of which had its specific diplomatic and strategic aspect. As far as the Russian empire was concerned, the advance on Peking resulted in the occupation of the enormous but sparsely populated wastes of Manchuria. At the same time, the opportunity was taken to occupy the ice-free ports of Port Arthur and Dalny. The first was to become a naval and land fortress, the second was intended to be a large commercial port. The European powers followed jealously each other's moves in Asia, trying to balance out the advantages which their intervention in the chaotic affairs of China permitted them to gain.

But far more important than a military occupation was the economic penetration, the establishment of concessions for building railways, for exploiting minerals, for cutting and exporting timber. The initiative lay often with private entrepreneurs, who tried to interest foreign investors and also pressed the various government departments for material and moral support and even for military help in securing these large-scale undertakings in the Far East. These activities also did not pass unnoticed by

the European powers, nor the Japanese government. The promoters and initiators of Russian economic concessions were later
accused of having provoked the Japanese and causing the
disasters of the Russo–Japanese War. This so-called scapegoat
theory appears, after a dispassionate investigation, exaggerated
to a large extent. True, some of these promoters known as the
Bezobrazov group, supported their claims for government aid
with somewhat fantastic ideological and strategic arguments:
according to their geo-political theory, the future of Russia was
in Asia, because Russia was essentially an Asiatic country. But
however unrealistic and dreamlike the ideas of a Bezobrazov
concerning camouflaged Russian military penetration may have
been, there was nothing essentially unsound in many of the
economic projects themselves, as more recent research tends to
show.[5] What is of far greater consequence is that the most
important sponsor of economic penetration was none of these
amateur financier businessmen, but the formidable Minister of
Finance, S. Yu. Witte (1849–1915) himself.

Witte—one of the most controversial figures of modern Russian
history—tried in his much-quoted memoirs to project an image
of himself for future generations which would make him appear a
paragon of honesty, modesty, humanitarianism, devotion to his
country and his monarch. This was to conceal his unsatisfied
longing for public admiration, honours and social status. Witte
comes into our story with only a small part of his many-sided
activities. He had never been foreign minister nor was he a regular
adviser of the Tsar on diplomacy. And yet hardly any of the
Tsar's ministers had more of an effect on the international
position of Russia. The acme of his career was the conclusion of
the peace negotiations with Japan, conducted in America at
Portsmouth (Maine); after this he dominated the political scene
in Russia and was awarded the coveted title of Count.

Witte had begun his career by building and exploiting railways
run by private firms whose modern economics he closely studied.
After serving as head of the department of railway communications, he followed I. A. Vyshnegradsky as Finance Minister.
Under Vyshnegradsky and Witte the Ministry of Finance became the centre of official political activity in Russia. By a
sustained effort, they managed to bring order into the Russian

finances, to restore the gold standard of the rouble, and to secure a flow of foreign capital in the form of state and private loans to Russia. Securing loans was naturally connected with diplomatic negotiations of far-reaching consequences.

Under Vyshnegradsky and especially under Witte, the Ministry of Finance which, under their predecessor, Bunge, used to be the bureaucratic administration of the state exchequer, became a kind of banking house, supporting or opposing various private enterprises, and using the enormous resources of the state for such far-reaching undertakings as the building of the Trans-Siberian and Chinese Eastern railways. All such operations under Witte were carried out rather high-handedly, and without sufficient coordination with the other branches of the imperial administration. Thus when, under the pressure of the British government, the Ministry of Foreign Affairs in 1898 was about to agree to a delimitation line in China, south of which the Russians would not claim any interest in the development of Chinese railways, it became unexpectedly known that the Russo-Chinese Bank, which operated with the support of the Ministry of Finance, had already acquired important concessions far beyond the delimitation line agreed to by the Ministry of Foreign Affairs.[6]

A further powerful means of exerting pressure was the right of the Ministry of Finance to agree to the ever-growing demands of the defence departments, although here the respective service ministers could, and often did, appeal to the Tsar for support. Using the enormous power in his hands, Witte furthered his own scheme of Russian expansion towards ice-free ports in China. His favourite project was that of the Chinese Eastern railway. This brought him into conflict with other competing projects, especially those directed towards Korea. When he later put forward the 'scapegoat theory' of the Russo-Japanese conflict, accusing the Bezobrazov clique of adventurous and bellicose activities, this was very much the case of the pot calling the kettle black. However this may be, it is still highly probable that war did not come as a result of Russian provocation but of a feeling in Japan that the time had come to make its presence felt on the Asiatic continent as a desirable technological and economic ally and militarily mature great power. Besides, Bezobrazov had already been eclipsed when, to his own surprise and that of the world at large, Witte was removed from his post of Minister of Finance and appointed to the honorific but hardly influential position of chairman of the Committee of Ministers.

Witte's departure from the Ministry of Finance was, apart from a concentrated intrigue against him, the result of a latent lack of confidence between the Tsar and himself, of which subsequent events furnish more evidence. Witte did not conceal his feelings from the Tsar, saying that although he would be ready to serve in the humblest position, he thought he could be of greatest use as Minister of Finance. Witte's removal was connected with plans for a new administration of the Russian Far Eastern provinces. Admiral Alekseyev, viceroy of the Far East, was to obtain wide powers at the expense of the authority of the St Petersburg ministers. Even diplomatic exchanges and the command of troops were at one time to be entrusted to him. He was to report to the Tsar, and obtain advice and directives after the Tsar had consulted his advisers.

The Ministry of Finance was then entrusted to Pleske, an honest bureaucrat of the traditional type, which meant a return to the times when the Minister of Finance was no more than the state cashier. Witte, in his position of chairman of the Committee of Ministers, continued to be influential. Count Lamsdorf, who took over the Ministry of Foreign Affairs after the death of Muravyov (1900), was ready to follow Witte's advice, and Witte's monetary and fiscal reforms remained a lasting and beneficial factor in Russian economics.

There was certainly no last-minute blunder which plunged Russia into the ill-fated war with Japan. There remained no diplomatic way of closing the gap between Russian and Japanese conceptions of future development in Manchuria and Korea. The only surprise was a tactical one, when the Japanese navy attacked the Russian naval squadron at Port Arthur before a formal declaration of war. Russia ran the war against Japan as a colonial war. Units deployed on the western frontier were used sparingly so as not to weaken Russia's position in the west. Slow communications on the partially completed Trans-Siberian Railway also contributed to the tactics of 'too little and too late' which characterised Kuropatkin's strategy and led to humiliating setbacks. But even so, as the Japanese clearly understood, it was always possible for Russia to increase its effort and redeem the situation on land. On sea, however, the Japanese position was dominating. Excellent port facilities in home waters, short lines of communication, modern equipment, and the sense of fighting at their own threshold, gave the Japanese advantages far exceeding the oft-mentioned higher speed of their warships.

The Tsushima naval disaster left no doubt that, despite a possible Russian victory on land, the naval situation made all Russian geo-political dreams of expansion in the Pacific unreal for a long time to come. The Japanese government, whose estimate of the situation was sober, approached the President of the USA with a request to act as a mediator in peace negotiations, provided he would agree to do so entirely on his 'own initiative'. In Russia, the military wanted at least one redeeming victory on land, while other ministers dreaded excessive and humiliating Japanese demands, which Russia should not consider before making a supreme effort in the war. On the other hand, they realised that the internal situation was becoming critical, with the threat of an imminent revolution. On receiving Roosevelt's suggestion, Nicholas II immediately thought of Witte as negotiator, but doubted whether the fallen Finance Minister would accept such an ungrateful task. Lamsdorf, having failed to find another suitable emissary, approached Witte, who accepted with alacrity but with no show of enthusiasm. This was his best chance to bid for the first place in Russian politics.

Witte's role in Russian foreign policy

Witte's attitude was determined by both personal and state considerations. In order to strengthen his position in the Russian government, the negotiations should lead to peace; if, however, the peace were bought at a humiliating price he would be blamed. Witte himself claims the merit of having persuaded the Japanese not to insist on an indemnity, something that the Tsar would not countenance. In fact, it appears that when the American envoy to St Petersburg tried to persuade Nicholas II to make further concessions to the Japanese demands, he was told with great firmness that as a last concession the Russian government would be prepared to abandon Port Arthur and Dalny and the southern part of Sakhalin, with the proviso that it should not be used for military purposes or fortified. Further guarantees should be given by the Japanese for the functioning of the Chinese Eastern Railway as a Russian concession. All demands for a war indemnity were refused. When proposals on these lines were made by Witte at the negotiating table, there was a moment of silence, after which the Japanese Foreign Minister, Komura, simply announced that the Japanese government accepted these conditions. The peace-treaty was signed on 5 September 1905.

Witte's return journey through Europe was like a triumphal march after the embarrassing rush to Portsmouth a few weeks before. The most important meeting, and one which gave him extreme satisfaction, was with Kaiser Wilhelm II in the hunting lodge of Rominten. Both Witte and the German Chancellor, Prince Bülow, record in their accounts of this interview the exceptional attention which the Kaiser showed Witte on that occasion. The Kaiser welcomed him outside the house, saw him off at the station, praised his achievements at Portsmouth, and stressed his complete agreement with Witte's conception of a continental European alliance to be brought about by restoration of the *Dreikaiserbund* and a rapprochement between Germany and France. More important than these generalities were the assurances the Kaiser gave Witte that he could reckon with the support of the German government in his political efforts in Russia, and an offer to maintain clandestine communications with the Kaiser's friend, Count Philip Eulenburg, and through him with the Kaiser via the German diplomatic service. According to Bülow the Kaiser revealed to Witte the secret agreement reached between him and Nicholas II a few days earlier in Björkö. Witte explicitly denies having been shown the Björkö agreement. Yet the subject was certainly discussed because on parting the Kaiser presented Witte with his portrait, inscribed 'Portsmouth–Björkö–Rominten', and signed 'Wilhelm Rex'.

The agreement in Björkö is in itself the most bizarre incident in the diplomatic history of the reign of Nicholas II. We know that, among the obsessive ideas of Wilhelm II, the theory according to which 'Germany's future lies at sea' was most persistent and led to the intensive German naval construction programme which naturally became a 'matter of ever-increasing concern' for the British government. This in its turn gave increasing weight to Kaiser Wilhelm's desire to conclude an agreement with Russia mainly directed against England. The Kaiser bombarded the Tsar with letters abounding with arguments in favour of such an alliance, but met with passive resistance. During the Russo–Japanese War, Germany went out of its way to help the Russian fleet proceeding from the Baltic to the Pacific, with fuel supplies, and the Kaiser did not miss an opportunity to boast of German generosity, contrasting it with the alleged passivity and coolness of Russia's perfidious ally, France. It so happened that in the summer of 1905, when Count Witte was on his way to America and Lamsdorf had his hands full with diplomatic exchanges preceding the peace negotiations, Nicholas II took a few days off for a cruise in Finnish waters. Kaiser Wilhelm crossed over, impromptu, and both monarchs met on board the Tsar's yacht *Pole Star* off the island of Björkö. The Kaiser was in an ebullient mood; the Tsar was depressed and shaken by the external and internal events which made 1905 one of the most difficult years of his reign. In a moment of weakness which it was not easy to explain, Nicholas II signed an agreement with Wilhelm, according to which both contracting parties promised to support each other against any attacker and not to conclude a separate peace. The Tsar undertook to inform France of this treaty and to invite her to join as an ally. The treaty was to come into effect after the ratification of peace between Russia and Japan, and could be repudiated by either party at a year's notice. In the absence of competent diplomats to countersign the treaty, an aged German official, Count Tschirsky, and the Russian Naval Minister, Admiral Birilev, put their signatures to the document. The Tsar kept the treaty secret even from the Foreign Minister, Count Lamsdorf, for almost three months. When Lamsdorf finally saw the text he immediately realised its incompatibility with the agreements with France. He made representations in this respect to the Tsar, and informed Witte of it. Witte claims that he then insisted on getting the treaty abrogated and succeeded. The clash between the Kaiser and his Chancellor, Bülow, who was strongly opposed to the Björkö agreement, made it particularly easy for the Russians, although they did not know why, to consider this agreement as null and void. The very existence of this document remained a secret until 1917, when it was first published by the Bolsheviks.

Whatever his attitude to the Björkö agreement may have been, Witte considered a continental alliance between Germany, Russia and France to be a guarantee of the further progress of Russia itself and of European security, in face of growing competition with other continents. In his memoirs he regrets that nothing has been built on the foundations he laid during his stay in Rominten and blames the Germans for it. At the Algeciras conference on Morocco, according to Witte, Germany annoyed France by petty and irritating demands.

In his memoirs Witte seemed disappointed about the Kaiser's departure from the Rominten standpoint, and he supposed that the unprecedented solicitude of Wilhelm was only the result of the latter's knowledge of how much the implementation of the Björkö agreement would depend on Witte. These surmises of Count Witte had every reason to conceal the character of the clandestine contacts which he maintained with the German court and government, and of which we have only fragmentary but conclusive evidence. When before his retirement from the premiership Witte planned to become the Russian ambassador in Paris, he met with opposition from the Tsar who he claims had promised him an embassy. It was then that Countess Mathilde Witte found it possible to write to Witte's banker friend in Germany, Ernst von Mendelssohn-Bartholdy, asking him to intervene with the Kaiser so that the latter could prevail on Tsar Nicholas to appoint Witte ambassador in Paris.[7]

Wittes support of France at Algeciras strengthened his chances of concluding a major loan in France. The conclusion of the loan increased Witte's reputation as a brilliant negotiator, and earned him the official gratitude of the Tsar. His retirement from the premiership only six months after his return from Portsmouth was due exclusively to the internal situation in Russia. He left office showered with signs of particular favour from Nicholas II, who bestowed on him the order of St Andrew. Yet nothing could conceal the profound antipathy which had developed between the two men during his stay in power and which was to contribute to the oppressive political atmosphere of the last pre-war years. The high honours he received did not protect Witte from the attacks and eventually ostracism of a snobbish society. On the other hand, nothing but a return to power could satisfy him. This urge explains why in the last years of his life he became an international intriguer of the most dangerous type.

Recently discovered documents in the German Foreign Office archives show that Witte renewed his private contacts with the German government to enlighten them on the situation in Russia. Using as agent a former employee of his, Joseph Melnik, who had made himself known in Germany as a writer on Russian affairs, Witte in 1913 gave him an 'interview' which was not meant for the press but was reported to the German ambassador in St Petersburg, Count Pourtalès. We recall that during the Rominten parleys Witte was encouraged to use, in case of necessity, German diplomatic channels for private communications to the German government. In this interview, Witte mentioned among other things that it was utterly impossible for Russia to go to war at the present, that the national minorities in Russia would support an aggressor, that Austria's policy towards the Balkans was the right one and that Austria should strike against her enemies in the Balkans. Witte spoke of his admiration for Germany's economic progress, army, administration and so on, and he regretted that neither the German nor the Russian diplomats were outstanding.[8]

The document speaks for itself. It has a possible direct bearing on the tragic circumstances of the summer of 1914. What credence could the German Foreign Office and Chancellor Bethmann-Hollweg give to Russia's assurances that she would certainly go to war if the sovereignty of Serbia was threatened, if the most brilliant Russian statesman, who chose to live in retirement instead of serving a régime which he despised, gave them such a solemn assurance that Russia was in no state to go to war? Why should Germany as 'elder brother' use a restraining influence on the hotheads in Austria if, even before the assassination of Archduke Franz Ferdinand, a Russian patriot, a monarchist, a man of conspicuous merit, had advised direct action by Austria against her enemies? The document remained secret until a couple of years ago, after many a pundit had pronounced the 'last word' on the July crisis of 1914. Is it too much to hope that academic prejudice will not prevent a revision of these findings in the light of this revelation?

We saw in the preceding pages how the desire to prolong the traditional alliance with the King of Prussia despite the basic changes brought about by the creation of Bismarck's empire, led Giers, in opposition to Alexander III's innermost convictions, to postpone a rapprochement with France which he himself had to accept seven years later. This meant losing seven precious years for consolidating a new situation in Europe. On the other hand, we saw Nicholas II caught up in a network of investment projects leading to diplomatic complications which finally, against his own will and without fault on the part of the faithful and tactful Lamsdorf, involved him and Russia in the disastrous war with Japan. We have followed up Witte's dubious and in the end treasonable activities, which demonstrate the danger of private initiative in diplomatic contacts.

It is impossible to deal with the last years of Russian foreign policy before the First World War without becoming involved in the controversies connected with the July 1914 crisis, for which there is no place in this chapter. We must say, however, that after the departure of Witte from power and the retirement of Lamsdorf shortly before his death, relations between Nicholas II and his successive Foreign Ministers, Izvolsky and Sazonov, were less affected by the tensions and conflicts which vitiated the Tsar's relations with their predecessors. Their task was particularly arduous. Russia's potentialities in the contest of power between imperialist systems remained considerable, despite a momentary loss of prestige through the defeat in the Far East and through the internal weakness exposed by the revolutionary events of 1905. True, the political experiment with limited parliamentarianism after 1905 did nothing to restore Russia's international standing; and far-going reforms of both land and sea forces prevented Russian diplomacy from taking any risks of armed conflict while in that state of unpreparedness. Yet, throughout this time, the main task was to persuade potential adversaries not to exploit Russia's temporary weakness in order to create a situation which would become intolerable as soon as she recovered the strength which her size and rapid economic development held in promise for a not too distant future.

Constitutional Law in Russia

LOTHAR SCHULTZ

Between 1894 and 1917 there were three distinct phases in the development of constitutional law in Russia. The initial phase had begun under Nicholas I, the first ruler to try to codify Russian law. The new statutes drafted under Nicholas, which were published in 1832 in Volume I of 'The Collected Laws of the Russian Empire' and came into force in 1835, incorporated all the constitutional norms previously covered by a great welter of legal documents. They remained the law of the land until the proclamation of the constitution of 1906 and firmly established the Russian empire as an absolute monarchy.

After 1832 various attempts were made to cut back the Tsar's autocratic powers and several draft constitutions were drawn up to this end.[1] Although none of these was successful, they none the less demonstrate the determination of the more liberal elements amongst the nobility and the bourgeoisie to introduce a certain measure of social reform.

The second phase in the development of Russian constitutional law began with the proclamation of the constitution of 1906, which changed the Russian empire from an absolute into a constitutional monarchy: the unlimited power previously enjoyed by the Tsars was then curbed by a freely elected parliament. Although various interpretations have been placed on this document—some historians have even described it as a 'sham' constitution—from the point of view of constitutional law it was an extremely important innovation.

The third phase of this development was ushered in by the revolution of February 1917, which brought about the dissolution of the monarchy and was followed by a brief period during which Russia might be said to have constituted a democratic republic.

The fundamental laws of 1832

The fundamental laws published in the first volume of the 'Collected Laws of the Russian empire' contain 179 articles arranged in eight sections.[2] Most of these sections deal with questions concerning the imperial family, such as the age of majority, the succession and the accession. In terms of constitutional law the most significant sections are those on 'The Nature of Autocratic Power' and on 'The Laws'.

Article I of the constitution was of major importance. It reads: 'The Emperor of All the Russias is an autocratic (*samoderzhavny*) and unlimited (*neogranichenny*) monarch; God himself ordains that all must bow to his supreme power, not only out of fear, but also out of conscience.' Thus, all power was vested in the monarch. He had absolute control of the legislature, the executive and the judiciary.

Prior to 1906 a lively discussion was conducted in Russian legal journals as to whether there was any substantial difference between the concepts of 'autocratic' and 'unlimited' rule without a definite conclusion being reached.[3] In actual fact, of course, these two terms are completely synonymous under an absolute monarchy. The word 'autocracy' had been in use in Russia for some considerable time, having been introduced during the reign of Ivan III.[4]

The Russian constitutional lawyers of the day attached great significance to Article 47, which reads: 'The Russian empire will be ruled on the firm basis of positive laws, institutions and charters established by the autocratic power.' They rightly considered that this reflected a transition from despotism to autocracy.[5] According to Article 47 the Tsar's commands were legally binding only in so far as they were based on legal criteria, which prompted M. M. Speransky to speak of a 'legitimate autocracy' in this connection.

The Tsar's unlimited power was implemented by two distinct executive bodies: the higher administration and the lower administration. This distinction was maintained in the constitution of 1906.

The members of the higher administration dealt with all matters which required a personal decision on the part of the

Tsar and, since all new laws had to be ratified by the Tsar (Article 51), most of these were of a legislative nature. As supreme legislator the Tsar was able to seek expert advice but was not bound to follow it. He was also authorised to formulate and enact laws *motu proprio*. In addition, the Tsar frequently promulgated declaratory statutes. Even his verbal commands were legally binding, although he was not able to rescind laws by word of mouth (Article 66).

In the executive sphere the Tsar had the power to appoint high-ranking officials of his own choosing and to declare states of war and emergency. He was also personally responsible for foreign affairs and was Commander-in-Chief of the armed forces. Moreover, Article 42 named him as 'head of the church'. As part of the establishment the Russian Orthodox Church enjoyed a privileged status: membership was mandatory for the Tsar, who otherwise forfeited his right to the throne. But, as head of the church, the Tsar was entitled to pass legislation for the administration of church affairs and so was able to exercise direct control over the structuring of ecclesiastical life. He did so with the help of the Holy Synod.

The members of the lower administration dealt with all day-to-day affairs which did not call for a personal decision on the part of the monarch. For the most part these lesser officials belonged either to the government ministries, which were empowered to promulgate decrees affecting the administration of the law, or to provincial administrative offices.

The absolute power vested in the office of the Tsar was also attached to his person. He was inviolable and could not be called to account for his actions. He was also afforded special protection under the law, for any attack on the Tsar was regarded as high treason and carried the death penalty.

The departments of state under the constitution of 1832

Under the constitution of 1832 the departments of state were the Imperial Council, the Committee of Ministers, the Holy Synod and the ministries.[6]

The *Imperial Council*, a brainchild of Speransky's, was created by Alexander I on 5 April 1810. It was a purely advisory body, whose principal task was to provide the Tsar with expert opinions on all matters pertaining to legislation.[7] Article 23 of its charter stated that matters calling for a decision or ratification by the supreme imperial power should first be submitted to the Imperial Council for examination. Once this examination had been carried out the Council sent a full report to the Tsar, who then decided whether to accept or reject its recommendations. Thus, the Imperial Council was not able to enact legislation on its own account. Nor was it authorised to issue decrees. The legal drafts, on which it was required to comment, were sent to it either by the Tsar himself or by the ministries. The Tsar was, of course, fully entitled to pass laws without obtaining the advice of the Council and as a result individual ministers cultivated the practice of seeking personal audiences in order to submit legal drafts for the Tsar's approval. In the course of time this procedure became extremely popular.[8] The Imperial Council was also required to give advice on fiscal matters. The individual ministries submitted their estimates to the Council, which then considered them in the light of the national budget. In the administration of justice the Imperial Council investigated cases of alleged corruption involving the three leading groups of government officials (members of the Council of Ministers, ministers, governors general, etc.) and advised the Tsar whether there was a *prima facie* case against them.

The Imperial Council was organised along departmental lines. There were five departments in all, which were responsible for the routine work of the Council. There was also a plenary assembly, which dealt with all really important issues. The members of the Council, most of whom were retired ministers or governors general, were appointed by the Tsar. No statutory limit was imposed on the size of the Council. In the early years there were thirty-five members, later there were ninety. The Imperial Council continued to function as an advisory body until the proclamation of the constitution of 1906.

After introducing the ministerial system into Russia, Alexander I went on to create the *Committee of Ministers* on 8 September 1802. This committee was supposed to handle all major administrative issues. Article 1 of its charter stated that it was 'to deal with the affairs of the higher administration'. In actual fact, however, we find that these affairs were also being dealt with by the Imperial Council and the Senate with the result that there was frequent overlapping and a certain amount of rivalry between these three government departments. But then imprecision in the allocation of departmental responsibility was one of the characteristic features of the absolute monarchy in Russia.[9] With the Tsar taking so many important decisions himself, the government departments were constantly being by-passed and so were unable to establish clearly defined areas of competence.

According to Articles 11–14 of its charter the Committee of Ministers bore a special responsibility for all administrative problems calling for concerted action on the part of different ministers. But it was also responsible for all matters affecting public order and security—such as the banning of books and journals and the proscription of clubs and societies—and for the supervision of the work of the provincial governors and officials. The Committee had to submit its decisions to the Tsar for his approval, a requirement which effectively demonstrated its subservience to the crown. In certain relatively unimportant and clearly defined spheres, such as the control of the press, this requirement was waived. The implementation of the Committee's decisions was the responsibility of the appropriate ministries.

The Committee of Ministers was headed by a chairman appointed by the Tsar and included among its members all the ministers of the crown, the heads of certain government departments, the heads of the five departments of the Imperial Council, and various persons specially appointed by the Tsar. It continued to fulfil its functions as an instrument of the higher administration until 1905.

In the course of the eighteenth and the early part of the nineteenth century the *Senate*, which had been created by Peter the Great in 1711, lost more and more of its original importance. Alexander I tried to reverse this process in 1802, when he issued an edict extending its powers. He wanted to make it the 'highest authority' in the land, to which all other authorities 'must be subordinated'. Thus the Senate was to have been placed in command of the whole administrative machine. In Article 1 of its charter the Senate was described as the 'protector of legality', which means that it was also supposed to prevent illegal practices in all departments of the administration. But because its objectives were so far-ranging, the Senate found itself in competition with the Committee of Ministers and the Imperial Council. As a result it was largely unable to fulfil its supervisory function. The ministers were in a far stronger position: they had frequent private audiences with the Tsar, who invariably backed them in any difficulties they might have with the Senate.

In the provinces, however, the Senate remained of some consequence. It had disciplinary powers over the local authorities in the *Gubernii* (or provinces) and was able to issue reprimands to leaders of those authorities. The Senate was also authorised to issue declaratory statutes and was further entitled to publish all new laws passed by the Tsar. Consequently, it was responsible for the publication of 'The Collected Laws and Decrees of the Government'. The duties of the Senate were completely changed in 1864 as a result of the legal reform carried out by Alexander II; it was then relieved of its supervisory function and became the supreme court of the Empire. Like the Imperial Council, the Senate was made up of various departments. The senators, most of whom were members of the nobility or high-ranking government officials, were appointed by the Tsar. Their number was not subject to statutory limitation.

Ministries were first introduced into Russia by Alexander I. Their charter was drawn up in 1811 and remained in force until 1906, during which time it was virtually unchanged.[10] Initially there were eight ministers but their number gradually grew until eventually there were fourteen. These men held positions of great power for they controlled the whole of the administrative machine in the absolute monarchy. They were appointed by the Tsar and were accountable only to him. They were also granted regular private audiences, which enabled them to acquire considerable influence and fully justified the contemporary view of Russia as a 'ministerial despotism'. Although both the Imperial Council and the Senate were entitled to supervise the work of the ministries, this right was purely nominal.

The ministers had the power to issue statements clarifying and complementing the laws and decrees passed by the Tsar. But that was not all, for the Tsar tended to leave them a very free rein in this sphere, which meant that they were able to influence the development of Russian legislation. For all practical purposes these ministerial statutes, which often dealt with important issues, had the full force of law. (Not surprisingly, therefore, the attempt undertaken by Professor N. M. Korkunov, the leading expert on constitutional law in Tsarist Russia, to establish fundamental distinctions between laws and decrees, was unsuccessful.)[11] The ministers were also authorised to appoint and dismiss high-ranking government officials. They could dismiss these officials without giving any reason, and there was no right of appeal against their decision.

The Ministry of the Interior was a particularly powerful department. It controlled both the security police and the gendarmes, who were responsible for tracking down 'revolutionaries' and 'anarchists' and uncovering projected coups. The Minister of the Interior was authorised to declare states of emergency in limited areas of the country, thus restricting the personal freedom of the inhabitants.

The basis for *provincial administration* in modern Russia was created by Catherine II in 1775 when she established new territorial divisions which enabled her to introduce a bureaucratic system under strict central control. The largest of these divisions were the provinces (*Gubernii*), of which there were eventually seventy-eight. These provinces were broken down into districts (*uyezdy*) and further subdivided into cantons or *volosts* (*volosti*). In a number of cases—primarily in Asiatic Russia—several provinces were joined together to form Governments-General.[12] Each Russian province had its own governor, who was appointed by the Tsar acting on advice from the Minister of the Interior. These governors were the Tsar's foremost representatives in the provinces, where they controlled all local administration. Although ultimately accountable to the Minister of the Interior, they enjoyed very considerable powers within their own provinces, where they were authorised to issue decrees, primarily for the maintenance of order and internal security.

The day-to-day running of the provinces was carried out by an administrative council, which was composed of a group of high officials and presided over by the deputy governor. The council also acted in concert with the governor in respect of certain issues which the governor was not authorised to decide on his own. Local administration in the districts was conducted by prefects appointed from the ranks of the aristocracy while in the *volosts* it was entrusted to special overseers.

The vast majority of the provincial towns came under the direct jurisdiction of the governors and their administrative councils. A few of the more important towns, such as St Petersburg and Odessa, had their own administrative systems under the control of the local mayor (*gorodskoy golova*).

In the constitution of 1832 the people of Russia were referred to as *subjects*, for the concept of 'the citizen' was unknown in the autocratic Russia of the Tsars. The rights granted to these subjects were based exclusively on considerations of rank and varied very considerably. At that time there were four estates in Russia: the aristocracy, the clergy, the bourgeoisie and the peasants.

The most privileged of these classes was the aristocracy, whose members were even allowed to form their own independent associations at provincial and district level. The peasants, who made up ninety per cent of the Russian population, were the worst off. As serfs, they were completely dependent on the goodwill of the estate owners. They were subjects in a dual sense, for they owed allegiance, not only to the Tsars, but also to their masters.

The reforms of Alexander II

The reforms carried out by Alexander II were a major factor in the development of constitutional law in Russia. The most important of these were the introduction of the Zemstvo system of administration in the provinces (1864) and the towns (1870), the emancipation of the serfs (1861) and the reorganisation of the judicial system.

The introduction of the Zemstvos was particularly significant, for these elective assemblies were destined to play an extremely positive role. Thanks to them the bureaucratic and centralist trend, which had been such a marked feature of provincial administration in Russia, was reversed and wide sections of the population acquired a new interest in political affairs.[13] The Zemstvos also produced a large number of liberal-minded politicians, who went on to play an active part in the Duma. But above all they eroded the traditional supremacy of the aristocrats, many of whom were forced out of local administration and obliged to go back to tending their estates. The Zemstvos were elective assemblies operating at both provincial and district level which, in their original form, were largely independent of the official provincial administration. This system was introduced in thirty-four Russian provinces under the law of 1 January 1864.

Remarkably enough, the Zemstvos were composed of representatives from all three secular estates, namely the aristocracy, the townsmen and urban classes, and the peasants, who met annually at plenary assemblies, where they passed resolutions laying down the general lines of local policy. These resolutions were then put into effect by special committees consisting of a president and at least two other members, who were appointed by the representatives. The representatives themselves were elected for a period of three years by their respective estates.

As far as the first two estates were concerned the franchise was restricted to those able to fulfil certain property qualifications. Thus, the aristocrats had to own a certain amount of land while the townsmen either had to be house-owners or else have a turnover of not less than 6,000 roubles in their trade or business. For the peasants there was no such qualification, but their representatives were elected by an indirect procedure. The number of representatives from each estate was fixed by statute.

This was the system used for all elections to the district Zemstvos, whose members then elected the representatives to the provincial Zemstvos. At this second election there was only one ballot, for the candidates were not segregated according to rank. Both Zemstvos functioned in the same way: annual plenary assemblies were convened to decide general policy, which was then implemented by elected committees.

The terms of reference of the Zemstvos were very wide. Among other things, they dealt with economic and social questions and with education. They were also authorised to issue decrees and raise taxes. However, they were subject to a certain measure of control by both the governor and the Minister of the Interior, for they had to submit all their resolutions to the governor before acting upon them. But they were only required to obtain his assent in certain stipulated cases.

Under the law of 16 June 1870 the principle of self-government was extended to the towns, thus enabling all social classes in Russia to be represented at local government level by men from their own ranks. Municipal administration was effected in three ways, by the town council (municipal Duma), the executive committee of the town council and the local mayor. The municipal Duma was elected for a period of four years. Here too there were property qualifications, for the franchise was extended only to those persons who owned real estate worth upwards of three hundred roubles or who ran a business in the town and paid taxes on it. The Duma elected its own president, who was also local mayor and the most important person in the administration. It also elected its own executive committee.

The small rural communities in Russia acquired self-government at the same time as the municipalities. Their affairs were administered by the *volost* assembly, which was made up of members elected by the *miry*, and by the *volost* elder, who was elected by the assembly.

From the point of view of constitutional law the second most important of Alexander II's reforms was the *emancipation of the serfs*. Although this did nothing to relieve the peasants' desperate need for land, it did give them their personal liberty, which was an essential prerequisite for the introduction of a constitutional monarchy.

The *reorganisation of the judicial system*, which was provided for by the law of 20 November 1864, was a further important reform introduced by Alexander II. Prior to 1864 the administration of justice in Russia was most unsatisfactory. There was no dividing line between the judiciary and the executive, for the judges were not judges by profession but simply members of the official class employed as judges. Moreover, there were separate courts for each of the four estates. In these circumstances there could be no question of equality before the law. The inequity of the system was largely eradicated by the new reform, which was modelled on western European procedures. Thus, the judges and courts became independent and the judicial and administrative functions were separated from one another. With few exceptions, the old practice of holding separate courts for the different estates was abolished.

The Constitution of 1906

The new constitution was proclaimed on 23 April 1906 and four days later the Imperial Duma—the first Russian parliament— was convened. The terms of this constitution, which was imposed by the Tsar, were worked out by a special commission whose report was published by Burtsev in *Byloe* (1917, volumes 5 and 6).

As a result of the revolutionary incidents of 1905 the Tsar was forced to relinquish part of his power in order to give greater rights to the people. Most of these concessions were made in the manifesto of 17 October 1905, in which the Tsar undertook to grant civic rights and to allow the Duma to participate in the drafting of any new laws. All these imperial manifestos and government decrees of the year 1905–6 subsequently became the basis of the new constitution. Incidentally, this was not referred to as a 'constitution' by the Russian government, which considered this word far too revolutionary and so preferred the old expression used to describe the constitution of 1832: the fundamental laws of the state.[14]

The constitution of 1906 contains two hundred and twenty-three articles set out in two parts and seventeen sections. Most of the sections, which contain one hundred and forty-three articles in all, are devoted to the question of the succession and the different institutions of the imperial house. The most important provisions in terms of constitutional law are contained in four sections dealing with the supreme power of the Tsar (articles 4–24), fundamental rights (articles 69–83), legislation, the powers of the Duma and the Imperial Council (articles 84–119) and the powers of the Council of Ministers (articles 120–124). In certain respects the Russian constitution of 1906 reveals the influence of the Prussian constitution, especially in its approach to fundamental rights.[15]

This new constitution met with a very mixed reception both

in the West and in Russia. Max Weber, the celebrated German sociologist, accused the Russian government of indulging in 'sham constitutionalism', claiming that the new fundamental laws were a mere 'caricature of constitutional government'.[16] Weber based his view, which caused a considerable stir at the time, on two principal points. On the one hand he argued that the introduction of the constitution had not reduced the Tsar's unlimited power in any real sense, while on the other hand he claimed that after the constitution had passed into law, the Tsar had broken its provisions on several occasions. Weber's view has been espoused by various western historians, such as V. Gitermann, N. Riasanovsky and J. Haller.[17] It was also discussed in Russia, where it found particular favour with the Kadets.[18]

In fact, the constitution of 1906 was not a sham. Those who adopt this point of view have been unduly influenced by western European conceptions of constitutional government and so have failed to appreciate the true nature of Russian autocracy.

The new constitution was an important turning point in the development of Russian constitutional law. It transformed the Russian empire from an absolute and unlimited monarchy into a constitutional monarchy. It is quite true that, by comparison with the rulers of western Europe, whose powers had been strictly curbed by the early twentieth century, the Russian Tsar continued to enjoy very considerable rights and prerogatives even after 1906. This was particularly the case in the legislative sphere, where the Tsar had an absolute right to veto any bill. It would be perfectly reasonable, therefore, to describe Russia after 1906 as a constitutional monarchy in which the monarch enjoyed considerable legislative powers. But that does not mean that the constitution was a sham. O. Hoetzsch, the German historian, has rightly pointed out that the concept of 'sham constitutionalism' coined by Max Weber was both 'exaggerated' and 'one-sided'.[19]

The advocates of Weber's theory point to the fact that in Article 4 of the constitution the imperial power is described as 'autocratic', from which they conclude that it was 'unlimited' and consequently opposed to the constitutional concept. But there is a fallacy here. In the constitution of 1832 the expressions 'autocratic' and 'unlimited' were both used to describe the imperial power. But in the constitution of 1906 this power is described only as 'autocratic'. The word 'unlimited' had been dropped, which can only mean that the two expressions were not in fact synonymous. The word 'unlimited' does recur, however, in Article 222 of the 1906 constitution, where it is used in conjunction with the word 'autocratic' to describe the Tsar's powers vis-à-vis the members of the imperial family. Thus, in respect of his relations the Tsar's power was both autocratic and unlimited while in respect of the nation it was merely autocratic. V. Gribovsky, the Russian constitutional lawyer, has pointed out that in this context the word 'autocratic' has a purely descriptive force: it simply denotes the Tsar's function as the representative of imperial power.[20]

The principal features of the new constitutional monarchy in Russia, which limited the absolute power previously enjoyed by the Tsar, are contained in the following six points:

(1) In accordance with Article 86 of the constitution no law could be passed without the approval of the Duma. Any bill that was not approved by the Duma was considered to have been rejected.

(2) In accordance with Article 108 of the constitution the Duma was authorised to question any minister whose actions appeared to contravene the law. This provision gave parliament a certain measure of control over the ministries.

(3) In accordance with Article 114 the budget had to be debated in the Duma. This provision gave parliament the right to control state expenditure. It also limited the Tsar's right to issue decrees.

(4) The right previously enjoyed by individual ministers to apply to the Tsar for a personal audience was virtually abolished when the Council of Ministers was created. In accordance with Article 120 of the constitution, decrees issued either by the Council of Ministers or by individual ministers had to comply with existing laws.

(5) The Tsar's right to promulgate emergency decrees (which was established under Article 87 of the constitution) was limited in two ways: first, no such decrees could be issued within the sphere of constitutional or electoral law, and, secondly, all such decrees issued in other spheres were to lapse at the end of two

months unless presented to the Duma in the form of bills within
that period.

(6) The constitution also contained a list of fundamental
rights (such as the freedom of the press and the right of the individual to domicile in any part of the empire), the first of its
kind ever published in Russia. The fact that these fundamental
rights were officially recognised by the state was highly significant.
It should be added, however, that the Tsar was able to limit these
rights by passing special legislation. Article 83 of the constitution
specifically refers to states of war and states of emergency in this
connection.

The departments of state after the constitution of 1906

We have already mentioned that the *Tsar* was *forced* to share
his authority with the Duma. None the less, he still retained very
considerable powers under the new constitution, which may be
briefly summarised as follows:

(1) The Tsar possessed an absolute right of veto. Article 9 of
the constitution stated that no law could be passed without his
assent.

(2) The Tsar alone was entitled to introduce bills designed to
change the constitution. The Duma was expressly excluded
from doing so by Article 8 of the constitution.

(3) Both the Prime Minister and the ministers were appointed
by the Tsar and were directly responsible to him (Article 17).

(4) The Tsar was able to dissolve the Duma at will (Article 98)
but was obliged to reconvene it annually. He also retained full
responsibility for the command of the armed forces and the
conduct of foreign affairs. But, despite these far-reaching powers,
Nicholas II frequently contravened the provisions of the new
constitution.

The constitutional monarchy in Russia lasted for ten years,
during which time there were four *parliaments*. The parliamentary charter was published on 20 February 1906. The electoral
law of August 1905 and the complementary imperial decree of
11 December 1905 provided for indirect elections based on
separate lists for the different classes. Thus, the electors were
divided into three *curias*: landed proprietors, citizens and

peasants. Each curia in each province elected a specified number of delegates, who then met at electoral assemblies to elect the deputies to the Duma. The landed proprietors' curia embraced both large and small estate owners, who had to fulfil a property qualification. The citizens' curia consisted of house owners and tradesmen. Under the electoral law of August 1905 the lower urban classes (the poorer citizens and manual workers) were still excluded from the franchise but this group was then granted the vote under the imperial decree of 11 December 1905. The workers' deputies were elected by the personnel of industrial concerns. The peasants' curia was exceptional in that its members were not required to fulfil any property qualification, a privilege granted to peasants because the government was confident that it could rely on their loyal support. The precise number of deputies elected by each curia was specified under the electoral law.

The activities, rights and duties of the Duma were defined in its charter, which contained sixty-three articles.[21] It was elected for a five-year term and normally met in weekly session; its principal task was to debate the bills presented to it by the government and the Council of Ministers, although it was also authorised to propose legislation on its own account. We have already observed that the Duma had the power to investigate the activities of the ministers, who were required to provide any information for its enquiries. Thus any illegal actions committed by the administration could be brought out into the open. One very important right vested in the Duma was the right to debate the budget, for this provided the public with an insight into the financial state of the nation. All opinions expressed by members of the Duma on matters subject to parliamentary jurisdiction were privileged. The personal liberty of members was also assured unless they were found guilty of a criminal offence.

The First Duma was convened on 27 April 1906. At the elections held in the previous month the liberal and democratic factions had obtained a large majority, which they immediately used to oppose government policy. Thus, in its address in reply to the speech from the throne, the Duma called for the establishment of a genuine democracy in which the ministers would be responsible to parliament, and for the expropriation of the great landlords. This last condition was particularly obnoxious to the government, which flatly refused to entertain any of the Duma's demands. The deputies then voted in favour of a motion urging an appeal to the people, with the result that the Tsar dissolved the First Duma on 8 July, little more than two months after its solemn opening.

The Second Duma began its work on 20 February 1907. This assembly was even more radical than the first. Of the 524 deputies 306 were left-wingers. The parties representing the national minorities had made heavy gains and both the Poles and the Ukrainians were demanding home rule, which the government found extremely disconcerting, especially in the case of the Ukrainians. On 3 June 1907, after a period of three months in office, the Second Duma was also dissolved by imperial edict.

In order to create a more compliant assembly the government then committed a breach of the constitution: on 3 June 1907 it contravened Article 87 by promulgating a new electoral law without consulting the Duma. The crucial provision in the new law was that involving the redistribution of the delegates to the various curias. The delegates representing the supposedly loyal peasant curias, who had proved so radical, were reduced from 43 to 22.4 per cent, the number of workers' delegates was reduced from 200 to 114 while the number of delegates allocated to the national minorities was also heavily cut back. The number of delegates representing the estate owners, on the other hand, rose sharply from 30 to 51.3 per cent. This new electoral law achieved its purpose: there was a conservative majority in the new parliament. But the democratic opposition continued to make its presence felt.

The Third Duma served its full five-year term, from 1 November 1907 to 9 June 1912. The Fourth and final Duma almost did so; it was opened on 15 November 1912 and dissolved on 26 February 1917.

In terms of constitutional law the Duma was an entirely positive institution. It served as a vehicle for liberal ideas, for parliament was the only place where the government could be openly criticised; it helped to bring the monarchy up to date, as the historian M. T. Florinsky has pointed out;[22] and, finally, it made a significant contribution to Russian legislation, primarily in the spheres of social insurance and agrarian reform.

Under the constitution of 1906 the *Imperial Council* served as an upper house, which means that its functions were completely different from those which it had fulfilled under the constitution of 1832. In point of fact, the manifesto of 17 October 1905 made no provision for an upper house. It was only after this had been issued that the monarch decided to create a second conservative chamber in order to restrict the powers of the Duma. The Imperial Council, which consisted of 196 members, debated all bills passed by the Duma. It also had the power to veto any bill which did not meet with its approval and so was able to disrupt the legislative programme of the lower house. All new bills were first examined by the Duma before being sent on to the Imperial Council. If the Council approved of a particular bill in principle but objected on points of detail, an arbitration commission consisting of an equal number of members from each house could be set up.

The Imperial consisted of elected members and members nominated by the Tsar. For the most part the Tsar's nominees—who were not allowed to exceed fifty per cent of the total membership —consisted of retired ministers and high-ranking officials. The elective members were representatives of five professional and class organisations. It is significant that in all disputes between the Duma and the Imperial Council the Tsar supported the Council.

The Council of Ministers was created by the decree of 19 October 1905. It was the first western-style cabinet in Russian political life and it effectively disposed of the 'ministerial despotism' which had dominated the political scene until then. One of the tasks performed by the Council was that of coordinating the work of the individual ministries. It was headed by a chairman who helped the Tsar to map out the general lines of administrative policy. The chairman also submitted regular reports to the Tsar on the activities of the Council. Both the chairman and the ministers were appointed by the Tsar, to whom they were directly and solely responsible. Although the Council of Ministers was authorised to promulgate edicts, these had to comply with existing legislation. All edicts and commands issued by the Tsar had to be countersigned either by the president of the Council or by one of the ministers. The chairman or the minister in question then accepted the political responsibility for the document which he had ratified.

The constitution of 1906 laid down a number of *fundamental freedoms* for the Russian people. These were based on laws which had been passed shortly before the proclamation of the constitution in the wake of the revolutionary incidents of 1905. By comparison with the conditions obtaining in the pre-constitutional period they constituted a very definite advance.[23]

The new provisions governing the publication of periodicals, which replaced the old law of 27 August 1882, came into force on 24 November 1905. Under their terms the wide administrative powers previously enjoyed by the authorities, which included the right to vet all periodicals, were abolished. As a result the editors of such periodicals were removed from the direct jurisdiction of the administration and could only be prosecuted in the civil courts. Only the courts had power to ban publication.

The law governing the founding of clubs and associations was passed on 4 March 1905. From then onwards associations could be founded without an official permit. They had to be registered with the competent officials in the province concerned, who also had to be provided with a copy of the associations' statutes. If the officials considered that the purpose of a particular association was contrary to the law, they could refuse to register it. But, in all such cases, the persons concerned could appeal against their decision to the Senate.

Finally, the government passed a law granting freedom of assembly on 4 March 1906. Under its terms notice had to be given in writing to the local police authority by anybody proposing to call a public meeting. The authority had power to forbid all meetings likely to cause a breach of the peace and endanger public security. The responsibility for ensuring orderly conduct at such meetings rested with the organisers.

These concessions, which the Tsar was forced to make to the constitutional cause, were by no means insignificant. However, under Article 83 of the 1906 constitution all fundamental rights were automatically suspended during states of emergency. The power to declare states of emergency was vested in the Tsar by the notorious law outlining 'measures for the preservation of national order and public peace' which was passed on 14 August 1881 during the reign of Alexander III. Originally, this law was to have been allowed to lapse at the end of three years, but it was repeatedly extended and actually remained in force until the February revolution of 1917. It specified three distinct states of emergency, which the Tsar was entitled to declare at his own discretion:

(1) a state of heightened emergency,
(2) a state of exceptional emergency and
(3) a state of war.[24]

During states of heightened emergency provincial governors and local mayors were authorised to introduce special regulations binding on all sections of the population for the maintenance of public order. Any infringement of these regulations was punishable by a term of up to three months' imprisonment plus a fine of 500 roubles. 'Suspect persons' could also be banished from certain localities.

During states of exceptional emergency the governors and local mayors received even wider powers: they could then impose three-month prison sentences without recourse to the civil courts plus fines of up to 3,000 roubles; they were also authorised to suspend publication of periodicals and to dismiss officials employed by the state and by professional and social organisations.

During states of war control of the administration passed to the Commander-in-Chief of the armed forces. Even the governors were placed under his command.

The development of Russian constitutional law from 1906 to the October Revolution

After the revolution of February 1917, which brought about the downfall of the constitutional monarchy, Russia became a bourgeois-democratic republic for a period of eight months.

In the early summer of 1915, when it became obvious that the Tsarist régime was quite incapable of prosecuting the war successfully, the Duma, which was the only representative body involved in the administration at a national level, gradually asserted itself as the most important organ of state. Even the conservative delegates began to press for a new government capable of inspiring confidence. As far as the future constitution of Russia was concerned, the Octobrists wanted to see a continuation of the constitutional monarchy whereas the Kadets were beginning to favour a democratic republic, an idea they advocated even more forcibly following their party conference in June 1915. Their preference was shared by the Social-Democrats and Socialist Revolutionaries, both of whom were firmly opposed to the Bolshevik conception of the dictatorship of the proletariat.

In November 1916 the leader of the Kadets, P. N. Milyukov, launched a fierce attack on the government in the Duma, in which he accused it of total incompetence. This was followed by an even more vicious attack on 14 February 1917, which persuaded the Tsar that the Duma was largely responsible for the unrest in the country, with the result that he dissolved the assembly on 26 February. The majority of the deputies were prepared to comply with the Tsar's wishes, although a small minority wanted to continue with their work in defiance of the imperial edict. In point of fact, most of the deputies remained in the Tauride Palace in St Petersburg—the seat of the Duma—and a number of private sessions were held after 26 February. None the less, it was on that date that the official business of the Duma was concluded, and any subsequent activities engaged in by its members can only be regarded as symptomatic of the revolutionary dynamism of the time.

On 27 February 1917 the revolutionaries carried the day. The government lost all power in St Petersburg and several ministers were captured by the insurgents. On 2 March 1917 Nicholas II abdicated in favour of his brother, the Grand Duke Michael. But on 3 March Michael refused the throne.

The Tsar's abdication constituted a turning-point in Russia's constitutional development: the constitutional monarchy was replaced by a bourgeois-democratic republic. Not that this republic was proclaimed by the new leaders. The representatives of the Provisional Government and of the Soviet of Workers' and Soldiers' Deputies, who ran the country between them, both considered that the future constitution of Russia must be decided in due course by a constituent assembly. The Social-Democrats and Socialist Revolutionaries also subscribed to this view. It was not until 1 September 1917, after General Kornilov's abortive coup, that the provisional government finally declared Russia to be a democratic republic.[25] This is a point worth noting, for it has been wrongly assumed by a number of western[26] and Soviet[27] scholars that Russia remained a monarchy until the October revolution.

Once the Tsarist government had been forced out of office an immediate replacement was needed. The Duma was well aware of this and, at an unofficial session on 27 February 1917, it authorised its Council of Elders to set up an executive committee. This committee was formed later the same day under the leadership of the president of the Duma, the Octobrist M. V. Rodzyanko. Between them its twelve members represented all the major political parties save those of the extreme right. Aware of the considerable prestige enjoyed by the Duma in the country at large, the committee regarded itself as the supreme organ of the post-revolutionary state. But this proved to be wishful thinking. It was involved to some extent in the formation of the new government, but once this had been accomplished its influence soon declined. Although there was no formal delegation of power, in point of fact the Provisional Government assumed responsibility for all major affairs of state. Its supremacy over the Duma was demonstrated beyond all doubt on 6 October 1917, when it abolished both the Duma and its executive committee.

Meanwhile, on 3 March 1917, the Duma executive committee had nominated the ten members of the Provisional Government, all of whom belonged to bourgeois parties with the single exception of A. F. Kerensky, the Minister of Justice. Subsequently the government was re-formed on three separate occasions, the last being in August 1917.

On 3 March, the day on which it was constituted, the Provisional Government published a policy statement announcing far-reaching reforms of a democratic nature. Constitutionally, the provisional government was the supreme organ of the Russian state in the period between the February and the October revolutions. It both fulfilled an administrative function and passed several new laws affecting the constitution. The Provisional Government also enjoyed powers normally vested in the head of state, for it represented Russia overseas and issued directives to the officers commanding the armed forces. In the telegram which he sent to the Chief of the General Staff on 4 March 1917 the Prime Minister, Prince G. E. Lvov, stressed the fact that his government had taken over 'all power' until such time as an assembly was convened to set up a new constitution.[28]

In practical terms, however, the power of the government was severely restricted by a second institution: the Petrograd Soviet of Workers' and Soldiers' Deputies. The Soviet—which was established on 27 February 1917 and had its seat in the Duma building—was controlled by Social-Democrats and Socialist Revolutionaries. It too had an executive committee, of which Kerensky was vice-president. It was not long before other Soviets were established throughout the whole of Russia and eventually these joined together to form the All-Russian Soviet of Workers' and Soldiers' Deputies.

The Petrograd Soviet set up a special committee which was instructed to make contact with the Provisional Government and to keep a close watch on its activities. It also had a hand in the formation of the Provisional Government, in which the vice-president of its own executive committee became Minister of Finance. Thus Kerensky played a double role, representing both the Soviets and the Provisional Government.

Shortly after it had been constituted the Petrograd Soviet put out a proclamation stating that no orders issued by the Provisional Government were to be obeyed unless they had been endorsed by the Soviet.[29] In July 1917, when the Provisional Government was re-formed for the second time, the Soviet insisted that it should submit a full report of its activities twice a week.

And so Russia was ruled both by the provisional government and by the Petrograd Soviet. But real power lay in the hands of the Soviet. No important legislation could be passed by the Provisional Government without its approval.

The activities of the Provisional Government

During its brief period of office the Provisional Government initiated a considerable amount of important legislation which changed the constitution of 1906 in many essential respects and prepared the ground for a new democratic and republican form of government. It also introduced far-reaching reforms in the administrative sphere which led to the adoption of a more democratic system for the management of public affairs.

A number of the *constitutional laws* passed by the Provisional Government were particularly important. These included the laws of 12 and 20 March 1917 which granted all citizens equality before the law,[30] thus banishing considerations of class, creed and nationality from the court room. This effectively disposed of the old class system whereby members of different estates were arraigned before different judges and also put an end to the discriminatory practices directed against the Jews. Thus, the law of 5 August 1917 gave equal rights to all women employed in the government service. Another crucial law was passed on 14 July 1917. This recognised the essential sanctity of the individual, of the home and of correspondence; it laid down that no arrests or house searches could be made without a warrant and it established the important principle that a state of emergency could be declared only in times of war.

The law of 14 July 1917 also granted religious freedom. The special privileges previously enjoyed by the Russian Orthodox Church were withdrawn and every citizen was entitled to change or renounce his confessional allegiance upon reaching the age of fourteen.

Meanwhile, under the law of 12 April 1917, the provisions governing the founding of associations and the right of assembly were amended: the government recognised the absolute right of the people to hold assemblies without obtaining special permission and also allowed far greater freedom than under the constitution of 1906 to those who wished to found associations. All such associations had to be registered at the appropriate district court but they could not be forcibly dissolved by any official body unless they violated the law, in which case they could be dissolved by a court order.

The new press law, which was passed on 27 April 1917, removed all restrictions previously imposed by the state. Upon attaining their majority all citizens were entitled to publish periodicals if they so wished. All that was required of them was to advise the local press office of their intention to do so. Under the new law it was also possible to run a printing press without special permission. Here too all that was needed was to notify the press office.

The law passed on 30 May 1917, which set up an entirely new judicial procedure for hearing complaints against the administration, was a very important measure, for it helped safeguard the fundamental rights granted to the people. Primary jurisdiction was provided by individual judges appointed to the *okrugi*, who dealt with the simpler issues themselves and referred any more complex cases to the District Court. Thus, the people had a right of redress against the administration at courts of first and second instance, something quite unheard of under the monarchy.

The Provisional Government also helped to evolve the democratic procedure to be followed for the election of delegates to the constituent assembly. Part of this electoral procedure was contained in the law promulgated on 20 July 1917, which provided for general, secret and direct elections based on universal suffrage. The minimum age for electors and candidates alike was fixed at twenty years (Article 3). The electoral system to be used was proportional representation.[31]

We have already seen that the Provisional Government introduced far-reaching reforms in the *administrative sphere* which were calculated to reduce the extreme bureaucracy that had developed under the Tsars. On 4 March 1917 a law was passed removing all governors from office and replacing them by the chairmen of the provincial Zemstvos, who became commissars of the Provisional Government. Responsibility for the administration of the districts was taken over at the same time by the chairmen of the district Zemstvos. Moreover, the general control previously exercised by the various departments of state over the activities of the Zemstvos was curbed. Consequently, although the state officials were still able to question the legality of any resolutions passed by the Zemstvos, they were not at liberty to question their efficacy. Under the provisions of the law of 21 May 1917 the Zemstvo system of self-government was extended to the small rural communities and also to those provinces where it had not been introduced during the constitutional monarchy. The law of 17 April 1917, which provided for the setting up of the militia, resulted in a large-scale restructuring of the police system. The old police units were replaced by militia units which came under the control of the Zemstvos both in the towns and in the country. The officers commanding the militia units were appointed by the Zemstvos.

Where the *administration of justice* was concerned the Provisional Government sought to ensure that the segregation of the administrative and judicial functions was strictly maintained. The law of 11 April 1917 withdrew the special protection previously accorded to officials employed in government service. Until then it had not been possible to prosecute such officials for misfeasance unless their superiors gave consent, which had meant that it had always been extremely difficult to call them to account. The death penalty was abolished by the law of 12 March 1917 and banishment to Siberia—a punishment *sui generis* under the Tsars—was replaced by confinement in a fortress by the law of 26 April 1917.

Thus, the Provisional Government laid the essential foundations of a constitutional state. Under its rule a democratic republic was beginning to emerge in Russia. But in its eagerness to ensure that this transformation of Russian society was achieved by strictly legal means the Provisional Government made three fatal mistakes which led to its downfall. In the first place, it repeatedly postponed the elections for a constituent assembly. Eventually an election was arranged for 12 November 1917 by the law of 9 August, which would have enabled the assembly to convene on 28 November. But this was forestalled by the successful October revolution, though the elections took place as arranged under the law. In the second place, the provisional government failed to find an immediate solution to the problem of agrarian reform, preferring to leave this crucial question for the constituent assembly to deal with. But the inflamed masses were not prepared to wait that long. Finally, the Provisional Government adopted the unpopular view that despite the progressive disintegration of the Russian army the war must be brought to a 'victorious conclusion'.

The Bolsheviks were quick to exploit these mistakes and skilfully turned the procrastinatory policies pursued by the Provisional

Government to their own advantage. Throughout the summer of 1917 they constantly won new followers and in September took over the leadership of the Petrograd Soviet of Workers' and Soldiers' Deputies. From then onwards there could be no question of collaboration between the Provisional Government and the Soviet, which meant in effect that the fate of the government was sealed.

The role of the political parties

ERWIN OBERLÄNDER

Soviet historians have consistently created the impression that prior to 1917 the Bolshevik wing of the Social-Democratic Workers' Party was the only really important political group in Russia and that its ultimate victory in the struggle for power was pre-ordained by the force of historical necessity. This view, which has also been espoused by the majority of western observers, is in fact quite false. After the establishment of the Imperial Duma, which sanctioned party political activities in Russia, a large number of different political parties were founded, many of which—including some left-wing groups—were far more important than the Bolsheviks. Although the Russian parliamentary system of 1905 to 1917 was far removed from the democratic systems in force in western Europe, politicians were none the less free to formulate and discuss in public a wide range of political programmes. These programmes and the attempts of the different parties to make their influence felt in the special circumstances prevailing in Russia from 1905 onwards will form the principal subject of this survey. We will not be dealing, however, with the political groupings formed by the non-Russian ethnic groups within the Russian empire. Although extremely interesting in themselves, these played only a minor role in the Duma, for their principal objective was to obtain autonomy for their respective territories within a federal framework.

The emergence of the parties and the revolution of 1905

The emergence of the Russian political parties and revolutionary organisations was accompanied by a growing diversification of Russian society. The rigid structure of traditional Russian society, in which neither the clergy nor the merchants had played any significant part and whose principal characteristic had been the antithesis between the nobility on the one hand and the peasants (mainly serfs) on the other, was disrupted before the end of the century when the industrial proletariat and the bourgeoisie entered the scene. The growing resentment of the peasants and of these newly emerging urban classes at the harsh treatment meted out to them by the autocratic tsarist régime found expression, from the turn of the century onwards, in peasant unrest, industrial strikes and urgent pleas for reform on the part of the bourgeois and even the aristocratic classes. And yet in the period prior to 1905 only two illegal parties were formed, the Socialist Revolutionaries and the Russian Social-Democratic Workers' Party, whose leaders—most of them living in exile—had only a small following in Russia.

Until the very end of the tsarist régime the spokesmen for the radical opposition groups all belonged to the so-called intelligentsia. They were a motley assortment, consisting of 'penitent nobles' and the sons of priests, merchants and peasants, who went among the people to preach their new doctrine, in which the main emphasis was placed on political and social revolution. Their movement, which began in the middle of the nineteenth century, was a philosophical rather than a sociological phenomenon. Unable to take part in practical politics, the intelligentsia were thrown back on to political theory with the result that they became alienated from reality, especially during the initial phase of their campaign when they steeped themselves in French utopian socialism. This was followed by a period of German scientific materialism which was then superseded in the 1880s by Marxism. In fact, not many of the ideas advanced by the intelligentsia were original: they were mostly imported from Western Europe. From 1900 onwards many of these crusading intellectuals were assimilated into the ranks of the bourgeoisie, then beginning to assert itself as an independent force. But, although this undoubtedly undermined the movement, its radical left wing—which was completely dedicated to the principle of revolutionary change— none the less succeeded in influencing the attitudes of the opposition parties, both inside and outside the Duma, right up to 1917. This influence, which was often far from beneficial to the cause of Russian democracy, was particularly strong amongst the peasants and industrial workers. Their social and political programme was virtually dictated by the radical intelligentsia.

The intelligentsia had, of course, based the whole of its revolutionary programme on the situation in rural Russia. The *Narodniki* (Friends of the People), who had formed the *Zemlya i Volya* (Land and Freedom) secret organisation in 1878, argued that Russia could proceed to socialism without passing through a capitalist phase by developing her system of village communities (the *mir* or *obshchina*), which would lend themselves admirably to the formation of a communist party organisation. Before the year was out the *Narodniki* had split into two separate groups. The first of these was the *Cherny Peredel* (Black Repartition), which concentrated primarily on propaganda and whose leaders subsequently helped to found the Russian Marxist movement when they were living in exile in the early 1880s. The second group, the *Narodnaya Volya* (Will of the People) preferred terrorist methods.

The members of the *Partiya Sotsialistov-Revolyutsionerov* (Socialist Revolutionary Party), which was founded in 1901, continued in the revolutionary tradition of the *Narodniki*. This revival of interest in their ideas was due, among other things, to the dogmatism of the Marxist doctrine, which had been introduced into Russia in the early 1880s but had failed to satisfy the essentially activist approach and anarchist aspirations of the Socialist Revolutionaries. The original conceptions of *Narodnichestvo* had been brought up to date by some of the early followers of *Narodnaya Volya*, who had founded the short-lived *Narodnoye pravo* party (People's Right) in 1894. But it was Viktor Chernov (1873–1952) who actually evolved a new programme based on firm theoretical premises which took full account of the role of the individual, the interests of the peasants, their revolutionary potential and the use of terror as a 'necessary evil'.

Between 1901, the year in which their group was founded, and 1905, the year of the first Russian revolution, the Socialist Revolutionaries made little contact with the working classes whom they claimed to represent. This was due partly to the heterogeneous make-up of this party—whose members were drawn from widely differing sections of the intelligentsia—and partly to the fact that its central committee and the main journal were both working in exile. The only Socialist Revolutionaries really active in

Russia during that period were the militants, who were responsible for numerous acts of terrorism and whose victims included the Minister of Education, Bogolepov (1901) and two Ministers of the Interior, Sipyagin (1902) and Plehve (1904). But in 1905 the party's image underwent a marked change. After having received virtually no support it suddenly acquired a large following consisting not only of peasants and village schoolmasters but also of industrial workers, democratically-minded members of the intelligentsia and, above all, the youth of the country. The Socialist Revolutionaries also enjoyed considerable influence in various professional organisations, such as the Union of Teachers, the Union of Statisticians, the Union of Railwaymen and particularly the All-Russian Union of Peasants, which was founded in 1905. By the end of 1905 the Socialist Revolutionaries had set up local party organisations in practically every part of the empire and at the first party congress, held at the end of December 1905, their leaders set out to persuade the different groups within the party to agree on a common programme.

The programme adopted by the congress openly subscribed to the conception of 'international, revolutionary socialism', thus reflecting the Socialist Revolutionaries' allegiance to the Second International, to which they belonged until 1914. In the political sphere the programme called for a democratic republic, large-scale decentralisation, self-determination for the different ethnic groups within the empire (who, however, were to be offered membership of a new federation), direct and secret elections based on universal suffrage, and the recognition by the government of specific norms for the protection of human rights.[1] It also demanded an eight-hour working day, the establishment of minimum wage levels and greater consultation between management and the 'workers' organisations'. A notable omission from the programme was the socialisation of industry: this the Socialist Revolutionaries preferred to leave over for future consideration. The agrarian problem, on the other hand, commanded their urgent attention. 'In the interests of socialism and the struggle against the bourgeois principle of private ownership' they tried to preserve the traditional working methods of the Russian peasant as embodied in the *obshchina* system and, over and above this, to uphold the widely disseminated view that the 'land belonged to those who worked it'. Consequently, the Socialist Revolutionaries advocated the nationalisation of all land in private ownership and its redistribution to those prepared to cultivate it either individually or collectively. The old *Narodnik* ideal is clearly discernible in this general policy statement. Chernov, amongst others, argued that if, after the land had been nationalised and redistributed, the peasants were offered free collective usufruct, it would be possible to establish a collective system of agriculture on a purely voluntary basis. However, it seems more likely that it was the promise to redistribute the land amongst the peasants and not this future prospect which gave the Socialist Revolutionaries an almost absolute majority in the constituent assembly of 1918.

Although the party programme was couched in very general terms it none the less led to defections. The left-wing *Soyuz maksimalistov* (Union of Maximalists) which advocated among other things the immediate nationalisation of industry, broke away because it considered that the programme was not revolutionary enough, while the right-wing *Narodnye sotsialisty* (Popular Socialists) broke away because they found it too unrealistic. Not quite as unrealistic, however, as the resolution passed by the party congress to boycott the forthcoming elections to the First Duma! This decision deprived the Socialist Revolutionaries of nearly all the influence they had gained in the course of the preceding twelve months and, although their refusal to take part in an election that left much to be desired in terms of democratic suffrage was prompted in part by a laudable determination to remain true to their principles, a further motivating factor was undoubtedly their failure to appreciate the true relationship between the power of the revolutionary movement and the power of the Tsarist régime. This overestimation of their own strength, which was characteristic of the maximalist outlook of the revolutionary intelligentsia, was to have fatal repercussions in 1905–6 for others as well as themselves.

Since the Socialist Revolutionaries believed that the working class movement that was destined to free Russia from the tsars would be made up not only of peasants but also of industrial workers, they were the natural rivals of the Marxists, who had united in the *Rossüskaya Sotsial-Demokraticheskaya Rabochaya*

Partiya (Russian Social-Democratic Workers' Party). Most of the leaders of this party, which was founded in 1898 but did not become an effective force until after its London Congress in 1903, also came from the ranks of the intelligentsia. They placed their faith almost exclusively in the industrial proletariat of the big cities, who constituted 2·3 per cent of the total population of the empire in 1905.[2] In the Marxist scheme of things these two and a half million men were supposed to become the mainstay of the revolution during the final phase of Russian capitalism. But, although the incidence of strikes amongst the workers, which had been increasing since the turn of the century, suggested that this was a viable proposition, there was one major problem which proved quite intractable for a number of years. The fact of the matter was that the intelligentsia found difficulty in establishing contact with the workers, which was essential if the workers were to be persuaded to sacrifice the immediate economic advantages of strike action in favour of the more distant goal of political revolution. Differences of opinion over the tactical and organisational procedures to be adopted led to the formation of numerous small action groups within the party and also resulted in the split between the Bolsheviks and the Mensheviks at the London Congress of 1903. (The terms 'Bolshevik' (majority) and 'Menshevik' (minority) were coined after the group led by L. Martov (1873–1923) had been defeated in a number of important votes by the group led by V. I. Lenin (1870–1924).) Formal party unity was restored in 1906 and prevailed until 1912.

Before the split took place the Second Congress ratified the party programme[3] evolved by Plekhanov and Lenin which, however, was soon revised by both sides. In this programme the RSDRP called for 'the overthrow of the tsarist autocracy and its replacement by a democratic republic' in which supreme power would be vested in a constituent assembly. The new constitution was to guarantee fundamental rights, including the right of self-determination for all ethnic groups, and was to provide among other things for 'extensive local self-government', the replacement of the standing army by a people's militia, and the segregation of church and state. These provisions were then followed by a long list of requirements promoting the interests of the 'working class', which amounted to what was virtually a comprehensive programme of social legislation. In order to facilitate 'the un-impeded development of the class struggle in the villages' the RSDRP called for the abolition of redemption payments and proposed that the peasants should be allowed to hold their land in usufruct. They further proposed that peasant committees should be set up to deal with any grievances still outstanding following their emancipation in 1861.

In restricting themselves to these demands—which they would certainly have regarded as constituting no more than a minimum programme of reform—the RSDRP acted on the assumption that the overthrow of the tsarist autocracy would be achieved by a bourgeois-democratic revolution which would enable Russian capitalism to develop its full potential. But, unlike the Mensheviks, Lenin soon came round to the view that following this initial revolutionary phase the socialist parties would need to be repre-sented in the new bourgeois-democratic government. According to Lenin, the RSDRP would then have to work for a coalition between the proletariat, the peasants and the middle classes, in order to prepare for the socialist revolution which would be the second phase in the revolutionary process. This raised the question as to whether they should join forces with the newly emerging liberal movement and make common cause against the Tsar or whether they should conduct a war on two fronts and oppose both the liberals and the Tsar.

But the really essential differences between the Bolsheviks and the Mensheviks lay in their attitude to party organisation. In this respect Lenin and the Bolsheviks represented the revolutionary tradition of the intelligentsia, for they insisted that the party should be restricted to a small group of professional revolutionaries under central control who would 'direct the struggle of the pro-letariat'.[4] By contrast, Martov and the Mensheviks wanted a broadly based workers' party organised along much the same sort of lines as the German Social-Democratic Party. What they expected from the bourgeois-democratic revolution was a parlia-mentary system in which they could play their part as a demo-cratic group. But apart from the brief interlude furnished by the revolution of 1905—which enabled the Russian Social-Democrats to make political capital out of the general dissatisfaction of the populace despite the serious divisions and general confusion existing within their own ranks—the Mensheviks were quite unable to assert themselves. For as long as the Tsar remained in power they made no headway whatsoever in pursuit of their democratic ideals. Like the other radical parties, they were forced to use conspiratorial methods and to delegate the major part of their political activities to a small group of professional revolutionaries, with the inevitable result that the workers and peasants, who were the ones most intimately concerned by the revolution, were completely dominated by the intelligentsia. This applied, not only to the Mensheviks, but also to the Bolsheviks and the Socialist Revolutionaries, and it meant that all three of these parties, most of whose leaders were living in exile, were really no more than splinter groups between 1905, when the first revolution failed, and the spring of 1917. It was only the rapid decline of the tsarist régime during the First World War, coupled with the monstrous suffering of the Russian people and the ineptitude of the provisional government, that gave the radicals a second chance.

Like the Socialist Revolutionaries, the Bolsheviks decided to boycott the elections to the First Duma in 1906 and to continue to fight for a constituent assembly. This left-wing boycott had a double effect. On the one hand it led the peasants—who had been allocated a relatively high proportion of seats by the government in the erroneous belief that they would vote for conservative candidates—to elect a large number of independent delegates; while on the other hand it resulted in the formation of an entirely new party—the *Trudovaya gruppa* (Labour Group). Apart from the liberals, this constituted the strongest single group in both the First and Second Dumas. As early as January 1906 a call had gone out for 'all who live by their labour' to elect delegates to the Duma who would represent the 'interests of labour'.[5] The candidates who stood on this platform were generally considered to be 'to the left of the Constitutional Democrats', a description which, incidentally, also fitted the many Socialist Revolutionaries and Social-Democrats who had revolted against the decision of their party leaders to boycott the elections.

The *Trudovaya gruppa* was not formed until after the elections. Unlike the Social-Democratic and Socialist Revolutionary parties, whose leaders were drawn from the ranks of the intelligentsia, this new group was not concerned with far-reaching revolutionary aims but with the concrete and immediate interests of the working population. In order to further this policy three of the new deputies—A. F. Aladin, Onipko and Shaposhnikov—opened a club in St Petersburg so that the peasants' delegates arriving there for the official opening of the Duma would have an opportunity of making contact with one another and evolving a common line of approach. Since most of the members of the new group were peasants' delegates, it is only natural that agrarian reform should have been the most important point in their programme. Like the Socialist Revolutionaries, they considered that this could only be effected by the nationalisation of the land. But initially at least the new group also embraced a number of industrial delegates. Consequently, in addition to the customary demands for fundamental rights, a democratic franchise and a new government that would be directly responsible to the Duma, its programme also included demands for an eight-hour working day and up-to-date social legislation. Because of its extremely heterogeneous composition in the first two 'revolutionary' Dumas (in which it had 107 (23·8 per cent) and 94 seats respectively) the *Trudovaya gruppa* had great difficulty in agreeing on common tactics. As a result the majority of its members tended all too often to back the Constitutional Democrats, who were the most powerful party in the First and Second Dumas and so led the opposition to government policy.

Between 1900 and 1905 the liberal *Osvoboditelnoye dvizheniye* (Liberation Movement) was supported by three groups: the Zemstvo nobles, the liberal intellectuals in various professional organisations and a number of so-called 'legal' Marxists and *Narodniki* who favoured a limited revolution designed to set up a new constitution and so make it possible for social reforms to be achieved within the legal process. The political programme of the Liberation Movement went under the title *Doloy samoderzhaviye* (Down with the autocracy), which one simple-minded provincial police official thought was a 'well-known Russian proverb'.[6] By leaving the details of their projected political, economic and cultural reforms to be worked out by the new representative government which they hoped to create, the leaders of this movement were hoping to obtain wide support for their activities.

In the very first issue of *Osvobozhdeniye* (Liberation), a Russian language newspaper published abroad which served as a rallying point for the Liberation Movement, the paper's chief editor, P. B. Struve, wrote: 'No single class, party or doctrine is exclusively or primarily responsible for the cultural and political liberation of Russia. It is a task . . . for the whole nation.'[7]

From the turn of the century onwards, at a time when the opposition forces in Russia were becoming more and more radical, a number of the liberal Zemstvo nobles embraced many of the ideas evolved by the intelligentsia concerning the extent of the constitutional powers to be vested in an elected government. This provided them with the necessary basis for a common organisation and, after holding preliminary discussions in Schaffhausen and Kharkov they founded the *Soyuz Osvobozhdeniya* (Union of Liberation) in January 1904. The principle objective of the Union was the overthrow of the tsarist régime, to which end it was prepared to use any means, including terrorism. The Union of Liberation was not a party. Rather, it was an attempt to unite as many different groups as possible in opposition to autocracy. In this it was only partially successful. In 1904, for example, when its leaders tried to create a united front of all Russian revolutionary organisations in Paris, the Social-Democrats and a section of the Socialist Revolutionaries refused to participate.

The Union was more successful in its dealings with the professional organisations, who had been made particularly susceptible to anti-government propaganda by their dissatisfaction with the Tsar's grandiose policies in the Far East and the military defeats which Russia consequently sustained in her war with Japan. The assassination of the Minister of the Interior, Plehve, also gave a considerable boost to the Union of Liberation, especially since Plehve was succeeded by the highly respected Prince Svyatopolk-Mirsky. But he too was powerless to stop the revolution. By then the Union of Liberation had evolved a three-point programme for direct action and in accordance with its terms the so-called 'banquet' campaign was staged on 20 November 1904. Under the pretext of commemorating the fortieth anniversary of the judicial reform carried out by Alexander II banquets were held in all major cities, at which virtually identical resolutions were passed calling for the convention of a constituent assembly to set up a democratic régime in Russia. A somewhat less blatant but equally significant step was taken at the third (secret) session of the Zemstvos, which was attended by delegates from all but one of the Russian Zemstvos, and at which the majority voted in favour of a resolution calling for a freely elected, independent parliament that would be responsible for the budget and for all new legislation and would also have control of the administrative machine. The minority, which voted against this resolution, wanted to see elected representatives of the people taking part in the government, in line with the Slavophil conception of the *Zemsky Sobor* (old Russian Land Assembly).[8] Meanwhile, progress was being made towards the realisation of the third objective of the Union movement, namely the amalgamation of all professional associations irrespective of their political allegiance, in a *Soyuz Soyuzov* (Association of Associations) which was eventually formed under the presidency of P. N. Milyukov, later to be the leader of the Constitutional Democrats.

By the end of 1904 the Russian government was faced with a critical situation. In the war with Japan its forces had suffered heavy defeats whilst at home it was being subjected to mounting pressure by a constitutionally-minded opposition, which was becoming more and more coordinated. One of the most serious weaknesses revealed by the Tsar and his intimate advisers was their inability to grant concessions until it was too late for them to do any good, which can only mean that they were completely oblivious of the consequences of their own intransigence. Thus it was that in December 1904 the Tsar—who could not abide the word 'constitution'—rejected Svyatopolk-Mirsky's proposal that representatives of the people should be allowed to participate in the drafting of legislation. Instead, he simply made vague promises of reform at some future date in the imperial ukase of 12 December. But, far from pacifying the opposition, this merely served to alienate the liberals, who had until then still been prepared to negotiate. Meanwhile, the incidence of strikes and peasant disturbances grew progressively more marked. In 1905 there were no less than 3,228 peasant disturbances which had to be put down by troops; there were also cases of mutiny in the army and navy, such as that on the battleship *Potemkin*. This mounting unrest in the country at large lent considerable weight to the demands made by the intelligentsia with the result that in August 1905, when the Minister of the Interior, A. G. Bulygin, published his draft proposals for a purely consultative Duma that was to be elected on a restricted franchise based on property qualifications and separate electoral lists, nobody was even prepared to consider such an offer. On 12 October a general strike was called and the government found itself with no transportation and no means of communication with the outside world. At first the Tsar thought he would be able to bring the situation under control by imposing martial law, but Count Witte, the most important Russian statesman of the day apart from Stolypin, taught him otherwise. And so, on 17 October, the Tsar issued a manifesto in which he granted national representation and civil liberties and gave an undertaking that no legislation would be passed without the consent of the Duma. From 17 October to the beginning of December—a period known at the time as the 'days of freedom'—these concessions were protected by the balance of power between the government and the revolutionary forces. But following the arrest of the St Petersburg Soviet on 3 December and the suppression of the Moscow rising on 18 December the government again began to assert its superiority, which found tangible expression in the imposed constitution of 23 April 1906.

The success of the revolution of 1905 was not due to any one party or any one political trend. On the contrary it was the result of a spontaneous mass movement, in which nearly all levels of society were involved. It was only after the Tsar had been forced to yield that this united front broke down and opposition to the government was again conducted at party level. The Union of Liberation produced, in addition to numerous splinter groups, two big and important parties: the Party of People's Freedom and the Union of 17 October.

From 12 to 18 October, while the general strike was at its height, the liberals were holding a conference in Moscow, where they formed the *Partiya Narodnoy Svobody* (Party of People's Freedom), which came to be known as the Party of the Constitutional Democrats or Kadets. This new party, which was led by the historian P. N. Milyukov (1859–1945), was a coalition made up of members of the intelligentsia and the major part of the constitutionally-minded Zemstvo nobles headed by the President of the Zemstvos in Tver, I. I. Petrunkevich (1844–1928), who was one of the pioneers of the constitutionalist cause. As for the party programme, which was also evolved in Moscow, this seems more radical than liberal to the western observer, an impression that is reinforced by the maximalist policies subsequently pursued by the leaders of the Kadets, which they refused to moderate even when the balance of power had shifted away from the revolutionary forces.[9] After demanding fundamental rights for the people, the authors of the programme went on to state that the political system to be adopted in Russia would be specified in the new constitution. Thus no direct reference was made to the constitutional monarchy, although many of the Kadets undoubtedly subscribed to the monarchic principle. However, it was the parliamentary principle that interested them most. They wanted a Duma elected by direct and universal suffrage, to which the government would be directly responsible and whose assent would have to be obtained for all new legislation. They also wanted local self-government to be extended to all parts of the empire and the old constitutional systems to be restored in Poland and Finland. Under their proposals the peasants would be given more land, which would be obtained partly from the compulsory purchase of estates with suitable compensation for their owners and partly from the expropriation of crown, apanage, church and monastery lands. As far as the industrial workers were concerned, the programme made provision for the right to associate, the right of assembly and the right to strike, and it also contained proposals for an eight-hour working day. It was further suggested that primary schools should be placed under the jurisdiction of local government bodies and higher education be made available to all children irrespective of their religious or social background. In the light of this programme it is perfectly obvious that the Kadets would not approve the imposed constitution of 23 April 1906.

In this they differed from the members of the *Soyuz 17 Oktyabrya* (Union of 17 October) who came to be known as the Octobrists because they based their policies on the October manifesto. The Octobrists accepted the shortcomings of the constitution in the belief that by pressing for liberal reforms in the

Duma, they could gradually amend it and so turn it into a more democratic instrument. This approach had its origins in the attitude adopted by the minority group of the Zemstvo nobles at the Zemstvo congresses of 1904 and 1905, when they had spoken up against the growing radicalism of their colleagues.

Under the leadership of D. N. Shipov (1851–1920) and A. I. Guchkov (1862–1936) who succeeded one another as leaders of the Union, the Zemstvo nobles represented the middle-of-the-road liberals among the estate owners. But the Octobrists were not all Zemstvo nobles. On the contrary, as their official title implies, they were a union made up of several different groups. The most important of these, apart from the Zemstvo contingent, were the two groups representing the merchants and the manu-facturers. Prior to the formation of the Union these sections of the community had been represented by a number of smaller groups such as the Association for Industry and Commerce and the Progressive Economic Party in St Petersburg, and the Moderate Progressive Party in Moscow. Although these groups had much in common with the Kadets and backed many of the demands made in their programme, they none the less openly expressed their disapproval of the Kadets' extreme radicalism.[10] Their general aim was to put a stop to the revolutionary move-ment of the peasants and industrial workers without making any real concessions to either of these classes.

Because of the widely differing views held by the two principal groups in the Union the delegates to the first Party Congress, which was held in Moscow between 8 and 12 February 1906, found difficulty in agreeing on a joint programme. What they had in common was their pan-Russian nationalism, which distin-guished them more than anything else from the parties of the left and which found expression in the concept of the 'unity and indivisibility of the Russian state', to which they all subscribed. They advocated the establishment of a constitutional monarchy and a democratic parliament based on general elections with the same unanimity that marked their opposition to the convention of a constituent assembly. They were completely at loggerheads, however, over the attitude to be adopted in the Duma to the question of agrarian and industrial reform. In their 'proclam-ations', which were published in 1905 and formed the basis for the discussion of the agrarian question within the Union, the Zemstvo nobles had gone so far as to call for the expropriation of land with suitable compensation for the landowners. Later, however, this demand was dropped in favour of a plea for 'greater productivity on the land'. Although this means that the Octobrists were amongst the very few groups to realise that low productivity was one of the root causes of the agrarian problem, they failed to make any concrete proposals for improving the situation. This was not the case in the industrial sphere. There the Octobrists called upon the Duma to subject all existing legislation to a thorough review. What was more important, they proposed that local self-government should be expanded, in both urban and rural areas, thus enabling all classes to participate and providing the people with 'the best possible training in political freedom'. Although these proposals were not worked out in detail, they reveal a considerable insight into the social problems of the day, for which the Octobrists were chiefly indebted to the Zemstvo nobles.[11] It was they who made the Union of 17 October a genuine centre party, the only party, in fact, that was prepared to base its policies on the reality of existing conditions. Because of this, the Octobrists were able to fulfil, in the Third and Fourth Dumas, the function which the Kadets had refused to entertain in the first two Dumas.

But while the Octobrists were determined to abide by the principles embodied in the manifesto and the constitution, the groups to their right sought to revoke both of these imperial concessions. M. Florinsky has rightly observed that in Russia, as in the rest of Europe, all right-wing parties were simply 'reflex movements' produced by the emergence of liberal and socialist ideas. This was even true of the *Russkoye Sobranye* (Russian Assembly), which was founded by representatives of the aristocracy, the bureaucracy and the clergy as early as 1900. The programmes of all such parties were invariably based on the formula evolved by S. S. Uvarov, the Minister for Popular Enlightenment under Nicholas II: orthodoxy, autocracy and popular patriotism (*narodnost*). Thus, in its election programme in 1906, the Russian Assembly stated: 'The Russian Assembly considers that, far from having been abrogated by the manifesto of 17 October, the autocratic powers vested in the Tsar are still

operative in Russia under the new dispensation and that the
Imperal Duma is neither qualified nor able to alter the fundamental laws of the state in any way.'[12]

It should be pointed out, however, that even right-wing circles
in Russia had come to accept that the best way of improving
relations between the Tsar and the people, which they considered
had been strained as a result of bureaucratic mismanagement, was
by granting popular representation. But where they differed from
the left-wing parties was in their insistence that any such representative body should be purely consultative (like the ancient
Zemsky Sobor). This was the principal demand made by the most
important of the right-wing organisations, the *Soyuz Russkogo
Naroda* (Union of the Russian People) which was founded at the
end of 1905 under the leadership of A. I. Dubrovin and V. M.
Purishkevich. Thanks to its fighting organisation, the *chernaya
sotnya*, or Black Hundreds as its members were soon to be
called, which played a leading part in nearly every pogrom in
Russia from 1905 to 1914, the Union of the Russian People
became notorious far beyond the borders of the empire. It has
even been suggested that this organisation was a forerunner of the
fascist movements of western Europe.[13] Incidentally, Nicholas II
thought nothing of appearing in public in the company of members of the Black Hundreds and he once accepted a gift of the
insignia of the Union of the Russian People for himself and the
heir apparent. But by February 1917, with the aid of the Tsarina
and her protégé Rasputin, the Tsar had none the less succeeded
in alienating even these dubious pillars of the constitutional
monarchy.

Another common feature of the right-wing parties—one which
not even V. A. Gringmut's *Monarkhicheskaya Partiya* (Monarchist Party) was able to avoid—was their pan-Russian nationalism, which found one of its principal outlets in wholesale
anti-semitism. This anti-semitism—which V. Levitsky has aptly
described as the 'socialism of idiots'—and the anti-bureaucratic
attitude mentioned earlier, were the only points held in common
by the leaders of the right-wing parties, most of whom were
aristocratic, and broad sections of the population. And even this
appeal to the baser instincts of a largely uneducated populace
failed to procure a really strong following for the parties of the

right. Their general objective, which was the re-establishment of the autocratic conditions obtaining prior to 1905, was too far opposed to the wishes of the vast majority. There were no right-wing delegates in the First Duma and only ten in the Second. In the Third and Fourth Dumas the right-wing parties had a majority. This, however, was due, not to a sudden swing to the right, but to the change in the electoral law of 3 June 1907, which ensured a conservative victory.

The parties in the Duma

From the very outset the auspices for the Duma were not good. Although the Kadets, who formed the centre party, were prepared to continue the struggle for further concessions within a parliamentary framework, the left-wing Socialist Revolutionaries and Social-Democrats were so dissatisfied with the powers vested in the Duma that they boycotted the elections, while the right-wing parties considered that these powers were far too extensive and were determined to curb them. In the circumstances much depended on the attitude of the Tsar and the Prime Minister. But Nicholas II and his Tsarina had only one political goal: to re-establish and preserve for their heir a completely autocratic régime. In their eyes the Duma was entirely suspect. As for I. L. Goremykin, the extremely weak Premier, who had been appointed to his office shortly before the official opening of the First Duma, he decided that it was best to ignore the new assembly. And since there was no one in his cabinet, apart from the Foreign Minister, A. P. Izvolsky, who approved of the new constitutional system, it is difficult to see how the Duma was to become a forum for a genuine dialogue between the state and society.

The elections to the First Duma showed that, although the electoral law was democratic only to a limited extent, it was still possible for public opinion to make itself felt. Of the 448 delegates present at the first session 153 (34.1%) were Kadets, 107 (23.8%) *Trudoviki*, 63 (14%) representatives of the non-Russian ethnic groups, 13 (2.9%) Octobrists, 105 (23.4%) Independents and the remainder members of various splinter groups.[14] Throughout all four Dumas the strength of the parties tended to fluctuate to some extent, which is what one would expect in a newly established parliamentary system. None the less, the First Duma produced a clear left-wing majority, which the government had certainly not bargained for and which there was very little it could do about. On 27 April 1906 the Duma was officially opened with a speech from the throne in the Winter Palace, after which the delegates proceeded to the Tauride Palace, where S. A. Muromtsev, one of the Kadet delegates, was elected president. It was a mixed gathering, which the correspondent of the *Morning Star* described in the following terms:

'You see dignified old men in frock coats, aggressively democratic-looking intelligentsia with long hair and *pince-nez*, a Polish bishop dressed in purple, who looks like the pope; men without collars; members of the proletariat, men in loose Russian shirts with belts; men dressed by Davies or Poole, and men dressed in the costume of two centuries ago.'[15]

After attending further sessions of the Duma the correspondent went on to discuss the standard of debate:

The second, and what is to me the principal impression of the Duma, is the familiar ease with which the members speak; some of them speak well, and some of them speak badly, but they all speak as if they had spoken in Parliament all their lives, without the slightest evidence of nervousness or shyness.

In the speech from the throne there was no mention of a legislative programme to be presented to the Duma by the Tsar. The delegates were quick to seize upon this serious tactical error and in their reply to the speech on 5 May they submitted their own draft programme which, as they adroitly suggested, was designed to promote a rapprochement between the Tsar and the people. The principal proposals made by the Duma were: the dissolution of the second house (the Imperial Council), the withdrawal of all emergency legislation, the creation of a new government directly responsible to the Duma and the transfer to the Duma of responsibility for all future taxation measures. The programme also provided for the drafting of new statutes guaranteeing fundamental rights, for the abolition of the death penalty and for social legislation involving a complete reorganisation of local government. Finally, it called for an amnesty for all political and religious detainees as a means of establishing a new relationship of mutual trust between the Tsar and the people.[16] It took the government until 13 May to prepare a reply to this unexpected initiative. It then rejected the proposals put forward by the Duma and stressed the need to strike a 'sensible balance between freedom and order'. The Duma responded by initiating discussions of the various bills outlined in its programme, attaching particular importance to the agrarian question. On 26 June the government published its own recommendations for a solution of the agrarian problem, whereupon the delegates promptly insisted that these should be debated in the house and eventually went to the extreme length of appealing to the people. This provided the government with the excuse it had been looking for and on 8 July P. A. Stolypin, who had meanwhile succeeded Goremykin as Premier, dissolved the Duma on the grounds that, by making this appeal to the people, it had exceeded its constitutional rights. A number of delegates then travelled to Vyborg in Finland, where they issued a further appeal, calling on the Russian people to refuse to pay taxes or report for military service. This call went unheeded. Unfortunately for those deputies involved, it also prevented them from standing for re-election to the Second Duma.

Apart from their official dealings the government and the Duma also conducted secret negotiations to consider the feasibility of appointing members of the Duma to ministerial posts. In these negotiations the Palace Commandant, D. F. Trepov, acted for the government and the leader of the Kadets, Milyukov, for his party. From the outset Milyukov argued from what he considered to be a position of strength and insisted that all governmental responsibility should be transferred to the majority group in the Duma. This, however, merely provided the reactionary elements in the government with a welcome pretext for sabotaging the negotiations. Sir Bernard Pares' analysis of the reasons underlying the failure of the First Duma was, therefore, essentially correct: 'We might say that the Emperor wanted a German Parliament, and that the Duma intended to be an English one.'[17]

The elections to the Second Duma, in which both the Socialist Revolutionaries and the Social-Democrats took part, produced an even more radical parliamentary majority which was made up of 99 Kadets, 98 *Trudoviki*, 37 Socialist Revolutionaries and 66 Social-Democrats (Bolsheviks and Mensheviks). Of the other groups the non-Russian ethnic minorities had 94 delegates, the Octobrists 12, the right-wing moderates 23 and the right-wing extremists 10. In addition, there were 52 independent delegates and 7 delegates representing splinter groups.[18] Given this preponderance of left-wing members it could only be a matter of time before the Second Duma, which was officially opened on 20 February 1907, met with the same fate as the First, especially since by then the new government under Stolypin had completely mastered the revolution so that the balance of power had shifted even further away from the left wing. Determined not to repeat the error committed by his predecessor, who had ignored the First Duma, Stolypin delivered a policy speech on 6 March, in which he laid before the house a detailed programme of reforms. In addition to numerous decrees based on Article 87 of the constitution this included draft legislation designed to ensure fundamental rights, improve the judicial system, extend the Zemstvo system of self-government, reform the administration and solve the agrarian problem. But although this programme was extremely liberal by comparison with the statement made by Goremykin the previous year and came some way towards meeting the demands of the majority groups in the Duma, they none the less decided to ignore it. In this way they were able to demonstrate their lack of confidence in a government which had used methods that contravened the principles of the October manifesto and the constitution of 1906 in order to suppress the revolution. Stolypin must have already realised at this point that there could be no question of collaborating with the Second Duma and on 3 June he published the resolution ordering its dissolution, together with a decree which altered the electoral law. Now that the balance of power had swung in the government's favour, Stolypin created a parliament with which he could confidently expect to work in harmony. In doing so he placed his faith primarily in the Zemstvo nobles and the Union of October 17.

Although Stolypin had contravened the terms of the constitution by revising the electoral law his action produced no serious repercussions. The revolutionary forces were exhausted and their leaders had either gone underground or fled the country. The Socialist Revolutionaries had completely withdrawn from public debate and were not represented in the Third and Fourth Dumas. As for the Social-Democrats, and more especially the Bolsheviks, although they still considered it expedient to use the Duma as a forum, most of their leaders were living abroad, where they continued to hope that the revolution would somehow receive a fresh impetus that would carry them to power. In the Third Duma, which ran its full term from 1 November 1907 to 9 June 1912, the 140 right-wing delegates and the 148 Octobrists had a solid majority over the Kadets, the *Trudoviki* and the Social-Democrats, who had 53, 14 and 19 delegates respectively. Although there were frequent regroupings on the right wing during the five-year term, this had little effect on the general distribution of power.[19]

On 16 November Stolypin again presented his liberal programme to the house, for which he gained the support of the moderates. With their aid and in the face of determined and sometimes bitter opposition from the right wing, he tried to give effect to measures which the Tsar and his advisers (amongst whom Rasputin was steadily gaining influence) eventually found so bold that it seemed as if Stolypin would shortly be dismissed from office. But on 1 September 1911 he was murdered by an agent of the secret police during a gala performance at the Kiev opera. Despite occasional stormy debates on both internal and external affairs (the latter arising out of the budget debates) the Duma was a consultative rather than a legislative body during Stolypin's term as Premier.

Although the relative strength of the parties in the Fourth Duma (which sat from 15 November 1912 to 26 February 1917) was virtually the same as it had been in the Third, the attitude of the parliamentary majority to the government was entirely different. The Third Duma had been extremely cooperative. The Fourth was not. But this was due neither to the tendency revealed by the right-wing parties in the course of the Third Duma to gravitate towards the centre nor to the tentative move towards the left made by the majority of the Octobrists. This sudden change was prompted, first, by what D. Treadgold has called the 'psychopathic tragicomedy' being enacted at the imperial court (in which Rasputin, who had also acquired political influence following Stolypin's death, played the central part), and secondly, by the general ineptitude of the Russian bureaucracy which from 1914 onwards showed itself to be quite incapable of prosecuting the war. The fact that Rasputin was able to prevail upon the Tsar to appoint totally incompetent persons to important positions was regarded by the left as evidence of corruption and by the right as an impediment to effective government.

Initially the Duma's attitude to the war was extremely positive. Commenting on the special session called on 26 July 1914 to approve the war credits, the Bolshevik deputy A. E. Badayev said that the brief meeting quickly developed into a 'patriotic orgy'. Apparently nobody even thought of pressing the government to give guarantees of future reforms in exchange for an assurance of full parliamentary support for the Tsar's war policy. Later, however, when the crushing defeats imposed on the Russian armies and the miserable role played by the responsible authorities became known, there was a complete reversal of feeling. The Duma majority then decided to take matters into its own hands, both by organising the provision of essential supplies for the army and by instituting political initiatives. In August 1915 the Progressive Bloc was formed. This was a coalition made up of parties ranging from the Kadets to the National Progressives and embracing about two-thirds of all Duma delegates. The two basic demands made by the coalition were:

'1. The creation of a united government composed of ministers who enjoy the confidence of the Russian people and are capable of putting into speedy effect, in collaboration with the legislative assemblies, a concrete programme.

'2. A complete revision of government practice to date, which has been characterised by its mistrust of all independent initiatives undertaken by society . . .'.[20]

It was the government's neglect, indeed its suspicion, of the organisations set up by public groups—such as the War Industry Committees and the Joint Committee of the Union of Zemstvos and the Union of Municipalities for the Supply of the Army

(*Zemgor*)—that had been mainly responsible for alienating public opinion. Unfortunately, this attitude remained unchanged, for both the Tsar and his Premier, Goremykin (Stolypin's predecessor and successor) refused to listen to the urgent representations of the Progressive Bloc. It has been suggested that this was the last real chance of saving the monarchy and ensuring an organic development in Russian political life. The suggestion is almost certainly true.[21]

It is not necessary to consider in detail the death agonies of the tsarist régime, which continued until March 1917. During that final period the Duma restricted itself to criticism and even the Progressive Bloc was not prepared to take the strong measures necessary to remove the incompetent Premier, B. V. Stürmer, and the corrupt Minister of the Interior, A. D. Protopopov, from power. As in 1905, so too in 1917, it was the people who acted, largely due to the growing shortage of food. They took to the streets. Violent disturbances broke out—especially in St Petersburg, where the garrison joined the revolutionaries on 27 February—with the result that on 2 March 1917 the Tsar was forced to abdicate. Such was the inglorious end of this bankrupt régime, which had been unable to renew itself from within, and thanks to the machinations of the clique that had gathered around the weak-willed Tsar, had refused to countenance any proposals put forward by other sections of society. The end was undramatic: the tsarist régime was not overthrown, it succumbed to its own inertia.

The downfall of the old régime sealed the fate of the Duma. It was superseded by a Provisional Government which was led by Prince G. E. Lvov and composed of former members of the old Progressive Bloc including the left-winger A. F. Kerensky, a member of the *Trudoviki* who later succeeded Lvov as Premier. As soon as it entered office the Provisional Government issued a proclamation in which it undertook to respect all fundamental rights and to call a general election based on universal suffrage and a direct and secret ballot, with the object of establishing a constituent assembly. But this government was far from being its own master. It was created largely as a result of an agreement reached between the Duma Committee and the St Petersburg Soviet of Workers' and Soldiers' Deputies, both of which were formed on 27 February. The ensuing situation, in which the Provisional Government and the St Petersburg Soviet ran the country between them, contributed in no small measure to the spread of anarchy. Because of the different views held by the parties who were represented in it and also because of the vastly different attitude of the Soviet, the Provisional Government was unable to take any really effective measures. Meanwhile, the majority parties in the Soviet (the Socialist Revolutionaries and Mensheviks) were biding their time and waiting for the Provisional Government to bring about the bourgeois revolution which, according to their ideology, would provide the 'objective' basis for the socialist revolution. But it was not long before they abandoned this waiting policy, and on 5 May 1917 six socialists (Socialist Revolutionaries and Mensheviks) were appointed to ministerial posts in the Provisional Government. This meant that the only important party not represented in the government were the Bolsheviks. They continued to place their faith in the St Petersburg and Moscow Soviets where, by appearing to identify themselves with the wishes of the anarchistic masses, they acquired a majority in September 1917. This majority was the base from which Lenin proceeded to his coup d'état, which was made considerably easier for him by virtue of the fact that the other left-wing parties were inclined to hold back in the first instance for fear of provoking a counter-revolution which might have destroyed everything that had been achieved up till then.

In November 1917 the elections to decide the membership of the constituent assembly were held. Of the 808 seats it seems that only 703 were filled, and these were apportioned as follows: Bolsheviks 168; left Socialist Revolutionaries 39; right Socialist Revolutionaries 380 (an absolute majority); Mensheviks 18; Kadets, Popular Socialists and right-wing parties 17; non-Russian ethnic groups 77.[22] On 5 January 1918, when the constituent assembly was officially opened, it elected the Socialist Revolutionary V. Chernov as its president and threw out a draft resolution presented by the Bolsheviks. It was then closed by the Bolsheviks on 6 January.

The Russian parliamentary experiment had ended long before this. It was a complex phenomenon, whose evaluation calls for more than a passing reference to the fact that Russia possessed a constitution, political parties and a house of representatives with legislative powers. The scope of those powers was not really important. What mattered was that the Russian parliamentary system was completely undermined by the lack of trust between the tsarist government and the First and Second Dumas, which were more or less representative of the people. One of the main contributory factors to these bad relations was undoubtedly the doctrinaire maximalism of many of the left-wing parties, including the Kadets. On the other hand, the leaders of these parties would not have made such importunate demands if the Tsar and his government had been more accommodating. Where concessions were concerned, it was invariably a case of too little and too late. This was a fatal error for if adequate political reforms had been granted in time this might have led to evolution rather than revolution. There were, after all, a number of positive features in pre-revolutionary Russia, especially in the economic sphere, which would have provided a basis for the future development of the country.

Russia's economic development

KARL C. THALHEIM

In the twenty-five years preceding the outbreak of the First World War Russia's economic problems were largely agrarian. This emerges quite clearly from the article contributed by Harry Willets to this book and is further demonstrated by the fact that, in 1914, three-quarters of Russia's work force was still employed on the land. However, this statistic also shows that Russia's agrarian problems could not be solved by means of agrarian policies alone. Such a high proportion of agricultural workers invariably means that there is an over-concentration of the available work force on the land, even though this may not be immediately apparent in the case of countries like tsarist Russia, whose agriculture was still largely based on primitive farming techniques. But in Russia this imbalance was further exacerbated by the constant and speedy growth of the population; for, although the mortality rate was high, the birth-rate was even higher, with the result that between 1901 and 1913 there was an annual population increase of between sixteen and seventeen per thousand. Nor was this offset to any appreciable extent by emigration, which was relatively insignificant in tsarist Russia.

In these circumstances it would only have been possible to expand and extend agriculture by providing considerably more land for cultivation. At first sight the enormous size of the Russian empire would suggest that this might easily have been done. But upon closer consideration we find that, due to the large areas of tundra, desert and mountainous terrain, only a relatively small part of this enormous expanse is arable and that only a relatively small part of this arable land has good quality soil and a really suitable climate. None the less, in the period under discussion agricultural expansion was still a viable proposition. In 1891 work had begun on the Trans-Siberian railway and when this was completed in 1904 it was possible to proceed with the colonisation of Siberia. This project, which played such an important part in Stolypin's programme for the solution of Russia's agrarian problem, was by no means entirely unsuccessful. However, it soon became apparent that only a small part of the new territory was suitable for immediate colonisation, and that before any additional areas could be taken over a completely new infra-structure would have to be created. This called for investment on a significant scale, for which the necessary capital was not available.

And so tsarist Russia found itself in the same situation as so many of the newly developing countries of our own day. It had to provide productive employment for its surplus population, thus increasing the social product and raising the standard of living, which was still very low for the broad mass of the population and was actually falling for a certain section of the peasant population. But this could only be done by creating new employment outside of agriculture and on such a scale that it would not only cater for the surplus population but would also make it possible to reduce the existing agricultural strength. The only possible solution to this tremendously complex and difficult problem was industrialisation. It must be remembered that industrialisation creates work both directly and indirectly: the building of new factories not only produces an expansion of trade and commerce, banking and insurance, it also leads to the development of service industries, provides the state with new administrative functions and opens up new cultural possibilities. Seen in this light, industrialisation is not just a starting-point for economic growth, it also leads to a greater diversification of social structures.

By the early years of the twentieth century this process of economic and social diversification had been carried to far greater lengths in western and central Europe than in tsarist Russia. And yet it was by no means inevitable that this should have been the case. By the beginning of the First World War it was perfectly obvious that as far as natural resources were concerned, the United States and Russia were the two countries in the world best equipped to become great industrial powers. But although Russia possessed large quantities of every conceivable type of raw material within her borders, she had failed to exploit these resources to the full. Thanks to her oilfields in Baku, Russia was the second largest producer of crude oil in the world. She also obtained practically half the cotton used in her textile industry from her colonial territories in Central Asia.[1] But although they were aware of the great industrial significance of the west Siberian coalfields, the Russian industrialists had made no serious attempt to open them up. Nor, for that matter, had any really effective use been made of the enormous Russian forests, which offered almost unlimited supplies of timber for any industry working in or with this material.

Of course, natural resources are not necessarily the same as economic resources. This was particularly true of Russia, where transportation difficulties excluded or severely restricted the use of many raw materials, especially minerals. Under the tsars, when Russian technology was in its infancy, the vast distances within the empire often had an inhibiting effect. In this respect there was no real comparison between Russia and the USA. The Americans certainly had their own transportation problems and, like the Russians, had to draw on foreign capital to finance their railroad system; but the difficulties with which the Russians had to contend in collecting their scattered resources and carrying them to their industrial centres were unique. Yet, taken all in all, Russia was none the less extremely well placed to become a great industrial power.

Russia's backwardness in the industrial sphere at the beginning of the twentieth century is also surprising in so far as during the eighteenth century, when Peter the Great was pursuing his mercantile policy, it seemed as if she might well become one of the foremost industrial nations in Europe. At the end of the eighteenth century she was the leading producer of low-grade steel in the world.[2] The French economic historian, Roger Portal, has reminded us that Russia's industrial growth in the eighteenth century 'was far more significant than is commonly supposed'.[3] The traditional cottage industries were also an important feature of Peter the Great's reign. Textile manufacturers, woodworking firms and other branches of the consumer goods industry all gave work out in this way.[4]

But these hopeful beginnings were not followed up by a full programme of industrial development of the kind found in western and central Europe and in the United States. None the less, they did enable Russian manufacturers to become acquainted at a very early stage with the new technological discoveries on which factory-based industries of the western world were built up. Thus, the first industrial spinning machine was imported into Russia in 1798 by a factory in Alexandrovo, a suburb of St Petersburg; in 1808 the same factory imported the first weaving loom; and in 1815 the first Russian steamship was built in St Petersburg. The first eight decades of the nineteenth century also saw the establishment of new factories, most of which produced essential goods, especially armaments. The famous Putilov Works was one of these. Founded in 1873, the Putilov Works became the largest industrial concern in St Petersburg and even before the First World War employed some ten thousand workers.[5] But these were all isolated developments which did not really affect the basic economic structure of the country.

The reasons *why* it took so long for modern economic structures to be developed in tsarist Russia, especially in the industrial sphere, cannot be discussed in detail within the framework of this present chapter. Certainly, the retention of serfdom until such a late date played an important part. So too did the inadequate formation of capital within Russia and the relatively late development of capital transactions. A further factor which undoubtedly contributed to the backward state of Russian industrial development was the lack of initiative displayed both by the government and by private enterprise. Until the end of the nineteenth century the majority of Russian entrepreneurs were merchants of the kind depicted in the novels and dramas of the period. From early times it was widely held that the Russians possessed a definite flair for commerce. Certainly, the famous fair at Nizhny-Novgorod (now Gorky) remained an important feature of Russian economic life long after similar fairs in other parts of Europe had been discontinued or—as in the case of Leipzig—transformed into exhibitions. The Russian textile industry was exceptional in that it was developed at a relatively early stage, due to the existence of a large home market for the simpler kinds of woven goods.

The following table, which was compiled by P. L. Lyashchenko,[6] shows the development of Russian industrial production between 1860 and 1876:

		1860	1876
Cotton spinning	(in millions of roubles)	28.7	44.2
Cotton goods	(in millions of roubles)	42.9	96.3
Woollen yarns	(in millions of roubles)	0.45	2.5
Woollen goods	(in millions of roubles)	34.9	52.7
Machines	(in millions of roubles)	14.0	43.4
Petroleum	(in millions of poods)†	0.6	10.9
Coal	(in millions of poods)	7.3	111.3
Pig iron	(in millions of poods)	18.2	25.5
Iron	(in millions of poods)	11.7	17.1
Steel	(in millions of poods)	0.1	1.1

† One pood (an old Russian weight) = 16.38 kg

Taken all in all, the growth rate shown in this table is by no means inappreciable. None the less, it was not until the last quarter of the nineteenth century that there was any really significant speeding up in the development of Russian industry. Subsequently—despite the severe economic crisis of 1900–1902—growth rates were very high indeed.[7] The following table shows the average increase in factory production in fifty provinces of European Russia between 1900 and 1913:[8]

	Total production in millions of roubles	Per capita production in roubles
1900	861.7	8.8
1913	1665.0	14.3

After allowing for price alterations we find that over this period total production increased by 74.1 per cent and per capita production by 46.2 per cent.

These are very considerable growth rates, especially in view of the fact that the figures make allowance for price alterations. It is quite clear from the per capita increase of almost fifty per cent that industrial production had more than kept up with the rapid population growth taking place at that time. None the less, the total output—even in 1913—was still very low compared with that of other industrial countries and shows how backward Russia still was on the industrial front.

Moreover, industrial growth in tsarist Russia was still not nearly strong enough to produce any profound change in the professional and social structure of the country save in certain strictly limited areas. Nor did it lead to any large-scale redistribution of the population. Between 1885 and 1914 the number of city dwellers in Russia rose from 10.6 to 13.3 per cent of the total population, which is only a relatively modest increase.[9] Now, it is perfectly true that at that time the rural population of Russia was not composed purely of agricultural workers, for a considerable number of country-dwellers were engaged in the various cottage industries. None the less, industry was concentrated primarily in the towns, and to this extent the relatively small increase in the size of urban populations reflects the slow rate of change in the economic structure of the country as a whole.

Initially, the more industrialised areas of Russia were like islands set in a vast agrarian sea. But the corporate potential of these islands was so great that by the outbreak of the First World War Russia was almost certainly the fifth largest industrial country in the world. On the other hand, the gap between Russia and the three leading industrial nations was extremely wide, especially when measured in terms of per capita production. And it must also be remembered that this assessment is based on the industrial output of the *whole* of the Russian empire within its *pre-1914* frontiers, which included Russian Poland and the Baltic Provinces, whose industrial output was well above the Russian average. The following table, which is based on the official statistics published at the time, shows the increase in factory production between 1887 and 1908:[10]

Year	No. of factories	No. of workers (thousands)	Total production (millions of roubles)
1887	30,888	1318.0	1334.5
1890	32,254	1434.7	1502.6
1897	39,029	2098.2	2839.1
1908	39,856	2609	4909

The increase of production in certain branches is illustrated by the following table:[11]

	1900	1909	1913
Production of pig iron (in millions of poods)	177	175	283
Production of steel (in millions of poods)	163	163	246
Production of steel rails (in millions of poods)	30.2	29.1	35.9
Production of copper (in millions of poods)	0.5	1.3	2.0
Production of coal (in millions of poods)	1003	1591	2214
Production of petroleum (in millions of poods)	632	563	561
Consumption of cotton (in millions of poods)	16.1	21.3	25.9
Number of spindles (in thousands)	6646	8064	9200
Number of spinning machines (in thousands)	151	200	230
Production of cotton yarn (in millions of poods)	14.6	20.2	22.7
Production of linen yarn (in thousands of poods)	2042	3088	3039

The serious economic crisis of 1900–02 and the depression to which this gave rise are clearly reflected in these figures: it took until 1909 for Russian industrial production to return to its 1900 level. This period of stagnation was then followed by a period of rapid growth in a large number of industrial spheres. Thus, from 1909 to 1913, coal and steel production both rose by nearly fifty per cent, a growth rate comparable with the kind of rates now being achieved in the Soviet Union.

Thanks to this period of rapid growth Russian industrial production received a very considerable boost and by 1913 it was running at a level that was significant even by international standards. This is readily apparent from the following tables, which are based partly on quantities or prices, partly on percentages and partly on the consumption of raw materials.

Unfortunately, the available statistics cannot be reduced to a standard measure.

Mineral production in 1912 (in millions of pounds sterling)

Source: M. Meisner *Die Versorgung der Welt mit Bergwerkserzeugnissen* I. 1 Stuttgart, 1925 p. 4		
USA	392
Great Britain	123
German Empire	104
Russia	83
France	29
Austria-Hungary	22

Consumption of rubber and gutta-percha in 1910 (in 1000 × 100 kg)

Source: W. Woytinsky *Die Welt in Zahlen* Vol. IV. Berlin, 1926 p 340		
USA	671
Great Britain	254
German Empire	225
Russia	73.5
France	38
Austria–Hungary	20.0

Production of pig iron in 1913 (in thousands of tons)

USA	31,462
(a) with Luxembourg Source: *Statistisches Jahrbuch für das Deutsche Reich* Jg. 41, 1920 p 15	German Empire (a)	19,312
	Great Britain	10,425
	France	5,311
	Russia	4,635
	Austria–Hungary	2,435

Steel production in 1913 (in thousands of tons)

USA	31,803
(a) with Luxembourg Source: *ibid.* Jg. 45, 1926 p 52	German Empire (a)	18,329
	Great Britain	7,787
	Russia	4,841
	France	4,687
	Austria–Hungary	2,683

Production of machines in 1913 (as percentage of world production)

Source: Bruno Dietrich and Hermann Leiter *Produktion, Verkehr und Handel in der Weltwirtschaft* Vienna, 1930 p 252	

USA	50
German Empire	20.7
Great Britain	11.8
Russia	3.5
Austria–Hungary	3.4
France	1.9

Electrical industry in 1913 (as percentage of world production)

Source: Dietrich and Leiter *ibid.* p 252

German Empire	34.9
USA	28.9
Great Britain	16.0
France	4.0
Austria–Hungary	3.2
Russia	2.2

Goldmining in 1913 (in thousands of kg)

Source: Dietrich and Leiter *ibid.* p. 232

South Africa	273.7
USA	133.7
Australia	69.1
Russia	39.9

Petroleum production in 1913 (in thousands of tons)

Source: *Statistisches Jahrbuch für das Deutsche Reich* Jg. 41, 1920 p 13

USA	33,132
Russia	9,139
Mexico	3,686
Rumania	1,885

Textile industry in 1913 (as percentage of European production)

Country	Cotton	Wool	Silk	Linen	Jute	Ready-made clothes	Art. Silk	Total
Russia	14.9	15.0	6.8	14.0	6.1	1.2	7.4	13.3
Germany	19.1	21.2	22.6	18.2	21.4	23.2	28.1	20.3
Gt Britain	28.6	21.5	4.9	22.4	31.4	29.3	20.0	24.2
France	10.0	15.7	32.9	16.9	16.6	29.1	21.1	15.2
Austria–Hungary	7.2	7.0	5.2	12.8	8.8	8.9	7.8	7.5

Source: Woytinsky *op. cit.* p 282
(Woytinsky's figures are taken from A. Kertesz *Die Textilindustrie sämtlicher Staaten* Brunswick, 1917, p 37)

Cotton spindles in 1913 (in thousands)

(a) with Poland (1,322) but not Finland
(b) with Czechoslovakia
Source: *Statistisches Jahrbuch für das Deutsche Reich*, Jg. 45, 1926, p 40

Great Britain	55,653
USA	32,149
German Empire	11,186
Russia (a)	8,990
France	7,400
Austria (b)	4,909

Total cotton consumption for the year ending 31 Aug. 1913 (in thousands of bales)

(a) with Poland

USA	5,483
Great Britain	3,825
Russia (a)	1,907
German Empire	1,702
India	1,698
Japan	1,581

Source: Woytinsky *op. cit.* p 292

Paper production in 1909 (in thousands of metric tons)

Source: Woytinsky *op. cit.* p 343 (Woytinsky's figures are based on an assessment made in 'Compass' Vol II, 1912. p 186)		
	USA	2,904
	German Empire	1,351
	Great Britain	866
	France	605
	Austria–Hungary	362
	Canada	257
	Sweden	235
	Italy	232
	Russia	223

Sugar beet harvest: average annual yield based on figures for 1909–1910 and 1913–14 (in thousands of metric tons)

(a) with Poland

German Empire	2,309
Russia (a)	2,120
Austria–Hungary	1,515
France	733

Source: Woytinsky *op. cit.* p 267

Alcohol production in 1913 (in thousands of hectolitres of 100% proof alcohol)

Source: Woytinsky *op. cit.* p 271

Russia	5,196
German Empire	3,753
USA	3,659
France	2,954
Austria–Hungary	2,928

In nearly every one of these tables Russia is placed fourth, fifth or sixth. By 1913 she had already overtaken France in the production of steel to become the fourth largest producer in the world. Her share in the cotton industry had also been greatly increased: measured in terms of spindles she was fourth and in terms of consumption third in the international table. In petroleum production she occupied second, and in goldmining, fourth place.

But it was not only in these branches of industry that Russia had established herself as a serious international competitor. By 1913 she had also become the fourth largest producer of industrial machinery and the sixth largest producer of electrical equipment in the world. These are extremely interesting statistics and, since they have been produced by leading German professional associations,* which carried out exhaustive research in these spheres, they would appear to be entirely reliable. It is of course hardly necessary to point out that the development of the various branches which go to make up these two highly complex industrial spheres fluctuated considerably.

The Russian chemical industry—for which, unfortunately, we possess no comparative statistics—appears to have been decidedly antiquated. Its total turnover for the year 1907 has been estimated at 15 million pounds sterling, which is less than the turnover figure for sugar beet.[12] The figures for the production of artificial fertilizers for the year 1913 are quite lamentable in view of the almost unlimited size of the potential home market.[13] In 1913 Russia's output of super-phosphates (354,000 metric tons, of which over half came from Russian Poland) was considerably less than Japan's; her output of basic slag (213,000 metric tons, of which 164,000 came from Russian Poland) was less than Luxembourg's and her output of ammoniac fertilizers (26,000 metric tons, of which half came from Russian Poland) was only a third of France's.

However, although Russia failed to develop her chemical industry as such, she was able to establish a powerful position for herself within the international economy in a closely related sphere: the processing of rubber. The Russian winter had created such a large home market for galoshes that this branch of industry was able to build up a significant export market as well, which was something of a rarity in Russia at that time. The Treugolnik rubber manufacturing company of St Petersburg, which was founded in 1860 with American backing, became one of the largest industrial firms in the whole of Russia.

But, despite the comparative failure of one of its major industries, it seems virtually certain from the figures quoted above that, by 1913, Russia had become the fifth largest industrial

* The Verein Deutscher Maschinenbauanstalten provided the statistics relating to Russian machine production.

power in the world. Her industrial capacity actually appears to have exceeded that of the Austro-Hungarian Dual Monarchy. It must be borne in mind, however, that the population of Russia (within its pre-1914 borders) was more than three times as great as the population of the Dual Monarchy: 174 millions as opposed to 51.3 millions. Thus, although Russia's industrial output appears impressive when considered in absolute terms, in actual fact it left much to be desired. One of the principal reasons for the poor per capita returns was of course the fact that such a high proportion of the work force was still engaged in agriculture.

A further reason appears to have been the lack of adequate mechanisation. Although the only available statistics date from the turn of the century and although Russia subsequently made considerable progress in the mechanisation of her factories, it seems highly probable that she continued to lag behind the rest of the world in this respect right up to the outbreak of war in 1914. The following table, in which the returns are based on different years, is admittedly only a rough guide. But the discrepancy between the Russian figure and the figures for the other industrial nations is so marked that the table none the less acquires some significance:[14]

Output in thousands of hp of motors owned by each country

Country	Year	Total	Of those used in industry
Russia	1900	863	863
German Empire	1907	8,264	8,008
Great Britain	1907	10,755	10,504
France	1906	3,551	3,191
Austria–Hungary (a)	1898/1902	2,053	1,823
USA	1910	23,284	23,284

(a) Hungary 1898, Austria 1902

We have already mentioned that Russia subsequently took steps to mechanise her factories. This process, which set in from about 1905 onwards and soon made considerable progress, had two principal facets. On the one hand Russian machine production was stepped up, although this proved a costly undertaking on account of the protectionist policies then in force, while on the other hand large numbers of foreign machines were imported. The value of Russian imports of machinery rose from 4.9 million pounds sterling in 1906 to 15 million pounds in 1912.[15] As a result Russia became by far the largest importer of machinery in the world, beating France—who came second with imports of 10 million pounds—by almost exactly one-third. But, although this extremely high import figure undoubtedly shows that the modernisation of Russia's industrial plant was proceeding at a very fast rate, it does not follow from this that the Russian industrial economy was in a satisfactory condition. The fact that Russian *exports* of machinery amounted to only 0.28 million pounds is also significant.

We see therefore that, during the period immediately preceding the First World War, powerful—but ultimately insufficient—forces had been set in motion within Russia with a view to creating a modern economic infra-structure. These forces were brought into play by two principal mechanisms. The first of these was provided by the government's economic and financial policies, the second by the flow of foreign capital into Russia and the influx of foreign nationals, who either set up in business on their own account or worked as skilled technicians in industrial and allied spheres. From 1725, when Peter the Great died, until late in the nineteenth century, the state and its monarchs, the 'autocrats of all the Russias', did little to help modernise the Russian economy. In order to pay for its imperialist policies the state made excessive demands on the people, most of whom lived at —or in bad years below—subsistence level. The impoverishment of the masses, the fluctuations in the value of the paper currency, the primitive system of taxation and the almost perennial deficit in state revenue created a general climate that was far from conducive to the development of commercial and industrial initiative. Moreover, when the peasants were granted their personal liberty under Alexander II in 1861—a measure long overdue—the vast majority were not properly provided for, and having gained their independence, found that they were unable to earn an adequate living. Consequently, because their purchasing power was so low, they were unable to buy consumer goods or agricultural machinery, with the inevitable result that the home market was subject to severe restrictions and could not be expanded to any significant extent. Fifty years later—by which time it was too late—Stolypin introduced his major reform, which is dealt with in detail in another chapter of this book and which was designed to create a new and viable peasant class. Clearly, if this project had been undertaken earlier it would have helped to promote the growth of industry by providing it with a strong home market. As it was, the only important industrial schemes initiated by the state prior to the late 1880s were various projects for armaments factories and railways, which were prompted largely by military considerations.

It is widely thought that the first conscious decision on the part of the state to promote economic and, more particularly, industrial expansion was taken by S. Yu. Witte, who was born in 1849 and served as Minister of Finance from 1892 to 1903. In point of fact, however, his predecessor I. A. Vyshnegradsky, who was Minister of Finance from 1887 to 1892, had already initiated policies essentially the same as those pursued by Witte. Amongst other things Vyshnegradsky tried to reorganise the Russian currency system, he sought to attract foreign investment (at the end of 1888 he arranged the first big Russian loan in the French money market) and he started to bring the Russian railways under state control.

Of course, Witte had a far more powerful personality than Vyshnegradsky and his politico-economic ideas were far more comprehensive and more daring. After working for a private railway company Witte entered government service in 1888 and was appointed Minister of Finance on 11 September 1892. During his term of office he became identified with the principle of industrial reform just as Stolypin subsequently came to symbolise the principle of agrarian reform. His influence in economic affairs was far greater than that normally enjoyed by a Minister of Finance.

Witte's policies were the subject of a fierce debate during his lifetime and have remained a source of controversy ever since. To this day scholars still differ, not only in their assessment of the wisdom and viability of his programme, but even in their analysis of his basic intentions. Whilst Theodore von Laue regards Witte's policies as a first step towards a planned economy, Nötzold considers that 'the era of Witte and Stolypin was actually the only time in the history of Russian industrialisation . . . that the main emphasis was laid on the development of a liberal policy.'[16] In the opinion of the present author both these views are too extreme, although of the two, that advanced by Nötzold (who also adopts a rather more moderate attitude elsewhere in his book) is the more acceptable. Otto Hoetzsch has rightly pointed out that Witte was strongly influenced by Friedrich List and by Bismarck's policy of protectionism.[17] Certainly, his long term objective was the establishment of a free economy, whose development would be vouchsafed primarily by private enterprise. He was well aware, however, that such enterprise was sadly lacking in Russia. He also considered that it was unlikely to appear until the imperial revenues were increased, the currency was stabilised and a favourable balance of payments was created. In pursuit of the first of these aims he brought the distilleries under state control and placed a tax on all spirits. This characteristically Russian method of raising revenue soon became the most important source of state income and remained in force until the outbreak of war in 1914. Witte also reduced the rate of interest paid by the treasury on redeemable stocks by arranging a conversion and completed the nationalisation of the major part of the Russian railway system that had been begun by Vyshnegradsky.

The introduction in 1897 of a new currency based on the gold standard was another important measure taken by Witte. Its principal object was to inspire confidence abroad, thus enabling the Russian government to raise loans with which to finance major state projects (such as the building of new railways) and persuading foreign capitalists to establish new companies inside Russia. Witte had realised that the only way of obtaining sufficient funds to ensure a period of rapid economic growth without placing an intolerable strain on the Russian people (whose standard of living was already extremely low) was by attracting foreign capital into the country.

Witte's protectionist policies, which were also designed to promote economic expansion, were embodied in the new tariffs introduced in 1891. These imposed considerable increases in import duties on a wide range of manufactured goods and even on raw materials (such as cotton) and industrial machinery. The protection afforded by the new tariffs, coupled with the high prices paid for manufactured goods and the low level of direct taxation, ensured a considerable profit margin for industrial firms operating in Russia and consequently helped home production. Many of the firms under foreign ownership made exceptionally high profits during this period.

But there were also serious disadvantages to Witte's protectionism. In the first place the interest paid out on the foreign loans and the interest and profits earned by foreign investors created a large deficit in Russia's balance of payments. This meant that the flow of foreign capital into the country was by way of being a mixed blessing, especially since the new firms financed by this foreign capital almost invariably concentrated on the home market and so did little or nothing to ease the balance of payments position by boosting exports.

In the second place, the high prices charged for consumer goods produced by industry had an adverse effect on living standards and greatly impeded the modernisation of peasant agriculture in Russia. At that time the vast majority of peasant collectives possessed only the most modest technical aids; many peasants were still using primitive wooden ploughs which simply hoed the ground without turning it, and many had no draught animals.

In the third place, this protectionist policy, which was maintained at the expense of the masses, produced within a relatively short space of time an industrial proletariat that was highly receptive to revolutionary ideas. With so many men out of work, the wages for unskilled workers were very low. This in itself was a constant source of resentment. But the situation was aggravated even further by the lack of a strong, legal trade union movement and by the inadequacy of Russian industrial and social security legislation, which was still in its infancy.

Witte was aware that his methods imposed a heavy burden on the people. Commenting on this aspect of his policy, he said:

'Protectionism is a nursery for industry, the cost of which is borne by all sections of the population. We must, therefore, try to devise some means of ridding ourselves of this burden. One way of doing so is by attracting foreign investment. We have [virtually] no capital of our own and what little we do have is tied up in immoveable assets. If we can attract foreign investment, the protectionist nursery will be cheaper. Certainly the flow of foreign capital into Russia will call for sacrifices. But would it be better to import foreign goods for hundreds of millions of people or would it be better to create our own industry with the aid of foreign capital, which would then remain in the country? We must do our utmost to ensure a protracted flow of foreign capital into Russia.'[18]

This quotation shows quite clearly that, although Witte considered protectionism (and state control) to be a necessary part of his programme for the modernisation of the Russian economy, he did not think of it as an end in itself. This was one of the many points that he had in common with Friedrich List, who regarded educational protectionism—what we would now call progressive protectionism—as a means and not an end.

It should be apparent by now that both foreign capital and foreign enterprise played a very large part in the economic development of Russia in the late nineteenth and early twentieth centuries. Not that Russia was unique in this respect! The USA could never have acquired her dominant position among the industrial nations of the world without contracting overseas debts. In fact, North America remained a debtor nation right up to the outbreak of the First World War. The importance of foreign enterprise for a newly developing country had been demonstrated by the Huguenots, who made a major contribution to the early industrialisation of Prussia. Manufacturers from England, the homeland of the modern factory-based industry, had also played a significant part in the industrial development of Germany and Austria.

But nowhere was the influence of the 'foreigner', both as initiator and as financier, as marked as it was in Russia. And nowhere were the indigenous financial and technical resources as weak as they were there.[19] Both the initiative and the financial backing for the Russian mining industry were supplied primarily by foreigners. This was true not only of the small coalfields in Russian Poland (which abutted on to the German coalfields in Upper Silesia) but also of the much bigger fields in the Donets basin, which was the only really important mining area in

Russia until the collieries in western Siberia were developed under the Soviet five year plan. The first foreigner to play a significant part in the development of the Russian economy was the Englishman John Hughes, who founded the Novorossisk Company in London in 1869. This company, which was floated with a capital fund of £300,000, built industrial installations in Novorossiisk to produce coal, iron and, more especially, iron rails. It was granted considerable privileges by the Russian government, which it undoubtedly needed in order to overcome the great difficulties encountered in this undeveloped territory where, among other things, there were no modern transportation facilities. In the event these privileges turned out to be a sound investment, for John Hughes's courageous enterprise provided a powerful stimulus for the subsequent exploitation of this important mining area. But even these later developments owed much to foreign initiative. Commenting on them in 1896, a Russian financial journalist wrote: 'Of the various concerns now in operation only two can be said to be genuinely Russian . . . The remainder either belong exclusively to foreigners (English, French and Belgians) or have been founded by foreigners in association with Russians.'[20] By the end of the century the Hughes company had over eight thousand workers on its payroll.[21] The town of Yuzovka (later Stalino, now Donetsk) was named after this great English industrialist.

The three Swedish brothers, Robert, Ludwig and Alfred Nobel played a similar role in Baku, where they helped to develop the Russian petroleum industry. When Robert Nobel visited Baku in 1874 he recognised the great potential of the local oilfields and five years later he and his brothers founded their naphtha production company. Like Hughes, the Nobels also had to contend with great difficulties during the initial stages of their venture and it was not until modern techniques had been introduced and considerable amounts of capital invested that it was possible to create a Russian oil industry capable of competing on an international scale.

We have already mentioned that relatively few Russian industrialists were represented in the mining industries. This was not the case with textiles. A large number of Russian manufacturers had been engaged in this industry from the outset, not only in central Russia but also in Russian Poland and more especially in Lodz, the centre of the Polish cotton trade. In Lodz there were also two important German cotton manufacturers, Louis Geyer from Saxony and Karl Scheibler from the Rhineland. Both these men operated on a large scale: in the year 1898 Scheibler's mills employed 6,500 people and produced goods to the value of more than thirteen million roubles.[22] The foremost foreign textile manufacturer in Russia proper was Ludwig Knoop, a native of Bremen, who first went there as an employee of an English firm. Later, when he set up in business on his own account, Knoop's early connections stood him in good stead, for he was able to obtain English capital with which to finance the construction of new textile factories.

Although these three were the biggest foreign manufacturers working in Russia at that time, there were many others—from England, Germany, France and Belgium—who either founded or managed new mills and whose combined influence on the development of Russian industry was very considerable, especially in the last three decades of the nineteenth century.

But although the initiative displayed by foreign industrialists was extremely welcome it was not enough in itself. As has already been mentioned, the Russians also needed to obtain foreign capital with which to finance their programme of economic expansion. In most of the loans transacted to this end the state itself was the borrower and the credits were made available from private capital, usually through the offices of banking houses such as Rothschild and Baring in England, Rothschild in Paris, Mendelssohn, Bleichröder and the Berliner Handelsgesellschaft in Germany. From 1888 onwards most Russian loans were raised in the French money market. This was an important development, the political consequences of which are only too well known.

But the principal reason why the Russians borrowed money abroad, initially at least, was to cover their military expenditure, which was often heavy. Thus in 1857, following the Crimean War, the foreign debts incurred by the state to cover its war expenses amounted to 521 million roubles, which was over thirty per cent of the consolidated national debt. Between 1884 and 1889 Russia's foreign debts rose to three and a half thousand million roubles, almost sixty-five per cent of the consolidated national debt. Arms purchases still accounted for a large part of these borrowings and continued to do so for some time to come. According to an analysis carried out by a group of Russian economists, the Ministry for the Navy spent 234 million roubles on foreign armaments and the Ministry of War 111 million roubles between 1901 and 1907.[23]

The state also incurred large foreign debts in order to finance its railway programme, although here too military considerations played a significant part, priority being accorded to any sections of line that would facilitate the transportation of troops. In Russia the railways were more important than in most other countries for, with the exception of the Volga, the Russian rivers were not capable of further development as inland waterways. Even in the Soviet Union the railways still account for a higher percentage of the total transport system than in any other industrial country. At first the vast majority of Russian railways were built and run by private companies, the most famous of which was the Chief Russian Railway Company, founded in 1857. But even during this early period the state was able to bring crucial influence to bear on the development of the rail network thanks to the financial backing which it provided, primarily by means of foreign loans. Subsequently, when the railways were nationalised, first under Vyshnegradsky and then under Count Witte, the state took over their capital assets and also assumed responsibility for any deficits in their current trading accounts. Nationalisation proceeded very quickly: whereas in 1889 only 23.5 per cent of the rail network was under state control, by 1900 this had been increased to 60.5 per cent.[24]

The overall length of the Russian rail network (including Finland)[25] rose from 31,000 km in 1890 to 62,200 km in 1913. This final figure was roughly the same as the length of the German rail network but considerably less than that of the United States, which contained some 411,000 km of track. At that time only very few of the more remote parts of Asiatic Russia had been opened up. But the Trans-Siberian railway had been completed and this provided a basis for the economic development of this vast and almost virgin territory. The agricultural colonisation of Siberia was promoted largely within the framework of Stolypin's agrarian reform and quickly assumed surprisingly large proportions. The attempt to establish industrial and mining colonies in the new territory was less successful. Apart from the goldmining settlement in the Lena district, run by an English firm, these colonies remained largely undeveloped until after the First World War. But the fact that in 1913 Siberian butter was being sold on the international market[26] shows what can be done when colonisation and communications go hand in hand.

The Russian merchant navy was decidedly underdeveloped prior to 1914. This was due partly to the severity of the northern winter, which denied Russia ice-free ports on the Baltic, and partly to the lack of a seafaring tradition. At all events, Russia's merchant navy was far smaller than one would have expected from the fifth largest industrial nation in the world. In 1910 the net registered tonnage of the world's merchant ships was 22.266 million tons, of which Russia and Finland together owned only 1.117 million tons. Moreover, the Russian fleet was extremely antiquated, for more than half her net registered tonnage (581,000) was accounted for by sailing ships. (By contrast, only ten per cent of the British merchant navy, which was then the largest in the world, was composed of sail.)[27] This modest fleet of merchant ships was not even able to cope with Russia's own maritime trade, with the result that large quantities of Russian goods were carried in foreign ships. This, of course, imposed a further burden on the balance of payments, already heavily strained by the deficit incurred as a result of the interest and capital repayments made on foreign loans.[28] Another, and by no means inconsiderable, deficit was created by the personal expenditure of Russian aristocrats when they visited western and central Europe.

Apart from continually raising new loans in order to pay off interest on the old, the only way of countering these balance of payment difficulties was by ensuring a favourable trading balance. Consequently, this was always regarded as one of the prime objectives of Russian economic and financial policy. Thus, the protectionism, which was one of the cornerstones of Witte's economic policy and which he introduced following a period of relatively free trading relations (1850–1877), was much more than a means of 'protecting the economic development of the country' as advocated by List. It was also designed to maintain a favourable trading balance by discouraging imports.[29] In this it was almost invariably successful, as is clear from the following table, which shows the value of Russian exports and imports for the years 1910 to 1913 in millions of roubles:[30]

Year	Exports	Imports	Favourable balance
1910	1383.6	953.0	430.6
1911	1514.0	1022.6	491.4
1912	1428.1	1036.7	391.4
1913	1420.8	1225.5	195.3

But despite this favourable balance, the general structure of Russia's foreign trade was not particularly satisfactory and clearly showed that the industrial development of the country still had a long way to go.[31] Two-thirds of Russia's exports to the western world were made up of foodstuffs, primarily cereals[32] but also sugar (from south and south-west Russia), meat, eggs, poultry and butter (chiefly from Siberia). The remaining third consisted almost entirely of raw materials: timber, flax, oil products, pelts, tobacco, wool and petroleum. The only manufactured goods exported by Russia went either to Asian countries or, on a very limited scale, to the Balkans.

About one-half of Russia's imports from western countries was accounted for by industrial raw materials and semi-finished goods, such as wool, rubber and woollen yarns, while a further third was made up of finished goods and industrial machinery. Purchases of foreign machinery, it will be remembered, increased very rapidly during this period so that by 1913 Russia was by far the largest importer of industrial machinery in the world. Of the commodities imported from Asian countries the most important was tea, the Russian national drink.

Russia's biggest supplier and her biggest customer during this period was Germany,[33] her second biggest Great Britain. In the conditions obtaining prior to the First World War Germany and Russia were natural trading partners. With their different economic structures they complemented one another extremely well and were able to build up what was by pre-1914 standards an extensive volume of trade. Apart from a slight drop in the volume of German imports in 1912 and 1913 this interchange increased steadily from 1908 up to the outbreak of war.

With exports of 3.33 million tons Russia was the largest supplier of wheat in the world in 1913, although she was closely followed by Canada with 3.28 million tons. At the time these Russian exports of wheat were frequently referred to, by critics at home as well as abroad, as 'starvation exports'. This was of course a reference to the undeniably low standard of living of the peasant population, many of whom suffered genuine privation, especially if the harvest failed.

Peasant distress was wholly due to the pressure of taxation and—until their abolition—of the redemption payments exacted under the agrarian reform of 1861. Commenting on conditions in central, eastern and northern Russia in 1912, Wiedenfeld said: 'The principal reason why the peasant is forced to sell his produce—and in many cases to sell more than he can really spare—is not because he hankers after consumer goods, not because he has come to expect more from life, but because he is subjected to oppressive taxation. In order to render unto the Tsar that which is the Tsar's he has to raise ready money by selling his corn, even if in a bad year this means that he is unable to appease his own hunger.'[34] Thus, Russia's favourable trade balance, which was based primarily on the export of corn, was not an entirely positive development, especially since it meant that Russian economic stability depended on the vagaries of the corn market.

But if Russia's trade balance was a doubtful quantity, so too was her trading position. The fact that she had acquired 3.8 per cent of the total turnover of international trade by 1913, thus becoming the sixth largest trading nation in the world (after Great Britain, the German empire, the USA, France and Belgium),[35] was less impressive than it looked.

What were the future prospects for the economic development of Tsarist Russia? Opinions differ widely—not only between east and west but even amongst western scholars and publicists. When Vladimir Ilyich Lenin wrote his early pamphlet on 'The Development of Capitalism in Russia' (published 1899) he was primarily concerned with the analysis and refutation of the views advanced by the Populists (*Narodniki*). His general conclusion concerning the development of the economy was as follows:

If we ask ourselves whether the development of capitalism in Russia proceeded slowly or quickly, we find that everything depends on what we compare this development with. If we compare the pre-capitalist epoch in Russia with the capitalist epoch (and this comparison has to be made if we are to answer the question correctly), it must be said that the development of the social economy under capitalism has been extraordinarily fast. But if we compare the actual speed of that development with the sort of speed that might have been achieved, given the present state of technology and culture, we are forced to the conclusion that the development of capitalism in Russia is, in fact, proceeding slowly. Moreover, it is bound to do so, for in no other capitalist country have so many traditional institutions survived, which are incompatible with capitalism, which inhibit its development and which have had such a pernicious effect on the position of the producers.[36]

The Soviet historian P. Lyashchenko has produced a great deal of evidence which would support the thesis that Russia entered into a period of prosperity between 1909 and 1913. But his general assessment of the state of Russian industry is none the less pretty devastating.[37] Non-Marxist western historians, on the other hand, who were writing about this period before the First World War, tended to be cautiously optimistic about the future of the Russian economy. This optimism is not shared by later western historians, who have been decidedly sceptical about the prospects of an economic policy based almost exclusively on the principle of a free market.

Two things emerge from any detailed analysis of the Russian economy during the period 1890–1914. In the first place we see the enormous difficulties with which the advocates of modernisation and industrialisation had to contend and in the second place we find that, despite many partial successes, the results of their endeavours were quite inadequate on the eve of the First World War. But we should not forget those partial successes. The most important advances in the industrial sphere were:

(1) The gradual emergence of a group of native industrialists.

(2) The gradual strengthening of Russian capital formation.
(3) The continuous expansion of the home market (due in no small measure to the creation of a new and economically viable class of peasant farmers).

True, these developments all took place very slowly. But in the course of time, and in conjunction with the new agrarian reforms, they enabled the Russian economy to break out of the vicious circle in which it had been caught up for so long. W. W. Rostow actually places Russia among the small group of nations who had already completed the take-off phase of industrialisation prior to the First World War. Although this may be going too far, it seems to the present author that she was certainly well on the way to doing so.

It was not the failure of its ill-conceived economic programme that sealed the fate of the tsarist régime but the overburdening of the economy—and the people—by the adoption of imperialist policies abroad, which not only provoked the Russo-Japanese war of 1904–05 but also contributed to the outbreak of the First World War. Arms purchases made heavy inroads on Russia's resources, reducing to an unacceptable level the money available for much needed industrial developments. The neglect of popular education, which was illustrated by the large number of illiterates in Russia, also seriously impeded the development of a modern industrial economy. And it was only by developing such an economy that Russia could have solved the pressing social problems which made her the 'weakest link in the chain of capitalist countries', for only then could she have offered her rapidly growing industrial proletariat a decent standard of living. But in order to carry out an effective programme of modernisation in her vast territory Russia would have needed a prolonged period of external peace and internal stability.[38] That she was denied this was a fate whose consequences no economic policy, however enlightened, could have mitigated.

The agrarian problem

HARRY T. WILLETTS

The three-cornered relationship between the state, the peasants and the gentry is the inescapable theme for all historians of Imperial Russia. Whatever their special interests, they must take account of, and seek explanation for, the feeble tempo of social and economic change in a richly endowed country, the debilitating and cramping effects of serfdom before 1861, and after the Emancipation the fitful efforts of a rigid autocratic régime which had grown up on the basis of serfdom to reconstruct society without endangering itself. The historian of thought, no less than the economic or social historian, must accustom himself to the usually inarticulate company of the *muzhik*, since in the nineteenth century Russia's peculiar institution, and later the results of the incomplete reform of 1861, became an agonising obsession among Russian intellectuals. Concern for the condition of the peasantry was not their monopoly: there was always a handful of enlightened bureaucrats to worry about the peasant question. But official anxiety resulted in bold action on two occasions only: in 1861, with the Emancipation, and after the 1905 Revolution, when the government wrestled purposefully with problems to which the terms of Emancipation, and subsequent neglect, had largely contributed. It is with the agrarian problem in the last decades of Imperial Russia that we are here mainly concerned, but any study of it, and particularly of official attitudes to it, must begin in the era of serfdom.

The Emancipation of 1861

The glimmerings of awareness that serfdom in its Russian form was a disgrace and a handicap can be seen at the very beginning of the imperial period. Peter the Great, though for fiscal and military reasons he added largely to the peasant's burden and tightened his chains, none the less complained (not quite accurately) that nowhere else in the world were people sold like cattle, and his protégé, the universal autodidact Pososhkov, urged regulation of relations between master and peasant in the interests of good husbandry. Peter's would-be emulator, Catherine II, embarrassed by the contrasts between Russia and Western Europe, anxious to win the approval of her fine philosophical friends, and conscious of the connection between economic backwardness and serfdom, explored in the early years of her reign ways of 'doing something for the peasant'. The discussions which she stimulated convinced her that the problem was intractable—'wherever they touch it, it won't budge'—and the Pugachev rising froze any lingering compassion for the peasants. As a result, her social legislation consisted largely of reinforcements and extensions of the landowner's privileges and his arbitrary powers over the serf.

Alexander I and Nicholas I thought of large-scale peasant disturbances as a likely consequence of precipitate change, rather than of reform delayed. Their active, if not very productive, concern with the problem sprang from a realisation that serfdom impaired Russia's strength and prestige. Both Tsars were convinced that serfdom must sooner or later be abolished, but the results of nearly half a century of bureaucratic project-mongering (Nicholas lost interest after 1848) were minor measures of relief for the peasants at large, and the creation of opportunities for discretionary emancipation, which benefited only a tiny minority of serfs.

The main difficulty, of course, was the irreducible hostility of the mass of the gentry to any policy—as, for instance, the introduction of fixed obligations between master and peasant in some of the western provinces under Nicholas I—which looked like a step towards emancipation. It should not be supposed that either Alexander or Nicholas much respected the gentry as a class: but they could not separate its interests from those of the state. The gentry, as they and the Tsars often reminded each other, were the main prop and support of the throne. There was no coherent and educated social group to balance against them, no alternative reservoir of state servants.

The thorniest problem for the eventual emancipator would

inevitably be the division of the land between landowner and peasant. Liberation of the serf without land would have been eagerly welcomed by a large section of the gentry in the middle of the nineteenth century. In the non-Black-Earth areas they would have expected compensation for their forfeited share of peasant earnings outside agriculture, but in the Black Earth provinces there were enthusiasts for instant and total liberation, without compensation, and with full civil equality for the peasant, provided that all the land, or all but a token plot for each peasant household, remained with the landlord. A policy of land clearance was, however, unthinkable, at least in the Russian heartlands of the empire. As Nicholas's wisest adviser on agrarian matters, P. D. Kiselyev, told him, the peasant mind could not separate the concepts of freedom and land. Freedom to the peasants meant precisely secure and untrammelled tenure of what they persisted in regarding as their land. Thoughtful bureaucrats did not merely fear the immediate reaction of the peasants to landless liberation: they were as eager as the first Russian socialists to spare their country the miseries of 'proletarianisation'. For this amongst other reasons, Kiselyev, for instance, was not merely opposed to any scheme for clearance, but, after some early vacillations, as staunch a supporter of the peasant commune as Herzen or Chernyshevsky.

It is not surprising that opponents of serfdom among Russia's rulers, like Kiselyev, should resign themselves to a policy of gradual erosion, or comfort themselves, like Mordvinov,[1] with the thought that sooner or later serfdom would prove economically unviable and liquidate itself; or pass the problem to the next generation, as did Nicholas I. More surprising is the vigour and determination with which Alexander II pressed through the Emancipation. As Tsarevich, he had shown, if anything, rather less enthusiasm for reform than his father. The débâcle in the Crimea convinced him that Russia's 'strength and might' depended on reform, and that its basis must be a real improvement in the life of the peasants.[2] Even amongst the bureaucracy, he had few ardent supporters. In most provinces, the gentry responded tardily and reluctantly when Alexander invited them to initiate local discussion of reform: and, for fear of sabotage and endless delay, Alexander allowed the provincial delegations of the gentry only to appear briefly before the bureaucratic drafting commissions. Though the gentry grumbled bitterly about bureaucratic high-handedness and about the authority entrusted to dangerous 'reds' like N. A. Milyutin,[3] their interests were more than adequately defended within the Drafting Commissions, the Main Committee, and finally the State Council. At every level, fresh means were found of minimising the inconveniences and maximising the advantages of the operation to the landowner. The results of anxiety to conciliate the Russian gentry can best be seen from a comparison between the enactments of 1861, affecting serfs on the estates of the gentry in European Russia at large, and the much more generous provisions for appanage peasants* (1863), the peasants of certain Western provinces (1863, as a punishment for rebellious Polish landowners), and state peasants (1866).[4]

It is misleading to speak of 'the abolition of serfdom' in 1861. The Act of 19 February did indeed peremptorily abolish the landlord's ownership of his peasants. But 'serfdom' was always something of a misnomer for a system under which landowners could buy, sell, mortgage and transport peasants, or detach them from the land. M. M. Speransky, with his usual acuteness, had long ago identified as the first step to reform the replacement of *esclavage* (personal attachment) by *servage* (attachment to the land). And this—promotion of the landlord's chattel to a higher status more nearly resembling serfdom—was the immediate effect of 'emancipation'. Within two years, the peasants were to enter the new phase of 'temporary obligation', in which the landlord retained full ownership of his estate (except for the peasants' homesteads but, by agreement with the peasants under the supervision of an arbiter, ceded to them a portion of land for use in perpetuity, in return for a fixed rent and services. To ensure that the peasant did not scamp his obligations, the landlord retained extensive disciplinary powers. This relationship, though 'temporary', was of indefinite duration. It could be terminated at any time, and the peasant could advance to a new status euphemistically described as 'proprietorship', by a volun-

* The inhabitants of estates carved out from the State land fund in 1797 for the maintenance of members of the imperial family not in the line of succession.

tary agreement between the two parties on the amount of land (within limits defined by law for particular areas and types of estate) which the peasant would redeem. The state would pay the bulk of the redemption price to the landlord in interest-bearing bonds, and recover it with interest by annual instalments from the peasant. Bargaining between many landlords and their peasants dragged on year in and year out. One party or the other often preferred to prolong the 'temporary' arrangements: the landlord, for fear of losing his supply of unpaid peasant labour, and the peasant, in the hope that the legislators would have more generous second thoughts.

In 1879, some fourteen per cent of former 'landlords' serfs' were still 'temporarily obligated' and the Tsar, grumbling that he had never expected the changeover to take twenty years, ordered in 1881 that it must be completed by 1 January 1883. The former appanage peasants, and the peasants in areas of Polish landownership, had become 'proprietors' at once in 1863. The state peasants entered the redemption phase in 1887. Former landlords' peasants were expected to reimburse the state within forty-nine years, and former state peasants within forty-four years from the conclusion of the redemption agreement. Few would be able to take advantage of the provisions for early settlement, but all of them under the original scheme, should have become unencumbered proprietors at some time between 1912 and 1932. The subsequent accumulation of arrears, and periodic deferments of debt, meant that in some cases redemption would have been completed in the 1950s.

With the inception of redemption, the former 'landlord's peasants' acquired a new, and not always easier master, the state, and the state peasants merely a prospect of eventual emancipation from their old master. The state exercised its hold over the peasants not only through its local apparatus but, more directly, through the 'rural community' (*selskoye obshchestvo*), comprising all peasants formerly under the jurisdiction of a single estate. In the preparatory stages of emancipation, there had been a good deal of discussion about the future of the peasant commune (*obshchina*) which was an almost universal feature of peasant life in Russia proper. As the defenders of the *obshchina* saw it, communal tenure was a guarantee against pauperisation, for the *obshchina*, by periodic redistribution of its lands, could provide for the livelihood of all its members, and adjust their dues according to ability to pay. Critics of the *obshchina* from the first complained that communal tenure inhibited individual initiative by placing an unfair share of the collective debts on the abler and more active members, and that periodic redistribution destroyed incentives to improve the land. Most of the themes which were to be so vigorously discussed some forty years later—the *obshchina* as a danger to economic progress, the *obshchina* as a barrier on the peasant's path to civic and legal equality, even the *obshchina* as a possible breeding-ground of Communism—were considered by the emancipators.

In the event, the legislators reached a compromise determined by administrative and fiscal convenience. The members of a rural community could decide for themselves, by a two-thirds vote, whether they preferred individual or communal tenure, and, if they kept the *obshchina*, when they should carry out re-partitions. Moreover, any peasant should be entitled to withdraw from the *obshchina* and become an individual cultivator on payment in full of his share in the communal redemption debt. But while providing, as they thought, for the eventual replacement of communal tenure by individual farming, the legislators simultaneously extended many of the disadvantages of the *obshchina* to those western and south-western areas where individual tenure was already the rule. For on the rural community (*selskoye obshchestvo*), whether or not it was also an *obshchina*, was placed joint liability for the redemption dues and tax payments of all its members. The distinct and inferior civic and legal status of the peasant was preserved, not only by the principle of joint liability and the limitations which it placed on his freedom of movement and disposal of his property but also by a special jurisdiction.

If, in many areas, the peasant joined half-heartedly in the official rejoicing of 1861, if his reaction was one of incomprehension or incredulous dismay, it was less because he was denied full civic equality than because he was promised too little land. Only a desperate minority demanded that all the land should be given to the peasant, but no peasant doubted his right to his pre-emancipation holding in full. The emancipators were advised from some quarters to leave the peasants with their existing holdings. They chose instead to define maximum and minimum allotments per male soul, or standard allotments for some areas. The landowner could retain one-third of his estate, or half in the steppe provinces, 'cutting off' part of the land previously used by his peasants, provided that they were not left with less than the minimum allotment. At the same time, the landlord was required to 'cut on' land where the peasant's present holding was less than the minimum. These rough and ready rules embodied, to the satisfaction of the legislators, the principle that the peasant should retain enough land to support his way of life, but they resulted in the overall reduction of peasant landholding.

The extent of the reduction is variously estimated, since no one quite knows how much land was 'constantly used' by the peasants before 1861, but Lositsky's figure of 5,250,000 *desyatins*[5] cut off as against 33,755,800 *desyatins* ceded by landlords in European Russia is widely accepted. Average figures for the reduction are meaningless, for peasant holdings increased slightly on the north-eastern periphery of Russia proper, and considerably in the north-western and south-western provinces, particularly in areas of Polish landowning. These gains were outweighed by heavy losses to the peasants in the Central Black Earth, Volga and steppe regions: in the provinces of Poltava, Kharkov, Tambov and Kursk respectively, peasant holdings were reduced by 37.2, 28.3, 20.6 and 18.9 per cent, and in the provinces of Samara, Saratov, Yekaterinoslav and Simbirsk by 41.8, 37.9, 37.6 and 27.8 per cent.[6] Such losses were the most deeply felt and persistent of peasant grievances—so much so that restoration of cut-offs was to be almost the whole content of the Bolshevik agrarian programme in its first form, while the Central Black Earth and Middle Volga regions would become the fiercest centres of unrest and the stronghold of the (neo-populist) Socialist Revolutionary Party. In this matter, as so often, the inhabitants of crown and state lands were much more generously treated: the appanage peasants increased their holdings by 14.3 per cent, and the state peasants suffered no reduction. A particularly miserable category of former serfs were those who accepted what came to be called the 'beggar's portion' —one-quarter of the local maximum allotment, unburdened by redemption payments.

The former 'landlords' peasants' had cause to complain not

only about the quantity of their land, but about its price, its quality and its structure. In fixing the redemption price, the legislators did not openly acknowledge that the peasant must buy his freedom as well as his land. It was equally impossible to avoid the fact that the gentry in the non-Black Earth areas expected compensation not merely for their land, which might not be very valuable, but for their share in the total earnings of their peasants, whether from agriculture, handicrafts, migratory labour, or industrial employment. The legislators escaped from their dilemma by relating the redemption price not to current land values, but to average local *obrok*, (originally a money payment in lieu of service) even where this was only nominally a land rent, and in reality a levy on total peasant earnings. As a result, the redemption price was often greatly in excess not only of average land values at the time of the Emancipation, but even of the prices obtaining a decade or so later. According to Lositsky's calculations, the redemption price of land exceeded its selling price in the decade after Emancipation (1863–72) in the Black Earth Provinces by 20 per cent and in the non-Black Earth Provinces by 90 per cent.[7]

The over-valuation would seem even grosser if we could take quality into account. The landlord had in the past often kept the best land to himself, so that old peasant land was by definition poorer land. Moreover, he could now reshape the peasant allotment with an eye to his own advantage. The peasants could scarcely avoid renting a wedge of manorial land awkwardly lodged in their fields, or paying for a right of way where their former landlord had cut across the path of their cattle to pasture or water. In both cases, payment could often be most usefully exacted in the form of labour on the manor lands. The landlord was not bound to include a definite proportion of pasture or meadow in the peasant allotment, and most peasants who had previously enjoyed timbering rights in the landlord's forest now lost them. Here were further profitable opportunities for the landlord, and further rankling inconveniences for the peasant. Once again, the appanage and state peasants fared much better. The state had no interest in making it difficult for them to farm— rather the contrary—or in placing heavy financial burdens on them.

The land endowment of the peasantry after the Emancipation varied greatly both from region to region, and as between land-lords' peasants on the one hand, and appanage or state peasants on the other. It was quickly brought to the attention of the government that, however satisfactory the average situation might be, there were very large numbers of peasants with insufficient land to support themselves and pay their debts. Professor L. V. Khodsky, arguing that the holding of the state peasant in particular areas could be taken as the necessary norm, calculated that by this criterion 32.6 per cent of peasants in all categories were generously endowed, and 27.7 per cent under-endowed. Moreover, the emancipators had taken no precautions against the aggravation of this problem in future. They can hardly be blamed for failing to allow for an impending increase in rural population from 55.3 million in 1863 to 82 million in 1897, or to foresee that their work, which they themselves certainly did not regard as complete, would for decades be modified only by some measures further restricting the mobility of the peasant, and others slightly reducing his financial load.

The condition of the countryside

The peasantry were immobilised, inadequately endowed, rapidly multiplying; a distinct estate with peculiar disabilities, and at the same time bound by galling economic ties to the gentry. This was a situation full of dangers to the economic development of the country, and in the end its peace.

The peasant could eke out his income by extending his land-holding, selling his labour or farming more intensively: the gentry had an abundance of land to sell, the greatest need for hired hands, the capital and education which should have enabled them to set an example of good husbandry to their poor and ignorant neighbours. In 1877 in forty-nine European provinces the peasants had 131,400,000 *desyatins* of allotment land, while private estates covered 93,000,000 *desyatins* of which the gentry owned 79,100,000. Already in the 1860s the gentry began to sell land on a large scale, and their holdings fell steadily to 65,300,000 *desyatins* by 1887 and 53,200,000 by 1905. Peasant purchases from all vendors amounted to 23,642,000 *desyatins* by 1905.[8] As the countryside grew more congested, and the average share in allotment land shrank from 13.2 *desyatins* in 1877 to 10.4 in 1905, prices soared: from 12.69 roubles per *desyatin* on the eve of Emancipation to 66.92 at the end of the century.[9] These are average prices for forty-five European provinces. In particularly fertile or particularly congested regions the price curve over the same period was steeper—from 17.76 to 119.80 roubles per *desyatin* in the Ukraine, from 11.34 to 123.97 roubles per *desyatin* in the southern steppes. Sellers, including the Peasant Land Bank, inevitably preferred to deal with those who could put down a deposit and were unlikely to default, so that it was not the needier who acquired most additional land.

Leasehold accounted for a larger addition to the area farmed by the peasants than purchase. No complete and reliable statistics are available to show the fluctuations in the leased area between 1861 and 1905. According to one authoritative, but not undisputed, calculation, peasants were renting 50,000,000 *desyatins* in the middle nineties at an average price of six roubles per *desyatin*.[10] Around three-quarters of the lessees paid money rents, but labour rents and sharecropping were still common in the central Black Earth area and the south west. Rents rose in sympathy with land prices, doubling or trebling in the Central Black Earth region and the southern steppes in the nineties.

The redemption payments and escalating land prices drained off an enormous annual tribute from the peasantry. Much of this money must have been put to productive use elsewhere, but very little of it was reinvested in agriculture. For far too many landlords and entrepreneurs, trading in land was much more remunerative than cultivating it. In over-populated areas, many landlords baulked at expensive improvements when they could obtain a quicker and surer return by leasing, or by letting peasants work the estate with their own animals and implements in return for a plot or a share of the crop. This pattern of agrarian relationships did not merely hinder improvement, it led in many places to progressive deterioration of the land. The peasant was notoriously reluctant to manure or cultivate carefully even his allotment strips when he might lose them at the next re-partition. He was naturally even less solicitous for land held on a short lease, or for fields which he tilled instead of paying rent. Yields on leased land were considerably lower than on allotment land. Not nature but primitive husbandry condemned Russia to yields one-half or one-third as large as those obtained in western Europe.[11]

The great mass of the peasantry had a static and archaic view of their calling. Where land was plentiful they tilled part of it to near exhaustion, then moved on to long-fallow soil. Elsewhere, they observed a three-field rotation, leaving one field fallow, scratching the others with their wooden ploughs, and planting them, for the most part, with 'grey' cereals—rye and oats. Between the short, back-breaking periods of ploughing, sowing and reaping, their preference was to wait God's will in patient lethargy. These primitive procedures, wasteful enough at any time, were suicidal in the decades of rapid population increase and growing land-hunger. Peasants from the more advanced western provinces might comment caustically on the 'lordly' mentality of their Russian brothers, those 'gentlemen at the plough' who, short as they were of land, kept a third of it permanently 'on holiday'. Such taunts, of course, were misconceived: only generous help and patient indoctrination could change the ingrained habits of the peasant. Until the turn of the century the government offered little of either, and the Zemstvos, though they often had the will, lacked the means to help significantly.

In the meantime, apart from poverty, ignorance and conservatism, the structure of land tenure (i.e. the peasant commune) was a major hindrance to modernisation. Enthusiasts for the commune had supposed that it would tend to adjust the holdings of its members to their needs. In practice, the principle of redivision was extremely variable: distribution might be to 'revision souls' (i.e. to males registered by the last pre-Emancipation census) or to all adult males (which was hard on predominantly female households) or to 'eaters' (all members). The attempt to provide fair shares, however defined, meant carving and recarving the land into irregular strips and patches. It was common for a peasant household to till twenty or thirty such strips, scattered over the good and bad fields, some of them miles away from each other and from the village. Strips were sometimes so narrow that they were called *shnury* (strings), and the peasant measured them in *lapti* (i.e., by the width of a bast shoe). That this system was enormously wasteful of time and labour is self-evident, but its absurdity can be fully appreciated only if we remember how fiercely individualistic the peasant was. Land was held in common, dues were raised communally, but there was precious little economic cooperation in the village. Peasants would cooperatively cut timber or mow a meadow, because the division of the wood and hay presented no difficulties. But as a rule, each household tilled its own land, guarding its boundaries, jealously garnering every grain of its crop, and if it needed to borrow a horse or an implement it would usually have to pay. The contradiction between communal tenure and individual husbandry greatly exercised the shrewdest and best informed observer of the post-Emancipation countryside, A. N. Engelgardt, who believed that unless peasants learned to pool their resources and their labour, an additional allotment, or a reduction of dues, would not go far towards solving their problems.[12]

The peasant, understandably, thought otherwise, placed all his hopes on extension of his holding, yearned for the fields lost at Emancipation, dreamt of a miraculous 'cut on' of state land, and more and more frequently took the law into his own hands. Illicit grazing or mowing on the neighbouring estate, moonlight timbering in private or state forests were everyday occurrences in the last two decades of the century, and affrays between trespassing peasants and estate employees often required military intervention. The incidence of peasant disorders was especially high in the Middle Volga and Central Black Earth provinces, soon to be the scene of the 'rural illuminations' of 1905–6.

The rise in land prices, in proportion to growing needs and not to any rise in productivity, would by itself have driven many to desperation. But there were many competing and exorbitant demands on the peasant's slender resources. He found it more and more difficult to keep up his redemption payments. The government, influenced by the findings of the Valuyev Commission of 1877 (which admitted the initial over-valuation of the land and the reason for it) and by Count Ignatyev's 'experts', substantially reduced redemption payments in 1881, and at the coronation of Alexander III in 1883 wrote off part of the arrears. Thereafter, concessions took the form of deferments or temporary remission of payment, but there was no general reduction of the total debt until 1904. That sheer inability was the commonest reason for non-payment can be inferred from the severity of the sanctions which the authorities freely used against defaulters. Peasants, and the elders of communes, could be flogged, the movables, crop, implements and cattle of a peasant household could be sold off to cover its debts, and in the last resort the household could be deprived of its allotment.

The main objects of Russian fiscal policy in the late 1880s and 1890s were to balance the budget and stabilise the rouble, to maximise exports (mainly agricultural) and to protect nascent Russian industries. The measures adopted to these ends involved great hardships for the peasantry. Financial stability meant rising taxes, and ruthlessness in collecting. By the middle nineties, half of the state's revenue was drawn from indirect taxation on consumer goods. Finance Minister Witte, in his euphoric way, could say that these taxes were paid by those who could afford them, since the rural masses were self-sufficient. This would have been true if all peasants had been content to eat none but unleavened bread, light their huts with tallow dips, abjure tea, sugar, alcohol and tobacco. But peasants hankered after these and other expensive commodities—boots instead of bast shoes, manufactured textiles instead of homespun—and Witte's budgetary calculations depended to a considerable extent on these rising expectations. The export drive took little account of fluctuations in output. The government's motto had been formulated by Count Vyshnegradsky ('let us go hungry—but export') and as much as fifteen per cent of the Russian crop might be exported in a famine year.

While a difficult world market and primitive trading habits depressed profits from agriculture, protectionist tariffs forced up the price of manufactured goods. A particular grievance for large agricultural producers and peasants alike was the cost of iron goods, which Witte's tariff increased by thirteen per cent. Like the Soviet enthusiasts for rapid industrialisation forty years later, Witte undoubtedly believed that his crash programme would in the end bring prosperity to the peasant. But, for the present, it brought the financial burdens we have mentioned. Witte, who saw Russia's huge reservoir of cheap labour as a powerful attraction to foreign capital, may have expected that industrialisation would quickly draw off millions from the countryside. In the event, the expansion of the settled labour force only slightly relieved the pressure on the land. The non-Black Earth provinces supplied the main contingent of new factory workers, while the tight-packed peasants of the western and Central Black Earth area relied as before on employment as agricultural labourers for their outside earnings. In some years as many as 300,000 Russian labourers made their way to the estates of East Prussia, and every year millions streamed from the central provinces to the Black Sea steppes and the North Caucasus. The spurious egalitarianism of the *obshchina* could not conceal the evidence of proletarianisation in the summer months, when the hungry rural proletariat roamed the countryside.

Already in the 1880s, the government had at its disposal a mass of information on the condition of the countryside, collected by its own agencies, by the Zemstvos and by private scholars. There was no lack of thoughtful suggestions for reform, from within the bureaucracy and from outside. As an example of a coherent programme for supplementing the legislation of the 1860s we may mention the work of Prince A. I. Vasilchikov,[13] who pleaded in 1877–81 for the delegation to the Zemstvos of responsibility for distributing tax-burdens, for the rationalisation of taxation, for the relief of land-hungry peasants in part by resettlement, for credits on easy terms to facilitate peasant land purchases, and for a great effort to raise standards of cultivation. The government did none of these things. Its one important concession was in the matter of resettlement. In the 1880s it had tried to stem unauthorised migration to empty lands beyond the Urals, but in 1889 it changed its mind, and the annual exodus to Siberia quickly rose from a few thousands to a quarter of a million.

A law of 1893 required that there should be an interval of at least twelve years between general re-partitions of allotment land, and prohibited partial adjustments. Later in the same year, the government took steps to prevent the shrinkage of allotment land, by forbidding the peasants to sell it and by qualifying the right of individuals, granted in 1861, to withdraw from the commune and hold their land as private property on payment in full of redemption dues. Henceforward, withdrawal was possible only with the consent of the village assembly. These measures show a concern with the problem of land-hunger, and its effects on husbandry, but fiscal and administrative considerations determined their form.

Only in the following decade did the rulers of Russia come to realise that institutional rigidity and rapid economic growth were incompatible, that for its own safety the régime must not blindly resist social change, but take control of it and direct it. This process of mental adjustment is nowhere more clearly seen than in the political evolution of Sergey Yulyevich Witte.

Witte's plans for reform

Witte took over the Ministry of Finance just as the worst famine of the century struck twenty Volga and central provinces. This disaster was the climax of a series of crop failures due to increasingly frequent drought. Half of European Russia's peasant population was unable to feed itself from harvest to harvest, and mortality in the stricken areas for 1891–92 was 400,000 in excess of the 'normal' figure (itself the highest in Europe). The government was not to blame, of course, for an unfavourable phase in the climatic cycle, but it could no longer shut its eyes to the realities of rural impoverishment, a term which now passed into official parlance. The conscience of Russia spoke through Tolstoy and Korolenko, and through the Zemstvos which played a large part in organising famine relief. The Tsar himself was dismayed, and put the Tsarevich at the head of a fund-raising committee.

Bureaucrats began to study more carefully the mass of disturbing information accumulated by the Zemstvo statistical services. Local committees to assist in a review of legislation concerning the peasants were set up by the Ministry of the Interior in 1894. In the next few years certain of Witte's colleagues expressed anxiety about the effects of his policies on the countryside. In particular Goremykin, Minister of the Interior, noted the impossibility of extracting his dues from the peasant, while Kuropatkin at the War Ministry took fright at the rapid increase in the number of horseless households reported by the Remount Department, and also at the annually growing proportion of peasant conscripts rejected as medically unfit. In 1898, determined to outmanoeuvre his rivals at the Ministry of the Interior, Witte put himself forward as an expert on the 'peasant question'. His earlier views on it had been hazy and conventional: in particular, he had professed a simple faith in the virtues of the peasant commune.[14] Now, in a series of representations to the Committee of Ministers in 1898, and in his report to the Tsar on the budget estimates for 1899, Witte pronounced, in his atrocious style, that 'the reason which retards the firm establishment of the economy of our peasants is concealed in the legal conditions of their way of life.'[15] In this verbal mud the first seed of the government's agrarian policy after 1905 was germinating. In the meantime, Witte made one practical proposal for the immediate relief of the peasantry: nothing less than the writing-off of redemption dues. Perhaps this was meant as a retort to those who grumbled about the burden of Witte's 'own' taxes. In any case, it found no favour with the State Council, where, according to his memoirs, he was asked: 'Why pamper the peasants? They are undisciplined and out of hand as it is.'

Witte's suggestion, also in 1898, for a 'special conference', with public participation, to consider the needs of agriculture, was finally accepted only in January 1902. 618 local committees were set up, with nearly 12,000 members, most of them land-owners, officials or Zemstvo delegates, and two per cent of them peasants.[16] The work of the committees went on simultaneously with that of the Stishinsky Commission, appointed in 1902 to report on the investigation which the Ministry of the Interior had been conducting since 1894; and that of another Commission, under Witte's associate, Kokovtsov, to 'enquire into the reasons for the impoverishment of the Centre', which went into action in October 1903.

The crop failures of 1901 led to the most serious disturbances in the Russian countryside since the 1860s. In 1902 and 1903, in the chronically hungry provinces of Poltava, Kharkov and Saratov, peasants in their thousands over-ran the estates of the gentry and plundered their barns. These events, coinciding with the first successes of the Socialist Revolutionary terrorists, the strike wave in southern Russia and the increasing radicalisation of the liberal movement, made agrarian reform a matter of desperate urgency. To the programme of reform which Stolypin would introduce in

1906 the Commissions under Stishinsky and Kokovtsov both contributed, but its essence was best anticipated by Witte, in his 'Note on the Peasant Question', based on the findings of his Special Conference, and published in 1904. Here Witte furiously attacked the *obshchina* and its devotees (still to be found in the Ministries of the Interior and Agriculture). His main recommendations were that the government should 'assist the transition of rural communes to individual tenure of consolidated holdings by permitting individual peasants to withdraw their plot from communal land use without the consent of the commune'; and secondly that the government should 'eliminate the distinctive peculiarities in the civil rights and personal property rights of the peasant. . . .'[17]

A series of partial reforms had already been initiated by the law of 12 March 1903 abolishing joint responsibility for peasants with communal tenure in most parts of Russia. On 11 August 1904, to mark the christening of the Tsarevich, an imperial manifesto forbade corporal punishment of peasants by local courts. Witte's old proposal to annul redemption payments was finally embodied in a decree of 3 November 1905. From these enactments it was clear that the government had pronounced against the commune and against continued treatment of the peasants as a distinct and inferior estate. Its declaration of intent passed almost unnoticed in the swelling clamour for land. On this subject the Tsar had already made known his will in a rescript to Goremykin in April 1905, insisting on the 'unconditional preservation of private landed property against all encroachments on it'. But in the panicky autumn months Russia's first 'unified' government, under Witte as Prime Minister, wavered in its resistance to peasant pressure. Indeed, some highly influential die-hards outside the government at the height of the revolutionary crisis thought that the Tsar must yield. D. F. Trepov, the Palace Commandant whose influence on the Tsar Witte so dreaded, said in October: 'I am a country gentleman myself, and I shall be very glad to give up half my land for nothing, in the conviction that only thus can I keep the other half for myself.' Panic in high places probably explains the initiative of Witte's Minister of Agriculture, N. N. Kutler, who in December put forward a plan for compulsory purchase for gentry land on a large scale to satisfy peasant needs. In his minute on Witte's report the Tsar reiterated that 'private property must remain sacrosanct'. Kutler was dismissed and sought a more congenial home in the new-born liberal 'Party of People's Freedom' (the Kadets).[18]

The agrarian problem in the First Duma

In the event, the task of handling the Duma fell, not to Witte, but to his successor, the notoriously inert Goremykin, who was in no hurry to put forward proposals of his own but determined to dismiss the Duma if it should raise demands for expropriation. It may seem tragic that neither the new executive nor, with few exceptions, the legislators, looked for a compromise on the biggest and most acute of all Russia's social problems. In the spring and summer of 1906, the government was faced with fresh revolutionary outbreaks in the countryside, and the dominant groups in the Duma—Kadets and *Trudoviki*—saw themselves as the advance party of an embattled people, triumphantly confronting a badly shaken régime with the terms of capitulation. The Kadets, as much as the *Trudoviki*, were no doubt sincerely convinced that the forcible expropriation of gentry land was necessary for the relief of rural poverty: but in making this the loudest and most insistent of their demands, the Kadets were also intent on mobilising popular support for the battle against autocracy on a much wider front.

Three main sets of proposals were put before the Duma by the dominant groups. The Kadets, in a note signed by forty-two deputies and presented on 8 May, made the demands:

Expansion of the area in use by those who work the land by their own toil, that is landless peasants, peasants with little land and other categories of cultivators, from state, appanage, cabinet, monastery and church lands, and by means of compulsory alienation for the same purpose at the expense of the state, and in the necessary proportions, of privately owned land, with compensation of its present owners at a just valuation. The alienated lands should pass into the state land reserve. The principles on which they are to be distributed to the population in need of them must be determined in accordance with the specific features of land tenure and land use in various regions of Russia.

The Kadet experts professed to see no 'basic differences in principle' between these proposals and those signed by 104 *Trudoviki* and presented on 15 May. The *Trudoviki*, however, spoke not merely of creating a state land reserve but of 'making the whole land with its minerals and waters the property of the whole people'. They would not merely, like the Kadets, expand the area in use by those who worked it by their own labour, but give agricultural land only to such people. They 'had in mind the compensation of private owners at state expense for alienated land', but on undefined terms, and they specifically envisaged 'the possibility of cases in which the land will be alienated without compensation'. On the face of it, the Kadets should have found much to quarrel with in this programme, and their tolerance seems explicable only by their need of the *Trudoviki* as allies. They could note with satisfaction that the 104 did not call for immediate and total nationalisation, and that they were willing to leave private owners in possession of land 'not in excess of the labour norm'. On their side, many of the *Trudoviki* deprecated the much more radical project put forward on 6 June by thirty-six members of their group, who wanted immediate nationalisation of all land, equal rights to agricultural land and forests for all citizens, and what is more, an equal say for all citizens in deciding how 'the other riches of the land should be extracted and distributed'.

It would seem, then, that the three main projects embodied three irreconcilable concepts: expansion of peasant holdings through a state land reserve but without general nationalisation (project of the 42), gradual nationalisation (project of the 104), and immediate, total nationalisation (project of the 34). In fact, party lines were much less rigidly drawn. There were, in particular, Kadets who envisaged almost total expropriation of the gentry. Others were concerned to reinforce the provisions in the Party programme for the protection of specialised or highly productive farms, and model estates. Some Kadets stood closer to the moderate conservatives in the Duma and envisaged expropriation only as an auxiliary measure for limited use. Amongst the *Trudoviki*, there was an apparent gulf between those who wished to avoid any suggestion of expropriating *peasant* proprietors, and those who would control all private property in

land at once: but there is no doubt that many of those who preferred the project of the 104 to that of the 34 did so for purely
tactical reasons.

On two matters the Kadets and the *Trudoviki* within the
Agrarian Commission would have found it very difficult to reach
agreement, even if the dissolution of the First Duma had not
curtailed their debates. These were the basic questions of compensation and the organisation of land distribution. On the first,
the attitude of the Kadets was clear: expropriated landowners
should receive a fair price determined by current income from
the land without taking into account profits from leaseholds. The
Trudoviki were evasive. They were saying in effect that the
peasant must please himself whether he paid compensation and
how much. To leave him a free hand they insisted that local
committees must determine the principles of redistribution, and
that the Duma should finalise the terms of reform according to
their instructions. The Kadets, for their part, wanted firm definition of principles by the Duma, and were willing to give local
committees only limited discretion in adjusting the terms of the
reform to regional conditions. They had no more liking than the
Duma conservatives for the 'thousand parliaments' of the *Trudoviki*. There was here a clash between two distinct political
concepts. The *Trudoviki* wanted to 'set the Russian people in
motion which it will be impossible to stop', as Aladin put it. The
Kadets relied of course on popular unrest to force a 'responsible'
government (one in which they could play a leading role) on
the Tsar: it was no part of their plan to abdicate the powers of
that government in advance to the caprice of the masses.

From these manoeuvres, and from other considerations too, it
is clear that the leading Duma parties did not even try to see the
problem of land-hunger in the context of what was ultimately
the much bigger problem of agricultural backwardness. Nothing
is more revealing in the proceedings of the First Duma than
the speeches of the Polish and Baltic peasant deputies, none of
them big farmers. They did not for a moment deny that the
poorer peasants of the central areas needed more land, but they
dismissed as illusory any idea that territorial expansion of primitive Russian farming was a cure for rural poverty. The cure
must be sought in rationalisation of land-use and intensified

cultivation. The majority parties argued that it was impossible, after so long a history of official negligence, to urge patience on the peasant. The extension of peasant holdings by expropriation of private land, said M. Ya. Gertsenshtein was 'a historical necessity created . . . by the criminal negligence of the government and the fact that the government had struggled with its land captains and its machine guns against those phenomena . . . which showed the need and urgency of a broad system of agrarian cultural and economic measures. The government by its actions and inactions has helped to create a situation from which there is no escape except forcible expropriation, and in general the extension of peasant landholding.'

But the immediate practical implications of expropriation were inadequately explored by its proponents. Their criticism of the government's intention to stimulate peasant purchases through the Land Bank was that this would not help the neediest. They themselves, however, did not explain how the transference of land was to be financed, unless expropriation became confiscation, nor how the needier peasants were to farm, unless they were also provided with draught animals and implements, nor yet how any equitable redistribution was possible without massive shifts of population.

The Stolypin reforms

The Kadets and *Trudoviki* in attacking the agrarian problem from this angle were also striking at the social class which they considered the only prop of the autocracy. They could not conceive that the government's own measures would have any intention beyond defence of the landed gentry, whose organisations passionately pledged their loyalty to the old order, and furiously condemned all encroachments on their property. The government, in the person of Minister of the Interior, Stolypin, was in fact contemplating an agrarian reform which would have as one of its objects the creation of a new and very different 'prop'. The insistence of the leading parties on expropriation precipitated the dismissal of the Duma, and Stolypin, now Prime Minister, initiated his reform with decrees promulgated under

Article 87 of the Fundamental Laws, which provided for emergency legislation between Duma sessions. In the event, the decrees of 9 November 1906 were formally translated into a law only on 6 June 1910, and even the much more congenial Third Duma produced by the new Electoral Law of 3 June 1907 gave the Prime Minister rather a rough passage.

Stolypin's great strength lay in a vision of a strong, capitalist, monarchical Russia which many did and many will always find displeasing, but which had the advantages of boldness and consistency. For the first time since the 1860s a Russian statesman addressed himself systematically to the problems of backwardness. Using the autocratic power to the full for the suppression of revolution, he none the less saw the need to strengthen and rationalise the monarchy by broadening its social support and winning the cooperation of the new legislature. His uncompromising defence of private property sprang from loyalty to the bourgeois future, not to the feudal past. He would not sacrifice the 130,000 landowners, because massive expropriation would undermine the institution of private property, and because large-scale redistribution could only 'put a plaster on a septic place'. But at the same time, he believed that the days of big landowning were numbered: the future of agriculture lay with the medium landowner, who might be a gentleman or a peasant. He set out to accelerate the transference of land into the hands of the most efficient, to release the peasant from restrictions on his enterprise, and to build up a new class of prosperous peasants who would be a force both for economic progress and for social stability. Though Stolypin confessedly 'put his stake on the strong' he did not ignore the problem of rural poverty. He proposed to remedy it by increasing sales of land on easy terms, and by speeding up resettlement. And he did not entirely exclude expropriation as an auxiliary and exceptional measure.[19]

The decrees of 5 October and 9 November 1906 released the peasant from the commune. Peasants could henceforward freely leave their communes and receive passports on the same terms as other citizens. The more important decree of 9 November permitted every peasant to apply for registration of his existing holdings as private property without consulting the commune, and 'to demand at any time that the commune should exchange his strips for a consolidated holding as far as possible in one place'. If the peasant's family had decreased since the last partition, so that his holding was disproportionately large, he would none the less retain it, paying for the surplus only if partition had taken place within the past twenty-four years, and then not according to current land values but according to the original redemption price. The 'separated' peasant would keep his share in the use of communal pasture, meadow and forest and other village amenities. The finalised law of 14 June 1910 introduced two important modifications: members of communes which had carried out no partition since the original land-endowment were declared outright proprietors without the formality of registration and households in the communes which had carried out partition but not under the law of 1893 were allowed to retain their existing holdings without paying for any surplus. Stolypin's object was to accelerate the exodus from the commune by all possible means.

The Stolypin reform preserved for the time being some legal disabilities peculiar to the peasant estate in the interests of the peasant himself. Thus, he could dispose of his land only to other peasants or to the Land Bank. The head of a peasant household became an individual proprietor if its other members were his wife and descendants (to whom alone he could bequeath his property) but otherwise the household owned its property communally. These, and similar survivals from the past, enabled Stolypin's critics to vary their attacks on him: he was both ruthless in destroying the peasant's cherished institutions, and hypocritical in pretending to have equalised the peasant with other citizens.

By 1 January 1916, 2,478,000 households (about 24 per cent of the total in forty provinces of European Russia) had obtained individual proprietorship of their land, and 747,000 applications awaited registration. About 1,200,000 households had concentrated their holdings, and of these 103,364 had moved from the village and set up house (with the help of a government subsidy) on their new consolidated holdings. The conversion of the peasant into an independent farmer proceeded rapidly in some provinces, and very slowly in others. Reasons for leaving the commune varied. The wish to farm more rationally and intensively was common, but there was also a large-scale exodus of peasants with small families fearing reduction of their holdings at the next partition, and of those who wanted to sell their holdings and migrate to new lands or to the town. The 'strong' peasant was not always in a hurry to leave the commune, where he could conveniently exploit his poorer neighbours, and the weak peasant often hesitated to consolidate a tiny holding on which 'the calf can't stand if the cow lies down'. Reluctance to move away from the amenities of the village, and to bear the high cost of building materials and well-digging, held up the conversion of consolidated holdings into homesteads in many areas. Consolidation, with the sometimes over-zealous assistance of local officials under pressure from the centre, often provoked friction and even violent resistance in the village.[20]

No study at once comprehensive and impartial, has been made of the social and economic effects of Stolypin's reconstruction. It is, however, noteworthy that his more balanced critics were willing to concede him a measure of success. The analysis by the Menshevik, Professor I. V. Chernyshev,[21] of replies to a questionnaire circulated by the Free Economic Society in 1910–1911 shows a majority opinion that consolidated holdings made possible a greater use of machinery, increased yields, and an improvement in animal husbandry. A like-minded writer, Professor A. E. Lositsky, who held that reconstruction 'leaves unsolved the problems of land-hunger and the peasant's lack of rights,' none the less recognised the majority of the new farmers as 'pioneers in the movement for technical improvement of husbandry recently observable among the peasantry,' and considered that the reform 'corresponds to the interests of a considerable mass of peasants.' The liberal A. A. Kaufman was also ready to recognise the soundness of Stolypin's political calculations. 'In the rising class of small proprietors,' he wrote, 'a conservative class was being created. . . . If Stolypin's successors had been given a little more time . . . who knows, it is very likely that the possibility of a decisive political overturn would have been averted for a long time, or that the overturn would have taken another direction.'[22] Lenin's much earlier reaction to Stolypin was not dissimilar. Stolypin's policy might make it necessary for the Social-Democrats to discard their agrarian programme (that is, their hopes of rallying the peasant mass to their support) and to rely on the support of the rural proletariat (wage-labourers) alone.[23]

Stolypin had set out not merely to reconstruct the countryside but to increase peasant landholding and resettle surplus population. Largely through the efforts of the Peasant Land Bank some nine million *desyatins* were transferred from the gentry to the peasants in 1906–15. Over half the purchasers were peasants with less than six *desyatins*, and a quarter landless: between them these groups acquired over a quarter of the land transferred. Peasant purchases were subsidised up to as much as 90 per cent, and repayment was scheduled over fifty-five and a half years. The whole scheme could, of course, be represented as a new redemption operation by those who held that all the land belonged to the peasant by right. But one of its effects was to make land available for a lower annual payment than prevailing leasehold prices, with a prospect of ultimate ownership, and to bring down leasehold prices themselves.

The third component of Stolypin's agrarian policy was his resettlement programme. Already in the 1890s the government had organised and subsidised emigration, but legal limitations on freedom of movement, obstacles raised by local officials, and the inadequacies of the resettlement machinery kept figures down. A law of 6 June 1904 had removed some restrictions on resettlement, but offered subsidies only to 'approved' settlers. Stolypin's Rules of 10 March 1906 gave complete freedom to resettle with government aid, and under the law of 9 November, migrants could expect to become owners of a consolidated farm. The efflux eastwards rose enormously. Stolypin, who toured Siberia and Central Asia with his Minister of Agriculture, Krivoshein, in 1910, was able to report that 'in three hundred years of our possession of Siberia a Russian population of only 4.5 millions grew up there, and during the past fifteen years, there has been an increase of about 3 millions, more than 1.5 million of them in the three-year period 1907–9.' In spite of some shortcomings, especially the over-estimation of the availability of easily cultivable land, the resettlement programme made a measurable contribution to the relief of densely populated areas, and in the end fostered in Siberia a relatively prosperous and independent-minded peasantry.

The policies which Stolypin initiated were not to run their course. He had said in 1910 that given ten years of peace, Russia would be 'unrecognisable'. In 1911 he was assassinated, and six years later the war which he had dreaded brought to power some of those who 'wanted great upheavals' instead of 'a great Russia' on the Stolypin model. The problems with which he struggled had been created or aggravated by a quarter of a century of myopic immobilism. The solutions which he devised were alien to a large section of educated Russian society, remote from the immediate aspirations of the Russian masses. They had, in many cases, a character of improvisation and incompleteness and, at times, of compromise with the views of those to the right or left of himself whom he needed to conciliate. In the event, he was too late. The historian may hesitate to pass judgement on the long-term prospects of Stolypin's policies. He must question the view put forward by those who suffer from no such inhibition, for instance, the author of a very thorough Soviet study, S. M. Dubrovsky,[24] who holds that the failure of the Stolypin agrarian reform was evident before the First World War.

The general improvement in Russian agriculture in the years 1906–16 was due in considerable measure to Stolypin's reconstruction. Still backward and poor by western standards, the Russian countryside was no longer stagnant. Its future, however, depended not only on the concentration and technical improvement of agricultural production, but also on the progress of industrialisation. As Maslov and others had demonstrated, the long-term problem was not that the peasants had too little land but that, however the land was distributed, there were too many peasants. Stolypin's policies involved intensification of agriculture and the transference of surplus rural population to the towns. Industry, after years of slump and revolutionary disruption, was again expanding rapidly, but it could not for a long time absorb all displaced or impoverished peasants. In Russia, as in all underdeveloped countries with a swollen rural population, the costs and hardships of modernisation would fall mainly on the peasant. It is very clear that the burden would have been lighter if the Russian government of the 1880s had been less myopic, and Witte in the 1890s less fanatically narrow. It is arguable that Stolypin could, without damage to his general programme, have done more for the direct relief of rural poverty. But neither he nor anyone else could base a programme of national reconstruction on the utopian fantasy of the peasant.

For purely tactical reasons, the Soviet régime would, in 1917, pander to this dream, and with fewer qualms in the NEP era. Perhaps, as one of Solzhenitsyn's characters came to believe, 'the peasant' was better off under NEP than at any time 'from Rurik to the latest unscrambling of amalgamated *kolkhozy*'.[25] But not all peasants. 'Socialisation' did not eliminate the landless peasant, nor the class of agricultural labourers. The NEP rescued the country from famine, but under it the gap between the prosperous and the poor peasant widened again after the initial 'mediumisation'. This is not the place to discuss whether a reasonably high rate of industrial development could have been achieved without large-scale collectivisation. Whatever alternative solution we envisage, there is no doubt that the interests of industry and of the towns were coming into ever sharper conflict with the peasant's interests as he saw them.

Collectivisation, in many respects, meant reversion to the pre-Stolypin period, or even to the era of serfdom. The peasant was partially dispossessed. Labour in the 'socialist sector' was often grossly and systematically underpaid, so that it looked to the peasant like a new form of *barshchina* (corvée). The peasant was attached to the land, except when it suited the state to release him, by a discriminatory passport régime. The residual property rights of the individual were largely merged again in those of the household. The state exacted unpaid labour on public works, and even levies in land on the produce of the garden plot. The new feudalism, of course, differed from the old in having as part of its purpose the planned creation of a prosperous society. We cannot compare the unrealised prospects of the tsarist government's policy in its last phase, and its probable social costs, with the results and costs of the Soviet solution of the agrarian problem. The independent historian must, however, examine very carefully Lenin's view that the *Stolypinshchina* 'had a smell of death,' and enquire whether it was not, in fact, a painful but hopeful new beginning.

The economic and cultural development of Siberia

NIKOLAUS POPPE

Apart from the Amur district, which was not incorporated into the Russian empire until 1858, the conquest of Siberia was completed by the mid-seventeenth century. Thus by 1900 Siberia had been a Russian dominion for much longer than the Caucasus, the Crimea or the Baltic territories. None the less, it long remained an underdeveloped territory and was widely believed to be a land of misery peopled only by exiles and convicts. Recognising that this popular misconception might well harm the development of the territory the celebrated Russian expert on Siberia, N. M. Yadrintsev, tried to correct it as early as the 1890s.[1] But the fact that the economic and social development of Siberia proceeded so slowly was due, in the final analysis, to the slow economic and social development of Russia as a whole. Consequently, if we wish to form an accurate assessment of Siberian history, we have to consider it within the general framework of Russian history.

Initially, the sole object of Russian policy in Siberia was the exaction of money from the native population, who had been laid under tribute following their conquest, in order to swell the imperial coffers. It was not until much later that Russian governments began to concern themselves with the economic and political integration of the territory. Siberia, as Danckwortt once observed, is the largest colonial territory in the largest land mass in the world.[2] Like all colonial territories, it had its share of social abuses, and at the turn of the century these were subjected to bitter criticism by the Siberian regionalists, the *Oblastniki*, who called for urgent reforms. But an even grimmer picture of pre-revolutionary Siberia has been painted by Soviet authors. M. Vetoshkin tells us that Siberia was simply used by Russian capitalists as a dumping-ground for shoddy goods and by the tsarist government as a place of confinement for criminal elements and political opponents.[3] Moreover, numerous authors have pointed out that by the late nineteenth century fifty-two per cent of the Russian population of eastern Siberia (east of Lake Baikal) was accounted for by exiles, a figure which did not include the prison populations. According to the Soviet historian A. A. Mukhin, the 'reactionary policy of the tsarist régime, which had transformed eastern Siberia into a land of exile, forced labour and deportation, [constituted] the principal reason for the slow development of the productive forces of that enormously rich territory.'[4]

The population of Siberia consisted largely of immigrants, most of whom—Soviet authors now insist—were very badly off because 'the colonisation policy pursued by the tsarist government catered exclusively for the interests of the estate owners and capitalists. . . . Because the colonisation programme was organised in such a way as to benefit the exploiting classes and because no assistance of any kind was given to the peasant settlers, the vast majority of these were ruined; many died on the journey or in their new settlements whilst the remainder swelled the ranks of the proletariat.'[5] The fact that so many Russians none the less chose to emigrate to Siberia, especially in the second half of the nine-teenth century, naturally called for some explanation. This has been furnished by Soviet authors, who claim that Siberia was used by the monarchists and estate owners as a safety valve to reduce the dangerous tensions created by the agrarian revolts in European Russia. It was, they say, in order to promote emigration that the tsarist régime spread the erroneous idea that Cossacks, Buryat Mongols and Tungus would receive thirty[6] and Russian peasants fifteen *desyatins* of land in Siberia (one *desyatin* was about 2.7 acres). In actual fact, we are told, the enormous tracts of forest and arable land in the new territory remained firmly in the hands of the Tsar, the Russian state, the kulaks, the churches and monasteries and the Cossack and Tungus leaders. A similar interpretation has been placed on the building of the Trans-Siberian railway. This, it seems, was designed to serve as a 'pump' for drawing off the wealth of the new territory and as a 'means of enforcing tsarist colonial policies'. (At the same time Soviet historians are obliged to concede that this railway created the necessary basis for the economic and, more particularly, the industrial development of Siberia.)[7] Reference is also made in Soviet historiography to the pernicious effects exerted on the original native population, especially the Yakuts, by the tsarist policy of russification. P. I. Petrov, for example, speaks of the 'severe oppression by the tsarist régime, and by the Russian and indigenous exploiting classes, of the peoples of the Yakut territory, who were reduced to extreme poverty, chronic malnutrition and near extinction'.[8]

It would seem from such accounts that Siberia was a really terrifying place prior to the revolution, which makes it difficult to understand why it was that in the year 1908 alone 758,812 people left European Russia in order to settle there. Moreover, of these new settlers 47.7 per cent were illegal immigrants and so received no assistance from the state.[9] In actual fact, of course, we find from a careful study of conditions in Siberia and of the historical development of this territory, that, although it was not exactly a promised land, it none the less provided millions of people with a better opportunity for building a reasonable life than they were able to find in European Russia. In the late nineteenth century Siberia was not a forgotten land with primitive and hopelessly rigid economic structures. On the contrary, it was passing through a relatively rapid phase of development.

Yadrintsev has rightly observed that the history of Siberia is the history of its colonisation. By the end of the nineteenth century more than eighty per cent of the population of this colony was composed of immigrants and this percentage has risen still further since then.[10] Siberia resembles North America in so far as there too the early history of the country saw the colonisation of a large territory within a relatively short period. The speed of the Russian advance in Siberia was due to the fact that the indigenous peoples were so few in number, were not organised into a corporate state and followed a way of life that was culturally inferior to that of Russian society. They were either nomadic tribes or tribes of primitive hunters. The Russian population of Siberia was already numerically superior to the native population in the eighteenth century, although it did not pass the million mark until the beginning of the nineteenth century.

European Russians who elected to emigrate to Siberia did so for one of two reasons: they went in search either of arable land or of personal freedom. Emigration began immediately the new territory had been conquered. Nor did all the early emigrants travel at their own risk; state-sponsored emigration started as far back as 1590.[11] The first criminals were deported to Siberia in 1593, although at that time such deportations were ordered more with a view to promoting colonisation than as a punishment. All deported persons were set to work and were paid for their labour. But it was not until the nineteenth century that more or less reliable records were kept of criminal and political deportations. These show that up to 1880 the number of criminals and political prisoners exiled to Siberia each year exceeded the number of peasant emigrants. At that point the government realised that 'by turning Siberia into a sort of drain for refuse disposal, the development of the territory [had been] brought to a standstill'[12] and that the time had come to redress the balance in favour of voluntary emigration. From then onwards a genuine attempt was made to curb arbitrary deportation orders and evolve an effective colonisation programme.

But the significance of colonisation had been appreciated long before this by M. M. Speransky, an important statesman who realised that the Siberian economy could be developed quite speedily if the right measures were adopted.[13] The imperial ukase of 10 April 1822 which he helped to draw up, authorised the emigration to Siberia of serfs from crown lands. Other liberal measures affecting the colonisation programme were also taken on subsequent occasions. In 1837, for example, when a government surveyor's office was opened in Siberia, provision was made for every new family settling in the territory to receive fifteen *desyatins* of land for each of its male members. Later the settlers also received financial aid and were absolved from all liability for taxation and even from liability for military service. As a result of these measures the state was able to resettle approximately 350,000 serfs from crown lands by 1860.

But, in addition to these sponsored immigrants, there were also illegal immigrants. Many whose applications for resettlement in Siberia had been turned down by the authorities and many more who wished to avoid the inevitable bureaucratic delays set out on their own initiative and at their own risk. Theoretically, such people were not supposed to receive any help upon arrival. On the contrary, the law provided for their immediate repatriation. In fact, they were invariably allowed to stay and the authorities also allocated them land. But they were not given financial support and remained liable to taxation and military service.

The settlement issue became particularly acute following the Emancipation of the serfs in 1861, which entitled twenty-two million peasants to leave their village communities (*mirs*). But, although many of these wanted to emigrate to Siberia, the government of the day failed to respond to the new situation and contented itself with half-measures. This then led to a steady increase in the number of illegal immigrants. In 1882 17,942 illegal immigrants settled in the Altai district alone. Two years later this figure rose to 30,544. Moreover, as illegal immigration increased, government-sponsored immigration almost came to a standstill. This was due partly to the bureaucratic attitude of the authorities and their inability to appreciate the great significance of the colonisation programme, and partly to the enormous distances involved and the lack of an up-to-date network of communications.

Until the end of the nineteenth century the only traffic routes in the whole of Siberia were those provided by roads and rivers. A journey to the eastern parts of the territory took several months. The building of the projected Trans-Siberian railway had long been under discussion and its desirability had been recognised by certain sections of Siberian public opinion, although Yadrintsev and the regionalists were opposed to it at first.[14] Later Yadrintsev changed his mind and commented favourably on the project: 'The construction of a main line through the whole of Siberia to the Pacific will be an innovation. After this main line has been completed a subsidiary rail network should be developed in Asia, its route being determined by the location of industrial concentrations and the local need for such a service.' S. Yu. Witte, the then Minister of Finance who later became Prime Minister, also recognised the need for a railway and, in a proposal which he submitted to the Tsar, he stressed its importance for the colonisation of Siberia, the development of the Siberian mining industry, the expansion of Russia's trade with Asia and her military plans in the Far East. His proposal eventually received the imperial assent. When the heir to the throne, Nikolay Alexandrovich, who later became Nicholas II, returned to Russia from his tour of the world and was staying in Vladivostok, he was commanded by Alexander III to conduct the initiation ceremony for the new railway, which was held in Vladivostok on 19 May 1891. Work started the same day on the 415-kilometre section of track between Vladivostok and Grafskaya. Shortly afterwards work started simultaneously on several other sections with the result that by 1898 the entire line had been completed. Thus, 6,500 kilometres of track were laid in seven years, which was no mean achievement.

The new railway was primarily intended to facilitate the establishment of further settlements in Siberia and of industrial developments in their immediate vicinity. In view of the great importance of these projects a special committee was formed at the end of 1891 (Committee of the Trans-Siberian Railway) to deal with all matters relating to the colonisation and economic development of Siberia. The chairman of the committee, who was appointed by imperial decree on 13 January 1893, was the heir to the throne. At the committee meeting of 8 March 1895 the chairman—who had meanwhile succeeded his father as Tsar—stated that the whole object of government policy was to secure the successful colonisation of the new territory and that consequently no illegal immigrants were to be repatriated. Shortly afterwards a special colonisation department was set up under the auspices of the Ministry of the Interior which was responsible among other things for the issue of emigration permits, for the welfare of settlers and for the administration of government subsidies. The numerous restrictions imposed under previous edicts were gradually relaxed and a new measure was introduced, which denied to illegal immigrants any of the benefits normally conferred by the state but freed them from any liability to prosecution. It was also decided that groups of intending immigrants could send a *khodok*—an authorised representative—to visit the area in which they proposed to settle and report back to them on local conditions before their departure. This measure proved extremely useful.

In 1894 and again in 1898 rail fares were reduced for all authorised immigrants travelling to Siberia. Field kitchens and medical posts were also set up at various points along the Trans-Siberian railway for which, in the year 1894 alone, the sum of three million roubles was set aside from the public purse. The scale of these welfare operations was quite significant: at twenty-seven of these centres over 3,000,000 meals for adults, 471,353 meals for children and over 1,000,000 kilos of bread were dispensed free of charge, and 519,274 people were given medical treatment between 1894 and 1901.[15]

It is not possible to enumerate within the scope of this present chapter all the measures taken by the authorities to promote emigration. Suffice it to say that the number of emigrants rose sharply following the introduction of rail travel. Many of these, it is true, were disappointed with what they found and returned home to European Russia with their illusions shattered. None the less, in the six-year period immediately preceding the opening of the new railway the highest number of emigrants in a single year (1892) was 92,146 as compared with 120,000 in 1895, over 190,000 in 1896, over 223,000 in 1899, nearly 568,000 in 1907 and over 758,000 in 1908. The proportion of illegal immigrants in this period fluctuated between 19.7 and 47.7 per cent. The repatriation figures also reveal a marked fluctuation: 29,915 in 1896 as compared with 121,204 in 1908. The total number of emigrants to Siberia between 1887 and 1913 was 5,375,353, of whom 4,983,498 went between 1904 and 1913.[16] This vast influx of settlers produced a rapid increase in the population of the territory, as can be seen from the following table:[17]

Year	Native population	Immigrant population	Total population
1858	648,000	2,288,036	2,936,036
1897	870,536	4,889,633	5,760,169
1911	972,866	8,393,469	9,366,335

We see from these figures that the population almost doubled between 1858 and 1897 and almost doubled again between 1897 and 1911. In this respect, therefore, the colonisation of Siberia proceeded more rapidly than that of comparable territories such as Canada. In 1851 the Canadian population was 2,436,297 and by 1911 this had risen to only 7,206,643.[18]

One of the consequences of the mass emigration of Europeans to America and Australia was the sudden decline, and in some cases the extinction, of the native tribes. In Siberia this was not the case. Although Russian colonisation brought no particular benefit to the indigenous peoples, neither did it do them any great harm. Only in very few instances did the Russian army resort to extermination tactics. As early as the seventeenth century successive Tsars had stressed the importance of establishing friendly relations with the native peoples whilst later immigrants were strictly forbidden to settle on the grazing grounds used by the nomads. As a result of this essentially benevolent attitude the native population constantly increased under Russian rule. The following table shows the growth rate of three of the original Siberian tribes in the nineteenth century:

	1831	1897	1911
Buryat population	152,000[19]	289,480[20]	332,656[21]
Yakut population	—	221,467[22]	246,405[22]
Tungus population	—	62,068	75,204[23]

Those Russians who emigrated to Siberia found that their standard of living was considerably improved. This was clearly revealed by a survey carried out in 1898 which was based on a sample of 93,312 settlers, all of whom considered themselves to be better off in Siberia and most of whom attributed the improvement to the greater availability of arable land. In this survey the settlers were asked about the number of horses and domestic animals, the number of agricultural machines and the amount of arable land which they had owned before and after emigration. The table on the next page gives some comparative figures for the years 1889 to 1893[24] ('after emigration' figures are in brackets).

The immigration into Siberia of over five million peasants within a twenty-five year period led to a considerable increase in the amount of land under the plough. In 1897 there were 3,481,000 *desyatins* of arable land in Siberia,[25] in 1911 there were 5,857,592

Year of emigration	1889	1890	1891	1892	1893
Percentage of settlers who owned:					
Horses	83 (94)	85 (94)	81 (94)	81 (96)	79 (94)
Cattle	83 (94)	79 (95)	82 (94)	81 (95)	76 (95)
Agricultural machines	77 (82)	78 (82)	73 (79)	74 (80)	71 (81)
Their own holding	83 (91)	86 (94)	82 (90)	85 (93)	80 (90)
Average area of arable land (in *desyatins*) owned by settlers:	2.7 (7.5)	3.6 (5.9)	3 (6.2)	2.8 (5.9)	2.6 (5.4)

$(6,527,591)^{26}$ *desyatins* and in 1916 7,133,100.[27] The grain harvest grew proportionately. In the period 1910–14 the wheat harvest averaged 3,247,200 tons and the rye harvest 828,576 tons.[28] A considerable amount was exported. In the period 1892–1910 Siberian grain exports rose from 164,000 to nearly 500,000 tons per year and by 1911 the value of Siberian wheat and flour exports was 0.7 million pounds.[29] In fact, agriculture was more advanced in Siberia than in most areas of European Russia. By 1911 west Siberia alone possessed 36,519 reaping machines whilst European Russia, whose population was several times greater than that of the whole of Siberia, possessed no more than 66,381. By 1913 there were thirteen factories and workshops in Siberia producing agricultural machinery and 767 distribution warehouses. The most popular machines were iron ploughs, winnowing machines, threshing machines and harvesters.

Cattle-rearing, which had been one of the traditional occupations of the native Siberian tribes, was carried on even more intensively than agriculture. Between 1904 and 1916 the total amount of livestock in the territory rose from 11.5 million to 38.5 million head.[30] By 1913 Siberia had 53 horses, 63 head of cattle, 61 sheep and 13 pigs per hundred of the population. According to the records for 1916, Siberian farms possessed an average of 20 farm animals as opposed to only 9 for the farms in European Russia. Animal husbandry was the cornerstone of the Siberian farmers' prosperity and exports of dairy produce soon became the most important item in Siberia's trade both with Russia and with foreign countries. Butter exports rose from 400 poods[31] in 1894 to 4.4 million poods in 1912 and during this eighteen-year period a total of 36 million poods (590,000 tons) of Siberian butter worth 500 million roubles was exported.[32] This trade in dairy produce also encouraged the development of cooperatives, which were to become such an important feature of the social structure of the new territory. The first cooperatives were formed in 1896 and by 1911 1,318 of the 3,102 butter factories and dairies in western Siberia were organised along cooperative lines.[33] Thanks to the Trans-Siberian railway Siberia's trade in other products, such as meat, wool and furs, was greatly intensified. In 1911 alone 70,000 Siberian sable furs found their way on to the international market. Meanwhile, imports of sugar, iron and steel products, textiles and agricultural machinery showed a constant increase.

There was no Siberian manufacturing industry worthy of the name under the Tsars, although metallurgical works had been founded east of the Urals as early as the eighteenth century. The Siberian mining industry also went back quite a long way and was reasonably well developed. Of the various branches which went to make up this industry the most profitable was goldmining. In 1912 the production of the Siberian mining industry was constituted as follows: gold 2,250 poods, copper 134,000 poods, zinc 120,000 poods, lead 9,000 poods, salt 10,500,000 poods and coal 123,000,000 poods.[34]

One of the distinctive features of the cultural and economic development of Siberia was the fast rate of urban expansion, which was a concomitant of the growth of Siberian trade. The precise rate naturally varied from town to town. Thus, whereas in the fifty-year period from 1860 to 1910 the population of a large number of Siberian towns increased by about 20 per cent, in Omsk there was an increase of 503.5 per cent and in Krasnoyarsk of 727.7 per cent. The table on the next page which shows the growth in the population of six Siberian towns between 1897 and 1909–11, gives some idea of the enormous changes that were taking place.[35]

We have already pointed out that the peasants who emigrated to

Town	1897	1909–11
Tomsk	52,430	107,711
Irkutsk	51,484	113,288
Omsk	37,470	127,869
Vladivostok	28,980	120,000
Chita	11,480	73,114
Novo-Nikolayevsk (now Novosibirsk)	8,473	70,000

Siberia found that their standard of living rose considerably. In point of fact, this appears to have been true of all sections of the community. In the nine-year period from 1901 to 1910 the number of securities held by people living in Siberia rose by 73.9 per cent whereas the average increase for the whole of Russia during this period was only 66.7 per cent. Moreover, the money invested in Siberian savings accounts between 1907 and 1909 came to 79.8 million roubles, which was 31 per cent of the total amount invested throughout the whole of the empire (253.7 million roubles), a very high percentage considering that the Siberian population accounted for only 11 per cent of the total population.[36] In certain parts of Siberia savings averaged 20 roubles per head of the population, which compared favourably with the savings levels in the wealthiest areas of Russia. The growing affluence of the Siberian settlers, especially the peasants, is also demonstrated by their greatly increased purchasing power. 1906 was the great turning point. In that year the peasants of the Yeniseisk district bought goods to the value of 223,400 roubles, which was twice as much as they had ever spent in any previous year. Furthermore, the Soviet historian V. A. Stepunin has established that in 1911, immediately following the Stolypin agrarian reforms, the peasants of Yeniseisk bought agricultural equipment to the value of 602,542 roubles.[37]

Siberia was not entirely lacking in culture and it also had an educational system of sorts. Basically, however, the literacy rate throughout the whole of tsarist Russia was much lower than in the countries of western and central Europe, and among the original inhabitants of Siberia it was much lower still; in fact, they were almost completely illiterate. According to the census of 1897, 29.3 per cent of Russian males and 13.1 per cent of Russian females were able to read as compared with 19 per cent of Siberian males and 5.1 per cent of Siberian females. In the years that followed this situation improved to some extent. In 1897 Siberia had only 3,468 primary schools with 117,410 pupils, 49 secondary schools (grammar and technical) with 9,877 pupils and one institute of higher education, the University of Tomsk, which was founded in 1888 and had 383 students. By 1911, however, there were 5,704 primary schools with 297,779 pupils, 125 secondary schools with 36,012 pupils and four institutes of higher education with a total of 2,849 students. By 1911, therefore, there was a grand total of nearly 340,000 pupils and students, although even this much improved figure was still very low by comparison with the rest of Russia. On the other hand, various Siberian towns, such as Tomsk, had excellent museums, learned societies and theatres.[38]

Medical services throughout the whole of Russia were bad, but they were worse in Siberia than in European Russia. In 1907, for example, there was one hospital for every 703 sq km in European Russia but only one hospital for every 29,250 sq km in Siberia. The distribution of doctors at that time followed a similar pattern. Russia had one doctor for every 288 sq km or every 7,700 persons while Siberia had one doctor for every 19,364 sq km or every 12,500 persons. But conditions gradually improved and by 1910 Siberia had 526 hospitals or one hospital for every 22,800 sq km. By 1913 it possessed 663 hospitals with beds for 15,990 patients, 163 polyclinics and 12 hydropathic establishments. Thanks partly to its extremely healthy climate and partly, no doubt, to its improved medical services, the average life expectancy in Siberia was greater than in any other part of the Russian empire immediately prior to the First World War. This is reflected in the fact that 48.1 per cent of the Siberian population was made up of people between twenty and sixty years of age whereas in European Russia this age group accounted for only 44.3 per cent of the population.

In the past Siberia was generally regarded as a land of exile. Nor was this view entirely unfounded, for the penal colonies and prisons of Siberia were undoubtedly highly populated. But although it would go far beyond the scope of the present chapter to deal with this highly complex question in detail, there are a few facts which ought to be mentioned. We are told, for example, by the Soviet historian M. N. Gernet that in the early years of the twentieth century the annual prison population for the whole of Russia averaged 1,859,314.[39] This compares with a total of 6,000 persons condemned to forced labour in 1903 and 32,000 in 1910, most of whom were common criminals. Of the 25,353 persons charged with crimes against the state between 1910 and 1914, 15,277 (or 69 per cent) were convicted. If we assume that all political prisoners were banished to Siberia at that time, then there must have been a large number of them in the territory by the early 1910s. Although the criminal elements deported to Siberia played no part whatever in the development of the territory, the political prisoners made an outstanding contribution, which has been rightly commended in Soviet historiography. To the immense satisfaction of the local settlers the deportation of criminals to Siberia was abolished under the law of 10 June 1900.

The living conditions of the exiles were not always as bad as is generally believed. An Englishman named De Windt who visited Siberia for the express purpose of investigating the local prisons, stated that rumours of terrible privations were exaggerated, that the general treatment of prisoners was decent and their food adequate. He also mentioned that the trains used to transport prisoners to Siberia were clean and heated.[40] According to De Windt, a certain Dr Landsdell went so far as to say that, if he were sentenced to a term of imprisonment and had the choice between Millbank Penitentiary in London and the political prison in Kara, he would prefer Kara. Although it certainly does not follow from De Windt's testimony that all political prisoners in Siberia were well treated, it would seem that some at least were better off than the prisoners in Millbank. De Windt also said that the prisons which he had inspected in Tomsk would have done credit to any European country. We must always remember, of course, that this was not a very humane epoch, either in Russia or elsewhere.

We have already seen that in the period preceding the revolution Siberia had achieved a higher standard in certain spheres than European Russia. This development, which was made possible by the construction of the Trans-Siberian railway and the intensive colonisation programme pursued by the tsarist government, has been confirmed by Soviet authors, who point out that, because agriculture was more highly developed in Siberia than in European Russia, the question of agrarian reform appeared less urgent there. In fact, the Siberian peasant was considerably wealthier than his Russian counterpart. Although the regionalists were wrong in claiming that there was no social basis for the development of a Social-Democratic movement in Siberia in 1905, it is none the less true that class distinctions were considerably less marked there than in other parts of the Russian empire. Why else should the Siberian peasants have afforded such 'ineffectual support'[41] to the workers in their struggle against the tsarist régime and why else should the Soviets of Workers' and Soldiers' Deputies formed in Siberia during the civil war have received so little backing from the populace? The reasons given by V. V. Ryabikov for the overthrow of the Siberian Soviets during the first phase of the civil war were the 'sudden intervention of foreign powers and the ineffectual part played in the struggle to establish Soviet power by the Siberian peasants, who had no personal experience of serfdom and had never been short of land. The wealthy Siberian peasants were producers of grain, meat, butter and wool, and both the abolition of free trade by the Bolsheviks and the introduction of fixed prices for grain were against their interests.'[42] From this Ryabikov concluded that 'the revolution in Siberia was not a revolution in its own right but merely a reflection [of events in Russia]. If the October revolution had not broken out in the heartland, there would have been no revolution in Siberia for decades.' Unlike their compatriots in European Russia, the people of Siberia had a standard of living to defend which was well worth defending, for the Siberian peasant was really a wealthy land-owner. During the twenty-five year period immediately preceding the October revolution, Siberia had passed through a rapid economic and cultural development and was well on the way to becoming one of the most affluent and progressive territories in the Russian empire.

The 'nationalities question' in the last phase of tsardom

VIOLET CONOLLY

Through successful wars and intrigues Russia was constantly expanding her frontiers from the sixteenth century until at the end of the nineteenth century they stretched from Poland in the west to Sakhalin in the Far East and from the Caspian Sea to the western borders of China. This advance had brought more than a hundred non-Russian peoples differing from the Great Russians in race, religion and culture within the imperial frontiers. The problems created by their multi-national ethos in a highly centralised empire came to be known collectively as the 'nationalities question'. It was an extremely complex and difficult question involving peoples as different as the Poles, the Turkestani Muslims, the Finns and the indigenous tribes of Siberia. The Russian attitude to these peoples differed enormously throughout the ages depending very largely on whether or not the monarch of the day was well disposed towards a particular people, as for example Alexander I was towards the Poles and Finns.

Russia had no fixed or consistent nationalities policy and switches were frequent with the rise and fall of influential statesmen. The period with which we are dealing, the apogee of empire, coincided with a rising tide of Great Russian nationalism which had the support of the Tsars Alexander III and Nicholas II and intimate advisers with the ear of these monarchs. Belief in the superiority of Russian culture, Orthodoxy and Slavdom led to an intensive policy of russification among the non-Russian peoples with the suppression of their native languages in schools and oppression of Roman Catholicism and other national religions. The national schools and churches were regarded as the strongholds of national feeling: they were thus the object of official attack and a threat to the unity of the empire in the drive towards the assimilation of all the non-Russian peoples in a Great Russian Orthodox unity. The ethnic minorities were not the only victims of the oppressive laws of the period. They also fell heavily on all, Great Russians alike, suspected of liberal views or aiming at a reform of the autocracy. It seemed that as the empire reached its greatest expansion, imperial apprehension about the separate national identity of its non-Russian subjects and their loyalty increased. This attitude led to a repudiation of the contractual basis on which some of the leading minorities originally acknowledged Russian sovereignty and destroyed their faith in the Russian monarch and state as the protector of their ancient liberties. All the western border states of Russia suffered the same collapse of rights at this time.

It is noteworthy that the policies followed among the Turkic Muslims of Central Asia, in the last colonial conquest of imperial Russia, were much less harsh in regard to native institutions and religion than the simultaneous russification of the Catholic Poles, Protestant Finns and Baltic Germans. But Russia lost the respect she might otherwise have gained by this policy of relative non-interference with the native way of life through the incompetence and corruption of the military government installed in Turkestan.

The civil liberties conceded by the Tsar under the pressure of the revolutionary events of 1905 introduced a period of temporary alleviation from russification for the minorities. The major groups were represented in the Dumas between 1906–7 but Turkestan lost its representation from the Third. The Dumas became increasingly reactionary and their performance was a disappointment for the minorities, to which they paid little attention.

A kind of mystic aura came to be associated in the minds of Russian nationalists with the principle of Russia 'one and indivisible' proclaimed in the preamble to the Fundamental Laws of 1906. The increasingly frequent minority demands for national autonomy or liberal reforms met with less than no understanding and even assumed a treasonable hue in the eyes of the more extreme reactionaries. And this attitude was later a major cause of the defeat of the Nationalist generals in the civil war against the Bolsheviks in the minority areas. 'Indivisible' Russia remained something sacrosanct and to be defended at all costs against disintegration in the form of federalism or autonomy.

Russification did not imply racial discrimination in tsarist Russia except in the case of the Jews, who were in a special category. Mother Russia, while always conscious of her superiority to the races of the empire, did not distinguish between her peoples on the score of race, and there were no barriers to inter-marriage or social intercourse at all levels of society. The Polish, Georgian and Tatar nobility for example, were welcome in the highest Russian society and married freely into it. The criterion of acceptance was not race but loyalty to the personal autocracy of the Tsar.

The Fundamental Laws also proclaimed the Russian language to be the language of administration, the army and the state and social institutions throughout the empire. The use of the local languages was to be a matter for special legislation. The need for an official *lingua franca* in the multi-racial Russian empire was well founded. The claims of the minorities for the use of their own languages in their schools and churches were also justified but in fact were more and more ignored after 1907, especially in regard to education. The central Russian bureaucracy seemed blind to the effect of its russification policies in the 'localities', and the inevitable exacerbation of outraged national feelings. The purely cultural national movements which had emerged in the latter part of the nineteenth century had gradually evolved into active political groupings and parties aiming at radical improvements in the position of the nationalities within the empire. As tsardom approached its end it may be said to have created the divisive attitudes to 'indivisible' Russia which were so dreaded. In Professor George Kennan's authoritative words: 'The revenge for this extraordinary blindness became apparent quite naturally in the form of the high percentage of members of the national minorities to be found in the revolutionary movement. It is impossible to say what 1917 would have been like without the Chkheidzes and Martovs, the Trotskys, Dzerzhinskiis, Radeks, Sverdlovs, Stalins and Ordzhonikidzes, but certainly the non-Russian component in the revolutionary opposition to tsardom was a great one, particularly after 1881, and it may be assumed to have added greatly to the difficulty of the predicament of the autocracy at that final moment.'[1]

In the following pages the implementation of these Russian

policies in some of the chief non-Russian territories of the empire will be discussed in greater detail. It is impossible in the space and time available to deal with all the nationalities but russification may be taken to have been the order of the day in them all.

Poland

The Polish lands appropriated by Russia through the various partitions at the end of the eighteenth century were consolidated and united to the empire as the Kingdom of Poland in 1815 by Alexander I under exceptionally favourable conditions. With a separate crown hereditary in the house of Romanov, this Kingdom of Poland was an entirely separate juridical entity from the empire and enjoyed a large measure of autonomy in the beginning. It was granted a constitution on relatively modern lines, a parliament and almost full self-government, and a special army linked with the 'Lithuanian Corps' was created. At the same time Vilna University was built up with the Tsar's blessing as a centre of higher education and Polish culture. The Poles for the most part kept their lands, though grants of church and state lands were made to Russian nobles. A distinction was made in the case of 'the western lands' (or Lithuania) which, not being ethnically Polish, were not returned to Poland but fully assimilated to the rest of the empire.

As a result of these measures, Poland was in many respects ahead of the political development of the rest of the empire. It is against this background of a liberal dispensation granted by Alexander I that the Poles' sense of outrage at subsequent Russian policy in Poland, and the justification for charges of broken promises and bad faith, have to be seen.

In spite of the liberal attitude of Alexander I, the proud and intensely nationalistic Poles resented their domination by Russia and the loss of their old independence. It was clear that only the most delicate handling of the situation would prevent an explosion of Polish national feeling. The rest of the century, and the first decades of the next, tragically belied this early promise of a better era of Russo-Polish relations. The trouble started under Alexander I's successor, Nicholas I, who had no love for Poland. There were bloody and disastrous risings in 1830 and 1863.

After the 1830 rising the Constitution of 1815 was supplanted with drastic consequences by the Organic Statute of 1832 by which the Kingdom of Poland became an integral part of the Russian empire but retained her civil rights, including the right to use the Polish language in the courts, schools and administration. These provisions in fact were soon ignored officially. School instruction in the Polish language stopped in 1837 and the University of Vilna, an old centre of Polish culture, was closed in 1832. Russians began to replace Polish nationals in the administration and in schools. The Catholic church also suffered persecution. Its estates were secularised in 1843. It has been estimated that about a tenth of the Polish landowners' land was confiscated after 1830 and much of it passed into Russian hands. From the point of view of Poland, one of the most serious results of the 1830 rising was the great wave of emigration of Poles seeking to escape reprisals and oppression.

The aftermath of the 1863 rising, which came after a period of limited reforms under Alexander II, was even more disastrous for Poland. A systematic programme of russification was enforced to destroy the cultural roots of Polish nationalism, in the first place in schools. The University of Warsaw, established with Alexander I's blessing in 1816, was completely russified in 1869 and not reopened as a Polish university until the end of Russian rule in World War I. A very heavy censorship plagued Polish writers and the press. A legal reform act of 1876 banned the use of the Polish language in the courts to the great confusion of the Polish masses. Earlier in the century, the Polish courts had lost their judicial independence to the Russian senate and Poland had had to accept a Russian-moulded criminal code in place of her own. According to a law of 1885, instruction in the primary schools had to be conducted in Russian except for classes in religion and in the pupils' own language.

Russification of the Polish secondary schools was often stupid and offensively carried out. The russification programme of the distinguished Mariinsky Institute in Warsaw was, for example, placed in charge of a Russo–German non-Polish-speaking bureaucrat who was unable in the course of his duties to communicate directly with the Polish staff from whom he was taking over.

As far as the peasants were concerned, this grim scene was

enlivened by the land reform of 1864 which was specially drafted, as in Lithuania, to gain their favour and break the landlords' hold over the countryside. The peasants at this time received several times more land and under much easier conditions than the emancipated serfs in Russia. In the end these promises were not always kept and lands taken from Polish landlords were settled by Russian officials and other non-Polish immigrants. The erection of a large Greek Orthodox cathedral in a prominent position in Warsaw (1894–1912) was a permanent reminder of Russian domination and further outraged Polish national feeling, in this most Catholic country.

Throughout the sixties, it was clear that more realistic views were gaining ground in Poland and that a number of people recognised the futility of 'romantic nationalism' in Poland's situation vis-à-vis Russia. It was significant that the cream of Polish society did not emigrate after 1863 but concentrated instead on building up Poland's economic strength. Educated Poles were welcomed in the simultaneous economic development of the new empire. The integration of the Kingdom of Poland into the Russian empire and the abolition of the customs' barrier with Russia (1850) had opened up the large markets of the empire to Polish goods. Full advantage was taken of these opportunities by the young Polish industries. The Polish contribution was regarded as important by the Russians and close economic ties developed between the two countries from the seventies. Polish nationalism remained none the less alive, if quiescent, and the Poles deeply resented the cultural restrictions imposed by Russia.

Strikes and demonstrations also marked 1905 in Poland, where socialist revolutionary movements had been gaining influence since the beginning of the century. Some concessions were extracted from the Tsar. The use of the Polish language was permitted in state schools for instruction in the Polish language and the Catholic religion, and private schools were allowed in which all teaching might be in Polish. As a result of the Tsar's edict on religious toleration, some 200,000 Uniates who had been fiercely persecuted and pressed into Orthodoxy in the seventies returned to Catholicism, a change now permitted by law.

In the First Duma (1906) Poland was represented by thirty-six delegates, but as a result of the new electoral law (1907) her delegation was severely cut in the third and fourth sessions. The 'preposterous' new electoral law allowed equal representation to the Russian population (one delegate) and the Polish population (one delegate) of Warsaw, though apart from military and officials there were few Russian residents in Warsaw at this time.[2] The Poles were unsuccessful in the Duma with a project under which there would be Polish autonomy in internal affairs, while external affairs would be reserved for the imperial government.

The period between 1907 and 1917 was marked by sharp divisions in the Polish political parties over their social-political aims in Poland and their attitude to tsardom. The leader of the Polish faction in the Dumas, Roman Dmowski, stood for a policy of collaboration with Russia, whereas Pilsudski and his Polish Socialist Party, intriguing against Russia abroad, urged another appeal to force. On the extreme wing of the socialist ranks, Rosa Luxemburg was active with agitation (from Berlin) for the class war and strict cooperation with the Social-Democratic movement in Russia. There was thus a great deal of ineffectual political thought and action during these years in Poland. It coincided with the renewal of tsarist reaction in Poland, under Stolypin's direction. The transfer of the district of Chelm (Kholm) to Russia in 1909 caused great indignation among the Poles. It had always been an integral part of the Congress Kingdom but was already the scene of scandalous Orthodox intrigues against the Catholic church. In the following years, the Poles were further incensed by the manipulation of the voting procedure for municipal elections, which in their view gave Russian bureaucrats a disproportionate voting power. Then, in 1912, the railway connecting Warsaw with the Austrian system and with Vienna, an important artery of Polish economic life which had remained in Polish hands, was expropriated by the state.

The outbreak of war in 1914 found Poland torn by internal disunity between the conservatives, fearful of revolution and anxious to preserve the new-found economic prosperity of their country, and the other group of more radical elements who aimed at sweeping away the old social-political order. There was also a deep division of opinion as to whether the defeat of Russia in the war would be advantageous or the contrary to Poland. Dmowski, unlike Pilsudski, held the view that the defeat of Russia would be a disaster for Poland because it would enable the hated Hohenzollerns to dictate the peace and would probably lead to yet another partition of Poland. On the outbreak of war in 1914 the Grand Duke Nicholas, Commander-in-Chief of the Russian imperial armies, issued a proclamation promising Poland freedom of religion, language and self-government 'under the sceptre of the Tsar' and claiming Polish help in the Slavonic cause. In the chaotic war situation nothing came of these promises, which in any case had no support at court. So matters rested politically until the fall of the Tsar. The Provisional Government in March 1917 (at a time when Congress Poland was already in the hands of the Germans) made an ineffectual promise of independence to 'ethnic' Poland.

So ended a century of russification in Poland. It had utterly failed in its objectives of winning Polish loyalty or assimilating Poles culturally if not politically to Russians. The Polish resistance to these policies, inspired by steadfast adherence to national-religious ideals, proved indomitable. On the Russian side, it must be added, there were some people who saw the folly of official policy towards Poland, for example N. A. Milyutin, a high official in the Ministry of the Interior in the reign of Alexander II, who exposed the futility of russification in the following terms: 'All our efforts to russify Poland remain in vain. We shall never succeed by means of education in attracting the Poles to us, merging them with Russia, changing the direction of their thought and political aspirations. . . . Repressive measures aiming at the russification of the region will only produce futile irritation.'[3]

The Ukraine

The reunion of the peoples of Little Russia (or the Ukraine) and of Great Russia, separated first by the Mongol invasion and later for centuries by the hegemony of Poland, started in the middle of the seventeenth century with the great revolt of the Cossacks under Hetman Khmelnitsky against Polish rule. The Cossacks appealed for help in their struggle for independence to the Russian Tsar and offered allegiance. By the Treaty of Pereyaslav in 1654, the Ukrainians swore homage to Russia which in turn promised to allow them to administer the country, collect taxes and other privileges. But for a time there was considerable Cossack autonomy with Muscovite influence gradually extending through a network of officials and garrisons. This situation rudely changed when the Ukrainian leader Mazeppa deserted to the Swedish side at the crisis of the Great Northern War, and Charles XII of Sweden was defeated at Poltava in Little Russia by Peter the Great in 1709. Under Catherine the Great, the country was completely absorbed in the administrative, financial, military and ecclesiastical system of the empire. The heart of the anti-Russian struggle, the Zaporozhian Cossack 'host', was broken up and their lands granted to new Russian settlers. But Russia also pursued an astute assimilation policy in the Ukraine by giving, in 1785, the same privileged status to the Ukrainian Cossack officers as the Russian gentry. Ukrainians mixed easily with Russians and were to be found in official posts all over Russia.

Against this historical background, a Ukrainian cultural movement emerged in the early nineteenth century which later inspired Ukrainian political nationalism with its demands for autonomy or separation from Russia. This concept of Ukrainian nationalism has aroused keen controversy not only in Russia but among historians and critics of otherwise widely disparate views abroad. Thus in Professor Sumner's view 'none of the Ukrainians have ever established a truly independent national state.'[4] Their separatist claims had therefore no historical basis in fact. The Polish-born Communist, Rosa Luxemburg, dismissed it as 'the ridiculous farce of a few university professors and students'.[5] The Ukrainian cultural movement, however, insisted on the distinctiveness of the Ukrainian people and language after four hundred years of separation from Muscovy, and their right to separate cultural existence with Ukrainian schools and other cultural institutions. These Ukrainian cultural ambitions awakened the suspicions of the Russian government and police from the beginning and were suppressed as a likely stepping-stone to more dangerous separatist political aims. The secret society of the Brotherhood of St Cyril and St Methodius, founded in Kiev in the forties, was an early landmark in this movement. Its programme called for the emancipation of the serfs and the creation of a federated Slavic republic based on broad national autonomy. It included among its members the historian P. A. Kulish, who advocated peaceful methods of propaganda, and the famous poet Shevchenko who was born a serf and held strong views about the tsarist social order and favoured revolutionary action. The members of the Brotherhood were soon arrested and Shevchenko was exiled for ten years to Orenburg and forbidden by the Tsar to write or draw. Reaction was in the air following the events in Europe of 1848 and the gendarmes of Nicholas I were highly suspicious of Ukrainian literary nationalism and its ideals.

The situation began to look more promising during the early years of the reign of Alexander II, and Ukrainian historians and writers pursued their activities advocating a 'federation of the Slav family of nations' in which the Ukraine would have an equal autonomous footing with the others. The publication of the archives of south-western Russia was begun and during the period 1860–90 an enormous amount of historical research was carried out by the universities of the Ukraine. Then in 1882 an important historical journal *Kievskaya Starina* began to appear. This historical research had interesting political repercussions because it later formed the basis of the theories promulgated by more politically minded Ukrainian leaders at the end of the nineteenth century. A main conclusion was that, from the fifteenth to the eighteenth century, Ukrainian nationality had been represented by the Ukrainian lower classes while the upper classes had been either Polish or Polonised until, in the seventeenth century, they had come under Russian influences. And in these Ukrainian masses, some Ukrainian 'national democrats' saw the germ of the 'Ukrainian national idea'.

In spite of Polish appeals, the Ukrainians had refused to join the rising of 1863 and thus removed any illusions which might have existed about the possibility of collusion between the Ukrainian national groups and the Polish patriots. But the Russian police and bureaucracy were increasingly suspicious of the Ukrainian literary movement owing to the encouragement given it across the frontier in Austrian Galicia. In 1863 the Russian Secretary of State for Public Instruction, P. A. Valuyev, issued a circular in which it was stated that 'no Little Russian language exists nor has it ever existed. . . . It is but bad Russian spoilt by Polish influences.' Under reactionary influences and fear of the links between Galicia and Kiev, Alexander II's early liberal policy relapsed into increasing russification as a means of checking Ukrainian nationalist tendencies. In the official mind, the use of native languages in the Ukraine as elsewhere in the empire was primarily inspired by political rather than cultural aims. In fact, the oppressive policies of the Russian autocracy went far to exacerbate the political element in the Ukrainian literary movement.

By a law of 1876, the printing of any books, pamphlets or plays in Ukrainian was forbidden. Even the printing of the Bible in Ukrainian was banned and, more important, Ukrainian could not be used as a means of instruction in schools. Ukrainian nationalists claim that this measure hindered the development of education in the Ukraine especially among the Ukrainian-speaking rural masses and divorced the educated classes from their Ukrainian nationality. The majority of educated Ukrainians, however, regarded Russian culture as their natural cultural medium and many Ukrainians achieved high place on an equal basis with Russians in the imperial service. Ukrainian nationalists, unchecked by the ban on publication in Ukrainian, continued to write and publish their works in Russian. The most famous of these Ukrainian-born writers was Gogol.

During the last years of the nineteenth century, revolutionary ideas of 'agrarian socialism' and other social-economic reforms aiming primarily at more competent government and the removal of major injustices and perhaps an autonomous Ukraine, but not separation from Russia, began to gain ground in the Ukraine, seeping into the country from Central Russia. This negative attitude to separatism was forcibly expressed, for example in 1882, by Mikhail Dragomanov, one of the most bitter critics of the imperial government:

There are no grounds whatever and never will be for political separatism. Little Russians and Russians have the same historical traditions, the same creed and, concerning many things, the same notions. Our languages are extremely similar; we have no natural boundaries and after all we are united by common interests. All talk of separatism is simply to be laughed at.[6]

In Galician Ukraine, however, the great nationalist Ukrainian historian Michael Hrushevsky was lending his talents indefatigably to the cause of a much more advanced nationalism and separatism. Though disturbing to the imperial gendarmes, these literary-political activities were of incomparably less importance within the Ukraine than the economic changes transforming the country at the turn of the century. In the first place, the population had grown enormously since the two and a half millions absorbed by Russia in the seventeenth century, and amounted to about twenty-five millions. Colonists had flocked into the country from Great Russia in the last century and then formed about twenty per cent of the population, while considerable numbers of German colonists, Jews, Tatars, Greeks, Moldavians and others made up another thirty per cent. Ukrainian peasants were also migrating in large numbers to Siberia and the Far East as well as to Canada and the United States from some overcrowded rural districts.

The Ukraine at this time was the scene of far-reaching economic development of its rich economic resources. Intensive development of the Donets Coal basin began in the eighties *pari passu* with the important sugar beet industry which in time became the sugar base of the empire. The mining (coal and iron) and metallurgical industries grew rapidly, encouraged by large investments of foreign capital. As a result of this economic development many new towns grew up and the urban population of the Ukraine greatly increased. The influx of Russian workers to all the industrial centres transformed many of them, like Kharkov, into Russian towns where Russian immigrants outnumbered the Ukrainians. These economic and demographic developments inevitably strengthened the links with Russia and the rest of the empire. The Ukraine had become an area of crucial economic importance to Russia with its valuable mining and metallurgical industries, its grain and sugar and the imperial significance of its ports and southern coastal frontier. It was not realistic to imagine that Russia would relinquish its hold on the Ukraine which was so closely bound to her in many ways.

The turbulent atmosphere of 1905 was followed by a period of mixed repression and longer official relaxation in regard to Ukrainian cultural nationalism. The Ukrainians voted with the other peoples of the empire for the four Dumas and had a strong delegation in the First Duma in 1906. The constitutional promises of 1905 permitted the printing of books and periodicals in Ukrainian. This was the signal for the return to Kiev of Michael Hrushevsky, who continued undisturbed to write his classic history of Ukraine-Russia. The last decade of tsarist rule in the Ukraine was marked by unusual tolerance of Ukrainian cultural activities. Indeed, one enthusiastic historian of the period has called it 'an Indian summer of liberalism'.[7] By one vote, the Imperial Academy of Sciences decided in 1906 that Ukrainian was not a dialect but a separate language from Russian. This gave a great impetus to publications in Ukrainian. The ban on the use of Ukrainian in the schools, however, continued. *Rada*, a daily paper, published in Kiev, won a fairly wide circulation.

During these years, the nationalist movement extended its influence especially among country schoolmasters, lower local officials and the cooperative movement, but its nucleus remained a small urban intelligentsia. It is extremely difficult to estimate its exact strength owing to the lack of impartial data and Russian suppression of the movement. On the available evidence, however, it seems to have remained a minority movement in the Russian Ukraine.

During World War I, when Austrian Galicia was occupied for some time by the Russian armies, the flourishing Galician Ukrainian movement with its schools, press and various scientific institutions was ruthlessly destroyed. A drastic policy of russification and oppression of the Uniate church was inaugurated and thousands of Ukrainians were deported to Siberia. These policies were of course reversed by the Germans when the Russians were forced out of Galicia in 1915. In Russia, the fall of tsardom was immediately followed by a spate of requests from the Ukraine for an autonomous government. But the Provisional Government 'either bargained, gave in or withdrew the concessions granted.'[8] So the matter rested with the Ukrainian Central Rada assuming the powers of a parliament and trying to extend its powers throughout the Ukraine, until the Bolshevik coup of November 1917. The Ukraine then declared its independence of Russia.

Unlike the political aspirations of the Poles and Finns, which had considerable support in tsarist Russia, even Russians of otherwise liberal views, had no sympathy for Ukrainian nationalism. In fact, it was generally regarded with derision if not condemned as overt treachery to Russia. In Professor Florinsky's words: 'To the man in the street, the separation of the Ukraine from Russia always seemed absurd and unthinkable.'[9] More than any of the other Russian borderlands, the Ukraine seems a natural extension of the motherland with no natural frontier separating it from Central Russia. A glance at the map shows the importance of access to the Ukrainian Black Sea ports and explains why Russia, tsarist or Soviet, would regard Ukrainian independence as 'unthinkable'.

Finland

After hundreds of years of 'personal union' with Sweden, Finland was annexed by Russia in 1809. Alexander I was very favourably disposed to the Finns, as he was to the Poles, and arranged exceptionally good terms at this time for their entry into the Russian empire and acceptance of Russian sovereignty. Finland's ancient rights and privileges, as recognised by Sweden, were confirmed by Russia. It retained its former title of Grand Duchy (the title of Grand Duke being personally assumed by the Russian monarch), its Diet or Parliament, and an entirely Finnish government. A Russian governor-general was to represent the Tsar in Finland and a Secretary of State would handle Finnish affairs in St Petersburg. The Finnish constitution remained in force. Thus, Finnish autonomy and the Lutheran church and schools seemed adequately guaranteed by the Tsar from undue Russian interference.

The annexation of Finland fulfilled a deep-seated Russian ambition to safeguard the approaches to St Petersburg from attacks through Finland and to acquire a foothold on the gulf of Finland. Throughout the first half of the nineteenth century, Russo-Finnish relations remained good and there was no reason to doubt Finnish loyalty to the Russian crown. The organisation of the state system and civil rights enjoyed by the Finns were far in advance of the domestic situation within Russia proper at this time. Taxation was only used for domestic purposes.

Finland's entry into the Russian empire opened the door to

thousands of Finns seeking a career in the Russian administration and the armed forces. Throughout the nineteenth century, Finns (many belonging to the Swedish minority) were eminently successful in imperial service and were greatly helped to succeed by the financial and educational assistance offered them by the Russian government. Nevertheless, the two countries continued to live almost separate lives and neither knew much about the other.

Finland remained untouched by the arbitrary measures imposed in other non-Russian areas of the empire by Nicholas I. As the century advanced, Finnish nationalism made great progress and a series of measures directed against the Russians by the Finnish Diet caused concern in St Petersburg. It decided, for example, that Russian-born subjects were to be considered foreigners within the Grand Duchy of Finland and were to be barred from practising medicine or engaging in railway construction. More politically sophisticated than the Russian bureaucrats, the Finns pushed forward with measures for the expansion of education, the emancipation of women and a greater liberalisation of their political life.

But by the 1890s the reactionary russification policies long familiar in other parts of the empire began to affect Finland also. In 1891 Russian was declared the official language in certain branches of government and Russian-born civilians were appointed to the Finnish civil service (where they were previously unknown). In 1898–9 the appointment of two utterly unimaginative ultra-nationalist Russian bureaucrats to the key posts of Governor-General (General N. I. Bobrikov) and Secretary of State (V. K. Von Plehve) for Finland initiated a disastrous period in Russo-Finnish relations. The turning point was the publication of an Imperial Manifesto in 1899 which provided that all legislation interpreted by the crown as of imperial concern would be enforced in the Duchy of Finland. All this spelt the doom of Finnish autonomy and was regarded by the Finns as a perfidious infringement of their constitutional liberties. It united the Finns as a man to dogged passive resistance and when, in 1904, the Governor-General Bobrikov was assassinated by a young Finnish patriot, the action reflected the outraged mood of the country. Following the Manifesto, the Diet was stripped of practically all its old legislative power. Finnish men hitherto exempt from military service except for the defence of Finland were to be conscripted within the imperial armed forces. The Finnish postal services were absorbed by the imperial post office and the Russian language made compulsory in the records of the Finnish Senate and other official agencies. Finns were further incensed by the right of Russian-born subjects to acquire land (1901) and the Governor-General's authority to dismiss police officers, judges and civil servants suspected of disloyalty and replace them with Russians.

The Finnish people opposed these measures by strict adherence to Finland's constitutional rights as understood in Finland, and united passive resistance. Cooperation between Finnish patriots and Russian revolutionary organisations became closer. By 1905 the tide of revolutionary events throughout the empire and the revolutionary mood in Finland, where a general strike was called, compelled the government in St Petersburg to adopt more reasonable policies in Finland. The Imperial Manifesto of 1905 revoked all the executive orders of Governor-General Bobrikov and much other legislation obnoxious to the Finns, including the statute of 1901 concerning military service. It did not alter the status of Finland within the empire. The Diet was promised permission to resume its work and it was replaced by a modernised new single-chamber parliament elected by universal free and secret ballot. Finland was ahead of the world at this time in granting the vote to women.

As reaction got into the saddle again in Russia under Prime Minister Stolypin (1906–11), this happy period of relaxation from Russian pressures came to an end in Finland. The old clash of views between Russians and Finns on the authority of the crown and Finnish constitutional rights developed into a fierce constitutional struggle. It was reopened by a Russian decree of June 1908 which granted the Russian Council of Ministers the authority to define in each case whether the proposed measures were concerned exclusively with the affairs of the Duchy or related to any extent to imperial legislation. The Russian jurists insisted that according to the Fundamental Laws of 1906 the empire was a single, indivisible state and denied that Finland had any of the claimed prerogatives, thus ignoring the obligations solemnly undertaken by three Russian monarchs. This official view was stated as follows by the Russian jurist F. F. Martens: 'The Finnish Duchy is an inalienable part of Russia; it is Russia's province. And if Finland has a constitution and various autonomous institutions, it is because the latter were granted to her by imperial authority, not introduced by mutual agreement between the Duchy and the Empire as two equal contracting parties.'[10] In this constitutional conflict the Finns were supported by many international jurists and notably by four eminent Dutch professors of law.[11]

As World War I approached, the situation in Finland had become extremely grave, thanks to the senseless policy of the Russian government. There had been a brief breathing-space in the Grand Duchy after the restoration of the Constitution in November 1905. But under Stolypin's premiership ultra-nationalist tendencies came to the fore in St Petersburg and Stolypin's hatred of Finland was unrestrained. The Finnish Diet was dissolved several times in succession between 1908–10 and the last government of Finnish patriots resigned in protest against the Tsar's Rescript of 1908, which like the coup d'état of 1899 virtually abolished Finland's legislative and administrative freedom of action. Russification of the administration of Finland proceeded apace, without any regard either for efficiency or Finnish sensibilities. The decision to bring pilots from the Caspian Sea with no experience of the Baltic to replace the skilled pilots of the Finnish Archipelago (with disastrous results for shipping) outraged the Finns and is a good example of the kind of legal absurdities imposed on them by the Russians.[12] 1912–17 was a specially trying period for Finland, when practically the entire court of appeal of Vyborg was gaoled in St Petersburg . . . for observing the laws of Finland.

When war broke out in 1914, Finland was in effect an enemy-occupied country and lived under martial law during the war. Many Finns hoped for a German victory so as to escape from the Russian yoke and a group of young Finns were trained in Germany and fought for a time on the Ost-Front.

After the collapse of tsardom, the Provisional Government in March 1917 restored Finnish autonomy. But this concession no longer satisfied Finnish aspirations and there were stormy clashes with the Finns over the demand for independence, which was refused. Russian stupidity and injustice had been the undoing of Russian influence in Finland and turned its formerly loyal and peaceful people into militant anti-Russians to whom independence from a hated and despised Russia had become a political obsession. It was at last achieved in December 1917 when Lenin recognised Finnish independence.

The Baltic provinces

The Baltic provinces were acquired by Russia in the eighteenth century, Livonia (Latvia) and Estonia from Sweden by the Treaty of Nystad (1721), Lithuania as part of Russia's share in the third partition of Poland in 1795. In their history and culture there were marked differences between these three Baltic countries. The dominant element in Latvia and Estonia was the Baltic German gentry (the *Ritterschaft*), the descendants of the Teutonic knights who had conquered the Baltic lands in the Middle Ages, whereas the dominant political-cultural influence in Lithuania was Polish.

The German gentry, only a small minority among the native Latvian and Estonian peasant masses, had maintained their peculiar position as the privileged landowning class and entrenched arbiter of local affairs under both Polish and Swedish rule in the Baltic. After the Russian annexation, Peter the Great also confirmed the privileges of the Baltic *Ritterschaft* according to the Privilegium Sigismundi Augusti declaration of 1560.[13] Thus until the nineteenth century, the official language in both countries remained German, the national church Lutheran, holding its services in German and with the great majority of its clergy Baltic Germans. The language of instruction in higher education was also German, as the majority of the children being educated belonged to the Baltic German group.

The position of the Baltic Germans in imperial Russia was in many ways anomalous. As distinguished statesmen, diplomats and soldiers, they had won a high place in Russian society and at the court. Their loyalty to the person of the Russian monarch was never in doubt. But this did not alter their belief in the innate superiority of German culture and institutions to Russia or their opposition in the *Heimat* to what they regarded as unwarranted Russian interference in Baltic affairs. The centralising russification policies of Alexander III (1881–94) and Nicholas II (1894–1917) seemed a gratuitous insult to the Baltic gentry. They never seemed to grasp the kind of provocation presented to an increasingly nationalistic Russian imperial government by their self-contained German province, isolated from Slavdom, politically and culturally, by religion and language.

From the middle of the nineteenth century, Russian policy tended to favour the growing national consciousness of the Latvians and Estonians and their hostility to the Germans, so as to weaken the German hegemony.[14] Tsar Alexander III's refusal to recognise the traditional 'rights' of the Baltic gentry initiated a period of severe repression of German religious-cultural activities in the Baltic.[15] The attacks on the special position of the Lutheran church had started under Nicholas I. A Greek-Orthodox bishopric was established in Riga in 1836 and in view of the small number of Orthodox then in the country was generally regarded as a centre for the propagation of the Orthodox faith. By the middle of the century, the Orthodox peasant converts were estimated to run into thousands. One of the major reasons for this was the unpopularity of the Baltic Lutheran clergy who, being almost entirely of German origin, were not only local spiritual leaders. They also formed a class of minor comfortably-off landlords, performed a number of quasi police-administrative duties as keepers of parish registers (*Metriken*) and exacted much heavy unpaid farm labour from the peasantry (of much the same order as the gentry). Many peasant converts were no doubt attracted by the hope of crown land believed to be in the gift of the Orthodox missionaries. Later, when these hopes did not materialise, or peasants were alienated by the strangeness of the Orthodox church ritual, there was a tendency to return to the more familiar Lutheran services. But whereas conversion to Orthodoxy was legal, it was an offence for a Lutheran minister to proselytise an Orthodox, even one of his returning sheep. The Lutheran clergy struggled doggedly against these restrictions on religious freedom and especially against the ruling that it was a criminal offence on their part to admit to Communion any *rekonvertiten* from Orthodoxy to

Lutheranism. Many court cases resulted from this measure and offending Lutheran clergy were prosecuted, jailed and exiled to Siberia in both Baltic countries, for so-called 'crimes against Orthodoxy'. The construction of an imposing Orthodox cathedral in Reval in 1893, and an Orthodox seminary in Pskov (Pleskau) to prepare priests for missionary work, were concrete expressions of Orthodox zeal in a Lutheran world.

The personal interest shown by Alexander III (1881–94) in the assimilation of the German pattern of life and culture in the Baltic provinces inspired the enforcement of harsh russification measures in the schools, the judiciary and the administration. In 1885–6, the Baltic school system was subordinated to the Russian (and simultaneously removed from local church supervision) and the national schools were russified except for instruction in the lowest grades in the schools, where teaching might be in the local languages. Later, this regulation applied also to gymnasia and private schools (1887–90). The University of Dorpat, a distinguished centre for German culture since 1802, was closed in 1893 and then reopened as the Yuryev University with a completely Russian staff. These measures were strongly but unavailingly opposed by the gentry who then withdrew their former voluntary cooperation from the educational system. In many cases, to avoid the russification of their children in the state system, they employed house tutors. Even the 'Froebel kindergartens' established by the landlords for their peasants' children were broken up, with nothing to replace them.

Apart from education, russification proceeded apace in the local administration, the judiciary and the police. Numbers of Russian officials were brought in to fill jobs formerly solely occupied by German Balts. The administration of justice was hampered by the use of Russian in court in a country where Russian was not generally known by the masses and the interpreters employed were often unreliable and even corrupt. Both in competence and integrity, the type of Russian official sent to the Baltic often compared poorly with his German predecessor, to the disgust of the educated Germans.

There was no Russian peasant colonisation of the Baltic provinces during this period and the estates of the Baltic German gentry remained intact. There was, however, a rising tide of agrarian discontent about the autocratic system of land tenure which blazed out in agrarian disorder in 1905–6.

The cultural concessions granted by the Tsar in 1905 somewhat alleviated the cultural-religious position of the Baltic Germans. Some of the restrictions on the use of local languages in the schools were removed but it remained obligatory to do the *abiturium* examination in Russian. Thousands of people re-entered the Evangelical church now that it was legally possible to do so. There was also an immediate revival of Baltic German schools and other cultural institutions.

In Lithuania, russification policies were enforced throughout the nineteenth century with much more animus and brutality than in the Baltic provinces of Latvia and Estonia. Racially and religiously, the Russians were confronted there with an entirely different situation. The landowning class was predominantly Polish or Polonised, the national church Roman Catholicism, both historically old enemies of Russia. Lithuania had been incorporated in the Russian empire following the third partition of Poland (to which it was formerly united) but did not share in any of the privileges then granted to the Kingdom of Poland by Alexander I. It was directly administered by Russian officials and governed by Russian law. Lithuanians (mainly of Russian extraction) entering government service were as a rule transferred to other parts of the empire.

The official separation of Poland and Lithuania did not at first cut the links between the two countries. Lithuanians participated in both the 1830 and 1863 Polish risings against Russia and were punished with savage reprisals, especially in 1863. Public executions, exile to Siberia and large-scale confiscation of landlords' property were ordered by the Governor-General 'hangman' Count Mikhail Muravyev during his two years of office (1863–5). (A great monument was none the less officially erected to him in Vilna.) Deported Polish landowners were ordered to sell their properties within two years and only Orthodox Russians were permitted to buy them. A land reform was also carried out under Count Muravyev's auspices by which the peasants' share of the land was greatly increased and their redemption payments on former serf land much reduced, in line with a similar agrarian reform in Poland.[16]

The Catholic clergy also suffered persecution during Murav-yev's reign of terror and there was renewed pressure on the peasants to join the Orthodox church during this period. Lithuanian schools were reorganised to eliminate Polish and Catholic influence. Teaching was ordered to be entirely in Russian except for the religious instruction of non-Orthodox children, which might be in the native language. Polish teachers and other officials were dismissed wholesale and replaced by Russians. These russification policies had the unintended effect of promoting the growth of national feeling in Lithuania and the development of the Lithuanian language, the language of the peasant masses.

The years preceding the 1905 revolution were marked by the appearance in the Baltic countries of a number of political groups of various colours all aiming either openly or clandestinely at reform of the political system. There were strikes in the chief towns of the area in 1905–6 and much destructive violence against the Baltic German landowners in Estonia and Latvia, which was eventually put down in 1906 by tsarist armed forces. The situation there was racially complex, the Estonian and Lat-vian nationalists working for the elimination of the German cultural-political influence while the Russians aimed at the assimilation of all three national groups by russification.

An all-Estonian Congress held in Reval in 1905 and a Lithuanian National Congress held about the same time in Vilna demanded local autonomy from the Russians. Political demands assumed more radical forms in Latvia. The Latvian Social-Democratic League aimed at an independent Latvia with an intermediate stage of autonomy within a federal Russian state. There was also considerable agitation for the use of the local languages in the schools. This had little success in St Peters-burg up to the fall of tsardom. Both Estonians and Latvians par-ticipated in the First and Second Dumas; Baltic German were only elected to the Third Duma as a result of the revised electoral law favouring the conservative landowning element in the empire.

Pari passu with russification, there were important economic developments in the Baltic provinces. The construction of the first railways linking Riga and Reval with the Black Earth regions of

Central Russia (1870) opened up a new era of prosperity for these ports and the hinterland. Riga, Reval and Windau soon became of major significance for Russia's foreign trade, accounting on average for twenty-six per cent of the Russian trade turnover across the European frontier for the period 1908–12.[17] Using new modern techniques, the old ship-building industry with its traditional skills flourished. Large manufacturing industries were also successfully established, including woollen and jute in Libau, cotton and cloth in Narva, engineering, woodworking and many light industries in Riga. The German estates supplied excellent timber and dairy produce for export. These economic developments gave rise to a new diversified social structure of factory owners and managers, skilled and unskilled workers anxious for education and social advancement, where some decades earlier there were only Baltic German landowners and native peasant masses working for them.

The native peoples of the Baltic had already moved far along the path of national consciousness and ambition when the Provisional Government assumed power in 1917. They had no desire to exchange Russian domination for German hegemony. The Provisional Government allowed the formation of an Estonian Diet but procrastinated about granting autonomy to any Baltic country until the future status of Russia should be decided by the Constituent Assembly. In the chaotic war conditions of 1917–18 they were soon struggling for complete independence from Russia and achieved their aim.

The Kazakh Steppes and Central Asia (Turkestan)

Since the eighteenth century, Russian power had been gradually advancing southwards from the borders of Siberia through the Kazakh steppes to the vast area bounded by the Caspian Sea and the western frontier of China. By the eighties of the last century, this expansion had reached its furthest limits through a series of sharp military coups. Tashkent was captured in 1865, the decadent emirates of Bukhara and Khiva reduced to vassals of Russia and territorially mutilated while the truculent emirate of Kokand was finally absorbed into the Russian *oblast* of Fergana in 1876. The subjection of the fierce Turkmen tribes then followed at the bloody battle of Gök Tepe. Thus, by 1881, Russia's last and most perilous colonial venture was successfully completed. By these conquests Russia secured a firm frontier with Persia and Afghanistan and Russian trade, long harried by local tribes on the desert trails between Orenburg and the Central Asian markets, would now be secure. Politically and economically these were important achievements.

In Turkestan, the Russians found themselves a tiny minority in a sea of Turkic-Muslim peoples alien to them by race, culture and religion and fanatically devoted to Islam. From their earlier experiences of the Muslims of Kazan and the Crimea, they were aware of the need to avoid an explosive situation in consolidating their hold on the country and were careful not to exacerbate Muslim susceptibilities unduly. Russification in Turkestan was therefore relatively flexible and cautious compared to the ruthless methods adopted in the European parts of the empire.

The administration of these colonial conquests was completely reorganised. The whole region was divided into two governorates-general of the Steppe Region and Turkestan. Throughout the tsarist period, the command of the military forces and the control of the civil administration in these areas was combined and headed by the governor-general, always a high-ranking military man. The old regional divisions were replaced by *oblasts* and *uyezds* on the Russian pattern in charge of military 'commandants'. Military personnel thus ran the administration. On the whole, this military establishment posted to Central Asia was of low quality and extremely incompetent. Count Pahlen's commission sent to Central Asia by the Tsar to investigate the administration (1908–9) reported a widespread state of corruption and misgovernment (for which numerous officials were cashiered) and advised drastic reforms, none of which were however executed before 1914.[18]

Native life at the *aul* (village) level was left almost intact by the Russians and run by *aksakaly* or headmen. Many native dignitaries also continued in office in Tashkent and other towns. The local aristocracy of education and wealth maintained its place but the former tribal and official establishment in Turkestan was soon removed and replaced by Russians. At higher levels, the judiciary was entirely Russian. But native courts were given jurisdiction (according to Muslim customary law or *adat*) over all criminal cases in the *aul*, except for those cases involving Russians or the general order of the region. The native peoples were not liable for conscription but they were not excluded from service in the imperial armed forces. Few applied to do so. Linguistic difficulties greatly added to the confusion of the uneducated masses of Central Asia confronted with an entirely alien, incomprehensible system of law and administration. On the other side, the Russian officials seldom bothered to learn the local language or to explain their orders locally, though the natives were expected to learn and understand Russian.

The reorganisation of the administrative divisions of Turkestan and the Steppe Region was accompanied by a basic reform of the traditional land tenure and taxation system. All the land in the annexed territories was nationalised and then assigned to the sharecroppers or leaseholders who actually worked it, thus abolishing automatically the rights of absentee landlords in the settled areas. The nomads' rights to any lands required for the pasture of their animals were recognised, the surplus reverting to the government. The imprecise wording of this measure opened the door to the later large-scale ruthless expropriation of native lands and caused the violent 1916 revolt in Turkestan and Semirechye. This far-reaching land reform, which destroyed the position of the former official and landlord classes in the village, was enforced without much difficulty by the Russians.[19]

The old oppressive taxation methods, which weighed heavily on the peasants, were eased and simplified by the new collection system. Theoretically, the native population should have greatly benefited by these measures; but they were at the mercy of the corrupt Russian tax officials and the native underlings employed at the lower level of the tax administration to assist them through the maze of native languages and customs (of which they were ignorant). Against this kind of chicanery, the natives had little or no hope of redress.

The possibilities of settling migrants from the overcrowded, impoverished districts of Central Russia in the annexed lands of the Steppe Region and Turkestan loomed large among the gains of the Russian conquest. The conditions for settlement differed enormously in both areas. From the end of the eighteenth century, waves of Russian peasantry had been moving in more or less haphazard fashion into the wide expanses of the Kazakh-Kirgiz Steppes. In the east, intensive colonisation of the Semi-rechye borderland with China started about 1868, continuing intensively until the violent Kirgiz revolt against the encroachments of these Russian settlers in 1916. Between 1893 and 1912, 2,513,000 *desyatins*[20] were appropriated from the natives for Russian settlement in Semirechye alone. In the four *oblasts* of the Steppe Region, Russians formed forty per cent of the population in 1911 or a total of some 1,500,000 people. There were plans on the eve of the 1914 war for even more intense settlement of the Steppe lands, which brutally disregarded the interests and reactions of the nomad or semi-nomadic indigenous population.

Turkestan was thickly populated at the time of the Russian conquest and further settlement depended on large-scale irrigation of potentially fertile desert areas. The Russians recognised the position and settlement was forbidden by the 1896 statute except to a limited extent, to workers in the towns and later in the railway depots. Pressure from the Centre and the Resettlement Department later forced the hands of the local administration, and Turkestan was declared open for settlement in 1907. The progress of irrigation had been disappointing and limited to two major schemes in the Hungry Steppe and the Murgab Imperial Domain. Most of the new Russian migrants therefore sought employment in the towns or the railways. By 1911, the Russian element of 406,500 only formed 6.3 per cent of the total population of Turkestan of 6.5 million, a tiny minority, mostly settled in Semirechye. 'In Turkestan,' declared the official publication *Aziatskaya Rossiya* in 1914 'there are no grounds for hoping at any time to bring the numbers of the Russian population in the already inhabited places to such levels as to change its ethnographical character. The basic state objective is that Turkestan while maintaining its ethnographical character should be an indivisible part of Russia and should become entirely Russian in political and economic relations.'

Russia used her new power over the oasis towns and steppe lands of Central Asia to promote her own commercial interests and to oust British-Indian competition in textiles and other goods (the main threat to her trade). Central Asia was of economic importance to imperial Russia mainly as a cheap domestic source of cotton for the Russian textile mills and a captive market for manufactured goods which it was difficult to export elsewhere. Apart from copper and gold-mining in eastern Kazakhstan and some oil production in the Fergana *oblast*, its natural resources remained for the most part undeveloped. But Russian scientists did a great deal of fine work in prospecting, exploring and mapping the area and thus prepared the way for later Soviet developments.

With Russian encouragement, the area under cotton constantly increased and the coarse native quality was improved by the introduction of fine American upland strains. By the end of the nineteenth century, Turkestan was supplying eighty per cent of Russia's raw cotton requirements. Cotton cultivation, and the irrigation on which it depended in the arid soils of Turkestan, remained in the hands of the native population, as both skills were unknown to the Russian settlers. The great expansion of cotton in the twentieth century, however, was not, altogether to the advantage of the peasant growers, though undoubtedly the more astute among them did prosper. Others fell victim to the usurious system of advance payment by which the crop was purchased by Russian buyers and which landed them heavily in debt, even to the extent of having to sell their lands and work as agricultural labourers.[21] Extensive cotton cultivation under Russian pressure also began to impinge on native cultivation of food crops and to make the area more and more dependent on imported food supplies. This Central Asian cotton base did not have one cotton mill before 1917 and local efforts to build up a cotton industry were frustrated by the Central Russian cotton magnates who feared any competition from this quarter.

Though lacking in most civilised amenities, Turkestan retained a fragment of its once great Islamic tradition in a network of schools (*mektabi*) and colleges (*medresses*) where instruction based on the Koran and Islamic traditions was given by Muslim teachers. The natives shunned the first Russian style schools, where their imams were banned from imparting religious instruction. It was thus soon early borne in on the Russians that it would be an extremely difficult and delicate matter to achieve russification, their long-term aim, through a reform of the native schools and the establishment of a western style Orthodox Russian system. It was therefore decided in 1884 to establish the so-called Russian-native schools where native children could get primary education in their own languages and religious instruction from Muslim teachers, and also become literate in Russian. The native schools were not closed but received no state support. The government was under the erroneous impression that by depriving these schools, which they regarded (and quite rightly) as pillars of Muslim tradition, of support and influence, they would die out. But they underestimated the enduring loyalty of the people to their own schools, now maintained at private expense since the government confiscated the Waqf (religious foundation) endowments which had formerly partly supported these schools. The more affluent families also employed itinerant mullahs from Kazan or Orenburg to teach their children privately. Up to the end of the imperial régime, there was only the loosest control of either of these forms of indigenous education, both of which were in the hands of Muslim doctrinaires mostly deeply hostile to the Russian infidel *ferangis*. It is significant of the Russian approach to Islam that, from the beginning of the occupation of Turkestan, Orthodox missionary work was forbidden there.

School population figures (unfortunately they do not distinguish between native and Russian children) show a rise from 11.6 per cent in 1897 (census) to 21 per cent in 1911, and a corresponding rise in literacy. In this work the native schools, far from dying out, had made great advances. In 1911 some 100,000 pupils were studying in these schools in the three main Turkestan *oblasts* of Syr-Darya, Samarkand and Fergana.[22]

Russian orientalists did much impressive work on the languages, peoples, flora and fauna of Central Asia and explored and mapped the region once it was opened up to their researches. Immersed in these interests, they lived in a world apart from the majority of ignorant, indifferent Russian officials. Their writings were published by the Imperial Academy of Sciences and other learned bodies in St Petersburg and did much to enlighten the world about the formerly closed world of the native emirates of Khiva, Bukhara and Kokand.

Before the Russian conquest, the huge area of the Steppe Region and Turkestan (larger alone than England, France, Italy, Denmark, Switzerland and Belgium combined) was without arterial roads, railways or other modern means of communication such as the telegraph or telephone. The Russians soon realised the necessity of establishing better contact with Central Russia than the slow and hazardous desert trails. A major programme of rail and road construction was undertaken and both the telephone and telegraph soon reached Tashkent and further. Uzen Ada on the Caspian was linked by rail with Tashkent via the great Karakum desert, the Amu Darya and Samarkand in 1898, a remarkable engineering feat. A decade later, another important railway connected Tashkent with Orenburg and thence with the Central Russian rail system. Branch lines were also built to Kushka on the Afghan frontier (1898) and to Andizhan (1899). It was planned to build another trunk line to connect Central Asia, which suffered from a grain deficit, with the Siberian grain fields, but construction was interrupted by World War I.

The state of public health was deplorable when the Russians arrived in Turkestan and some rudimentary medical services were established. But they were incapable of coping with the widespread and endemic tropical diseases such as malaria and the rampant syphilis and tuberculosis. According to statistics of the Central Statistical Committee there was only one doctor per 50,000 population in Central Asia in 1907 and in some areas like Semipalatinsk only one per 100,000.[23] These doctors were assisted by some hundreds of partly trained medical orderlies or *feldshers*. The distribution of the hospitals was exiguous in the extreme with one hospital serving an area of 26,140 *versts*. The military establishment had well-equipped separate medical facilities and the Russian settlers were also better supplied with official medical care than the natives.

Misrule and oppression in Central Asia during the last decades of the tsarist régime exploded as has been said in the 1916 revolt, which was savagely repressed. The abdication of the Tsar and the formation of the Provisional Government in March 1917 was followed by immediate demands in Turkestan for national-territorial or cultural autonomy culminating in a regular 'blueprint of the autonomy of Turkestan' proposed at the Extraordinary Regional Muslim Congress in September 1917, on the eve of the Bolshevik Revolution.[24]

The tsarist colonial record in Central Asia was far from exemplary but neither was it the unmitigated oppression and exploitation of the Soviet propaganda picture. It introduced the native people of Central Asia, formerly living in the medieval conditions of a particularly cruel type of oriental despotism, to ideas of western civilisation. It forbade slavery, capital punishment and whipping. After the original harshness of the conquest, it seemed to have taken the right course for gaining the favour of the native populations with an enlightened land and tax reform, while Islam retained its mosques and religious schools with little interference from the government.

The acclaim which the Russians might have gained among the native peoples through these measures was however lost, and bitter hatred aroused, through the intolerable behaviour of the Russian colonial officials recruited from 'the scum of military society',[25] and the uncontrolled greed of the Russian settlers in seizing native land. A stage had been reached when Russian colonial aims could only be achieved by the use of naked force and a wanton disregard of native interests. Under these circumstances, the official identification of Russian national and native interests was supremely unrealistic. In his report on the results of tsarist policy, written in 1916, the last Governor-General of Turkestan, General A. N. Kuropatkin, the embodiment of Russian chauvinistic patriotism, made no bones about Russia's failures as a colonial power in Central Asia, though to the end he seemed blind to the yawning gulf between Russian and native interests. 'Russian power for half a century did not succeed in making the indigenous peoples loyal servants of the Russian Emperor and devoted servants of the Russian government,' he wrote, nor did it succeed in implanting in them a realisation of the unity of their interests with the interests of Russian tsardom.[26]

The Muslim revival in Russia

HANS BRÄKER

One of the first proclamations issued by the Soviet government after the October revolution was addressed to 'All Muslims in Russia and the East'. In issuing this proclamation the Soviet leaders were trying to gain the confidence and active support of all Muslims both at home and abroad with a view to consolidating their own régime and pacifying Russia's border areas in the Near and Middle East, thus enabling them to concentrate their energies on internal affairs.

On the other hand, the declared intention of the Soviet government to sovietise all minority groups within Russia by amalgamating their different national cultures into a monolithic socialist culture, was calculated to provoke all those minorities whose sense of national identity presupposed allegiance to Islam. These particular minorities included the peoples of Caucasia and Trans-Caucasia, the peoples of the Crimea, the central Volga district and of that part of Turkestan situated between the Caspian Sea and the Pamir Mountains. They all differ greatly from the Russians in respect of their historical backgrounds, their religious allegiance and their national languages (which are still consciously cultivated to this day).

In view of the objectives pursued by the Soviets vis-à-vis their religious and ethnic minorities, and the extreme measures which they have taken in their efforts to achieve them, it is perhaps surprising to find that, by their own admission, the Soviet state and party functionaries have 'only a vague idea of the number of believing Muslims [in Russia] today and of their spiritual world, their psyche'. The Soviets are particularly alarmed on this account since 'an enquiry into the present state of religious belief amongst the population has shown that the proportion of believers in the Soviet Republics of the East is considerably higher than in other Soviet Republics.'[1] Thus, contrary to all rational expectations, Islam has been preserved in the Soviet Union. This is a phenomenon which calls for some explanation. But for the time being at least we should not expect to receive that explanation from the Soviet branch of Oriental studies. Although they have made a number of remarkable contributions in this field, Soviet scholars have failed to appreciate as yet that the crucial reasons for the 'survival' of Islam must be looked for in Islam itself.[2] It is, of course, all the more essential that they should do so since it was in Russia that Islam underwent such a marked revival at the turn of the century, one whose repercussions reached far beyond her borders and are still being felt in the Soviet Union today.

Russia and the Islamic minorities

When Russia conquered the Islamic peoples of Asia, it seemed as if this might bring to an end the dissension which had long existed between them. In fact this was not the case. The incorporation of these Islamic territories into the Russian empire did not lead to their pacification. On the contrary: by the 1880s they were again resisting the tsarist régime. Their opposition was directed against two major points of Russian policy. The first of these was the attempt made by the Russian government to neutralise the influence exerted in the economic and cultural spheres by the Tatars on their co-religionists in the Urals, in the Steppes of Kazakhstan and in Turkestan by the introduction of new and far-reaching legislation. The second was the readoption by Alexander II of the traditional proselytising policy that had been abandoned by Catherine II in 1785 when she granted religious freedom. This second point also explains why it was that virtually every resistance movement mounted by the Islamic peoples up to 1917 quickly assumed a religious character.

One of the principal reasons why this resistance proved so effective, and continued to make its influence felt long after the October revolution, was that it received its impetus from an internal reform movement that was designed to revive and modernise the whole of Islamic culture. This movement was evolved in the first instance by a group of religious thinkers. Acting in concert with other reformers, who were chiefly interested in modernising the antiquated educational system in the Islamic territories by introducing new curricula and new teaching methods, they paved the way for a really remarkable upsurge in the religious and cultural life of Islam in Russia.[3]

In the case of the Tatars this development reached such a high peak that it was frequently referred to as the 'Tatar' or 'Muslim renaissance'. From 1900 onwards Kazan became one of the focal points of the Muslim culture, not only of Russia but of the whole Islamic world. By the beginning of the twentieth century there were 7,000 students attending lectures at the Islamic university in Kazan, while in 1902 the Koran printing press attached to the university published 250 volumes and had a total book production of 25 million copies. In 1907 the Islamic library in Kazan had 18,700 readers.[4] According to reliable Russian sources there were 24,321 Muslim communities in Russia at the beginning of 1912, which were cared for by 45,399 'divines'.[5] In the same year 48 social welfare organisations, 34 study groups and 87 'law' (*Sharia*) associations were recorded in the various Islamic territories of Russia. Between them these societies ran 194 libraries and 23 printing presses and published 18 periodicals. These are just a few examples of the kind of activities that accompanied the upsurge in Islamic culture prior to 1917, which was accomplished despite, or perhaps on account of, the growing pressures being brought to bear on the Muslim minorities.

For purposes of this present study it is important that we should enquire into the general intellectual and cultural background from which this Russian reform movement drew its sustenance, and in doing so we shall also have to try to establish the precise relationship between Russian and international Islam. Although no comprehensive account of these intellectual currents has yet been produced, enough is now known for us to be able to say with certainty that the Islamic reform movement in Russia was not only in line with the cultural and intellectual trends developing in other parts of the Islamic world but was, in fact, directly influenced by them. Thus, the activities of the Russian conservatives or traditionalists, especially those in Turkestan, were influenced by the Wahhabis.[6] The so-called Vaisite movement of Kazan tried to impose the Wahhabite doctrine, which was based on the purity and asceticism of the original Muslim faith, by militant methods, for which, incidentally, the revolutionaries of 1905 provided the model. This doctrine also emerged, albeit in a very different form, in the Basmach movement of the early 1920s. Virtually all attempts undertaken by the conservatives to introduce reforms were prompted by their desire to preserve the traditional Muslim faith and to ensure that it continued to play its part in the cultural development of the oriental peoples of Russia. Consequently, they objected to change of any kind in the structure of Islamic society and were, therefore, naturally opposed to the anti-Islamic policies of the tsarist régime. Their activities produced no immediate practical results, but they did impress on the Muslim minorities the value of their independent Islamic culture.

Although it was brought to bear in a variety of ways, the influence exerted by the nineteenth-century reformers of south Asia on the modernists in Russia was much more direct and much more obvious. Like the conservatives, the modernists wanted to see the Islamic doctrine preserved in its original form. Thus, the basic tenets of the faith were never called into question. Where the modernists differed from the conservatives was in their insistence—which they shared with the Muslims of India and Pakistan—that Islam could not hope to come to terms with the present simply by reiterating its traditional position but that, on the contrary, if the Islamic peoples of Russia wished to retain their independent culture, they would have to introduce reforms designed to bring Muslim teaching up to date. The problems of 'modernity' were posed in the first instance by confrontation with the west. But whereas, in the other countries of the east, new and progressive western attitudes were associated with the two great imperial powers (France and England), in Russia they were associated with the imperialism of the tsarist régime.

The reform movement launched by the modernists in Russia was also greatly influenced by their recognition of the relative superiority of Christianity, which was one of the principal intellectual weapons used by the Russians in pursuit of their colonialist policy in the Caucasus and Central Asia. The Muslim reaction to the Christian challenge was as divided in Russia as it was in India and Pakistan. Some Russian Muslims rejected Christianity out of hand and opposed the missionary activities of the Russian Orthodox Church by every conceivable means, while others sought a new orientation in the philosophical and political concepts inspired by the Christian faith. This second group was particularly interested in Slavophil ideas. This is hardly surprising in so far as pan-Slavism provided them with a model for the pan-Turkish community which they envisaged for the Islamic minorities in Russia. But—and it is an important but—these Russian Muslims were concerned only with the general attitudes evolved by the enlightened thinkers of Christian Europe: their belief in progress, their positivism and their scientific approach. They were not interested in the spirit of Christianity as such.

Thus the links between modernist movements in Russia and other eastern countries are unmistakable. The principal reason for this interdependence was the influence exerted on the Russian modernist Muslims by their counterparts in the subcontinent of India, chief of whom were Saiyid Ahmad Khan, Saiyid Amir'Ali, al-Afghani and Muhammad Abduh.

Theological reforms

It was doubtless because of the direct influence brought to bear by these Indian thinkers that the Muslim reform movement in the Central Asiatic areas of Russia also developed as a result of reforms carried out in the religious sphere. The leaders of this movement wanted to break away from the traditionalism of conservative Muslim thinking but without calling into question the basic tenets of the faith. Their object was to ensure the survival of Islam in the modern world, whose progressive and essentially scientific attitudes Muslim intellectuals tended to regard as typical manifestations of the Russian ruling class.

The Kazan theologian, historian and archaeologist, Shihabeddin al-Marzhani (1818–1889),[7] was probably the most important of the early Muslim religious reformers. He was the first Tatar to press for far-reaching reforms in the traditional system of education employed in the Koran schools and the first to work for the adoption of a scientific and historical approach to theological research. He was radically opposed to religious authority and insisted that every individual was entitled to seek his own answers to all religious questions by reading the Koran and the traditions. Marzhani also believed that Islam's salvation lay in the rediscovery of the purity and simplicity of its original form, as exemplified by the life of the Muslim mystic al-Ghazzali. But in his view this process of rediscovery could not be achieved simply by resurrecting the outmoded forms of a bygone era, which more puritanical Muslims like the Wahhabis regarded as the pre-requisite for any cultural or social revival of Islam. Marzhani argued in fact that, far from burying himself in the past, the Muslim who wished to penetrate to the pure theological core of Islam must combine his religious quest with a lively concern for the achievements of modern scholars. Consequently, he urged all Russian Muslims to learn European languages in order to study western literature, which meant of course that they would have to attend Russian schools.

These, briefly, were the kind of ideas that paved the way for the Muslim modernist movement in Russia.[8] A number of Marzhani's disciples then carried his ideas much further and within a few decades had succeeded in completely revitalising Russian Islam. Two of them deserve special mention. The first of these is Rizaeddin Fakhreddin Oglu (1859–1936), a Tatar mullah who was *Qadi* to the Muslim Ecclesiastical Assembly in Orenburg for many years, and then, from 1922 until his death, served as mufti in the interior of Russia and Siberia. Oglu is generally regarded as the most important member of the new school of reforming theologians in Russia. The second is Musa Bigi (1875–1949) who came from a Tatar mullah family in Rostov-on-Don. After attending the theological colleges in Kazan, Bukhara, Cairo and Constantinople, Bigi returned to Russia to complete his studies at the University of St Petersburg, where he helped to produce a number of periodicals dedicated to Muslim reform.

Both these men were regarded by their contemporaries as essentially orthodox theologians. In point of fact, however, their daring ideas carried them far beyond the pale of orthodoxy for, like their great mentor, they argued that the traditional Islamic faith must be brought into line with the findings of modern research.

The most important outcome of the teaching of Marzhani and his disciples, Oglu and Bigi, was the struggle which de-veloped between the new modernist Muslims and those sections of the Muslim clergy who had corrupted the 'purity' of Islam by making it dependent on the priesthood. In Marzhani's view, Islam in its original form had not presupposed the existence of a clerical order, and it was this 'reformatory' thesis of his that eventually led to the division of the Russian Muslim community into two distinct factions: the modernists or *Jadids* on the one hand and the conservatives or *Qadims* on the other. The *Jadids*, who constantly attracted new followers, sought support for their reforms from the younger and more progressive members of the bourgeoisie, while the Qadims obtained their backing from a minority group of Tatar intellectuals who had succeeded in retaining, and in some cases extending, their influence in the rural areas and the Steppes. The Muslim Spiritual Assembly in Orenburg, which represented Islam to the Russian government in St Petersburg, also remained under conservative control right up to 1917.

The relative strength of the two factions fluctuated considerably from one area to another. Whereas Turkestan remained a conservative bastion until 1917, the theories advanced by Marzhani and his disciples were received with enthusiasm in the Crimea. Moreover, Azerbaijan, which had always belonged to the Shi'ite camp and consequently to the Persian sphere of influence, became a stronghold of anti-clerical feeling and gave little encouragement to religious conservatism.

Cultural and educational reforms

Theological modernism provided the basic framework for subsequent attempts to introduce cultural and educational reforms. It also created the necessary conditions for the emergence within the Russian Islamic territories of a sense of national identity, which was to create friction between the Soviet leaders and the Islamic minorities after 1917.

One of the principal reasons why the Muslim peoples of Russia always found difficulty in acquiring a true sense of their independent cultural status was the language barrier. This problem was particularly acute during the early stages of the reform movement, for until the mid-nineteenth century instruction at the Koran schools was given in Arabic (the language of religion), Persian (the language of literature) and Turkish (the language of

Islamic doctrine). Thus, apart from faith, the most important factor in determining the unity and cohesion of Islam was the extent to which its followers were acquainted with these three languages. And in Russia such knowledge was the prerogative of a relatively small élite, which meant that the great mass of the Russian Muslim population could not participate in the intellectual life of their community. Consequently, if the cultural level of the Islamic minorities was to be raised in the way envisaged by the modernists, then this problem had to be solved.

The first practical attempt to do so was made by three Muslim intellectuals. The first of these was Abdul Qaiyum Nasiri (1825–1902), the son of a Tatar mullah from Kazan and a contemporary of Marzhani's. He was the most popular of the Muslim reformers in Russia. After training at a theological college in Kazan Nasiri taught from 1855 to 1875 at a Russian Orthodox seminary, where he was professor for the Tatar language, and at a Russian Tatar school, both of which were situated in Kazan. It was largely as a result of his intimate contact with Russian culture that Nasiri came to realise that the principal reason for the backwardness of Islamic culture in Russia lay in the failure of the Muslim minorities to cultivate their mother tongue, which had been consistently repressed in favour of 'acquired' languages. He then devoted the rest of his life to the creation of a new Tatar literary language based on the local Tatar dialect, which quickly replaced the artificial language of Muslim tradition.

Meanwhile, similar developments were taking place in the Kazakh steppes, due primarily to the lead given by the Trans-Caucasian, Hasan Bey Melikov-Zerdabi (1837–1907).[9] He too came into close contact with Russian culture, for he attended a Russian college in Tiflis before going on to complete his studies at the university in Moscow. From Moscow Melikov-Zerdabi returned to the Caucasus, where he taught at a school in Baku. Then in 1875 he began to publish the first periodical ever produced in a Muslim language, one which he himself had evolved from the Muslim dialect spoken in the local villages and which was, therefore, largely free from Arabic or Persian influences. This language, which Melikov-Zerdabi had made 'presentable', was soon adopted by the Azeri press and even served as a medium for various writers and poets.

The third of the Muslim intellectuals to emerge as a linguistic innovator was Abai Kunanbayev (1845–1904), the son of the head of a Kazakh clan. Shortly after Melikov-Zerdabi had created his village-based language, Kunanbayev evolved a Kazakh literary language which was also readily understood by the common people.[10]

The detailed ramifications of this development do not fall within the scope of this present chapter. Our principal object in referring to Nasiri, Melikov-Zerdabi and Kunanbayev is to show the extent to which the secular reforms—which were inspired in Russia, as elsewhere, by the example set by the early theological reformers of nineteenth-century Islam—helped to create a new and much more broadly based sense of national identity amongst the Muslim minorities. The modernisation of the Muslim languages was, in fact, one of the chief contributory factors to this process. It also led to the development of a new type of Muslim literature, which was concerned primarily with contemporary problems and not with the romantic aspects of Islam treated by traditional writers, who drew heavily for their material on religious legends and epics. The new school of Muslim writers emerged as champions of religious and educational reform, they fought for the emancipation of Muslim women, called for equal rights for Muslim minorities and eventually even demanded complete cultural and political autonomy.

But there was an element of danger in all this, for by developing different literary languages for the different Muslim minorities, the reformers ran the risk of destroying the old cultural unity of the *Umma*. It was thanks to one of the most remarkable of all the nineteenth-century Muslim reformers, the Crimean Tatar Izmail Gaspraly (1851–1914), that this danger was recognised and averted. Gaspraly's personal development was typical of the progressive Muslim intellectuals of his day. After spending his formative years at the Military Academy in Moscow, where he received his formal education, he travelled extensively in France and Turkey before settling in the Crimea. There he became rector of a theological college and later mayor of Bakhchisaray.

The pan-Turkish literary language which he created was probably the most important single contribution to the cultural and social development of the Russian Islamic peoples in the late

nineteenth and twentieth centuries. Thanks to his achievement it
was possible to counter and, subsequently, to avert the centrifugal
tendencies created within Russian Islam by the individual reform
movements in the various Muslim territories. Gaspraly's work also
had a significant effect on the confrontation between Islamic
belief and Soviet ideology after the revolution. The attempts
made by the Soviet government—especially in the period 1918–
1929—to promote the cultural development of the individual
Muslim territories with a view to destroying the unity of the
Islamic movement in the Soviet Union, leave little doubt as to
the success of Gaspraly's reformatory activities.

Gaspraly's linguistic reforms were all the more important and
their influence was all the more enduring in that they provided
him with the necessary basis for the reorganisation of the educational system within the Islamic territories. Gaspraly's new
system was first introduced in his native Crimea with the establishment there of the *Jadid* schools, which were its central feature.
Shortly afterwards *Jadid* schools were also opened in the other
Islamic territories, and by 1916 there were over 5,000 of them in
different parts of Russia.[11] It was thanks primarily to these new
schools that the educational standard of the Russian Muslims
showed such a marked improvement during the late nineteenth
and early twentieth centuries. By the early 1900s Russian Islamic
culture, especially in the Crimea and among the Tatars of the
Volga, had reached a new and unprecedented peak. Many of the
theological colleges founded in these districts were amongst the
finest in the whole of Islam.

The development of political nationalism

The *Jadid* reforms provided the necessary basis for the development of political nationalism among the Russian Islamic minorities. The leaders of this movement were far more fortunate than
their counterparts in the Islamic territories outside Russia, who
found themselves faced with the serious dilemma of having to
decide whether to base their nationalism on religious, racial or
national considerations. The fact that this problem was solved
in different ways by different Muslim countries is one of the
major reasons why the relations between these countries have

been in a state of almost perpetual crisis ever since. This is particularly true of the Near East.

Although the Russian Muslims also had to consider this question, it was nowhere near as urgent for them as for their co-religionists in other parts of the world. Consequently, they were spared the kind of tensions which arose out of the clash between the pan-Islamic and pan-Arab movements in the Near East and between the Ottoman 'ideology' and the pan-Islamic and pan-Turkish movements. There were, of course, many other such trends, but these were the most important from the point of view of the Muslim minorities in Russia. However, one point on which all these non-Russian Muslim reform movements were agreed was that Islam and its peoples were threatened, both by the religious impact of Christianity and by the political power of the Christian countries of the western world. The principal protagonist of this view, which emerged in the early years of the twentieth century as a result of Islam's confrontation with Europe, was al-Afghani.

This sense of confrontation was shared by leaders of the Muslim reform movements inside Russia. However, their opposition was provoked not by Europe but by Russia herself. For them the intellectual and political superiority of the west was embodied in the Russian Orthodox Church, the Russian intelligentsia and the tsarist régime. None the less, only one small, albeit extremely active, group (whose members subscribed to the pan-Islamic ideas of al-Afghani) advocated a policy of total non-cooperation with the Russians. The leader of this group, the Siberian Tatar Abdul Rašid Ibragimov,[12] was one of the most interesting figures in the whole of the Muslim modernist movement in Russia. He was a disciple of al-Afghani, and as such an inveterate enemy of the west in general and of Russia, the Russians and the tsarist régime in particular. His extremist attitude was due in the first instance to a strict Muslim upbringing. After being educated at the theological college in Kazan and subsequently in Medina, he became *Qadi* to the Muslim Ecclesiastical Assembly in Orenburg before embarking on extensive journeys to Turkey and Egypt, where he entered into close contact with modernist Muslim circles and was introduced to the teachings of al-Afghani. On his return to Russia in 1904 Ibragimov conducted a lively campaign, both as a journalist and as a politician, against Muslim orthodoxy and Russian socialism. In 1910 he left Russia for good and after visiting Japan and India settled in Turkey, where he played an active part in the pan-Islamic and pan-Turkish movements. His implacable aversion to Russia and the Russians was clearly demonstrated by the fact that he lived in Berlin during the whole of the First World War and engaged in anti-Russian propaganda among the Muslim prisoners of war. He died in Japan in 1944.

The small extremist group of Muslim nationalists led by Ibragimov was opposed by a very much larger group led by Izmail Gaspraly and embracing the great majority of Muslim intellectuals. This group limited its demands to equal rights for all Muslims living in Russia. Its policy, which presupposed allegiance to the tsarist régime, was prompted by the conviction that open revolt on the part of the Muslims would be a hopeless and consequently a senseless venture. Gaspraly considered that the only way in which he could attain his objectives was by adopting a positive attitude, thus promoting 'friendly co-existence' and even active collaboration between Muslims and Russians. In his view, this was the only way to advance the cause of Muslim reform inside Russia.[13]

But this policy was profoundly influenced by two events: the Russian revolution of 1905 and the Russo–Japanese war of 1904–1905, both of which showed that the power of the tsarist régime was nowhere near as great as Gaspraly and his followers had imagined. Of the two events the Russo–Japanese war was by far the more influential. Here, for the first time ever, a European power had been convincingly defeated by an Asiatic power. Russia had effectively demonstrated to the world at large the vulnerability of Europe and, like all the other peoples of Asia, the Russian Muslims were deeply affected by this development. These two events had far-reaching consequences. Above all, they confirmed the essential validity of the radical line adopted by the small group of Muslim nationalists under Ibragimov, who had already started to arrange secret meetings between leading Muslims as early as 1904 with a view to creating a comprehensive political organisation representing all the Islamic minorities in Russia.

It was also due largely to the initiative of Ibragimov's group that the first Muslim congress was staged at Nizhny Novgorod in August 1905. A second Muslim congress was then held in St Petersburg between 13 and 23 January 1906 and a third in Nizhny Novgorod between 16 and 20 August 1906. We do not propose to deal in detail with the individual resolutions passed at these congresses.[14] By and large the delegates were able to agree without undue difficulty on the general objectives to be pursued on behalf of the Islamic minorities. Among other things they demanded: a democratic form of government for the Islamic territories with independent legislative and executive bodies; equal political, civil and religious rights; condemnation by the Russian government of the anti-Muslim propaganda put out by the Russian Orthodox missionaries; and educational reforms based on the reform programme drawn up by Gaspraly. They also agreed on the broad outlines of the proposed reorganisation of spiritual administration in the Muslim territories: the four spiritual districts of Orenburg, Tiflis, Baku and Bakhchisaray were to be restructured and all four were to come under the jurisdiction of the mufti of Orenburg, who would be the religious head of the Muslim communities and would represent their religious interests vis-à-vis the Russian central government.

Difficulties arose when the delegates came to discuss the methods to be adopted in order to achieve their common objectives and in the event these proved insuperable. At the first congress it was proposed that a union should be created consisting of representatives from all Muslim territories in Russia. At the second congress this proposal was put into effect when the All-Russian Union of Muslims (*Ittifaq al-Muslimin*) was founded. But when the Union delegates came to discuss the question of tactics serious divisions were immediately revealed. Despite determined resistance from representatives of the Crimean and Caucasian Muslims (one of whom was Gaspraly) representatives of the Volga Tatars (one of whom was Ibragimov) succeeded in carrying a motion in the praesidium of the second Muslim Congress calling for close collaboration with liberal elements in Russia and, more especially, with the Constitutional Democrats in the struggle against the tsarist régime. They hoped that by making common cause with these opposition groups, they would obtain support for Muslim reforms. But their hopes were quickly dashed. Not only were the Constitutional Democrats completely uninterested in helping the Muslims, it also became apparent to the leaders of the Union that members of this party had the same 'imperialist leanings' and entertained the same feelings of hostility towards the non-Russian minorities as the right-wing monarchists. In point of fact, since the All-Russian Union of Muslims had a ridiculously small number of representatives in the Duma and was therefore quite unable to bring effective pressure to bear in support of its demands, collaboration between the two groups was virtually ruled out from the start. Inevitably the Union slowly disintegrated. After the suppression of the 1905 revolution it grew progressively weaker and in 1914 it ceased to exist.

The demise of the Union had far-reaching consequences for the subsequent development of the Islamic minorities in Russia and was a major factor in their struggle with the Russian Communist Party and the Soviet government after the October revolution. As has already been indicated, the founding of the All-Russian Union of Muslims—the first and only attempt to unite the Muslim peoples of Russia at a political level—did not meet with the approval of leaders of all the Muslim minorities. Consequently, when the Union broke up, the Islamic nationalists turned their attention once again to the individual regions where their nationalism had its roots and where their activities were likely to prove more effective in so far as they would be directed towards concrete, if more limited, goals. And so this pan-Russian Muslim movement failed to achieve its national objectives prior to the downfall of the tsarist régime in 1917. It failed to obtain equal rights or cultural autonomy for the Russian Muslims, it even failed to create a united front in order to oppose the discriminatory policies of the tsarist régime. Far from helping the Muslim leaders, collaboration with the Constitutional Democrats actually harmed their cause, for from 1908 onwards the tsarist régime was more adamant than ever in its refusal to grant concessions to non-Russian minorities.

Meanwhile, however, Muslim religious unity remained unimpaired. Although 1908 was the beginning of the end of Russian Muslim attempts to secure political unity, it was also the point of departure for a serious reappraisal of the bonds uniting Russian Muslims with the rest of the Islamic world.

One of the principal reasons for this reappraisal was the highly complex development that had taken place in Turkey. The successful revolution of the Young Turks on 24 July 1908 was followed by the reintroduction of the parliamentary constitution that had first been introduced in 1876 only to be set aside shortly afterwards by Abdul Hamid II. This convinced intellectual Muslims in Russia that the day would come when Islamic countries would be able to compete both intellectually and politically with the western world. After their bitter experience following the abortive rising of 1905, the Russian Muslims welcomed the successful revolutions of Kemal Atatürk and the Young Turks as a sign that a democratic movement could prevail over an autocratic system. But, although the Young Turk movement called for the modernisation of the economy and the establishment of a parliamentary democracy, it also insisted that the introduction of western institutions must be accompanied by a campaign to promote a sense of national identity.

This dual approach was bound to appeal to leaders of the Islamic minorities in Russia. By stressing the importance of nationhood the Young Turk reformers were really arguing in favour of the dissolution of the Ottoman Empire and its replacement by a collection of nation states, an idea that could only strengthen the Russian Muslims in their determination to obtain national independence. It was no accident, therefore, that after the failure of the 1905 revolution and the negative outcome of the attempt made by the All-Russian Union of Muslims to collaborate with the Constitutional Democrats, Ibragimov should have decided to emigrate to Turkey, where—with one eye on its possible application in Russia—he played a major part in the pan-Turkish movement. At the same time Gaspraly, who had always been an advocate of Slavophil ideas, also came under the influence of the Young Turk 'ideology'.

Although the October revolution put an end to the Russian Muslim reform movement as such, its influence continued to make itself felt until the early 1920s. G. V. Safarov, the Soviet Commissar for Semiryechensk, pointed to the threat posed by Russian Islam for the young Soviet state when he spoke of the stubborn resistance mounted by the people of Central Asia to the Soviet régime. Safarov's comments on that occasion were

prompted primarily by two groups of Muslims, whom he described as 'conservatives' and 'modernists'. The conservatives, he
said, clung to their traditional culture, refusing point-blank to
adopt progressive ideas of any kind; they refused to consider
themselves as members of any nation and insisted that they were
simply 'Muslims'; but although this generic term effectively
disposed of the smaller nationalities and blurred their specific
social and cultural characteristics, it also created a new and equal
nation, namely the 'Muslim nation'. According to Safarov the
second group, the modernists, tended towards a chauvinistic form
of nationalism, in other words the nationalism of their own
specific Muslim group. In so far as they were bent on reform
and were threatening to establish themselves within the Communist Party Safarov regarded the modernists as particularly
dangerous.[15]

Quite apart from bringing the intellectual and cultural life of
the Islamic minorities up to date, the Muslim reform movement
in Russia also strengthened their sense of national identity and
helped them to resist the russification policy pursued by the tsarist
régime. This resistance was not broken until the Soviet leaders
mounted their anti-Islamic policy, which was considerably more
rigorous and aggressive than its predecessor. The observer of
present-day Islam finds himself faced with a strange and apparently paradoxical situation, for the Muslims of the Soviet Union
are really more 'orthodox' than their co-religionists in the Islamic
countries of western, southern and south-eastern Asia. This
surprising development poses a highly complex problem which
really calls for a much more detailed discussion involving many
aspects of Islamic cultural history but which can only be briefly
touched upon within the framework of the present chapter. Basically, what we have to ask ourselves is whether the persecution of
the Islamic minorities, both in tsarist Russia and in the Soviet
Union, has helped to preserve religious customs which would
otherwise have gradually disappeared and which are in fact disappearing to an ever increasing extent in many other Islamic
countries. In other words, have present-day Muslims in the Soviet
Union—having been deprived of any really meaningful outlet
for their religious feelings—simply turned to traditional orthodoxy as a last refuge?

On the whole, it seems unlikely that the Islamic peoples of the Soviet Union, who have undoubtedly retained a strong religious sense, would be content merely to perpetuate the traditional observances of Muslim orthodoxy. Moreover, there are various indications which would suggest that there are still modernists among the Soviet Muslims who are continuing the reform movement started in the late nineteenth century by working for Muslim nationalism.[16]

Church, state and society

GERHARD SIMON

The Russian state church

Although it is perfectly true that the Russian Orthodox Church was the prototype of a state church, the accusation that has constantly been levelled against it—namely that at the turn of the century it was a completely rigid institution caught up in compulsive rituals—is only partially valid. At that time the Russian church was still capable of initiating reforms and adapting to a changing world. The picture that we have of an institutionalised church needs to be diversified and its sombre background illuminated by some light and shade.

But first the background has to be sketched in. The monopolisation and tutelage of the Orthodox Church by the state were made manifest in the paradoxical arrangement whereby the state church was granted extraordinary privileges. In the Fundamental Laws of the Russian Empire the Orthodox Church was described as the 'first and dominant' church. It alone was entitled to engage in missionary activities. Up to 1905 nobody was allowed to opt out of the state church and apostasy was treated as a punishable offence. In defence of orthodoxy the church was authorised to call on the civil power and the police, who were required to prosecute all persons suspected, either by the police themselves or by the clergy, of attacking the church by word or deed, and all persons who broke away from the church to join the Old Believers or the dissident sects. Orthodox religious instruction was compulsory in all schools and in many colleges of further education, the cost of such instruction being borne by the state.

The Orthodox Church also received large subsidies from the public purse for the maintenance of its theological schools and academies and, from the 1890s onwards, for the support of its clergy and the financing of a crash building programme to provide new ecclesiastical schools for primary pupils. These subsidies rose from 19.8 million roubles in 1897 to 29.3 million roubles in 1905 and 53.9 million roubles in 1914.[1] But although these increases were very considerable, they really only reflected the extraordinary growth of Russian state revenue during that period. In fact, subsidies paid to the church never accounted for more than two per cent of state expenditure in any given year. Moreover, a certain proportion of these monies, especially those allocated to the primary school programme, was used for supra-confessional purposes. Incidentally, other religious communities, such as Evangelical Lutherans and Roman Catholics, also received money from the public purse, and by the end of the nineteenth century the Lutheran and Catholic priests working in the Baltic Provinces, Finland and Poland were economically and socially far better off than Russian Orthodox priests working in the rural areas of Central Russia.

The pre-eminence of the state church in Russia is best illustrated by its close links with the tsarist autocracy. Under the fundamental laws of the empire the Tsar and the Tsarevich and their ladies had to belong to the Orthodox Church. This provision preserved in a watered-down form the right vested in the mediaeval church to watch over the religious allegiance of the Grand Duke and the Tsar and to refuse to recognise the Tsar as ruler if he turned away from the Orthodox faith. On the other hand, the church also elevated the Tsar far above the rest of the faithful by the sacred rite of coronation, in which he was declared to be the 'Lord's anointed'. The Tsar, for his part, undertook to be the 'foremost defender and preserver of the dogmas of the dominant faith and the guardian of orthodoxy'. In this connection he was also referred to on occasions as the 'head of the church', although this did not mean that he possessed an ecclesiastical rank under canon law. In point of fact, however, the tsars who ruled Russia during the hundred years preceding the revolution had absolute control of church administration and finance and of all ecclesiastical appointments. Nicholas II and his Tsarina even went so far as to submit names to the Holy Synod for canonisation, thus interfering in the most intimate of all ecclesiastical spheres.

During its final period the Russian Orthodox Church came to regard the will of the monarch and the will of God—to whom absolute allegiance was due—as virtually identical. From the reign of Peter the Great onwards the church became increasingly subservient to the secular power, with the inevitable result that it lost its traditional influence in political affairs and had no say in the formation of government policy. In the end the voice of the church went unheeded even by the peasants, who realised that in all secular matters their priests were simply puppets of the tsarist régime. This is an undeniable fact which is not to be dispelled by statistics on church membership, however impressive these may appear at first sight.

According to official statistics, the Russian Orthodox Church had 88 million members in 1904—about 70 per cent of the population of the empire. In 1904 there were 61 eparchies (which had increased to 67 by 1917). In a number of these eparchies— which corresponded more or less to Russian provincial divisions —the eparch was assisted by one or more vicar-bishops. During the last hundred years of tsarist rule only the bishops of St Petersburg, Moscow and Kiev were still referred to as metro- politans and even in their case this was purely a courtesy title, for there were no metropolitan sees as such. In 1904 Russia had some 40,000 ecclesiastical parishes which were tended by 106,620 clerics, of whom 47,743 were priests, 14,701 deacons and 44,176 psalmists. In 1914 there were 1,025 monasteries and convents with a total population of 94,629 monks, lay brothers, nuns and lay sisters. Of this total, more than three quarters were women. But although the number of churches, monasteries and religious showed an almost constant increase during the life of the Holy Synod, this growth rate was considerably less than that of the Russian population as a whole. Whereas in 1738 there were 106 churches for every 100,000 Orthodox inhabitants, in 1890 there were only 56. Moreover, by the outbreak of war in 1914 the number of monasteries and convents in Russia had dropped by several hundred.[2]

The only real expansion of church activity during this period took place in the sphere of primary education. Thanks to the initiative of the Director General of the Holy Synod, a large number of new parish schools were opened at the end of the nineteenth century, which provided peasant children between 8 and 11 years of age with a rudimentary knowledge of reading, writing and arithmetic over a period of two to three winters. But the most important subject in the curriculum, and the one on which the pupils spent most of their time, was religious instruction. Educationally, these church schools were anything but progressive and consequently they aroused the mistrust of liberal Zemstvo circles and intellectuals. It was hardly surprising that the more enlightened members of Russian society should have disapproved, for the children were taught to read from texts written in Church Slavonic and instead of learning about geography and the natural sciences, spent much of their time singing hymns. Instruction in the church schools was given either by religious or by badly trained and badly paid secular teachers, most of whom were women. None the less, church schools helped considerably towards reducing the high level of illiteracy in Russia and at their peak in 1904 the 43,407 church schools then in existence provided 1.9 million children with a rudimentary education that they would not otherwise have received. In the 1890s the church actually had more primary schools than the state (although the number of pupils attending the state schools was greater).[3]

From these statistics it is clear that the Russian state church had at its disposal a vast organization, whose administration needed to be extremely flexible if it was to meet the needs of successive generations. In point of fact, however, we find that in the course of the eighteenth and nineteenth centuries church administration passed more and more into the hands of the state. It was only at a parochial level that the church retained any degree of autonomy. Its higher dignitaries, from the eparchs upwards, came under the direct control of the government.

In 1721, when Peter the Great reorganised the Russian clergy, the office of patriarch was abolished and the Orthodox Church was placed in the charge of the Holy Synod. During the eighteenth century this ecclesiastical body was composed of seven or eight eparchs and representatives of the parochial and monastic clergy. Later, during the nineteenth century, membership was restricted to the three metropolitans and the eparch of Georgia, who were permanent members, and three or four eparchs, who were appointed on a temporary basis by the Tsar. The Synod deliberated on all important administrative and religious questions and was also expected to deal with an enormous amount of routine business. But it possessed no independent authority: any decisions which it reached on major administrative or legislative matters had to be submitted to the Tsar for his approval. It goes without saying that all new eparchial appointments required official sanction.

By the nineteenth century, however, the Russian tsars were no longer able to administer the affairs of the church on their own, although they were of course entitled to do so under the constitution. Consequently this task was delegated to an official: the Director General of the Holy Synod. From the beginning of the nineteenth century the Director General was the sole mediator between the tsar and the church and in the course of time he became virtual head of the state church. Although this office had already existed in the eighteenth century, the Directors General of those days had fulfilled a purely supervisory function. But in the nineteenth century they gradually built up their department and extended their responsibilities until they held what were virtually ministerial powers. K. P. Pobedonostsev, who was Director General from 1880 to 1905, had sole responsibility for all aspects of ecclesiastical policy. True, Pobedonostsev was still required to submit all new proposals to members of the Holy Synod; but this was a pure formality. In actual fact, the Synod had become a rubber stamp and all real power had passed to the tsar's representative, a development that was, incidentally, far more radical than anything Peter the Great had ever intended. There was one exception to this general rule, however. In certain cases, especially those involving ecclesiastical appointments, the President of the Synod—who was usually the Metropolitan of St Petersburg—was able to exert his authority to a limited extent.

The administration of the institutionalised church was extremely bureaucratic, which meant that the Director General's subordinates were able to interfere in church affairs right down to parish level. The principal instrument of church administration in the eparchies was the secretary of the eparchial consistory, who received his instructions from the Director General. All eparchial appointments were made at the instigation, although not in the name, of the Director General, who also took it upon himself to move the eparchs from one eparchy to another in complete defiance of canon law. This enabled him to display favour and disfavour vis-à-vis the episcopacy on a sliding scale, thus ensuring that the eparchs remained servile towards their superiors and tyrannical towards their subordinates.

But, despite their subservience to the Holy Synod and the Director General, within their own provinces the eparchs enjoyed very considerable powers. Like the members of the Holy Synod, they were overburdened with bureaucratic duties and responsibilities and so had little opportunity to concern themselves with pastoral care. Instead of acting as shepherds to their flocks they tended to be remote and authoritarian figures who seldom came into contact either with the parochial clergy or with the faithful. The vast majority of eparchs were the sons of parochial priests, which meant that they had improved their social standing beyond all recognition. Not all eparchs, however, owed their success to any particular outstanding gifts. On the contrary, for most of them social advancement had been the automatic outcome of completing a course of further study at one of Russia's four theological academies and, more especially, of embracing the monastic life. Because there were so few monastic aspirants in the late nineteenth century most young monks made rapid progress in their careers and found no particular difficulty in acquiring eparchial rank. The friction that had always existed between the 'black' monks and the 'white' or secular clergy (who had to be married and were consequently debarred from all responsible positions in the administration of the church) was greatly aggravated in the nineteenth century. But in view of their common origin and the great social and hierarchical gap that was opening up between them, this is hardly surprising.

Traditionally, the parochial clergy had two main sources of income: church land and voluntary or agreed contributions from their communities. Nearly every village church owned a piece of land which the priest either cultivated himself or leased to local peasants. In addition, dating from the days when Russian communities chose their own priest, every priest had a prescriptive right to receive financial support from his parishioners. But although the right had been retained, the custom had been suppressed as far back as the seventeenth century. By then the Russian church had become an institutionalised and strictly hierarchical organisation in which the parish priest was regarded simply and purely as an instrument of church policy at parochial level. This combination of subservience to eparchial authority and dependence on community support often placed the clergy in an invidious position. Squabbles with parishioners over fees for baptisms, weddings and funerals were a common occurrence and the popular conception of the village priest was of a man prepared to deprive the starving peasant of his last chicken.

The only way in which this situation could be improved was by giving the parochial clergy a regular stipend. The first steps in this direction were taken quite early on under Nicholas I. But it was not until the 1890s that the new policy was consistently applied. From then onwards reasonable progress was maintained, so that by 1904 some 27,000 parochial churches had been brought into the new scheme. Between them these received annual grants from the public purse amounting to 11.5 million roubles. By 1916, despite determined opposition from certain sections of the Duma, this sum was increased to 18.8 million roubles, which was divided among 31,000 of the empire's 41,000 parochial churches. Even so, the situation remained highly unsatisfactory. According to an estimate made by the Holy Synod in 1910 it would have taken 75 million roubles per year to make the parochial clergy completely independent of their traditional sources of income.[4] Thus at the end of the tsarist régime the parochial clergy still found themselves without a secure economic base and consequently unable to perform their duties effectively. Feared or shunned by the peasants, ridiculed or defamed as a stronghold of reaction by the estate owners and liberal intellectuals, they formed an isolated social group, whose influence on the masses had been severely undermined and which had no contacts whatsoever with members of the upper classes.

The Revolution and preparations for the Church Council in 1905

Although the general condition of the Russian state church was far from being satisfactory, this was certainly not due to apathy on the part of its members, who had made a determined effort in the early years of the century to put their house in order. Spurred

on by the revolutionary climate of the times and recognising their
own shortcomings, they had accepted the need for change. It was
due in no small measure to this inner vitality that the Orthodox
Church was subsequently able to survive under an atheist
government.

The Revolution of 1905 and the turbulent years immediately
preceding it produced a sudden spate of self-criticism in the
church involving all aspects of church life. By their outspoken
comments, the eparchs, professors at the theological academies
and members of the parochial clergy revealed to the public at
large the full extent of the church's failure to fulfil its duties.

It was generally agreed that before ecclesiastical reforms could
be introduced the church must first re-establish the principle of
canonical self-government. This led to the formulation of two
major demands: the removal of state tutelage, and the convention
of a Russian church council that would enact reforms in all areas
of church life. At that time nobody advocated the total segregation of church and state. The church wanted to retain its privileges, but it also wanted to administer its own affairs without
government interference. A large body of opinion within the
church argued in favour of the restitution of the patriarchate and
confidently expected that this would be one of the proposals
adopted by the council. However, this was opposed by many of
the secular clergy, who wanted the church to become a completely democratic institution at all levels.

Public discussion of the projected reforms was carried on at
considerable length in ecclesiastical journals from 1902 onwards
and reached its peak in the years following the 1905 Revolution,
when censorship was temporarily lifted. But the reform proposals
also elicited a warm response from the secular press and, in the
spring of 1905 especially, the liberal newspapers hailed progressive
churchmen as allies in the struggle against autocracy. In doing so,
they failed to realize that political liberalism and the quest for
ecclesiastical reform were motivated by totally different considerations and that, amongst the higher religious orders at least,
nobody questioned the existing political system.

On the contrary, the whole object of the proposed ecclesiastical
reforms was to bring about a revival within the church itself,
which was to be achieved in the first instance by a return to

canonical tradition. Many members of the church and, more especially, of the secular clergy, also wanted to see parish priests elected by their communities and eparchs by both religious and lay members of their eparchies. There was, in fact, a general feeling that the laity ought to play a larger part in the life of the church and it was proposed, therefore, that the various community councils and community elders should be given greater responsibility. Over and above this, the parochial clergy wanted their communities to become largely independent of the eparchial consistories and to be recognised in law as independent corporations.

Many of the projected reforms were concerned with the social and political role of the church and the clergy. A proposal that this role should be intensified received almost unanimous support and it was agreed that the clergy should press for representation in the Zemstvos, the Duma and even the Imperial Council, since this would enable them to make a responsible contribution to the socio-political life of the country while at the same time re-establishing the former social pre-eminence of the Orthodox Church.

Severe censure was levelled at theological schools, especially seminaries, which had long failed to fulfil their principal function of training aspirants to the priesthood. These seminaries were anachronistic institutions which combined general education with theological instruction. They were attended by sons of parish priests, most of whom held enlightened views and were intent on gaining entry to a university but who were subjected to a regimen of hymn-singing, church services and brutal discipline by the staff in the hope that this would give them a sense of vocation. Because of their antiquated teaching methods the seminaries entered into a progressive decline in the 1890s. There were about sixty such seminaries in different parts of the empire and every year cases of student unrest were reported in a number of them. The outmoded curriculum, the incompetent teachers and the draconian and unhappy atmosphere combined to produce strikes, cases of assault and even of attempted murder, in which the victims were the rectors or teachers. And more and more frequently the authorities uncovered revolutionary groups in the Orthodox seminaries. Radical remedies were called for, and many of the reform proposals put forward by members of the church actually envisaged the dissolution of the traditional seminaries and their replacement by theological schools. Attendance at these schools —which it was proposed should be open to students of all classes[5] —would be restricted to candidates intending to become priests.

This lively public debate on the need for reform within the state church bore fruit early in 1905 when the Committee of Ministers held a special conference to consider the feasibility of establishing religious freedom in Russia. The conference was presided over by S. Yu. Witte, head of the committee, who invited Antony (Vadkovsky), the Metropolitan of St Petersburg, to take part. This invitation already constituted an initial success for the reformers since it undermined the authority of the Director General and enabled the church to speak and act on its own initiative in a matter of major public concern. The Committee of Ministers assumed from the outset that 'the beliefs of the individual are not subject to control by the state. . . .' For his part, the Metropolitan of St Petersburg stressed that he had no intention of asking for legislation forcing people to return to the Orthodox Church and that, on the contrary, he would welcome new measures to enable those people for whom membership of the church was simply a bureaucratic necessity to leave. He also spoke up against the persecution of dissident sects by administrative or police action. In doing so the President of the Holy Synod abandoned an important principle of traditional church policy and paved the way for a new relationship between church and state and between the church and dissidents.[6]

As a result of this special conference the law 'On the Consolidation of the Principles of Religious Tolerance' was passed on 17 April 1905. Under its terms all Russians were legally entitled for the first time ever to leave the state church in order to join other confessions or sects. Significantly, no provision was made for those who wished to renounce religion altogether. Moreover, the state church was still the 'first' and 'dominant' church in Russia and continued to enjoy special privileges. Thus, the law prohibiting all other religious communities from engaging in missionary work remained on the statute book and was still strictly enforced.

But, despite the continuing pre-eminence of the Orthodox

Church, its relationship to the other religious communities in
Russia was completely transformed by the new law of 1905
because under its terms nobody could be prevented from publicly
renouncing Orthodoxy. According to the official statistics 301,450
people, who had been Orthodox under duress and had previously
had no right to declare their true allegiance, left the church. More
than half of these were Christians—chiefly from the territory
around Kholm—who had been united with Rome until they
were forcibly converted to the Orthodox faith in the nineteenth
century. These people embraced the Latin rite of the Roman
Catholic church. The Muslims of the Volga district, who had
been forcibly converted following the Russian conquest of their
territory, also seceded. So too did the Estonian and Latvian
peasants in the Baltic Provinces, who reverted to their native
Lutheranism. The Protestant sects and the Old Believers also
acquired many new members.

Apart from working out the terms of the law on religious
tolerance, the special conference of the Committee of Ministers
was also prepared to discuss the whole question of the relationship
between the state and the church with a view to its possible
revision and to consider the problems of reform within the church.
Although this discussion—which was suggested by Metropolitan
Antony of St Petersburg—was frustrated by Pobedonostsev,
who persuaded the Tsar to intervene, by then both Antony and
Witte had submitted their draft proposals, which had been drawn
up with the aid of professors from the academy in St Petersburg.

In his draft Antony argued that the Old Believers and dissident
sects would be in a 'more favourable position' following the
promulgation of the law granting religious tolerance than the
state church because they would have been guaranteed 'autonomy in their religious affairs', whereas the Orthodox Church
would still be hindered and restricted by the state. Antony then
went on to ask whether the time had not come 'to abolish or at
least moderate the constant tutelage and all too vigilant control
exercised by the secular authorities over the life of the church and
the activities of its administrators; for this deprives the church of
its independence and [lames] its initiative, so that its activities
are restricted almost entirely to divine worship and the performance of routine religious rites whilst its voice is not heard at all

either in private or in social life.' Although the concrete proposals which Antony advanced in this draft were cautious, it was none the less quite unheard-of in the age of Pobedonostsev for the first Metropolitan of the Holy Synod to make programmatic statements of this kind, which called into question the rights of the state.

In the draft which he submitted to the Committee of Ministers Witte criticised the state church far more openly. He quoted Dostoyevsky, who had said that since the days of Peter the Great the church had been in a 'state of paralysis'. He then pointed out that the church had abandoned the conciliar principle and become an instrument of state policy under the direct control of the bureaucracy and the police. The life of the church, Witte suggested, had been 'rigid and cut off from the problems which now move society'.[7]

Although the Tsar prevented the Committee of Ministers from pronouncing on these problems and commanded that they should be dealt with by the Holy Synod instead, it soon became apparent that the eparchial college was also determined to speak its mind. It too had been infected by the general atmosphere of unrest which preceded the Revolution of 1905. In March of that year the Synod duly discussed the question of church reform and its three metropolitans were then afforded the highly unusual opportunity of conferring with the Tsar in person over the outcome of their deliberations, thus completely by-passing the Director General. In their address they urged the Tsar to give his assent to the convention of an all-Russian church council authorised to elect a patriarch and put through essential ecclesiastical reforms. Of the measures specifically mentioned by the metropolitans the most important were the decentralisation of church administration, the re-organisation of the parochial clergy and the reform of church schools.

This sudden and completely unexpected action on the part of the Holy Synod was warmly welcomed by the public and gave rise to a general assumption, both in the church and in society at large, that the re-establishment of the patriarchate was not far removed. But all hopes of a speedy renewal of the Orthodox Church were dashed on 31 March 1905 when the Tsar published his resolution in reply to the address from the Synod, in which he declared that 'in the present unsettled conditions' he considered it 'impossible' to embark on such a 'great matter' and merely promised to convene a church council 'at a suitable time'.[8]

Despite the Tsar's procrastinating tactics the Synod none the less went ahead with its preparations by forming a special committee to work out a draft agenda for the council. But this committee, which was presided over by Antony (Vadkovsky) and was made up of ten eparchs, twenty professors and a number of other experts and prominent public figures, was regarded with growing concern by the arch-conservative backlash, with the result that its activities were seriously curtailed; after meeting from March to June and from November to December 1906 it was dissolved by order of the Tsar. The committee none the less did valuable work, although its recommendations bore the unmistakable imprint of conservative eparchial thinking and for this reason were felt to be disappointing by the progressive section of the ecclesiastical press which was arguing for more far-reaching reforms.

The committee called for the restoration of the patriarchate and the creation of a permanent Synod consisting of twelve eparchs to assist the patriarch in the conduct of church affairs. But under this scheme all important decisions taken by the patriarch, the Synod or the church council would still have been referred to the Tsar for his approval (*blagousmotreniye*). The only difference would have been that the responsibility for submitting such matters to the Tsar would have rested with the patriarch and not the Director General, who would once again have exercised a purely supervisory function. In this respect the committee's recommendations differed completely from the ideas put forward by the liberal ecclesiastical press, which wanted to see the office of the Director General abolished. The press approach appears to have been more or less in line with Metropolitan Antony's original attitude, for in the draft reforms which he presented to the preparatory committee for a church council he made no reference whatsoever to the Director General. In its proposals for the re-organisation of the eparchies and parishes the committee also failed to satisfy the liberals, who were demanding democratisation and lay participation in the life of the church.[9]

Once the committee had been dissolved the preparations for a church council virtually came to a standstill and no serious attempt was made by the government to revive this project during the lifetime of the tsarist régime despite the considerable pressure brought to bear by sections of the parochial clergy, the Duma and society. The 'pre-Council conference' established by the Synod in 1912 was conceived as a means of deferring the council, not of promoting it. It seems clear that after its painful experiences with the Duma, the government was not prepared to run the risk of creating a second forum capable of criticising the autocracy in public, especially since in this case the criticism—however moderate—would have been seen to come from one of the last remaining bulwarks of the autocratic system.

Right-wing radicalism and socialism

After 1905 the state church was made to feel the right-wing backlash very quickly and very forcibly. Because of this, and because the church leaders offered no resistance to the new reactionary line, little or nothing came of their optimistic plans and ideas. Instead of carrying out the urgently needed reform of the seminaries the Synod decreed in 1908, and again in 1909, that all secular subjects taught in these institutions were to be removed from the curriculum and replaced by additional religious instruction and that new punitive measures would be taken against any seminarists engaging in revolutionary activities.

The theological academies were treated in exactly the same way. Although they had been pressing for a number of years for the right to administer their own internal affairs, under the new statute of 2 April 1910 they remained accountable both to their eparch and to the Holy Synod. This statute also laid down that teachers at the academies were to inculcate a sense of 'allegiance to the throne and the motherland' in their students. Because of this clause, which had never appeared in previous legislation, the church leaders dared not submit the bill to the Third Duma, even though the conservatives had a majority at that time. It was passed into law by the Tsar himself under the emergency powers vested in him by the constitution, of which he made such frequent use. When the statute appeared the Duma bitterly attacked the

Holy Synod and refused to authorise subsidies for the theological schools for the following financial year.

The Holy Synod also failed to take any steps to reorganise ecclesiastical life at parochial level, although the need for action in this sphere had long been recognised by all concerned. The bill providing for parochial reform passed backwards and forwards between the administrative departments of the church and the Duma for years and was finally dropped from the legislative programme in 1915 because the ecclesiastical hierarchy refused to accept the draft drawn up by the Duma, which would have authorised the laity in each parish to elect their own priest and have given the parochial communities the legal status of corporations. This bill, incidentally, received strong backing from the Octobrists.

And so, far from producing a revival in the Orthodox Church, the period following the Revolution of 1905 saw a growing identification between the official church and the reactionary policies of the régime. Progressive factions within the church were brushed aside and forced to adopt extremist attitudes. This polarisation between right and left undermined the whole of the church and threatened to split it right down the middle, with the result that it was unable to provide the necessary stability to counter the disruptive forces that were then rending the empire.

The alignment between the church and the forces of reaction was due in part to the belief held by certain religious leaders that they must preserve a strictly neutral attitude in all political questions. Men like Antony (Vadkovsky) thought that it was possible for the church to stand above political parties and failed to realise that, by doing so, it was accepting the status quo and condoning the reactionary policies of the autocratic tsarist régime. Other religious leaders adopted a more radical view, declaring quite openly that the church should come out in support of the threatened autocracy and in opposition to the conspiratorial forces of constitutionalism, socialism and Judaism.

The growing extremism of the political orientation adopted by the state church is well illustrated by its attitude towards the radical right-wing Union of the Russian People. Although Metropolitan Antony (Vadkovsky) refused to bless the flags of this conspiratorial group of reactionary monarchists in November 1906, the eparchs and religious in many Russian eparchies actively collaborated both with the Union and with other 'patriotic' organisations. Initially, when asked by individual eparchs whether it was permissible for them to work with the Union, the Holy Synod had replied that there was no objection to this. But on 15 March 1908, after being urged to do so by the Union, the Synod sent an official directive to all eparchs informing them that they should 'not only permit but give their blessing to any of the Orthodox religious under jurisdiction who wish to collaborate with the Union of the Russian People and other patriotic, monarchist associations'.[10]

Not content with actively promoting the radical groups of the extreme right, the Orthodox hierarchy also condemned any members of the church who had dealings with the parties of the left. In the First and Second Dumas several Russian Orthodox priests had joined the ranks of the socialists, much to the annoyance of the church leaders. In May 1907, when five Orthodox delegates gave vent to anti-monarchist sentiments in the Duma, the Synod made a pronouncement to the effect that membership of 'parties dedicated to the overthrow of the state, the social order and even the Tsar' was incompatible with the duties of the priesthood. Only one of the delegates concerned heeded the Synod's warning and disassociated himself from his party. Three others who belonged to the *Trudoviki*, and one who belonged to the Social-Democrats, refused to conform and were arraigned before an ecclesiastical court.

Later that same year, when the Tsar arbitrarily altered the electoral law and so ensured a conservative majority in the Third Duma, it seemed as if all grounds for conflict between church and parliament had been removed. One of the most outspoken representatives of the reactionary episcopacy, Archbishop Antony (Khrapovitsky) of Volhynia, who saw Russia's salvation in the restoration of the patriarchate and the consolidation of monastic authority within the state church, preached on the results of the election to the Third Duma in Zhitomir Cathedral as if he were delivering the Easter message: 'Our Holy Russia has risen again.' Now these 'fiends in human shape' can no longer 'parade themselves as spokesmen of the people'. The newly elected 'true spokesmen' know that any 'undermining of the tsarist autocracy is the first step towards the destruction of Russia'.[11]

Meanwhile, the links between the state church and the right-wing extremists had become much closer. Many of the local branches of the Union of the Russian People were led by members of the church and many had their headquarters in churches and ecclesiastical institutions. The monk Iliodor (Trufanov)—who operated first from the Pochayev monastery in Volhynia and later from Tsaritsyn, and who was at one stage in his career intimately associated with Rasputin—was notorious for his inflammatory diatribes on behalf of the Black Hundreds. Iliodor wrote and preached against Jews, Poles and revolutionaries and urged the people to take the law into their own hands in dealing with these 'Mongol bands'. He defended the terrorist methods employed by the right-wing extremists and incited the people to anti-Jewish pogroms. This anti-semitic campaign constituted a cynical attempt to acquire influence among the Russian peasants by providing them with a scapegoat on whom they could wreak their vengeance with impunity. The Synod was quite powerless to restrain Iliodor.

But, although the church maintained these close ties with the monarchy and the forces of reaction, this does not mean that social questions were completely ignored by Orthodox churchmen, as had virtually been the case prior to 1905. In 1905 especially, but also in the period immediately following the first revolution, both the liberal and ultra-conservative groups within the church called for better social conditions for the workers and peasants (shorter working hours, improved social security etc.) As far as the institutionalised church was concerned this issue remained largely theoretical and was really no more than an exercise in Christian apologetics that had been prompted by the need to come to grips with socialism. But from articles published in progressive ecclesiastical periodicals (such as *Tserkovno-obshchestvennaya Zhizn*) it is quite obvious that many individual priests were prepared to devote themselves wholeheartedly to social problems. Between 1905 and 1917 various members of the parochial clergy acted as treasurers for peasant credit associations while others helped to combat alcoholism by founding temperance societies or engaged in similar welfare activities.

Meanwhile, although the church itself did nothing in an official capacity to encourage social work either by precept or example, it embarked on a searching analysis of the theoretical aspects of atheistic socialism in an attempt to eradicate the deep-rooted attachment to this doctrine which had been revealed by both the workers and the intellectuals during the Revolution of 1905 and which had taken the church completely unawares. From late 1905 onwards the Orthodox periodicals and newspapers published a large number of articles on socialism. In addition, discussion evenings were held in many metropolitan parishes and the Holy Synod sent out synodal missionaries to counter the spread of socialist ideas in working-class suburbs. The dangers of revolutionary socialism formed the focal point of interest for Orthodox publicists at that time, from the Director General V. K. Sabler (who wrote a two-volume treatise on the subject) down to contributors to the provincial ecclesiastical press.[12] Socialism was also the main item on the agenda of the fourth missionary conference, which was held in Kiev in 1908. Moreover, a special course was introduced in all Orthodox seminaries and academies on the 'History and Unmasking of Socialism'. Those responsible for promoting this intensive campaign revealed a fairly subtle grasp of Marxist and socialist doctrine and will no doubt have contributed to the dissemination of socialist ideas. A point worth noting is that the Orthodox apologists based their arguments almost exclusively on the theoretical writings of German, French and English socialists. They appear to have had no knowledge of the works of Russian Social-Democratic authors. They also completely ignored the Bolsheviks.[13]

All Orthodox publicists were agreed on the need to improve social conditions, but they insisted that all such improvements must be achieved within the existing social order. One of the leading spokesmen of the anti-socialist movement was Ioann Vostorgov, a synodal missionary. At the missionary congress in Kiev he declared that Russian socialism owed its power and success to the 'failure of Christianity to make its presence felt in our mutual relationships' and to the 'imperfections of our social life as exemplified by pauperism and the more extreme forms of capitalism'.[14] Director General Sabler deplored the 'workers' difficult living conditions' and the 'ruthless exploitation of the workers by wealthy capitalists'. In order to raise the 'moral and material well-being' of the workers he recommended that western-type cooperative societies and agricultural bulk purchasing and vending associations should be established and cooperative banks, similar to those founded by F. W. Raiffeisen in Germany, should be introduced. Sabler even went so far as to suggest that at some future time the workers should be allowed to become 'partners or shareholders' in industry. But no firm proposals along these lines were put forward and it is difficult to escape the impression that such ideas were never anything more than window-dressing. For, while Sabler was making his enlightened declarations, another Orthodox writer, I. P. Pokrovsky, was defending poverty as a gift from God that must be preserved to enable Christians to exercise their charity. Pokrovsky justified the principle of private ownership by quotations from the New Testament and maintained that Christ had 'paid only scant attention to man's material needs'.[15]

In their writings the Orthodox polemicists all stressed the incompatibility of Christianity and socialism. 'Socialism promotes the class struggle and enmity, Christianity promotes unity and love.'[16] This was the essential message. The people were told that, whereas the socialists were bent on destroying the state and the present social order by violent revolution, the church wanted to engender a spirit of charity and achieve social reform by appealing to men's consciences and bringing its moral influence to bear; that whereas socialism merely undertook to free people from material need, Christ had come to save the world 'not from the oppression of the capitalists . . . and the tyranny of despotic government, but from the tyranny of sin and death'.[17] Why, the apologists asked, were the socialists trying to change social conditions when the root of all evil was to be found in the depravity of man? What was needed was for man himself to be reborn through the Christian faith, for then the social order would reform itself.[18] In other words: socialism was concerned with society, Christianity was concerned with the individual.

Most of the Orthodox writers also dealt at considerable length with the socialist vision of the future. This, they suggested, was a dangerous and utopian fantasy. The fact of the matter was that in a truly socialist society the individual would lose his human dignity and be completely suppressed by an all-powerful state *Apparat*. Family ties, patriotism and tolerance, it was said, could not survive in such conditions. As for the socialist contention that alienation would disappear in a socialist society, this was rejected out of hand: 'There is no reason to suppose that with the dawn of a new [socialist] era people will undergo a complete transformation.'[19] For all these reasons the church was adamantly opposed to 'Christian socialism', which it regarded as a misguided attempt to bridge the gap between irreconcilable opposites.

The reason why the Orthodox polemicists devoted so much of their time to attacks on Christian socialism was that a number of fringe groups within the state church had actually tried to base a programme of direct and progressive political action on Christian concepts. The St Petersburg Society of Russian Factory Workers was formed at the beginning of the century with the approval of Metropolitan Antony and under the leadership of Georgy Gapon (1870–1906), an Orthodox priest and a highly ambiguous figure. This association, which had over 10,000 members by 1905, constituted a novel attempt to channel the revolutionary movement of the Russian industrial classes into controlled paths, where it could be kept under surveillance. But, despite his ulterior motives, Gapon pressed for real reforms and created a kind of trade union organisation which was meant to be much more than a mere political instrument of the authorities. On 9 January 1905, when the strike movement was at its height, Gapon led a procession of St Petersburg workers bearing icons and church flags and armed with a petition in which they demanded freedom of the press, a parliament with constituent powers, an eight-hour working day and the redistribution of the land. This petition was to have been handed to the Tsar at the Winter Palace but when the workers appeared before the palace gates they were greeted with a volley of rifle fire from the guards. It seems that Gapon did not make contact with the police until after the disastrous outcome of this 'Bloody Sunday'. At all events, he was murdered by a group of workers in March 1906 for acting as a police agent.

And so the attempt to establish a Christian trade union movement was hopelessly discredited. But there were other ways of promoting a sense of social commitment amongst Orthodox Christians. Such, certainly, was the declared intention of those taking part in the discussions of the Religious and Philosophical Meetings which were held in St Petersburg from 1901 to 1903. At these assemblies members of the intelligentsia with religious inclinations, who came to be known as the 'Godseekers' (*bogoiskateli*), met representatives of the church in an attempt to establish a common approach to the urgent social questions of the day. But it soon became apparent at these meetings, which were organised by Dmitry Merezhkovsky and his wife Zinaida Gippius, that the mystical and highly speculative view of religion held by the intellectuals had little in common with the scholastic theology of the Orthodox churchmen. None the less, the Religious and Philosophical Meetings constituted the first attempt to bridge the great gap which had developed between the church and the intelligentsia, although it should be added that the philosophers who took part in these discussions and whose speculative approach to religion was based on the ideas of Vl. Solovyev were only a relatively small group of the intelligentsia. The ultimate object of the meetings was to discover a socio-ethical ideal acceptable to both groups since both wished to see a modernised church regain its former influence in the social sphere. 'The lack of a socio-religious ideal on the part of the churchmen is the real cause of the hopeless situation [which now exists],' declared the theologian and author V. A. Ternavtsev in the programmatic report with which he opened the discussions. In his view the church had neglected its earthly duties, which were now being performed by the intelligentsia in accordance with 'Christ's commandment that we must serve our fellow-men'. Although prompted largely by wishful thinking, the idea that the revolutionary intelligentsia was inspired by religious considerations and guided by an unconscious or subconscious form of Christianity, played an important part in the attempt to bring about a rapprochement between the church and the St Petersburg intellectuals by discovering a common socio-ethical mode of action. It was also one of the principal concepts underlying the work of the *Vekhi* authors. At one of the St Petersburg meetings V. V. Rozanov claimed that 'God resides in the intelligentsia' while Ternavtsev considered that the intelligentsia 'would assuredly find its way back to the Christian faith by way of rationalism'.[20] In actual fact, however, the barriers of language and thought which separated even these religiously-minded intellectuals from the representatives of the church often proved insuperable.

But there was one group of intellectuals which actually did return to the Orthodox Church after the turn of the century. This group included P. A. Florensky and his associates and also men like S. N. Bulgakov, N. A. Berdyayev, S. L. Frank and P. B. Struve, who had been disenchanted with Marxism. Even after their return to the church Berdyayev and Bulgakov still gave their assent to many of the socio-political reforms demanded by the Marxists and consequently subjected the state church to severe criticism for its lack of social commitment and its lethargy. Bulgakov founded a Union of Christian Politics which called for equal rights throughout the whole of the empire and for the nationalisation of the means of production. These ideas were derived, not from the Marxists, but from the early Christians, who had applied socialist principles in their communities and so set an example for the whole of Christendom. In Bulgakov's view, Christianity must, therefore, inevitably lead to 'political emancipation and religious revival'.[21] Although Bulgakov was widely regarded as the founder of Russian Christian Socialism, in actual fact his decidedly anti-revolutionary attitude meant that he was poles apart from the leaders of the socialist parties.

Conversely, there were certain groups within the Orthodox Church who felt a growing affinity with the socialist parties and who adopted many important facets of their policy. These groups, who caused a great stir amongst the general public, also affected the attitudes of many members of the parochial clergy. The originators of this particular brand of Christian Socialism —in which Orthodox religious took their political orientation from the parties of the political left—included the Group of 32, which was formed during the 1905 Revolution by 32 St Petersburg clerics, many of whom had taken part in the Religious and Philosophical Meetings. On 17 March 1905 this group submitted a petition—the first of several—to the Metropolitan of St Petersburg, in which they urged him to introduce ecclesiastical reforms as a matter of urgency. The Group of 32 called for the democratisation of the church, the limitation of eparchial power and administrative autonomy for the parochial clergy. In a declaration in 1906 the group went even further by stating that it was the duty of the clergy to protect the workers from the capitalists, to sympathise with the peasants and work for a speedy solution of the agrarian problem. One of the spokesmen for the group, Grigory Petrov, who openly proclaimed his allegiance to the 'fathers' of the revolutionary intelligentsia, Herzen and Belinsky, demanded a fundamental revision of all social structures and measures to prevent the exploitation of man by man. Petrov was elected to the Second Duma as a representative of the Kadet Party. But by then he was already under severe pressure from right-wing circles in the church on account of his 'anti-Christian, socialist doctrines'. This eventually led to his being banished to a monastery, whereupon he left the priesthood.[22]

But Petrov was not the only priest serving in the Duma to come into conflict with the hierarchy. There were six ecclesiastical delegates in the First Duma and four of these held markedly progressive views. In the Second Duma there were thirteen ecclesiastical delegates, only four of whom—two eparchs and two priests—belonged to conservative parties. Of the remaining nine three joined the Kadets, three the *Trudoviki* and one the Socialist Revolutionaries. The most outspoken of these left-wing priests was Fyodor Tikhvinsky, one of the *Trudoviki*, who not only wanted the Russian ministers to be responsible to parliament but also demanded the nationalisation of all land and its redistribution to the peasants. Thanks to the new electoral law of 1907 and the pressure brought to bear by the church, there were no left-wing ecclesiastical delegates in the Third and Fourth Dumas.

Even the St Petersburg Group of 32 abandoned its activities once the right-wing reaction set in. But there were others who still continued to discuss the feasibility of combining Christianity with socialism. In 1907 Archimandrite Mikhail (Semyonov), who was a professor at the ecclesiastical academy in St Petersburg, published a pamphlet entitled 'How I Became a People's Socialist', in which he argued that the social problem in Russia could be resolved only by renouncing the principle of private ownership and creating a completely new social infrastructure.[23] The title of the Archimandrite's pamphlet, incidentally, was prompted by Pastor Paul Goehre's publication 'How a Priest Became a Social-Democrat'. Pastor Goehre had joined the German Social-Democratic Party in 1900 together with Christopher Blumhardt.

Similar ideas were expressed by Nikolay Smirnov, who helped to clarify the theoretical premises of Christian Socialism. He contended that the reason why the Christian-Socialist thinkers of nineteenth-century Europe—from Wichern to Stoekker and Naumann—had failed to deal with the social problem was that they had not taken the essential step from the individualistic ethic of Christianity to the group ethic of socialism. In Smirnov's view charitable intentions and an appeal to the goodwill of the individual were not enough. The problems created by industriali-sation and the emergence of the new proletarian class could not be solved by the kind of 'total personality change' that the Christian-Socialist movement had in mind but only by 'reorgan-ising ... the structure of society and industry'. Consequently, Smirnov argued, if the new problems facing society were to be overcome, socialists and Christians would have to work together to promote new socio-political measures designed to bring about the 'rule of the working proletariat and the absorption of all other classes into the proletarian class'. According to Smirnov the socialist ideal was not only compatible with Christian aspirations, it was actually the most desirable way of furthering the Christian cause. Incidentally, in establishing this parallel between Christian and socialist hopes Smirnov expressly referred to the German revisionists who, in his opinion, no longer regarded atheism and materialism as an integral part of their political programme at that time.[24]

The ideas propounded by Smirnov and others in the Christian-Socialist camp were given a more radical turn by the Union of the Democratic Orthodox Clergy and Laity, which was formed in St Petersburg after the February revolution of 1917 and included among its founders the surviving members of the Group of 32. The Union, which supported the political programme of the Socialist Revolutionaries, called for the redistribution of the land to the peasants, the transfer of the factories to the industrial workers and the 'liquidation of capital in the name of Jesus Christ'. In fact, it sought to promote a socialist revolution, which it confidently expected to see in the immediate future. This

Democratic Orthodox Union, to which both A. I. Vvedensky and B. V. Titlinov belonged, was a forerunner of the 'Renewal Movement' (*obnovlenchestvo*) and the 'Living Church' (*zhivaya tserkov*) which were founded after the October Revolution. Both these splinter groups were strongly opposed to the patriarchal church; they welcomed the Bolshevik revolution as the fulfilment of Christian aspirations and regarded themselves as the executors of the revolution within the church. The attitude adopted by the Living Church to the Soviet régime was taken over by the patriarchal church from the mid-1920s onwards.

From the triumph of reaction to the election of a patriarch in October 1917

In the years immediately preceding the First World War it became increasingly apparent that the state church was beginning to break up and that the authority of its leaders was being progressively undermined. Later, when Grigory Rasputin— the 'Saviour' and 'Bearer of the Faith'—began to assert his dominance over church leaders, the situation grew still more threatening. Metropolitan Antony of St Petersburg and S. M. Lukyanov, the Director General of the Holy Synod, tried in vain to have Rasputin removed from the imperial court. But worse was still to come. In May 1911 Lukyanov was succeeded as Director General by V. K. Sabler, who was completely under the influence of Rasputin's group and who remained in office until June 1915. Sabler had been Pobedonostsev's deputy from 1892 to 1905 and during his own period as Director he modelled himself on his former chief. In fact, if anything, he was even more reactionary. Thus, after a period in which the Holy Synod had been acquiring growing independence under successive Director Generals, none of whom had possessed expert knowledge of church affairs or remained in office long enough to acquire it, the church found itself led by a man who knew exactly what he was about and was determined to use his power in order to prevent any further progress towards modernisation. Thanks to Sabler, Rasputin was able to bend the Synod to his will. This Siberian peasant, of whom the Tsarina once said that he made his dispositions 'through God', enthroned and transferred eparchs and abrogated synodal resolutions. The Synod was forced to appoint Varnava (Nakropin), a semi-illiterate peasant, as Archbishop of Tobolsk and Rasputin's friend Pitirim (Oknov) as Metropolitan of St Petersburg. A. D. Samarin, who succeeded Sabler as Director General in July 1915, tried to stem the worst abuses but fell foul of Rasputin and the Tsarina and was obliged to relinquish his post in September of the same year. The church was put completely to shame by the endless chain of Rasputin scandals, which were discussed at length by the public, the press and the Duma, and which therefore gravely undermined the church's authority. Rasputin and the subservient church leaders were subjected to particularly bitter censure by the conservatives who were forced to watch the state church, which was one of the last remaining pillars of the old order, being compromised and degraded by this exalted dabbler in the occult.

As for Sabler, he was criticised on all sides in the Duma for consistently by-passing parliament and rejecting proposals for really urgent reforms submitted by the moderates. In March 1912 the Nationalist deputy, V. M. Purishkevich, stated in the course of a debate in the Duma: 'In the past three, four or ten years neither the left-wingers nor the revolutionaries, neither the Social-Democrats nor the *Trudoviki*—nobody has done as much harm to the Orthodox Church as the present Chief Procurator.'[25]

After Sabler's retirement, which was welcomed by all parties in the Duma, a group of delegates from the ranks of the lower clergy submitted a memorandum to his successor, in which they criticised every aspect of church life. Church administration and the arbitrary exercise of power by the eparchs and consistories were severely castigated. The eparchs were described as arrogant and career-minded young monks who looked down on the secular clergy, although they themselves were quite incapable of providing spiritual guidance and pastoral care. In many eparchies, it was said, the practice of transferring priests from one parish to another had become almost habitual. In their memorandum the delegates insisted that eparchial authority must be curbed and greater power given to the assemblies of eparchial clergy, many of which were no longer being convened for fear of the parochial clergy. They also wanted greater independence for individual parishes and suggested that they should be encouraged

to undertake more educational and welfare work. In their assessment of the church's influence on the people these ecclesiastical
deputies were extremely pessimistic. They spoke of a 'decline in
religious feeling' and of the 'cool reserve (of the people) vis-à-vis
the church'. 'The authority of the clergy,' they said, 'seems to be
disappearing more and more' and they suggested that the only
way of preventing a further decline was by convening a church
council without delay.

In the decade preceding the 1917 revolution the Orthodox
Church undoubtedly lost a great deal of ground. During that
period church leaders became politically isolated from the
conservative parties, the ecclesiastical press constantly bemoaned
the clergy's diminishing influence on the peasants, and with
very few exceptions, the progressive intelligentsia looked down on
the clergy with undisguised contempt. By 1914 the Rasputin
scandals, the interference of the Tsar and Tsarina in the most
intimate spheres of church life and, above all, the failure of the
church leaders to introduce long overdue reforms had produced
a situation which was regarded as completely hopeless even by
the eparchs.

Consequently, when the Romanovs were deposed in 1917,
nobody in the Orthodox Church raised a hand to restore the
monarchy or halt the revolution. If proof of the wholesale
disintegration of the empire was still needed, it was furnished by
the fact that the overthrow of the monarchy was welcomed even
by the state church. On 27 February the Synod refused to
condemn the revolution, as requested by the Director General,
N. P. Rayev, and a few months later, on 13 July 1917, it issued
a solemn statement in which it referred to the events of the
preceding February as 'the hour of universal freedom for Russia
[when] the country . . . rejoiced over the new bright days of its
life'.[26]

In all important political issues the Orthodox Church supported
the Provisional Government. Among other things, it issued proclamations and launched appeals to encourage the war effort and
recommended that all socio-economic decisions should be left to
a constituent assembly.

The overthrow of the monarchy led to disturbances among the
parochial clergy in many eparchies. Assemblies often ended in

uproar and in a number of eparchies the clergy announced the deposition of their eparch. At the urgent request of the new Director General, V. N. Lvov, the Synod introduced legislation in June 1917 whereby all eparchs had to be elected by the clergy and laity of their eparchies. Elections were duly held and most of those already holding office were reinstated for the future. Many of the Orthodox clergy held distinctly liberal views at that time and were in favour of the redistribution of the land and the introduction of modern industrial legislation.

But this did not save the clergy from the repercussions of peasant unrest. The peasants frequently took over church and monastery lands, they drove priests from their villages, refused to contribute to their upkeep, and in some cases even subjected them to violence. None the less, this unrest was not really anti-clerical. The peasants were after the land, not the priests.

Although the church and the Provisional Government were agreed on many important aspects of policy, tensions soon developed between them once it became apparent that the Provisional Government regarded itself as a 'purely secular power' with no particular religious allegiance. Its ultimate objective was the complete segregation of state and church and although this constituted no more than a possible future threat in the spring and summer of 1917, it was quite enough for the conservative elements in the church to accuse the new government of 'godlessness'. The fiercest conflict broke out over church schools, which the Provisional Government removed from ecclesiastical jurisdiction on 20 June and placed under the Ministry of Education. Thus the standardisation of primary education was achieved at the expense of the church, whose antiquated educational methods had found few supporters, even among conservative politicians.

The man appointed as Director General by the Provisional Government, V. N. Lvov, was a Nationalist deputy who had headed the Committee for the Affairs of the Orthodox Faith in the Third and Fourth Dumas and was one of the most outspoken critics of abuses in the church. Lvov, who was an extremely energetic Director General and quite as authoritarian as his predecessors, immediately submitted a comprehensive programme of reforms to the Holy Synod. But although his proposals met with the approval of the eparchial clergy, they encountered resistance from the hierarchy. The impetuous Lvov reacted to this opposition by dismissing the Synod early in April 1917 and forming a new one which included four representatives of the secular clergy, two of whom were professors at Orthodox academies. The principal task of the new Synod was to make the necessary preparations for a church council, which was now treated as a matter of urgency.

On 2 August 1917 the All-Russian Church Council was convened in Moscow in the presence of the Premier, Kerensky. It was the first of its kind for over two hundred years, and thanks to the February revolution was far more liberal than had been envisaged by the special preparatory committee set up in 1906. Membership of the council was extended to all eparchs and to two elected representatives of the clergy of each eparchy and three elected representatives of the laity. There were about six hundred members in all, of whom roughly fifty per cent were laymen. All members were entitled to vote but a three-quarters majority of the eparchs enjoyed the right of veto.

During the opening ceremony A. V. Kartashev, who had succeeded Lvov as Director General a few days before, announced that for the time being the Provisional Government would continue to exercise its authority over the church and would reserve its opinion on any proposals put forward by the council for the reorganisation of relations between the state and the church.

On 5 August Kartashev, who was a Constitutional Democrat, changed the office of Director General into a 'Ministry for Creeds'. In doing so, however, he was merely paying lip service to the principle of church autonomy, for the powers of the Director were simply transferred to the minister.

The confused state of Russian affairs and the tensions which existed between the church and the Provisional Government enabled the anti-liberal forces in the council to gain the upper hand, which led to the adoption by the council of a completely unrealistic political posture. Thus, the eparchs openly sympathised with General Kornilov's attempt to stage a counter-revolutionary *putsch*, whereas later a considerable number of liberal clergy and laymen walked out of the council in protest. Even after the Bolshevik coup the council clung to the traditional conception of the Orthodox Church as the 'dominant' religion. In its recommendations to the constituent assembly it continued to demand exemption from taxation for all church property, recognition by the state of the church's laws governing marriage and divorce, compulsory religious instruction at all state schools and the provision of public funds for the support of the church. Thus the council rejected any idea of the segregation of church and state.

But although these resolutions were swept away by the Bolshevik revolution of October 1917, there was one important resolution passed by the council that has remained in force until the present day. This was the decision to restore the patriarchate. In the impassioned debates which preceded this resolution, various spokesmen for the laity and the secular clergy opposed the election of a patriarch on the grounds that the government of the church should be based firmly on the conciliar principle. But in the end, and to the accompaniment of cannon fire from the Moscow batteries, the council decided to place a patriarch at the head of the church, and on 31 October three prospective candidates were chosen by ballot, all of whom held distinctly conservative views: Archbishop Antony (Khrapovitsky), Archbishop Arseny (Stadnitsky) and Metropolitan Tikhon (Belavin). Lots were then drawn and Tikhon, the candidate with the least number of votes in the ballot, was appointed patriarch on 5 November.

Although neither the patriarch nor the council made any secret of their anti-Soviet attitude, the council was allowed to remain in session until September 1918 and as a result of further resolutions passed during that period the patriarch acquired a position of great power within the church, a fact which was to prove extremely beneficial in the coming decades of persecution. The other reforms introduced by the council failed to survive. They had come too late.[27]

The Old Believers and the Protestant sects between the Edict of Tolerance and the October Revolution

The Old Believers and the dissident sects were religious communities whose members had broken away from the Orthodox Church in the course of history. Since, in the eyes of theological tradition and Russian law, they had been called into existence by illegal acts, these communities were persecuted over long periods by both the state and the church before their right to exist was officially recognised. They never achieved equality with the Orthodox Church under the tsarist régime. The Soviets, however, did not discriminate between the different confessions: they persecuted them all with equal tenacity.

Of the dissenting religious communities in tsarist Russia the biggest by far was that of the Old Believers; at the turn of the century they had a following of several millions. But although smaller, the Protestant sects—which came into being in the 1860s —were none the less very important because of the extraordinary speed with which they spread throughout the empire from their stronghold in the Ukraine. It was for this reason that they were persecuted on such a massive scale both by the state and by the established church.

The edict of 17 April 1905, which granted religious tolerance to all religious communities in Russia, brought special relief to the Protestant sects because, under its terms, the law of 1894, which had deprived the 'Stundists' of the right of lawful assembly, was repealed. The term Stundists was originally used by the Protestant sects themselves but was later dropped by them only to be taken up by the Orthodox propagandists, who used it as a generic term to describe the Russian Baptists, Evangelical Christians and all such 'rationalist' or 'protestant' groups. These Stundists were referred to in a circular put out by the Minister of the Interior as 'one of the most dangerous and most harmful factions from both a theological and a political point of view'. The main reason given by the Minister for his assessment was that the sects preached 'socialist principles'. It was not long before this charge was shown to be completely unfounded and in 1905 the Stundists were exonerated of all seditious intent at the special conference held by the Committee of

Ministers. Metropolitan Antony (Vadkovsky) of St Petersburg, who took part in the conference, informed the Council that in their persecution of the Stundists the Orthodox clergy had displayed an unwarranted zeal that was quite unworthy of them.

After the declaration of religious tolerance in 1905 many nominal members of the state church, who had been secret adherents of the Old Believers or dissident sects, were able to leave the Orthodox fold and openly profess their true allegiance. This led, among the Protestant sects especially, to a great increase in missionary zeal. Under the terms of the new law religious communities were allowed to open their own churches, prayer rooms, monasteries, schools and welfare centres. They were even allowed to assemble in public places, which had been strictly forbidden under the old dispensation. During the reactionary period, that was soon to follow, this last concession was gradually withdrawn on the grounds that the Old Believers and dissident sects were trying to convert members of the Orthodox faith, which had remained an offence even after the declaration of tolerance.

The composition and activities of the various communities were defined in the ukase of 17 October 1906, which also granted them the legal rights of corporations. But the authorities were still able to keep a close watch on the Old Believers and the sects and to curb their activities if necessary. Since all communities and all priests were required to register with the authorities, surveillance was a relatively simple matter.

However although the dissenting communities did not achieve equality with the Orthodox Church under the new law, their position was none the less infinitely better than it had ever been before. From 1905 onwards all these religious groups became extremely active. Previously they had had to smuggle their sectarian literature in from abroad. Now they were able to print their own newspapers and periodicals and did so in every part of the empire. They also published a large number of books and pamphlets and held regional and all-Russian congresses in rapid succession. With their great energy and drive the dissenting communities were very different from the rigidly traditionalist communities of the Orthodox Church. But then they had been formed in response to a genuine demand and not by an administrative act. For the dissenters it went without saying that their priests and elders should be elected by the community and that the laity should participate in the administration of the church. It is hardly surprising, therefore, that they should have developed warm human relations with one another. It was this sense of unity, coupled with a rigorous moral code and an absolute abhorrence of drunkenness, coarseness and licentiousness, that constituted the principal appeal of the Protestant sects.

During this period the Old Believers were trying to overcome the many internal divisions which had reduced their movement to a collection of various uncombined groups. By far the most important of these groups was the Convention of Belokrinitsa which founded its own eparchial hierarchy centred on the see of Belokrinitsa in Austrian Bukovina in the early nineteenth century. From 1905 onwards this group was able to consolidate its position and to win back some of its followers, who had broken away as a result of the famous circular letter of 1862. Between 1905 and 1914 the Convention of Belaya Krinitsa built more than two hundred new churches and in 1912 it opened an institute for training priests and teachers at its centre on the Rogozhsky Cemetery in Moscow. One of the main reasons why this particular community was able to achieve so much was that it received both financial support and political protection from a number of its members, who happened to be extremely successful manufacturers and business men.[28]

But although the Old Believers displayed great energy between 1905 and 1917, they were not nearly as active as the Protestant sects. The Union of Russian Baptists, which had existed as an illegal community ever since the 1880s, held regular all-Russian conferences under the leadership of D. I. Mazayev and V. G. Pavlov and supported a missionary society from 1907 until it was closed by the authorities in 1910 for contravening the provisions of the edict of tolerance. By 1917, thanks largely to the activities of the Union of Russian Baptists, the Protestant sects had some 200,000 members, of whom more than 30,000 were Evangelical Christians.

The political attitudes adopted by both the Old Believers and the Protestant sects provoked speculation, suspicion and massive reprisals on the part of the state. The revolutionary intelligentsia

held the view that the dissident communities were engaging
in what Lenin once referred to as 'political protest in a
religious guise' and prompted the Social-Democrats to pass a
resolution at their second party congress calling upon their
members to campaign for the support of the sects. To this end
the Social-Democrats founded a special journal entitled *Rassvet*
(The Dawn) in 1904, though it only ran to nine issues. But the
Old Believers and the dissident sects none the less remained
suspect in the eyes of the state and the state church. Both these
bodies were firmly convinced that the sectarians sympathised,
certainly with the liberals, and perhaps even with the revolutionaries. This was why they were subjected to such severe persecution, which was invariably justified by the Orthodox leaders on
the grounds that the dissenters posed a threat, not only to the
state church, but to the state itself. In point of fact, both the
revolutionary and the Orthodox leaders were quite mistaken. The
revolutions of 1905 and 1917 showed quite clearly that the
dissenters had no extremist political ambitions.

During the municipal strikes and peasant disturbances of 1904–
1905, it is true, a few of the dissident communities felt called
upon to support the revolutionaries but the leaders of the Baptist
and Evangelical christians came out against the use of violence
and were able to persuade their followers to adopt an essentially
moderate attitude. After the proclamation of the October manifesto a group of Mennonites, Baptists and Evangelicals also
formed a short-lived political party that was loosely associated
with the Kadet party. This party—the Union of Freedom,
Truth and Love of Peace—was led by the Mennonite P. M.
Fritsen, and had its headquarters in Sebastopol. The Union's
programme included demands for such things as equal rights
for all religious confessions, universal suffrage based on an
equal franchise and free education for all irrespective of rank.
The Union favoured a constitutional monarchy and opposed the
convention of a constituent assembly. But, despite its impressive
programme, the Union was divided over many issues, both theological and political, and was evidently quite incapable of maintaining a united front over a prolonged period.

After the failure of this first attempt to form a political union
among the members of the Protestant sects, I. S. Prokhanov, a

dynamic churchman with a highly inventive mind, formed in 1908 a Russian Evangelical union, which he envisaged as an inter-denominational body and for which he even sought the co-operation of progressive elements in the Orthodox Church. On this non-sectarian basis Prokhanov hoped to initiate a Russian 'reformation' that would make it possible to avoid the 'bloodshed of fearful and constant revolution'. He wanted to banish revolution and the class struggle by promoting legal reforms but, more especially, by bringing about the 'moral rebirth of each and every individual'.

The political position of the Protestant sects is well illustrated by the statements made by Pavlov in 1917 when he joined the traditional school of Christian socialists, who placed their faith in the power of charity and preferred to appeal to the conscience of the individual rather than try to effect social changes by direct action. 'According to evangelical teaching,' Pavlov said, 'the solution of socio-economic problems must be preceded by a preparatory phase—the revolution of the spirit.'[29]

In the end even the tsarist authorities were convinced that the socio-political views and activities of the Evangelical sects were harmless: both the Ministry of the Interior and various police departments stated on repeated occasions that there was nothing to connect these sects with the revolutionary parties.[30]

The Old Believers adopted much the same sort of approach to politics. Although certain groups—especially among the proletariat—took part in revolutionary strikes and openly sympathised with the socialist parties, the head of the Convention of Belokrinitsa, Archbishop Ioann (Kartushin), declared in December 1905 that the October manifesto had been obtained under duress and that any further attempt to restrict the power of the Tsar must be resisted. On 21 January 1906 a delegation of Old Believers representing a large number of different sects presented a humble address to the Tsar, to which more than 76,000 signatures were appended and which expressed the gratitude of all their members for the religious and political freedom granted to them by the autocrat. At a special congress held in 1906 the Old Believers of Belokrinitsa condemned both the right and left-wing extremists and drew up a political programme which reflected the kind of approach advocated by the Kadets and the Octobrists. Among other things they called for a constitutional monarchy,

fundamental rights, the abolition of class privilege and the redistribution of the land to the peasants with compensation for the
previous owners. This liberal platform provided the basic framework for the political thinking of the Old Believers right up to
the February Revolution.

We see, therefore, that the tsarist régime had no real grounds
for regarding either the Old Believers or the Protestant sects as a
danger to the state. With skilful handling these groups could
easily have become reliable pillars of a constitutional monarchy.
But the reactionary forces in Russia would have nothing to do
with constitutionalism and in their blindness they continually
alienated the dissident sects until they too felt little sympathy for
either the state or the monarchy.

In the provinces the reactionary backlash made itself felt immediately. The local authorities there simply disregarded the
edict of tolerance. They continued to break up Stundist meetings,
arrested and meted out summary justice to presbyters and closed
down the churches of the Old Believers as if Pobedonostsev were
still in power. Later, from about 1908 onwards, the authorities
in the major cities also reverted to repressive and discriminatory
policies. Although the Old Believers were certainly affected by
the new measures—among other things they were barred, under
the terms of a circular letter sent out by the Minister of the
Interior in January 1914, from all teaching posts in state schools
—it was the Protestant sects who provided the real target for
the forces of reaction. They aroused particular resentment because their communities were continually growing at the expense
of the Orthodox Church.

On 4 October 1910 the Minister of the Interior introduced
new regulations governing the conduct of all meetings held by the
dissident sects. These regulations were typical of the restrictive
policy being pursued by the tsarist régime at that time. Under
their terms permission had to be obtained from the governor for
all meetings except divine worship. Consequently, if one of the
sects wished to hold a discussion evening, a reading, a lecture or
even a business meeting, it had to apply for permission on each
separate occasion. Children's services and catechisms were completely forbidden. Furthermore, a police officer had to be present
at all meetings, including prayer meetings.

These regulations made life very difficult for the Protestant sects from 1910 onwards. They were designed to restrict the activities of these religious communities to the holding of divine worship, thus ensuring that they did not appear in public or engage in missionary work of any kind, and preventing their children from receiving any formal religious education. Incidentally, the religious policy carried out by the Minister of the Interior under the tsarist régime corresponded in all essential respects to that subsequently pursued by the Soviets. This is an interesting example of continuity within Russian history that would merit closer investigation.

But despite the wholesale discrimination to which they had been subjected, the Old Believers and Protestant sects were none the less caught up in the wave of enthusiasm which swept the country following the outbreak of war in 1914. This, however, made not the slightest difference to their persecutors, who refused to abandon their repressive policies. In fact, the reprisals taken against the Baptists and Evangelicals were actually stepped up during the war because these groups, who had maintained close contacts with German Protestant settlers in Russia, were suspected of being German sympathisers and even of conspiring with the enemy. They were also branded as pacifists and traitors because some of their members had refused to bear arms on conscientious grounds. Thanks to the reactionary policies of the tsarist régime, the Old Believers and Protestant sects, who had pledged their full support to the monarchy in 1906, unanimously welcomed the overthrow of the Romanov dynasty in 1917.

The outlook for philosophy and the fate of the Slavophil Utopia

HELMUT DAHM

It is well known that Friedrich Engels considered the 'relation-ship between thought and being, between mind and nature' to be the 'supreme question in the whole of philosophy'.[1] This was undoubtedly a grave error on his part and one that has affected the subsequent development of the history of philosophy. Engels classified all philosophical systems which postulate the supremacy of the mind over nature, as idealistic, and all opposite systems, which postulate the supremacy of nature over the mind, as materialistic.

But although it has been effectively demonstrated that this antithetical classification is simply not applicable in the countries of western Europe, it is applicable in Russia since, with very few exceptions, Russian thinkers have eschewed critical realism. Given this, however, the question arises as to whether we are justified in speaking of an independent Russian branch of philosophy.

The argument over Russian philosophy

Reputable Russian historians such as Ernest Radlov (1854–1928; co-editor of the works and editor of the letters of Vladimir Solovyev), Mikhail Gershenzon (1869–1925; editor of the writings and letters of Pyotr Chaadayev), Gustav Shpet (1879–?) and Boris Yakovenko (1884–1948) have emphatically maintained that we are not.[2] According to Gershenzon, nineteenth-century Russian philosophy was made up entirely of ideas borrowed from successive foreign schools. Thus, it faithfully reflected the transi-tion from Schelling to Hegel, from Hegel to Saint-Simon and

Fourier, then the advent of positivism and finally of Nietzsche. In his book, *Fundamental Problems in the Criticism of the History of Idealistic Russian Philosophy*, Viktor Malinin subsequently pointed out that only one philosophical trend was not represented in this 'kaleidoscope' of foreign influences, namely materialism. But as far as the various forms of idealism were concerned, Malinin tells us that in Gershenzon's view the Russian nineteenth-century thinkers had made no independent contribution to their development.[3] This deprecating attitude, which was shared by other Russian bourgeois historians, was forcefully stated by Yakovenko in his *Outlines of Russian Philosophy*, where he wrote: 'Everything that Russia possessed and expressed in the sphere of philosophical thought was produced either as a conscious imitation or as a result of the unconscious assimilation of foreign influences or by a process of selection. . . .'[4]

All that these bourgeois critics were able to discern in Russian philosophy was a pale, trivial and vulgar reflection of the full-blooded and original philosophy of western Europe. As Malinin has pointed out, 'not only Yakovenko but Shpet, Radlov and Gershenzon considered it right and proper to regard the subject matter of Russian philosophy (at one particular stage in its development) as a derivative of French philosophy and (at a later stage) as a derivative of German philosophy. For, according to them, not only were there no independent philosophical ideas [in Russia], but the discussion of western European ideas, although conducted with passionate enthusiasm, was not calculated to produce a national school capable of original philosophical thought. We may say, therefore, that for Yakovenko, Shpet, Radlov, Gershenzon and other bourgeois historians of Russian philosophical thought there could not be a specific science devoted to the history of Russian philosophy because, in the strict sense of the word, there was no history of Russian philosophy.'[5]

Those who adopted this extremely derogatory attitude were supported in their view by a man of great eminence and unquestioned authority: Vladimir Solovyev (1853–1900). In Part III of a review of the works of Danilyevsky and Strakhov, which was published in 1888 under the title 'Russia and Europe', Solovyev dealt with the question 'What has Russian philosophy achieved?' His answer was far from encouraging: 'During the last two decades writings of greater or lesser seriousness and interest have appeared in Russia on a variety of philosophical subjects. But everything that is philosophical in these works is completely un-Russian whereas everything that is Russian has nothing whatsoever to do with philosophy and, in some cases, is completely unsubstantiated. We are unable to detect any real signs of an independent Russian philosophy; everything that has laid claim to independence has turned out to be a mere pretence.'[6] Solovyev contended that up till then the Russians' undoubted talent for speculative thinking had been demonstrated only at a receptive level: 'Although we have understood and assimilated foreign philosophical ideas extremely well, we have not produced a single important philosophical work because we have either been satisfied with fragmentary schemes or have subscribed to the extremist and unbalanced ideas of European thinkers.' In Solovyev's opinion, the fact that Nikolay Stankevich (1813–40) and his associates had adopted the Hegelian viewpoint was an indication that Russian thinkers lacked the 'positive drive' that was needed if they were to develop an original philosophy: 'This philosophical movement of select minds (of the 1830s and 1840s), which began in such splendour and with such high hopes, has ended—from the point of view of philosophy at least—with literally nothing.'

Malinin considered this 'severe judgement' to be unobjective only in so far as it 'swept away the materialist tradition' along with everything else and because it formed the basis for 'Solovyev's own pretence' that the 'beginning of . . . Russian philosophy could be dated to the precise point of time when his own mystical-philosophical works had appeared.'[7] But there are a few Soviet historiographers who have tried to reconcile the disturbing phenomenon of Vladimir Solovyev with the Marxist view of Russian philosophy and who have interpreted his works in accordance with Marxist criteria. In their *History of Russian Philosophy*, Anatoly Galaktionov and Pyotr Nikandrov concede that Solovyev, who was undoubtedly the most important of the nineteenth-century Russian philosophers, created a 'metaphysical system of integral knowledge', in which the 'synthesis of knowledge philosophy and religion is presented as man's highest duty and the ultimate objective of all intellectual development'. They also refer to Solovyev's 'large and thematically complex literary heritage', which included translations into Russian of foreign works such as Kant's *Prolegomena* and a number of Plato's Dialogues. In their concluding remarks these two Soviet writers point out that Solovyev's system found many imitators and was already being compared with Marxism in the last decade of the previous century. It seems that the members of the *Vekhi* group were influenced by Solovyev.[8]

From theosophy to phenomenology

In 1877, in its March, April, June, October and November issues, the periodical published by the Ministry of Education in St Petersburg printed Solovyev's 'Philosophical Principles of Integral Knowledge'. In the second part of this work, subtitled 'On the Three Types of Philosophy', Solovyev defined 'free theosophy' as an 'organic synthesis of theology, philosophy and the science of experience'. The proposed synthesis covered a very wide range, but this Solovyev regarded as essential if it was to produce 'true integral knowledge'. However, he considered that this wider synthesis had to be preceded by a narrower synthesis, which would unite the three basic trends within the philosophical sphere, namely: empiricism (with its affinity to the science of experience), rationalism (with its affinity to philosophy) and mysticism (with its affinity to theology). According to Solovyev's 'general analysis' the 'subject' of this 'integral knowledge' was 'that which truly is', not only 'within itself' but also 'in its relationship to the empirical reality of the subjective and objective world', in other words the 'absolute principle of that world'. From the relationship of 'that which truly is' to 'empirical reality' Solovyev developed the three fundamental components of his philosophical system of integral knowledge: 'For if two elements, namely the absolute principle and the second reality arising out of that principle, form the subject matter of philosophy, these two elements can only be conceived in three relationships. First, in direct unity, secondly, in antithesis [to one another] and, thirdly, in actual, differentiated [recognised] unity or synthesis. Thus, we acquire three philosophical sciences: the first of these considers the absolute principle in its own general and necessary terms, which embrace their opposite, namely finite and contingent existence. . . . The second [philosophical science] considers the absolute principle as that which produces or brings forth, outside of itself, finite reality. . . . And, finally, the third [philosophical science] is concerned with the absolute principle as that which reunites the finite world in actual, systematic unity.' The 'condition of direct unity' corresponded to 'organic logic', the 'condition of disintegration' to 'organic metaphysics' and the 'condition of reunification or synthesis' to 'organic ethics'.

Solovyev regarded theosophy as the logical, theocracy as the ontological and theurgy as the ethical components of this total organic system. Like Marx in his Feuerbach treatises, he considered it was not enough 'to look upon the absolute totality of being as a [mere] idea'. He argued that, unlike earlier generations, 'the new world' could not 'restrict itself to contemplation', it had to 'live and act with the force of the divine principle [which had been manifested in the world] by refashioning itself after the image and example of the living God'. According to Solovyev, this active 'collaboration between the deity and humanity [which was designed] to raise humanity from its corporeal or natural condition to a condition of spirituality and godliness' did not involve an original act of creation or 'creation from the void' but merely the theurgical transformation of the world for the purpose of 'transforming matter into spirit'.

In his *Biographical Sketch* Ernest Radlov pointed out that 'Solovyev completed only *one* part of his philosophical system, namely the ethics.' Not surprisingly, we find that ethical questions loomed large in his *Critique of Abstract Principles* (1877–1880). Solovyev's interest in ethics was promoted by the conviction that it was only through morality that man could approach the absolute. Consequently, when Sergey Bulgakov maintained that Solovyev's ethics were not particularly original and represented the Achilles' heel of his philosophy, he was really saying that Solovyev's whole philosophy was of little or no consequence. Radlov did not agree and pointed out that in Solovyev's view, man constituted the essential 'link between two worlds' (namely, between personal and universal being on the one hand and empirical reality on the other): 'God and creation must unite in man, which is why both the life of the individual and the historical development of humanity are essentially meaningful.'⁹

But by the time he came to write his most important work, *The Justification of the Good* (1894–8), Solovyev regarded ethics as a completely independent discipline and not simply as an appendage to religion or theoretical philosophy. He justified this view in the opening pages of his new work by providing a phenomenological description of the feelings of shame, compassion and reverence, which he subsumed under the general heading of feelings of sympathy and defined as the 'principal components of morality'. Despite religion and theoretical philosophy, Solovyev contended, man would be incapable of moral actions unless his nature was structured in such a way as to allow objective goodness to impinge on him. From this he argued that moral philosophy—by which he understood the objective assessment of the ethical relationship between the individual and his environment—must be based on an analysis of the 'fundamental moral factors in man's consciousness', for it was man's feelings of sympathy that determined his relationship to all things. Thus, his attitude to everything inferior to himself (all material things) was regulated by his sense of shame; his attitude to everything equal to himself (his fellow-men), by his sense of compassion; and his attitude to everything superior to himself (God) by his sense of reverence. As for man's ability to recognise in the objective factors present in his own feelings of sympathy the universal and necessary principles underlying all morality, this was vouchsafed by his power of thought.

And so, at the end of *The Justification of the Good*, Solovyev summarised his thesis as follows: 'These feelings [of sympathy] and the sense of conscience to which they testify contain the corporate or, to be more precise, the tripartite basis of the process of moral perfection. Reason, which is a derivative of conscience, gives universal validity to the impulses emanating from [man's] good nature and raises them to the status of a general law. [And so] the content of the moral law is simply an abstraction of the factors present in man's good feelings which appears in the form of a universal and necessary (or binding) demand or commandment.'

Consequently, Solovyev maintained, man's 'moral duty must

lie in the perfection of the factors present [in his good nature]',
which means that his relationship to the tripartite value datum
has to be 'transformed' into an appropriate 'norm of mental
and volitional activity'. In other words: 'Man's preordained
subservience to the highest power must be changed into a conscious desire to serve [the cause of] perfect goodness; his natural
sense of solidarity with his fellow men must develop into active
collaboration based on sympathy and understanding; and his
inherent superiority over physical nature must be transformed into
a rational control of nature, both for his and for its sake.'

In his *Theoretical Philosophy* (1897–9) Solovyev applied the
phenomenological approach—which he had already used in *The
Justification of the Good* for the investigation of man's feelings
of sympathy and which had been preceded by a draft version of
an *ordo-amoris* theory in *The Meaning of Love* (1892–4)—to the
basic principles of cognition. His chief concern at that time was
with the immanent contents of human consciousness. Previously
Solovyev had subscribed to the Cartesian view that cognition presupposes not only perception of external forms, but also of
essences, on the grounds that 'that which truly is' forms the real
basis of human consciousness and consequently the basis of
thought. ('Je vois très clairement que pour penser il faut être.')
But in his *First Principles of Theoretical Philosophy* (1897)
Solovyev criticised the Cartesian view: 'The evidence of the immanence of consciousness as an inner fact does not vouchsafe the
external reality of the objects which impinge on consciousness.
But then is it not [also] impermissible to deduce from the fact of
consciousness the actual reality, the special and independent
essence or cognitive substance, of the subject who possesses this
consciousness? Descartes considered such a conclusion to be both
permissible and necessary and, until now, many [including,
amongst Russian thinkers, Lev Mikhailovich Lopatin (1855–
1920)] have agreed with him. For a while I too subscribed to this
view, in which I now detect a crucial fallacy.'

Thus, in Solovyev's later view, the feeling of self-certainty
induced in the individual by the fact of consciousness did not
provide any reliable guarantee of the reality of either the subject
or the external world. In putting this argument Solovyev was not
trying to deny that the fact, or the objects, of consciousness

possessed a certain phenomenological reality. But he insisted that this phenomenological datum did not necessarily presuppose the existence of a subject conceived as an initiator of ideas: 'The pure subject of thought is a phenomenological fact which is neither more nor less credible than any other [fact]; in other words, although it certainly exists, it exists only as a content of consciousness or as a phenomenon in the strictly literal sense of the word.' Thus, the subject in the act of thinking appeared, not as the originator of ideas or states of consciousness, but merely as their passive and insubstantial centre. And Solovyev insisted that nobody was entitled to attribute unequivocal certainty to this subject or, for that matter, any degree of certainty that exceeded the 'limits of its phenomenological condition'. For no matter how many different states of consciousness were associated with this static centre 'it in no sense follows that this "ego" is not [merely] a thought but something different,' namely the real or sufficient cause of its ideas or states of mind. From this Solovyev concluded that he was only ever conscious of himself as the subject of his psychic states or affects and never as their substance. Consequently, he maintained, there 'are no grounds for attributing to the subject of consciousness as such anything but a phenomenological reality'.

From the psychic certainty of consciousness and the facts of consciousness Solovyev advanced via the logical certainty of formal abstract thought to the phenomenological certainty of the personal mind which 'transforms thought into the emerging reason of truth'. The relationship underlying this concept of the 'emerging reason of truth' was that between the pure subject of thought as a phenomenological fact on the one hand, and the insubstantiality and transintelligibility of the total person as the mode of existence of the spirit on the other. In short: it was the actual dimension of the potential field of intentional phenomenology.

In Solovyev's moral philosophy the points of reference for this dimension were provided by those objects whose immanence and structure tend to promote the feeling functions of shame, compassion and reverence. In acts of thought and volition these objects are transformed into intentional objects of truth and goodness and consequently into ideas. 'Ideas as objects or as the content of that which is' embrace on the one hand 'objects of contemplation for us' (in other words, all objects of perception, both our own and other people's, which are relevant to the theory of knowledge and which can be related to a psychic ego) and on the other hand 'subjects of existence as such'. In this second sense, namely as subjects, ideas are phenomenological, they are 'what the person who is wants, what he imagines, feels or senses'; they are 'his actual object or content'. Through his partial acts of will, imagination or feeling, which merge with one another because of the affinity of love and perception within the total act of loving, the person who is actually becomes 'the subject or vehicle of ideas'. Initially he had no more in common with Being than the ideas. Both 'receive their being only as a result of their reciprocal relationship or interaction,' for 'in themselves' they merely constitute 'forces of Being'.

And so we find that whereas will, reason and feeling are component forces of a unifying spirit, the objects of whose intentional acts appear as 'various forms of love', the 'vehicle of an idea, or that idea as a subject, is a person'. For the 'vehicle of this idea or its subject (to be more precise: the idea as subject) has to distinguish itself from others [other vehicles] subjectively or existentially; in other words, it must possess its own separate reality and be its own independent centre. Consequently, it must possess self-awareness and a personality.' If this were not the case, in other words if 'the ideas were distinguished merely objectively, merely in terms of their recognisable properties, and not in terms of their inner Being, then they would simply constitute concepts for another [person who is] and not real essences, which, as we know, is unacceptable.' Thus, the proposition that a person who is becomes the vehicle of an idea (as a result of the existential illumination of its knowledge-transcending centre in its acts of volition, imagination and feeling) appears as the phenomenological definition of the mind: concrete mind, in other words 'a process of thought' which refers 'in the [very] act of thinking' to an object (purposiveness), becomes a person as a result of volition, imagination and feeling or, alternatively, as a result of the total act of loving, for 'every being is what it loves'. 'This notional person or this idea that has become a person is merely one individual form of the total system of multiplicity in unity, which is indivisibly present in all of its individual forms.'

The passages quoted above show beyond all doubt that the ideas evolved by Solovyev, especially in the seven-year period from 1892 to 1899, anticipated the essential methodology of German phenomenology. His *Meaning of Love* appeared twenty-one years before Max Scheler's eleven treatises on the *Overthrow of Values* (*Umsturz der Werte*, 1915) while his *Justification of the Good* (1894–8) pre-dated Scheler's *On the Phenomenology of the Feelings of Sympathy* (*Zur Phänomenologie der Sympathiegefühle*, 1913) by fifteen years and Scheler's major work *Formalism in Ethics and Objective Moral Philosophy* (*Der Formalismus in der Ethik und die materiale Wertethik*, 1913–16) by eighteen years. But most important of all was the fact that Solovyev's essays on *Theoretical Philosophy* (1897–9) were completed two years before Edmund Husserl's *Logical Investigations* (*Logische Untersuchungen*, 1900–1), which are generally regarded as the starting-point of phenomenology.

However, this is not the popular view of Solovyev. Both bourgeois Russian scholars, such as Vasily Vasilyevich Zenkovsky 1881–1962) and Nikolay Onufrievich Lossky (1870–1965),[10] and Soviet scholars have failed to appreciate his revolutionary significance. Only Wladimir Szylkarski (1884–1960) has referred to this aspect of his work, to which I had drawn his attention. In the postscript to Volume VII of the German edition of Solovyev's collected works Szylkarski stated: 'In the second and in part of the third chapter [of his *Theoretical Philosophy*] Solovyev developed thoughts which anticipated the essential ideas underlying German phenomenology—two years before the publication of Husserl's *Logical Investigations* and independently of Bolzano and Franz Brentano, whose 'objectivist' philosophy of Essences and Being was extremely important for Husserl's phenomenology.'[11]

But in his commentary on the *Theoretical Philosophy* Szylkarski cancelled out this positive assessment. There he maintained that if Solovyev's new ideas are carried to their logical conclusion, they must inevitably 'lead to great difficulties in the construction of the Christian conception of "multiplicity in unity" ', to which Solovyev had always subscribed. This criticism was prompted by Solovyev's statement that man is only ever conscious of himself as the subject of his psychic states and never as their substance.

Szylkarski—who was evidently ignorant of Scheler's intentional phenomenology—interpreted this as a 'denial of the substantiality of the human soul'.[12] In actual fact, of course, Solovyev attributed the 'emerging reason of truth' to the *philosophical* subject, which he distinguished both from the *empirical* subject or soul and from the *logical* subject or intellect. And the '*philosophical* subject in the real sense' he defined as spirit.

Commenting in his *Critical Introduction to the Philosophy of Max Scheler* on the insubstantiality of the spirit, which he distinguished from 'anthropological impersonalism', the religious philosopher Johannes Hessen wrote: 'If . . . modern theory rejects the conception of the person as a substance which stands behind human acts, it is perfectly right to do so. But it does not follow from this that the person is simply a "link mechanism" for its acts. If this were the case, the person would simply be a mosaic of acts, whereas in actual fact it is the real unifying principle of those acts.'[13] In his book *On the Phenomenology of the Feelings of Sympathy*, Scheler himself stated that spiritual persons are by no means devoid of substance. On the contrary, they are 'act-substances' and, as such, are in fact the 'only substances which possess a genuine individual nature and whose diversity of *Dasein* derives in the first instance from their individuated *Sosein*'.[14]

By now it should be clear that Solovyev was not the mystic he has been made out to be and that anybody who still insists on classifying him as such cannot possibly have understood his writings. Ludolf Müller's observation that the German philosopher especially should ask himself whether it would not be simpler to study Schelling's works at first hand rather than read them in a Russian adaptation[15] loses its point once Solovyev's work is considered from a phenomenological point of view.

The sudden shift in Solovyev's thinking produced a certain amount of irritation amongst his contemporaries, which led to misunderstandings. As a result Solovyev was accused of anthropological impersonalism and pantheism. Zenkovsky, for example, stated that he did not find 'the greater prominence accorded by Solovyev to impersonal motifs particularly surprising' in so far as his general outlook had 'always been pantheistic' and 'revealed the influence of Spinoza'. Mochulsky and Lopatin, for their part, considered that Solovyev's new doctrine contradicted the whole of his earlier philosophical system.[16]

Yevgeny Ryshkov, the Soviet scholar, holds a very similar view. In an article published in the Moscow periodical *Nauka i religiya* in November 1968 he stated that initially 'Solovyev placed all his energy and knowledge in the service of the religious conception of universal salvation.' But Ryshkov then went on to outline Solovyev's subsequent development, which appeared to him to constitute a direct antithesis to his early phase: 'But life destroyed the illusions which Solovyev had created and induced in him a growing sense of disappointment and alienation from earthly pleasures. In the end Solovyev realised that his hopes for the realisation of the "kingdom of God" on earth were vain and would come to nothing. With this, life lost all meaning for him. His fear of death, which had never left him, was transformed into a fear of life, a fear of the future.'[17]

Incidentally, Ryshkov spoke highly of Solovyev as a philosopher and is the first Soviet scholar to attach importance to his work. He opened his article with the following appreciation: 'Of the many names in the history of philosophy there are few as illustrious as that of the Russian idealist and theosophist Vladimir Sergeyevich Solovyev.... That is why Solovyev's writings are also of interest to us atheists. We have to examine Solovyev's ideas and, by subjecting them to the Marxist philosophical method, trace their earthly origins and establish their actual significance and their position [in the history of philosophy].'

The new religious philosophy

In the preface to a series of articles, published in 1903 under the title *From Marxism to Idealism*, Sergey Nikolayevich Bulgakov (1871–1944) wrote: 'I must confess that for me Kant was always less dubious than Marx. That was why I considered it necessary to check Marx by reference to Kant and not vice versa.' Bulgakov's object in making this comparison was to establish 'an acceptable form for the positivist doctrine of economic materialism' and 'to free it from its absurdities'. His preference for Kant will doubtless have been due in part to the influence of Solovyev, for in a study which he produced on his compatriot in the same year he wrote: 'Solovyev's philosophy offers the contemporary mind a total and consistent Christian *Weltanschauung*.'[18]

But unlike Pyotr Berngardovich Struve (1870–1944) and Nikolay Alexandrovich Berdyayev (1874–1948), with whom he had previously been associated in the 'legal Marxist' movement, Bulgakov soon abandoned the new philosophical orientation which he had adopted in the early years of the century. Immediately following the breakdown of tsarist society he made a radical switch to a theological view of the world. In *Quiet Thoughts*, a collection of articles published in Moscow in 1918, Bulgakov suggested that, with his wide and unusual mystical experience, Solovyev was 'far more important, original and interesting as a *mystic* than as a *philosopher*'. Between these two assessments of Bulgakov's lay the epoch of the 'new religious philosophy'. For Bulgakov himself the peak of this development came between 1911 and 1916 when he was writing his *Immortal Light*,[19] which appeared in Moscow in 1917 and in which he turned once again to the slavophil-theosophical conception of 'multiplicity in unity' which Solovyev had discarded as a spent force during his final phenomenological phase. *And so the opportunity created by Solovyev of establishing a new realistic school of Russian philosophy that would have been capable of breaking away from theology and asserting its independence by evolving a sound and convincing methodology remained unexploited because nobody had recognised it.*

On 31 July 1900 Vladimir Solovyev died in the arms of his friend Sergey Nikolayevich Trubetskoy (1862–1905), on the estate of Uzkoye. Sergey Trubetskoy, who was then Professor of the History of Ancient Philosophy at Moscow University, became the first elected rector of the University on 2 September 1905 and subsequently acquired a reputation as a liberal politician. He and his younger brother Yevgeny Nikolayevich (1863–1920), who was Professor of the Philosophy of Law in Kiev and later in Moscow, were appointed literary executors for Solovyev's early writings (from the 1870s and 1880s). They also managed the literary estate of Kireyevsky and Khomyakov, editing their writings on the slavophil-theosophical conception of 'multiplicity in unity', in which both ecclesiastical and national considerations played their part.

In his own works—*Metaphysics of Ancient Greece*—(dissertation for Master's degree in 1889), *On the Nature of Human Consciousness* (1889–91), *The Foundations of Idealism* (1896) and *The Doctrine of the Logos in History* (dissertation for Doctorate in 1900)—Sergey Trubetskoy tried to reconcile the autonomy of the individual human consciousness with the 'impersonalism' of 'universal consciousness' by evolving a metaphysical system based on an absolute essence. Unlike Hegel, however, he did not identify thinking and being. This philosophical system, which Lapshin described as 'concrete idealism' or 'critical metaphysics', is summed up in Trubetskoy's 'hypothetical' formulation that 'consciousness' can be neither 'impersonal nor personal (individual)' because it is 'more than personal', namely 'integral' (*soborno*). Consequently, in all our ethical and theoretical acts we 'maintain within ourselves the link (*sobor*) with all things'. The conception of the 'integral character' (*sobornost*) of consciousness, which Sergey Trubetskoy developed into an individual system of 'metaphysical socialism', also constituted one aspect of 'communal personalism' (*kommyunitarny personalizm*)' which Berdyayev used at a later date, and of Lossky's supposedly 'intuitive' but in actual fact 'constructive' view that 'everything is immanent in everything'.

While Sergey Trubetskoy was content to write a 'biography of Solovyev (which was published by the Moscow *Vestnik Evropy* in 1900), Yevgeny Trubetskoy produced a work in two volumes, *The Philosophy of Vl. Solovyev* (which appeared in 1913). Yevgeny's two dissertations (for his Master's and Doctor's degrees) were devoted to 'The Socio-Religious Ideal of Western Christianity in the Fifth Century' (Augustine; 1892) and the 'Eleventh Century' (Gregory VII; 1897). These publications were followed in 1917 by *Metaphysical Assumptions of Knowledge: An Attempt to Come to Terms with Kant and Kantianism* and in 1918 by Yevgeny's major philosophical work, *The Meaning of Life.*[20] This development gives a clear indication of Yevgeny's spiritual affinity to the slavophil-theosophical conceptions of the new religious philosophy. Not surprisingly, therefore, he paid little attention to Solovyev's *ordo-amoris* theory, his objective moral philosophy or his phenomenology. Consequently, the claim made by Yevgeny in his *Metaphysical Assumptions of Knowledge* that his thinking was 'directly and consistently in

line with Vl. Solovyev's *Theoretical Philosophy* and constituted
an attempt to 'carry out the exact programme announced by
Solovyev' was largely unfounded.

In his *Theoretical Philosophy* Solovyev developed certain ideas
which he had first stated in his *Lectures on the Divine Principle
in Man* (1877–81) and so arrived at his conception of the philosophical subject as the living form of the spirit. Later, in his
Metaphysical Assumptions of Knowledge and his *Meaning of
Life*, Yevgeny Trubetskoy sought to clarify the relationship between conditional or human consciousness and unconditional or
absolute consciousness. He argued that 'every act of cognition is
an assertion that a specific content of consciousness is true, i.e.,
unconditional' and consequently that the quest for truth consists
of 'seeking unconditional consciousness in my own consciousness'.
Thus, 'unconditional consciousness' appears as a precondition
which, although unable to explain 'the origin of cognition, does
confirm its existence'.

From the striving of conditional knowledge after unconditional
truth Yevgeny Trubetskoy assumed the participation of human
consciousness in an unconditional or absolute consciousness,
whose reality he considered to be vouchsafed by the fact that
without such participation true cognition would be impossible.
Since 'all temporal phenomena really are given enduring form
in unconditional consciousness, either there is a truly unconditional consciousness that regards both the past and the future in
an infinite realm or else the whole of the temporal world is a lie.'

In his development of the philosophical subject as the living
form of the spirit Solovyev had also considered this argument and
rejected it. His phenomenological approach, which he first outlined in the *Philosophical Principles of Integral Knowledge* and
the *Lectures on the Divine Principle in Man* and subsequently
amplified in *The Justification of the Good* and the *Theoretical
Principles*, was firmly based on the intentional nature of man's
relationship to objects. But if objects can be apprehended by intentional acts and if all acts, no matter how disparate, have their
origin in the being of a person, then it follows that any world that
is conceived as a totality of intentional objects must be the
world of a person. Thus, the personal counterpart to the cosmos
would be furnished by what Max Scheler called 'the conception

of an infinite and perfect spiritual subject, whose acts would be given for us in intentional phenomenology in accordance with the conditions governing its essence' (which would of course apply to the acts of all conceivable persons). But, as Scheler subsequently pointed out, 'we would never be prompted to form this conception of God by philosophy but only by a more concrete person who was in direct contact with something corresponding to this conception and whose concrete being would itself be "given". Thus, the reality of "God" is invariably grounded in a possible manifestation of God, [i.e.] in a concrete person.'[21]

These views of Scheler's, which had been anticipated in all essential respects by Solovyev, were based on the ontological links between acts and objects, between the individual person and the world, between God and creation. But Yevgeny Trubetskoy seems not to have noticed these phenomenological links. He regarded the relationship established by Solovyev between God and creation—which arises by analogy with the correlation between the individual and the world—as a pantheistic amalgam of the absolute and the essence of the world. In order to correct this pantheistic aberration and draw attention to the radical difference between God and creation he insisted that, although God was the omnipresent centre of the world and of its evolution, he was 'not its subject'. Yevgeny Trubetskoy argued this view, which led away from phenomenology towards transcendental philosophy, not only in his *Metaphysical Assumptions of Knowledge* and *The Meaning of Life*, but also in his two-volume work, *The Philosophy of Vl. Solovyev*.

At the same time as Bulgakov and the brothers Trubetskoy were evolving their religious philosophy, a 'new religious spirit' began to emerge, which was prompted in the first instance by the need to overcome the antinomy between secularist decadence and historical Christianity. This new spirit found expression in the neo-romanticism of the younger Berdyayev and in the utopian 'religious community', which was proclaimed by Dmitry Sergeyevich Merezhkovsky (1865–1940) and his followers (Ternavtsev, Gippius, etc.) and was conceived in terms of Solovyev's 'free theocracy'. Both these movements formed a link between the Russian neo-Kantians and Russian metaphysical transcendentalism.

The best known representatives of the Russian neo-Kantian movement were Alexander Ivanovich Vvedensky (1856–1925), Georgy Ivanovich Chelpanov (1863–1936), and Ivan Ivanovich Lapshin (1870–?).

Between them, the cognitive approach of the neo-Kantians and the ontological approach of the new religious philosophers provided the necessary basis for metaphysical transcendentalism, whose principal exponents were Pavel Ivanovich Novgorodtsev (1863–1924), Pyotr Berngardovich Struve (1870–1944), Boris Petrovich Vysheslavtsev (1877–1954) and Ivan Alexandrovich Ilyin (1883–1954). Boris Yakovenko (1884–1948) and Fyodor Stepun (1884–1965) occupied a position midway between the neo-Kantians and the transcendentalists. There was also a Russian Leibniz school, which was led by Alexey Kozlov (1831–1901) and Nikolay Bugayev (1837–1903) and from which a personalist movement subsequently developed under Lev Mikhailovich Lopatin (1855–1920) and a pan-psychist movement under Sergey Alexeyevich Askoldov (1871–1945). Nikolay Lossky (1870–1965), who later founded Russian intuitionalism in conjunction with Semyon Lyudvigovich Frank (1877–1950), also belonged to the Leibniz school during his early phase. The theosophical metaphysics of the great sophiological systems of Sergey Bulgakov, Semyon Frank, Lev Platonovich Karsavin (1882–1952) and Pavel Alexandrovich Florensky (1882–1943), which also owed much to Solovyev, were evolved from intuitionalism, although they did not assume their final form until after the overthrow of the Romanov dynasty.

By and large, the representatives of these idealistic trends tended to close their ranks in opposition to the often naïve positivism of the Russian 'scientific philosophers', who were entirely empirical in their approach, would not hear of metaphysics and insisted on the relativity and historicity of all knowledge. The best known of the academic spokesmen for this movement were Vladimir Viktorovich Lesevich (1837–1905), Nikolay Yakovlevich Grot (1852–99), Ilya Ilyich Mechnikov (1845–1916) and Vladimir Ivanovich Vernadsky (1863–1937). Their positivism and the naturalism of a number of leading Russian scientists—such as the physiologists Ivan Sechenov (1829–1905) and Ivan Pavlov (1849–1936), the chemist Dmitry

Mendeleyev (1834–1907) and the botanist Kliment Timiryazev (1843–1920)—acted as a ferment for the anthropocentrism of Nikolay Chernyshevsky (1828–89), Pyotr Lavrov (1823–1900) and Nikolay Mikhailovsky (1842–1904), which was to make such an enduring impression on the radicals and Socialist Revolutionaries. The unmistakable influence exerted by these socially critical trends, especially on the Russian students, led to concerted resistance on the part of various secular and scientifically-minded groups to the autocratic and Orthodox régimes, which was subsequently exploited by Marxist thinkers like Georgy Valentinovich Plekhanov (1857–1918), Vladimir Ilyich Lenin (1870–1924) and Alexander Alexandrovich Malinovsky-Bogdanov.

But at the turn of the century this social criticism provoked an idealistic reaction, which appeared quite spontaneously and assumed one of two forms. There were those who sought to revive Solovyev's theocratic conception while others were fascinated by the highly individualistic ideas of the 'Russian Nietzsche', Vasily Vasilyevich Rozanov (1856–1919), whose biocentric aphorisms with their sexual, metaphysical and psychopathic connotations exerted a considerable appeal at that time. In the spheres of cultural philosophy and anthropology Rozanov espoused the views of Konstantin Nikolayevich Leontyev (1831–91) but in the religious field he went very much his own way.[22] In St Petersburg in 1901 Merezhkovsky organised the first public discussions of religious and philosophical questions, which were reported in the periodical *Novy put*. These were followed, after certain initial difficulties had been overcome, by the founding of Religious and Philosophical Meetings in St Petersburg, Moscow and Kiev.[23]

It was at about this time that the *Bogoiskatelstvo* or 'Search for God' was instituted. Most of the members of this movement, who included Berdyayev, Bulgakov, Filosofov, Gippius, Merezhkovsky and Minsky, were centred around the St Petersburg Religious and Philosophical meetings and publicised their views in various periodicals: *Novy put* (St Petersburg 1903–4), *Voprosy zhizni* (St Petersburg 1905), *Vesy* (Moscow 1904–9) and *Pereval* (Moscow 1906–7). The 'Godseekers' argued that the Marxist doctrine was a distorted form of religion and consequently could only be overcome by 'true' Christianity, in other words by a new form of Christianity that had been set free from the restrictive influence of the historical and institutionalised church. Thus, while opposing revolutionary secularism, the Godseekers also indulged in social criticism on their own account. Their 'true' Christianity, incidentally, was based on a new interpretation of Solovyev's *Lectures on the Divine Principle in Man*.

Although this movement had little to do with philosophy, it proved so effective and caused such a stir that during the 're-actionary period' (1907–10) a section of the Social-Democratic intelligentsia considered it necessary to compete with it on its own terms and so founded a new 'religion without God'. The principal spokesmen for this atheistic trend—who were known at the time as the 'God builders'—were Vladimir Alexandrovich Bazarov-Rudnev (1874–1939) and Anatoly Vasilyevich Lunacharsky (1873–1933). For a while Maxim Gorky (Alexey Maximovich Peshkov; 1868–1936) was influenced by their ideas.

The ever-increasing polarisation of Russian philosophical and sociological thought into an idealist and a materialist camp had its origins in a development of the late-nineteenth century. The Russian 'intelligentsia', who are defined in the Soviet Philosophical Encyclopedia as a 'social group made up of persons concerned in a professional capacity with intellectual work', had evolved from the *raznochintsy*, who had come into prominence in the course of the 1860s. These *raznochintsy* were intellectuals 'from different social classes' who played an important part in the ideological and political struggle against the tsarist autocracy of their day. Initially, the political and social ideas adopted by this group were based on nihilist and anarchist theories but subsequently these were displaced by populist and Marxist conceptions. By the end of the nineteenth century revolutionary populism (*narodnichestvo*) and Marxism were firmly established and commanded the support of the socially and politically active sections of the educated classes of Russia. At the same time positivism and materialism began to dominate the philosophical sphere, atheism (or indifference) the religious sphere, utilitarianism the ethical and aesthetic spheres and democratic or critical realism the sphere of social protest.

In 1901 Berdyayev published a book entitled *Subjectivism and Individualism in Social Philosophy*, for which Struve wrote a very long and detailed preface. This joint production, which announced the transition from positivism to metaphysics, outlined a programme for a series of future books to be undertaken on a collaborative basis which were designed to protect the state against seditious doctrines. The first of these, *Problems of Idealism*, was published in Moscow in the following year. This work, edited by Pavel Novgorodtsev and furnished with a brief preface by Lopatin, contained contributions from twelve different authors including the philosophers Askoldov, Berdyayev, Bulgakov, Frank, Novgorodtsev, Struve and Sergey and Yevgeny Trubetskoy.

Essentially, this anthology constituted an attempt to come to terms with recent trends in positivism and to defend metaphysics in religious-metaphysical terms. It assigned only a limited function and consequently only a limited significance to the science of experience, rejected dogmatic judgements in favour of the critical approach developed by students of the theory of knowledge, denied utilitarianism by insisting on absolute principles and stressed the importance of morality for the understanding of idealistic philosophy.

These arguments were, of course, by no means new. Boris Nikolayevich Chicherin (1828–1904), who held that no really important questions in the sphere of political theory could be solved without recourse to philosophy, and Vladimir Solovyev, had already subjected positivism to similar criticisms in the 1870s. But in his introduction to the second edition (Paris 1967) of the anthology *From the Depths* (Moscow 1918), in which he provided a comprehensive review of the three most important literary products of the 'intellectual renaissance in Russia', Nikolay Poltoratsky maintained that there was none the less a considerable difference between these two periods, since by the early years of the twentieth century idealism was no longer being considered in purely philosophical terms but in close conjunction with social and political questions.[24]

Problems of Idealism was followed by *Signposts* (Moscow 1909), in which Mikhail Gershenzon and six other authors, including the philosophers Berdyayev, Frank and Struve, tried to win over the Russian intelligentsia, whose philosophical and sociopolitical beliefs had been severely undermined meanwhile, and to secure their support for the state.[25] 'The intellectual attitude,'

Berdyayev observed in his article on the theoretical truth of the philosophers and the practical truth of the intelligentsia, 'needs to be reformed, and philosophy has been chosen to play the not insignificant part of the cleansing fire in this important operation. It would seem from a detailed analysis of the relevant historical and psychological factors that the Russian intelligentsia can only acquire a new mental attitude from a synthesis of knowledge and belief. Only a synthesis of this kind would be able to gratify the positive need felt by the intelligentsia for an organic link between theory and practice, between "real truth" and "real justice".'

Struve took a similar view. In his article, which dealt with the essential connection between man's belief and his sense of responsibility, between his philosophical and political attitudes, he suggested that the 'apostasy of the Russian intelligentsia [and their defection] from the state' was the 'key to the [correct] understanding of the revolutionary movement both in the past and in the present.' Although he conceded that the majority of the people considered that the kind of attitude adopted by the intelligentsia to religion could not possibly have any effect on political developments, Struve contended that this view was based on a fallacy. In his opinion, it was by no means 'accidental that—in the inner sense with which we are concerned —the Russian intelligentsia were *both* irreligious *and* politically fanatical, unobjective and frivolous. They were credulous but had no faith, they worked hard but were uncreative, they were fanatical without enthusiasm, intolerant without reverence. In a word: they displayed all the outer forms of religion but none of its inner meaning. Although this contradiction is encountered in every materialistic or positivist form of radicalism, nowhere is it as pronounced as in the case of the Russian intelligentsia. Radicalism or maximalism can only be justified by revering and serving some higher principle.'

In his memoirs Frank stated that the contributors to *Signposts* had planned to publish a further collection of articles in the following year (1910), in which their new philosophy would have been expressed in *positive* and programmatic terms. (Previously, of course, their writings had been more concerned with the negative aspects of revolutionary and secularist thought.) In the event, however, this project was not carried out.

After being appointed Governor of Grodno in 1902 and of Saratov in 1903, Pyotr Arkadyevich Stolypin (1862–1911) became Minister of the Interior under Goremykin in April 1906, and finally, in July of the same year, Prime Minister. He remained head of the tsarist government until he was shot by the Socialist Revolutionary Bogrov during the interval of a gala performance at the Kiev Opera. Four days later, on 5 September 1911, he died from his wounds in the Makovsky hospital.

The death of Stolypin put an end to the aspirations of the religious-philosophical thinkers. Their hopes of an intellectual revival and socio-political reforms that would have lent stability to the constitutional monarchy, were completely dashed by this tragic event. Stolypin's daughter, Maria Petrovna Stolypina-Bok, explained the reasons for this in the closing pages of her *Recollections*. She tells us that by 1911, although her father had then been in power for some five and a half years, his ideals had not really taken root: 'They had not yet been absorbed by the Russian people. And once he was dead, the whole edifice that he had created fell to pieces.'[26]

The festivities held in 1913 to commemorate the 300th anniversary of the founding of the Romanov dynasty, were staged in the artificial atmosphere of 'marble palaces', full of illusion and self-deception. In this calm before the storm of the First World War, when the court and the aristocracy were living in the eye of a hurricane, the sedition then rampant throughout Russia caused no apparent concern to those most affected. In his memoirs, published under the title *In the Marble Palace*, Grand Duke Gavriil Konstantinovich analysed this condition of paralysing uncertainty and dark foreboding with considerable perspicuity: 'I gained the impression that the jubilee of the House of the Romanovs was greeted without any special enthusiasm. And it seems to me that the reason for this was that the revolution was already in the air at that time. Of course the invited audience in the theatre shouted hurrah and the orchestra played the [tsarist] hymns. But the mood of the people was very different. Everything was conducted in a bureaucratic manner and one did not have the feeling that the whole Russian nation had joined together to celebrate the anniversary of the dynasty.'[27]

Five years later, after the overthrow of the monarchy, the

authors of the third book published under the auspices of this
group of religious-philosophical thinkers, who had been opposed
both to the utopian rationalism of the revolutionary intelligentsia
and to the irrationality of the monarchy, could only try to explain
what had happened and why. The collection of articles on the
Russian revolution of 1917, edited and compiled by Struve
under the title *From the Depths*, was printed by the Kushnarev
publishing house in Moscow and was ready for despatch to
booksellers by the autumn of 1918. But due to the wave of
Bolshevist terror that followed Kaplan's unsuccessful attempt
on Lenin's life, the anthology (which contained articles by
eleven authors including the philosophers Askoldov, Berdyayev,
Bulgakov, Frank, Novgorodtsev and Struve) could not be distributed at that time, and when it did eventually appear in 1921,
sales were almost entirely restricted to Moscow.

These were the three chief phases of the religious-philosophical
renaissance in Russia. The point of departure for this development was provided by the critique of positivism (*Problems of
Idealism*, 1902). This was followed, after the revolution of 1905,
by a critique of philosophical and political secularism and radicalism and a defence of the intellectual and moral foundations of the
state (*Signposts*, 1909). Finally, the Bolshevik coup of October
1917 prompted a critique of the atheist ideology and a defence
of the religious principles underlying social and cultural life.
According to Poltoratsky this development marked the 'transition
in socio-political terms from the residue of legal Marxism to the
national philosophy that was later described as "conservative
liberalism" or "liberal conservatism".'

The cadre of the religious, philosophical and socio-political
renaissance movement in Russia was formed by four philosophers:
Nikolay Berdyayev, Sergey Bulgakov, Semyon Frank and Pyotr
Struve. The fact that they, and they alone, contributed to all
three of the anthologies described above will scarcely have been
accidental. Incidentally, these four men had already revealed
their commitment to the new movement at the turn of the century
when, under the influence of Solovyev's writings, they were
'converted' from materialism to idealism. Like Yevgeny Trubetskoy, however, they failed to perceive the change in Solovyev's
thought which took place in the 1890s when he abandoned his

philosophy of integral knowledge in favour of phenomenology and advanced from a theocratic conception of the state to a new ethic based on natural morality. And so the opportunity of creating a school of Russian philosophy that would have been independent of both theological and theocratic considerations was missed. Instead of embarking on this new venture, the Russian philosophers of the early twentieth century reverted to the traditional conception of a Slavophil Utopia. Inevitably, this had an adverse effect on the development of Russian social and political life, for it blinded the conservative leadership to the real extent of popular discontent and persuaded the monarchy that it was far more powerful than it actually was, with the result that the Tsar refused to entertain even legitimate demands for reform.

Although the shadow of the great Solovyev lay over the contrasting philosophies of idealism and materialism which dominated this period, the reception accorded to western philosophy by the modernists was so stereotyped that any specifically Russian contributions to philosophical thought made at that time were almost entirely disregarded. The article on philosophy in the nineteenth volume of the *Great Encyclopaedia* (Ed. Sergey Nikolayevich Yuzhakov; 1849–1910) accurately reflects the kind of attitude adopted in Russia to original native thinkers, for the only Russian achievements listed in this article are translations of philosophical works by foreign authors. Thus, one result of the new importance attached to traditional theosophy by the twentieth-century religious-philosophical thinkers was the revival of the antithesis between Slavophil and western thought.

The more recent antithesis between the increasingly speculative intuitivism of the religious-philosophical school on the one hand and the 'strict objectivity' claimed by the positivist school on the other, assumed such proportions that it appears to have blurred the perceptive faculties of contemporary philosophers. Consequently, we find that even Gustav Gustavovich Shpet (1879–?) and Alexey Fyodorovich Losev (born 1893), who were disciples of Husserl and the only representatives of phenomenology in tsarist Russia, failed to perceive the revolutionary significance of Solovyev's work, although some of the ideas advanced by Shpet in his theory of personality were in fact very similar to those expressed by Solovyev in his *Theoretical Philosophy*.

Another equally incomprehensible and no less serious omission on the part of the early twentieth-century Russian thinkers was their almost total neglect of philosophical anthropology, whose essential principles had also been anticipated by Solovyev in a variety of works including *The Meaning of Love* (1892–4), *The Justification of the Good* (1894–8), *The Life of Plato* (1898) and *The Three Conversations* (1899–1900). The living core of this magnificent ethic is to be found in the revolutionary stipulation that man is 'on no account to be regarded as a means to an end for others'. He should not be used 'either for the benefit of another person or for the benefit of a whole class or for the so-called common good, in other words for the benefit of a majority of other persons'.

Significantly, contemporary Marxist writers, who are opposed to the existing socialist régimes in eastern Europe, are making the same sort of demands today. They are now trying to make good the deficiencies of philosophical anthropology at the turn of the century—which passed unnoticed by the leaders of the intellectual renewal movement in Russia until it was too late— by pressing arguments which clearly show that they too are determined to defend man as the 'principal criterion', as 'an end in himself and never as a means'.[28] The similarity between the social conditions obtaining then and now is obvious. Incidentally, this also seems to be the reason why present-day Marxist thinkers are beginning to show a greater interest in Solovyev's anthropological writings.

In 1905 Viktor Ivanovich Nesmelov (1863–1920), a Professor of Religious Philosophy at the Theological Academy in Kazan, published a two-volume work on the *Science of Man*, which was based in all essential respects on the ideas formulated by Solovyev in his *Lectures on the Divine Principle in Man* nearly thirty years before. By contrast, Solovyev's objective moral philosophy, which he evolved in the 1890s and which was completely independent of both theology and theoretical philosophy was not mentioned by Nesmelov.

It was only after the calamitous events of the First World War had shown the full extent of the terrifying malaise of Russian society that contemporary thinkers began to consider the problem of human existence in the kind of terms suggested by Solovyev.

Berdyayev, especially, focused his attention on questions of personal ethics. His book, *The Meaning of Creation*, which appeared in Moscow in 1916, was the first recent attempt to establish a justification of man. In his preface Berdyayev explained why he had undertaken this task: 'Many justifications of God, many theodicies, have been written. But now the time has come to write a justification of man, an anthropodicy. Perhaps an anthropodicy is the only way to approach a theodicy, the only way that has not yet been tried and is still open to us.'

Both Berdyayev and Lev Isakovich Shestov (Shvartsman; 1866–1938) embarked on this anthropological experiment, from which they developed a form of religious existentialism after their emigration to western Europe. Berdyayev's major works in this field were: *On the Destiny of Man* (Paris 1931), *The Fate of Man in the Modern World* (Paris 1934), *Selfknowledge* (Paris 1945) and *The Existential Dialectic of the Divine and the Human* (Paris 1952) while Shestov is best known for *The Power of the Keys* (*Potestas Clavium*; Berlin 1923), *Kierkegaard and Existential Philosophy* (Paris 1939) and *Speculation and Revelation* (Paris 1964). It is worth noting in this connection that I. F. Balakina, the Soviet researcher into the history of philosophy, has also traced Russian existentialism to Solovyev.[29]

It only remains for us to assess the importance of this period of Russian philosophy and to compare it with the Marxist ideology of the Soviet period.

This is best done perhaps by recounting the story of Mihajlo Mihajlov, a young Yugoslav philosopher who visited the Soviet Union in the summer of 1964 when he was employed as an *Assistent* in the Philosophical Faculty of the University of Zadar, Croatia. After his return Mihajlov wrote a critical report of his visit under the title 'Moscow Summer 1964', which was accepted for publication by the Belgrade periodical *Delo*. But the first part of this report, which appeared in the January 1965 issue of *Delo*, was far too truthful for the Yugoslav authorities, who confiscated the entire February issue, which contained the second part, and forbade the editors to print the third. They also had Mihajlov arrested. Later, after his release, the Jugoslav weekly *Tošović* (a supplement to the newspaper *Politika*) carried an unsigned article, in which Mihajlov was accused of denigrating the Soviet Union and branded as an 'agent of White Russian and anti-Communist circles'. Mihajlov responded to this attack with an open letter to the editor of *Tošović* in which he said: 'I make no secret of the fact that I consider Vladimir Solovyev, Shestov and Berdyayev to be more profound thinkers than any of the Marxist philosophers writing today. Nor do I deny that I regard myself as a Christian and that in my opinion only Christianity, as a free religion, offers a [viable] basis for a just social order on earth. By contrast, the so-called "inevitable laws" of "scientific" socialism are not suitable for this purpose.'

Mihajlov's choice of philosophers from the period when Russia was entering the twentieth century could not be bettered. Nor could his assessment of their importance as compared with their Marxist successors.

Russian literature from 1890 to 1917

ELISABETH STENBOCK–FERMOR

I serebryany mesyats yarko Nad serebryanym vekom styl

Anna Akhmatova

'And the silver moon rose brightly over the silver age.'[1] There is a double meaning in these lines: *mesyats* means both moon and month, and *vek* means primarily a century, though it is also used in the meaning of 'historical period'. Anna Akhmatova wrote 'Poem without hero' (*Poema bez geroya*) in the 1940s about a winter night of 1913. As the last great survivor of the literary circle described in her poem, she knew that the 'silver age' did not last long, and died a violent death.

Before he returned to Russia, where he perished in one of the purges, Prince D. Svyatopolk-Mirsky stated about the writers of that period: 'One may dislike their style, but one cannot fail to recognise that they revived Russian poetry from a hopeless state of prostration and that their age was a second golden age of verse inferior only to the first golden age of Russian poetry—the age of Pushkin.'[2] Yet if we open a contemporary Russian textbook on the history of Russian literature, we find the following statement about the same writers: '. . . their creative works as a whole signified the lowering of high artistic values and the morbid degeneration of art.'[3] A chapter which speaks of these writers is entitled 'Prose of bourgeois decadence'. In another we find 'Poetry of bourgeois decadence' with 'Symbolism, acmeism, futurism' as a sub-title.[4] In a book published in 1964, which recognises certain positive aspects of the new trend, we read the statement that it was 'an expression in literature of the social forces of the old decayed world', a counter-attack of the bourgeois camp against democracy, and therefore of lower quality than the 'critical realism' of the same period.[5]

It seems strange that having finally granted recognition to many great writers of the more distant past, literary historians in the Soviet Union still repeat the half-a-century-old clichés condemning the 'modernists'. As late as 1946 Zhdanov affirmed that 'all these "fashionable" trends vanished into Limbo and were dumped into the past together with the classes whose ideology they reflected.'[6]

In the period which interests us, we deal with two main groups of writers. One was old-fashioned and believed that one could express new radical social opinions while sticking to the old and hallowed literary genres tested by the realists of the recent past. The other was a new group of daring innovators, who rebelled against the old forms and subject matter of literature. Some writers who belonged to the first group, for whom the principles established by Belinsky, Dobrolyubov, Chernyshevsky and Pisarev were sacrosanct, also felt the urge for something new, and searched for new devices without accepting a definitely new theory. For most of them their literary trend was part of their *Weltanschaung*. A few representatives of both groups achieved success and even fame in their lifetime; their reputation spread abroad. Then, by decree of a new administration, one of the groups, the one which continued the older trend of faithfully rendering only certain aspects of material reality with the aim of propagating definite political opinions, was pronounced progressive. The other group, which attempted to renovate art by expressing the reality hidden behind the sensuous world, was declared reactionary, and persecuted as such. One of its ramifications, futurism, was permitted to survive for a short time because it identified revolution in literature with social revolution.

In a recently published book on Russian literature, the authors admit that though 'modernism, decadence, and symbolism' represented a tendency which actively opposed socialism, they gave birth to lasting artistic achievements, but the most important event of the period was the emergence of Gorky and 'revolutionary romanticism'.[7] We will, of course, examine both groups as well as writers who cannot be completely identified with any of them, e.g., Chekhov. The aim of this chapter is to describe the literary trends of this particular period, independently of the social and political opinions of the authors and their subsequent role in the world of politics and letters. We will start with the second group.

Symbolism, acmeism, futurism

The literary movement which became controversial in the early nineties was in the making earlier. This was one of the assertions of D. Merezhkovsky in his famous lecture of 1892, entitled 'On the Causes of the Present Decline and the New Currents in Contemporary Russian Literature'.[8] This lecture is usually accepted as marking the emergence in Russia of the new trend later designated under the names of 'modernist', 'decadent', and 'symbolist'. The term 'symbolist' is the one Merezhkovsky used. His book of poems published after the lecture was entitled *Symbols*. He saw signs of symbolism, which for him was synonymous with idealism, in contemporary writers of many countries. He was certain that all the great writers of which Russia was legitimately proud were great in so far as they had kept their faith in a mysterious and unattainable ideal. They had implied, in their realistic descriptions of human life, the existence of a higher and more important reality linked to the visible world, as a symbol is linked with the concept it symbolises.

The word 'decline' (*upadok*), as used by him, referred to the works of contemporary writers who refused to acknowledge these values and stuck to photographic representation of the visible world, and to rational, scientific explanation of whatever could be perceived by the senses. They simply denied anything that did not fit into this category, even though it was 'felt' by men. For Merezhkovsky materialism and positivism were responsible for the decline of letters, and he welcomed any sign of idealism reborn.

The new movement was at first identified with the already existing French literature of *decadence*. By preserving the French term in Russian as *dekadans* and later giving it a russified form, *dekadenstvo* with its derivatives *dekadent, dekadentsky*, the Russian representatives of the trend seemed to stress that they did not take the word in its literal meaning (which in Russian would be expressed by *upadok*—'downfall') but as a literary genre. This genre came into being at the end of the millennium, —and this was also accepted as a symbol—when an uphill trend in the material and intellectual development of culture had reached its peak, had hit a wall of dissatisfaction and unfulfilled hopes, and could only start downhill or on a search for new roads. The new generation was expressing both its despair and this search for new roads towards new vistas in philosophy and art.

But by translating the word *decadence* and using its Russian equivalent *upadok* and its derivative *upadochny*, which means something morally weak and of poor quality, the enemies of the new poetic school finally created a confusion which became prevalent in the Soviet Union and spread abroad. An article by Gorky written on the occasion of the death of Verlaine in 1896 accuses the French 'decadent' poets and their followers of physical and moral degeneration.[9] V. Solovyev's articles and parodies of 1894–5, which ridiculed the Russian decadent extravaganza and Tolstoy's condemnation of French and Belgian contemporary poets in 'What is Art?' are a proof that *dekadentstvo* and the symbolist school of literature were confused and frequently identified with each other. In Russia, we can find the term 'decadent' applied to all the authors of the first half of the twentieth century who can be classified as individualists. An article by Frid, 'Socialist Realism and Contemporary Decadent Literature', includes Valéry, Camus, and D. H. Lawrence in the list of decadents.[10]

In 1901, A. Bely and A. Blok, future representatives of the younger generation of symbolists, lived under the spell of Solovyev's philosophy and poetry. They knew, of course, how he had ridiculed the decadents a few years before his death, but for them and for many who had joined the new movement there was much more in it than a desire to startle the public, or morbidly enjoy one's own weaknesses, as it could seem from the early poems of V. Bryusov. The first Russian decadents had mainly imitated a French literary school, but as their movement gained impetus they turned towards the principles which gave birth to that school and to signs of similar principles in neglected Russian poets and German romantic philosophy. They considered that Merezhkovsky had been right when he described the new trend as idealism returning to fight the positivism that had ruled over literature for a long period.

The beginnings of the symbolist school are well known. First came articles and poems of little-known poets in two reviews,

'Russian Wealth' (*Russkoye Bogatstvo*) and 'The Northern Messenger' (*Severny Vestnik*). Then the lecture and poems of Merezhkovsky mentioned earlier, and above all, in 1894, the bombshell of Valery Bryusov's 'Russian Symbolists' (*Russkiye simvolisty*). This was a literary hoax, as he signed by different names poems of which he was the author. He remained ostracised for several years, because of these stormy beginnings. The public and publishers could not help feeling that his poetry was the product of deliberate intellectual composing rather than the sincere expression of faith in the revelations of symbolism. In the meantime, other poets achieved recognition. They found in the Russian language and background the necessary raw material for expressing the emotions created by a new concept of reality, a reality so different from the old tangible one that it needed new devices and a new form to put words describing it into organised sentences.

Bryusov's mastery and versatility were vindicated later, but for several years, the most popular poet was Konstantin Balmont (1867–1943). His musicality and virtuosity in using refined techniques of rhyme and rhythm without breaking with the classical pattern of syllabic-tonic verse conquered the public without shocking it. He was as prolific as he was shallow. There was just enough longing for the vague, beautiful and hopelessly distant eternal truth in his melodious poems to keep emotions alive, and not enough despair to awaken a feeling of sacred horror. His poems in the collection *Let's be like the Sun! (Budem kak solntse! Kniga simvolov)* sounded like an optimistic trumpet breaking through the minor key of the *fin de siècle*. His translations from various literatures, though often inaccurate ('The Raven' by Edgar Allan Poe is one of the most successful) helped to create the feeling of kinship with other cultures which was to become one of the important features of Russian symbolism.

Merezhkovsky's wife Zinaida Gippius (1869–1945) and Fedor Sologub (F. Teternikov, 1863–1927) belong also to the so-called older generation of symbolists. Their art, both in poetry and prose is deeper than Balmont's or Merezhkovsky's. They do not rely exclusively on the singing quality of verse, beloved by the symbolists who remembered Verlaine's rule: *de la musique avant toute chose*. But they struggled to find the right word.

They reached the reader's emotions by the combined effect of several devices: rhythm, sound, and image. The accusation of being 'morbid' which is still applied to the decadents and symbolists as a whole, refers mostly to these two, because Bryusov's morbidity, even 'necrophilism', lacks the sincerity which would make it effective. Gippius was also a first-rate critic (she signed her clever and often biting articles Anton Krainy). Sologub's novel *The Little Demon* (*Melky bes*) proved that in the probing of man's devious and repulsive instincts Dostoyevsky's *Notes from the Underground* (*Zapiski iz podpolya*) could be surpassed in horror if not in depth. It is remarkable that Sologub, whose chief preoccupation in the choice of subjects seemed, according to Mirsky, to be 'dark and cruel evocations of the evil diversity of the world', could also write the most delicate love poems. His cycle of poems on the imaginary Don Quixote-Dulcinea relationship is the work of an idealist of the highest order.

Another symbolist writer who belonged to the older generation but joined the group late because of his studies abroad, is Vyacheslav Ivanov (1886–1949). His amazing erudition, his refined taste and genuine mysticism (he died a Roman Catholic monk in 1949) made him the leader and teacher of the St Petersburg group of symbolists who met in his penthouse on Wednesdays to read poetry and discuss philosophy. He wrote a series of perfect sonnets. His work on Dostoyevsky brought a new insight into the possibilities of interpretation of the great novels. While the radical critics had long ago tried to write off Dostoyevsky as an exponent of reaction and religious obscurantism, the symbolists followed Solovyev, Merezhkovsky and Ivanov and saw in Dostoyevsky a precursor and even a prophet.[11]

In the first years of the twentieth century the symbolist movement was important enough to have several branches, each with a distinct philosophy. There was by that time the Muscovite group headed by Bryusov, and the religious philosophical circle of the Merezhkovskys, who lived in St Petersburg but spent much time in Moscow and abroad. Besides his poems and still valuable articles on Tolstoy and Dostoyevsky, D. S. Merezhkovsky (1865–1941 was the author of a trilogy of historical novels built around the antithesis of Christ and antichrist. Its second part, 'Leonardo da Vinci', was immensely popular and immediately translated into many languages. The historical background of the novels permitted the creation of romantic situations and colourful settings, in harmony with the aesthetic revival of the period. He was also able to use this background to formulate his belief that world history moves between opposing forces of good and evil, asceticism and joy of life, Christ and Dionysos, and that supreme harmony can be achieved only if they merge. Thus the poetical device of contrasts and juxtaposition of opposites favoured by the symbolists was carried by Merezhkovsky into the sphere of metaphysics: form and subject matter merged. Merezhkovsky's dichotomy was however rather superficial, as is evident in his next trilogy which attempted to recreate the era of Paul I, Alexander I and the Decembrists. It was popular mainly because it was a forbidden subject. As to the syncretic role of poetry—the mystical value of art, the concept of the poet as an intermediary between the Absolute and men, and therefore of the supreme importance of every aspect of the poet's verbal creation—these principles were developed more success-fully by Ivanov and the next generation of symbolists. The affirm-ation of the identity of form and content was taken over later by the formalist school of literary criticism, but without its mystical foundation.

In 1902 the Merezhkovskys founded a review, *The New Path* (*Novy put*) with a 'decidedly mystic and religious character'.[12] One of the contributors was Bryusov. Two years later Bryusov was himself the head of a purely symbolist review, *The Scales* (*Vesy*). Thus through ambition, stubborn work, and talent, he became leader of the new school, as had been his dream from the first. He was not, as many had thought, a freak; he was very well-educated, knew several languages, and had become well-acquainted with foreign literatures, and he was genuinely interested in poetics. His erudition—of another kind than Ivanov's, who was particularly versed in the classics of antiquity—took the form of an amazing accumulation of knowledge. Since 1894 he had continued to study, had published new books of verse, contributed to a serious historical review, and finally become an important collaborator in the publishing house Scorpion, which specialised in new poets. He was a first-rate organiser. His own poetry, written in meticulously polished verse, proclaimed the pre-eminence of poetry in its own right, without any regard for moral, religious, or political loyalties. In this he disagreed with several important symbolists, who also polished their verses as well as their prose, but for whom art never ceased to be a manifestation of the divine. Bryusov proclaimed that 'perhaps all in life is only a means for bright melodious verse.' He also wrote prose novelettes in which he displayed his capacity for assimilating foreign cultures. He was a poet who never ceased to theorize, and both Bely and later Gumilyov, the exponent of a new theory, considered him their teacher in the art of versification.

1900 marked the death of Vladimir Solovyev, the man who was to become the spiritual father of the two most important writers of the period: Andrey Bely and Alexander Blok. His parodies of their extravagantly decadent forerunners were a proof that the movement had been taken into account: not all extravagant poetry obtains that treatment from a noted philosopher and literary critic.

Solovyev had been a nihilist in his youth, later, after an emotional shock, a mystic. He became a brilliant lecturer who promoted the cult of Dostoyevsky at a time when no one else did. In 1881 he had incurred the censure of the administration and had to resign from his position at the university because he publicly disapproved of the execution of the murderers of Alexander II. He was a man of faith and a theologian (his faith and theology are still being debated) who strove towards a union of churches. The actual presence of another world beyond the material world was for him a certitude of which he could speak as a logician in lectures and treatises, and as a poet in his verse. Good and evil for him were separate entities, but the limit between flesh and spirit was not clear, and could merge in love. His critical essays brought to the public's attention neglected poets of the nineteenth century: Tyutchev, Fet and A. K. Tolstoy, who had been scorned by the radicals as adepts of 'art for art's sake', which was not exactly true. While Bryusov was still defining the life of a poet as a search for 'combinations of words' even at the price of martyrdom, but without any other definite aim, Solovyev's poems were infecting the 'younger symbolists' with the belief that being a poet was a priestly vocation.

Andrey Bely (Boris Nikolayevich Bugayev, 1880–1934) became a writer in the home of Solovyev's brother. The influence of Solovyev's metaphysics on the young Bely is undeniable, but it is Bely, the stylist, who has an important place in Russian literature. By 'style' I do not mean exclusively the way he used language to produce new effects, or his brilliant but seemingly irrelevant digressions. He wrote novels on burning contemporary themes and succeeded in giving profound historical meaning to a sequence of events that ran in various directions through a labyrinth of symbols. His two main novels are *The Silver Dove* (*Serebryany golub*) and *Petersburg*. The characters in the latter are direct descendants of the heroes of nineteenth-century novels. The background and participant is the capital of the Russian empire whose literary genealogy started with Pushkin's grandiose evocation in *The Bronze Horseman*. The city became the stage for a devil's tricks in Gogol's stories, a nightmarish town in Dostoyevsky's imagination, and the citadel of social evil for Tolstoy. All these aspects of the city are in Bely's novel, but for him St Petersburg is above all an illusory, senseless, gigantic madhouse built of geometrical figures. The high official in *Petersburg* (A. A. Ableukhov), is a development of the type represented by A. A. Karenin in Tolstoy's novel. He has the same initials and his last name reminds us of Karenin's ears (ear—*ukho*) which suddenly shocked Anna. Like Karenin, he is abandoned by his wife and turns into an official automaton, seemingly heartless yet adoring his son. Bely builds his novel around the impossibility of communication between such a father and his grown-up son, a 'superfluous man' of the twentieth century, who gets involved in terrorist activity and has to plant a bomb in his father's apartment. In *The Silver Dove* Bely uncovers the darkest recesses of Russian peasant society, and shows the peasants in murderous conflict with another 'superfluous man'. It is impossible to give an idea of the wealth of images, symbols, literary reminiscences, comic and dramatic interpolations accumulated in Bely's prose. It is closely linked with the art of Gogol and Dostoyevsky. His poems are less important, but Bely's deep insight into Gogol's art was a revelation. He is also the author of a theory on the musical quality of the Russian iambic tetrameter and its dependence on the place and number of true stresses. This opened the road to all subsequent analysis of the subject. He was the most important exponent of the symbolist theory. This survey is too short to enumerate all his works, but it should be remembered that most of the best prose of the revolutionary years and even later is indebted to Bely.

The other, and greatest, poet of this generation was Alexander Blok (1880–1921). He discovered Solovyev and symbolism only after he had himself written hundreds of verses without giving much thought to the literary school which should claim them. In 1910 he wrote an article on Solovyev the title of which, 'Knight—Monk' (*Rytsar—monakh*), points to the medieval source of Blok's inspiration. The neo-Platonic doctrine of Sophia (God's wisdom), which was part of the Byzantine heritage in Russian Orthodoxy, blended for the symbolists with the romantic Eternal Feminine worshipped by Solovyev. It was exactly what Blok needed to give substance to his youthful dreams of ideal love.

Blok's 'Verses about the Beautiful Lady' (*Stikhi o Prekrasnoy Dame*) which he himself considered somewhat similar to Dante's *Vita Nuova*, were published in 1904. At first the Eternal Feminine could be incarnated in his bride, later in any other woman, or blend with the vision of an unearthly being which represented the Russia of past centuries and future tribulations. No matter what he wrote about, his lyrical reaction to the event, and the poetical expression of it, were for him of ultimate and exclusive importance. Even when he did not mention his own emotions, when he seemed to be simply describing an accident or social ills, he was in fact suggesting to the reader his own poetic interpretation of the event. His poetry also expressed his premonitions of impending doom, of moral decline for himself, and later of a cataclysm threatening his individual world as well as Russia —for example *A Voice from the Chorus* (*Golos iz Khora*). His growing dissatisfaction with the life he was leading finally drained him of all creative energy. When the revolution came, he fastened to it his eschatological hopes of a new, better world to be born after the collapse of bourgeois culture. His last great poem 'The Twelve' was written on that subject in January–February 1918.[13] Symbols transform the frightening and real incident of a group of drunken men—shooting at random, killing a prostitute, planning burglaries—into the presentation of the metaphysical meaning of a historical catastrophe. To achieve this, Blok uses all the means upon which the symbolists had elaborated in previous decades: variety of rhymes and rhythms, alliterations, repetitions and a deliberate vagueness, unfinished statements or hints, and sentences which can be variously interpreted.

Thanks to notes in Blok's diary, we know that the conception of 'twelve men and poems' as a poetic unity was planned from the first, and that a line from a ballad by Nekrasov about twelve robbers, as well as a probable allusion to the repentant robber in the Gospels, were the axis around which the imagery of the poem revolved. Ten years earlier Blok had adapted for the Russian stage Rutebeuf's 'Miracle of Theophilus' in which a repentant sinner composes a poem of twelve stanzas to honour the twelve Apostles without mentioning them. Nekrasov's ballad tells us that the robber's sins were forgiven only when he killed a wicked landowner who was the scourge of the countryside. Seen from that angle, the figure of Christ, rejected by the Twelve yet leading them towards a goal they do not themselves realise, is explainable: the Twelve were destroying a world that was more criminal than they were. We know from Blok's poems and letters that the Revelation of St John was for him the highest poetry, and that an apocalyptic vision of the world ending in fiery destruction was familiar to him.

As a versifier, Blok broke all the accepted rules and created new ones. The purely tonic versification popularised by him prepared the road for the masterpieces of Akhmatova and the innovations of the futurists.

His theatre consists of 'lyrical dramas' and a play with the symbolic title *The Rose and the Cross* (*Roza i krest*), whose prevailing theme is Joy equals Suffering. The plays are not important *per se* but they required very special stagecraft to express their symbolism and irony. In an era which carried the Russian theatre from Stanislavsky's productions of Chekhov's plays, via interpretations of pure symbolism to Meyerhold's experiments, they left their mark.[14]

Although Blok remained a symbolist to the end, symbolism as a leading poetic school was dead by 1910, and he knew it. When he published his *Verses about a Beautiful Lady* or his next series of poems, people did not ask for interpretation: they understood the message. A poetic line, though nebulous in meaning, stirred up a wave of emotions; the intellectual generation of the period seemed to be attuned to the same key and reacted in the same way. Bely and Blok had not yet met, but when they read each other's poetry they simultaneously wrote to each other and discovered that they were in complete understanding on matters of poetic technique as a means of expressing metaphysical beliefs. Then the spell broke. The crisis of symbolism became obvious when a member of the group, M. Kuzmin, complained of the lack of clarity in symbolist poetry. N. Gumilyov replaced the motto 'clarism', suggested by Kuzmin, with 'acmeism', and a new school was born which would be made famous by two more names: Osip Mandelshtam and Anna Akhmatova.

A new review entitled *Apollon* published the poets' literary discussions and manifestos. The creation of a Society for the Promotion of Belles-lettres (Obshchestvo Revnityelyey Khudozhestvennogo Slova) was a sign that the intellectuals were in search of a new principle to guide them for poetic expression. Nikolay Sergeyevich Gumilyov (1886–1921) found his teachers in the French *Parnassiens*. He created the Guild of Poets (*Tsekh Poetov*) which he wanted to perform the double activities of publishing house and writers' academy. He believed in the exotic in art, travelled through Africa, and used all the imagery and legendary reputation of distant or ancient lands to glorify courage and even hopeless struggle. His poetry had distinctly martial overtones, and even though it holds premonitions of an early death there is no confession of weakness in it. Following his own poetic principles, he chose his words carefully, used them with parsimony, and obtained amazing effects through clashes of sounds, rhythm, and the juxtaposition of names of distant cities, evocations of tropical nature and heroic deeds. Some of his poems, 'The streetcar that lost its way' (*Zabludivshisya tramvay*) and 'The Worker' (*Rabochy*), carry the reader into the world of nightmares, but he never abandons his rule of speaking in terms of tangible objects.

He volunteered during the First World War, and was executed by the Communists in 1921. Part of his poetry was found outside the USSR and his complete works have been published in the west.

Osip Emilyevich Mandelzshtam (1891–1938) is more classic in form, and much of his inspiration derived from classical literature: Homer, Ovid, Tibullus and Catullus. He is sometimes cryptic, because his familiarity with antiquity and literature in general fills his poems with allusions and situations which are alien to the uninitiated, but a single line may be saturated with such powerful emotion through the use of a few meaningful words, that the rest is accepted as one accepts music, without trying to understand at once. Some of his best poetry is devoted to the city of St Petersburg. Much of it has been lost. Whatever remains of his poetry and prose is proof of an outstanding mastery of verbal means. Like Gumilyov's and Akhmatova's works, it is being published outside Russia.

The same mastery, joined to deliberate conciseness and simplicity in the choice of poetic vocabulary, is the distinctive feature of Anna Akhmatova (1888–1966), for seven years Gumilyov's wife, and first published in his review *Sirius*. By 'simplicity' I mean that she was never afraid of using colloquial expressions and phrases that were considered non-poetical to convey the fleeting emotions of a woman's intimate life. Her greatest achievements belong to the next period, and cannot be discussed here. Her formative years, however, were in the 'silver age'. She was first recognised as a great poet by Vyacheslav Ivanov, who was not inclined to leniency whether the poet was man or woman. The three collections which made her name famous before the October revolution are *Evening* (*Vecher*), *The Rosary* (*Chetki*), and *The White Flock* (*Belaya staya*). Much of her poetry later circulated in manuscript. Her importance in the world of letters was probably the reason why Zhdanov singled her out for attack in 1946.[15]

Maximilian Alexandrovich Voloshin (1877–1932) was another writer whose work also circulated in manuscript and was only partly published. His poems on the revolution, written during the civil war, are not political (any more than Blok's *The Twelve* is). They attempt, sometimes successfully, to relate the horrors of the present to those of Russia's past as part of a supernatural purposeful plan. This poet, who before the revolution had the reputation of a brilliant cosmopolitan, found words to convey a genuine feeling of mystic awe as he unfolds a Dantesque description of the Hell—or Purgatory—to which his country willingly descended.

All these writers belonged by origin to different social groups, but they had one feature in common—they were highly educated. The palm in that respect belongs perhaps to Ivanov and Bryusov, but all the others I have named were acquainted with world literature, knew languages and travelled; most of them were university graduates. Bryusov was the grandson of a serf. His father, born a serf, was a successful merchant. Ivanov was the son of a minor official. Sologub's father was a modest tailor, and his mother a maid; he himself became a teacher in a small community. Through his mother Blok belonged to the enlightened landed gentry: his grandfather was Rector of St Petersburg University, and his father Professor of Law. Bely's father was Dean of the Department of Mathematics at Moscow University. Mandelshtam was the son of a particularly unsuccessful Jewish businessman (his autobiographical sketch depicts a world as remote from the world of Blok as Bryusov's). Gumilyov and Akhmatova were children of naval officers; Mandelshtam and Ivanov studied in Russian and German universities, Gumilyov partly in France. Sologub graduated from a teachers' college. Blok studied law and switched to philology. Bely graduated brilliantly in Natural Science. I. Annensky, a most interesting precursor of symbolism and the prevailing influence of Gumilyov and Akhmatova, was an important official in public education. Though they were accused of being apolitical, they took sides and quarrelled over political issues. They sided with the revolutionaries in 1905 and hoped for liberal changes. Their creative work sometimes reflected their opinions, particularly since after 1905 there was a lifting of the censorship for a number of publications. The events of October 1917 and the ensuing hardships and restrictive measures of the Soviet administration influenced their future. Gumilyov was executed and Mandelshtam died in prison. Many emigrated and did not return. Of those who returned, A. N. Tolstoy, who started as a symbolist and was at the time of the revolution considered a promising writer, made a brilliant career in the USSR. Marina Tsvetayeva, a most original and interesting poet, returned only in 1939—and committed suicide. G. Ivanov, Khodasevich, and several others who were beginning to make a name for themselves around 1917, tried to stay, finally left the country, and continued to write abroad.

One of the outstanding features introduced by the new movement into Russian intellectual life was the publication of 'artistic' journals and almanacs. They were very different from the traditional 'heavy journals', each with its definite political reputation, which directed the social opinions and literary tastes of the reading public. The new publications were mostly concerned with the arts, lavishly illustrated, with beautiful covers and frontispieces. Each of them represented a certain trend in the new movement and was linked with a different publishing house and with one or another of the intellectual circles of Moscow and St Petersburg. They were usually shortlived. The first one, *The World of Art* (*Mir Iskusstva*, 1899–1904), was founded with money from two patrons of art, Princess Tenisheva and S. Mamontov, and kept alive until the Russo-Japanese war by the financial support of Nicholas II. It was not exactly a literary review, though it published critical articles by Russian and foreign writers. Most of the first symbolists were represented in it. S. Diaghilev, promoter of the Ballets Russes, was its first editor; A. Benois and L. Bakst were important contributors. It promoted all branches of modern art, but was not a purely symbolist review. In 1902 the Merezhkovskys started *The New Path*, which lasted about a year and reflected the religious revival of the period. In 1904 Bryusov became editor of *The Scales* (*Vesy*) which represented symbolism until 1909. Another symbolist review, beautifully illustrated, was *The Golden Fleece* (*Zolotoye Runo*), 1906–9, and in 1909 *Apollon* took over and became the representative of the new literary movement. This lasted until the Revolution. *Sofia*, published in 1914 by P. Muratov, specialised in problems of Russian religious art and published reviews of contemporary literature. Bely's *Petersburg* was discussed in it. Periodicals and almanacs of that period (not all of which are mentioned here) are now collectors' items in Russia and outside it.[16] They are proof of the high standards of creative writing and literary criticism of the time. Polemics, bickering and quarrels were frequent, and because of divergent views in various circles, young writers could be almost sure of finding a place to publish. Blok did not hesitate to patronise the 'peasant' poets, Klyuyev and Yesenin. Mandelshtam was adopted by the editors of *Apollon* when he was nineteen, because of the quality of his verse. Although personal, political and literary quarrels may have divided them at times, poets were united by special bonds, as is evident in the poems addressed by Anna Akhmatova to four important poets of her young years: Blok, Mandelshtam, Pasternak, and Mayakovsky.

Symbolism and acmeism looked for new modes of expression, discussed the aims and devices of poetic language, but never rejected old masters. They treated them as teachers outdistanced by their pupils, and they found in the past the roots of their own credo and strivings. Lermontov's 'There are words . . .' (*Est' rechi* . . .) and Tyutchev's *Silentium* were reinterpreted in the symbolist way. But a new generation of poets, tired of the vagueness and 'otherworldliness' of symbolism, rejected also the elaborate, sophisticated simplicity of acmeism. Symbolism and acmeism had been the products of a cosmopolitan education, of philosophy and of a renascent, specifically Russian, religious consciousness. The next generation, confronted with the growth of a mechanised, materialistic, urban world, found inspiration in the contrast between rudimentary passions and the conventions of civilisation. Their reactions were uninhibited and they needed words to express them. Like the acmeists, they wanted to free the word from the many interpretations which the various schools of thought permitted; they did not stress the importance of the thing the existing word stood for, however, but focused their attention on the 'word as such' and its possibilities.

They called themselves 'futurists', as did a new generation of Italian writers; yet their premises were not the same. They acted in protest against the aesthetic rules and mysticism of the symbolists, and also revolted against the sentimental narrative poetry of the preceding age. They scorned the romanticism of the old masters. They wanted to be craftsmen of the word and therefore transgressed all canons of word formation and syntax. They borrowed freely from all levels of colloquial speech. They coined new words. The most unexpected associations of seemingly unrelated concepts created a new poetic language. The futurists first emerged in 1910 and their beginnings were very much like those of the decadents, a *succès de scandale* which they deliberately provoked and fostered. It exploded in 1912 with the manifesto 'A Slap in the Face of Public Taste' which contained the advice 'to throw overboard from the ship of modernity Pushkin, Dostoyevsky, Tolstoy, etc'.[17] It was signed by Burlyuk, Kruch-enykh, Khlebnikov, and Mayakovsky, the great poet of the movement.

The life and work of Vladimir Vladimirovich Mayakovsky (1893–1930) have been described in detail in the Soviet Union because he joined the Communist revolution and helped it with all his talent. Yet in many biographies his early futurism has been minimised or altogether ignored. Most of his innovations that transformed Russian poetic language belong to the period before October 1917. Neologisms and archaisms, bold images built on contrasts or distant analogies, insults and self-glorification; new metres, new rhymes and blank verse were all present in these early poems. They were lyrical poems. Revolutionary themes were frequent and related to his own intimate experience of un-requited love, as if a social revolution would solve his personal tragedy or offer an escape from it. In fact his poetry was a poetry of escape from unavoidable human suffering, and all his dreams of a better future for himself and the world were utopian dreams of a suddenly transformed material world. Mayakovsky was an early and active member of the Bolshevik party. He was in tune with the generation which later made the Revolution and hoped for the speedy advent of a social paradise where even human passions would become painless. The violence of his language was deliberate: words were his revolutionary arsenal. The im-portance he attributed to the poet's role is best expressed in the lines he addressed to Igor Severyanin:

> How do you dare call yourself a poet,
> And be grey, and chirp like a quail!

This Igor Severyanin (Igor Lotarev 1887–1942) proclaimed himself the leader of an early branch of futurism called 'ego-futurism'. For a while he was the most popular Russian poet, but it did not last. Very few of his poems are important. They had a musical quality and a vocabulary which at first seemed new and daring, but rapidly lost its charm.

While Mayakovsky rose to political fame and personal disaster, V. Khlebnikov, the founder and interpreter of futurist theory, died of exhaustion and malnutrition in 1922. Yet he wrote enough poetry and prose to influence not only his fellow poets but also a school of literary criticism. Though the public at large and some of the futurists themselves regarded futurism as the manifestation of a destructive revolutionary force, its influence on literature was mainly intellectual. The desire to shock the bourgeois often took the form of hooliganism, and hooliganism was a necessary corollary of the Bolshevik revolution; but Khlebnikov's interest in 'the word as such', his breaking up of phrases for the sake of analysis of poetic devices, became the basis of a new school of criticism. It took the name of formalism. In 1916 the Society for the Study of Poetic Language (*Opoyaz*) was founded in St Petersburg. Its aim was to study verbal organisation for aesthetic purposes. As it neglected the social aspect of literature, formalism was persecuted and finally destroyed by victorious Communism, but it left its impact on all literary criticism.[18]

The name of Boris Leonidovich Pasternak (1890–1960) is usually linked to futurism; he was a member of one of the early futurist groups. In 1912 he was a young man still hesitating between poetry and music. His first verses, published in 1914, attracted attention; the next classified him as a poet with immense possibilities. His futurism was more evident in his arbitrary use of syntax and unexpected associations than in word formation. The freshness of his vision, when he referred to day-to-day realities or nature in relation to his personal emotions, was striking. His autobiography and *Dr Zhivago* tell us how much he owed to the old Russian tradition and to the air of the 'silver age' which he breathed in his youth.[19]

New trends in realism

The two literary trends which opposed each other in the early nineties had in common one essential feature: writers searched for something new. They were both heirs of the same realistic trend which aimed at reproducing human life in its actual setting and at explaining rationally the motivation responsible for human actions. The aesthetic possibilities of this literature had been exhausted. There was too much fragmentation, too much attention to detail—and no synthesis, unless the reader would accept as a synthesis the morality of the story. Konstantin Leontyev was speaking of Russian literature in general when he wrote in 1890 about Tolstoy, who was still considered the greatest writer, though his avowed aim was to be only a teacher of morals and prophet of a new kind of Christianity: 'He [Tolstoy] probably guessed that he would never write anything better than *War and Peace* and *Anna Karenina* in the former genre, the former style . . .'[20]

Tolstoy had renounced his former manner and was adapting an ultra-simplified style (which required a lot of refined workmanship) to rewriting medieval legends and popular tales. Leskov was doing the same in an ultra-ornate style which would later be revitalised by symbolism and taken over by A. Remizov.

An interesting case, demonstrating the need for new modes of expression, is that of P. Yakubovich. In 1884 he was condemned to prison, and later to hard labour, for revolutionary activity. He is better known because he attempted in *A World of Outcasts* (*V mire otverzhennykh*) to give a description (new since Dostoyevsky) of the life of convicts. His poetry is revolutionary and depicts the sufferings of the poor, but there is nothing powerful or original in it. He was, however, the first Russian to publish translations of Baudelaire's poems. The first appeared in 1879, and between that date and 1887 he published a selection from *Les Fleurs du Mal*, translated by him in prison. As interest in decadent literature was not to the credit of a revolutionary, the translations were not much publicised. Yakubovich explained in 1909 that, though he did not approve of the caricature features of *dekadenstvo*, he realised that 'the gloomy scepticism and angry misanthropy of the French poet had their source in his passionate striving towards light, his aching love of beauty and harmony, and the impossibility of seeing them incarnate in life and reality.'[21] Thus he put into words that desire for an escape not only from a dreary life but from the dreariness of literature unable to formulate this striving. We saw how the symbolists tried to solve the problem.

Those who considered that the solution was merely a matter of correcting social ills by reform or violence, continued the realistic trend in the 'literature of indictment'. Others sought beauty in a new romanticism, now labelled 'revolutionary romanticism'. They were also considered realists, because they spoke of the hardships of material life and gave vivid descriptions of moral and physical misery, but their characters were colourful, often exotic—non-Russian. Passionate feelings became important; actions were often irrational. The author pretended to be one of the characters and this permitted the use of emotional, poetic language. This romantic outgrowth of the literature of indictment was represented in the nineties by Gorky and Kuprin, and by an older and less violent writer—V. G. Korolenko, a populist. All three considered that the duty of the writer was to lead the readers towards a better life. Tolstoy at that time preached the same thing, but the meaning of the words 'better life' was different for him.

Vladimir Galaktionovich Korolenko's (1853–1921) topics belonged to the old school. *Makar's Dream* (*Son Makara*) takes up the story of the down-trodden, exploited 'little man', but it lifts the plot from the details of unfair treatment and physical sufferings into the realm of divine pity and justice. The setting is magnificent—winter in Siberia—and the language highly poetic. In other stories he described with tenderness and irony those members of the community who, for reasons of national origin, religion, or accident, did not quite belong to the majority, and were made to suffer for it. He was exiled to Siberia and was for a long time under police supervision. He went to the Chicago Exhibition of 1893 as a journalist, and the story *Without Language* (*Bez yazyka*) inspired by his visit stresses the discovery that political freedom, security, and love are not sufficient to make a man perfectly happy in this world. There still remains an inexplicable striving for the unattainable.

For some time the Russians thought that Maxim Gorky (Alexey Maximovich Peshkov, 1868–1936) would be the renovator of Russian prose, but his talent was captivated too early by revolutionary ideas which he had to express through the confrontation of stereotyped characters. He could not create something completely new. In his early stories, features of the new romanticism crystallised around characters who broke laws, were thieves, liars, even murderers, but nevertheless had redeeming qualities: generosity, sincere passions, boundless daring, disregard for any lasting material security. Gorky pitted them against a social structure represented by people who also had vices, but none of these qualities—the smug, self-satisfied, often self-made men with a middle-class mentality—the *meshchanstvo*. This word once denoted a legally recognised social class; now it took on the meaning of a despicable way of life devoid of any higher interests. Gorky had one feature in common with the poets of the decadent school: the border between good and evil was obliterated in his early stories, and the generally accepted moral code was turned upside-down. The trespasser became the positive hero. It was, though Gorky would have been the last to admit it, the Nietzschean idea without the Nietzschean philosophy. He realised the necessity of a new style; in 1900 he wrote to Chekhov: 'You are killing realism. This form has outlived its time. . . . You will kill realism. And it delights me. Enough of it. Let it go to the devil.'[22]

Gorky was at first careless in his choice of epithets, and often diffuse, but the images were bright, if not clearly delineated, the colours violent, the conflicts dramatic. He sometimes wrote in rhythmic prose, and this increased the emotional appeal of his revolutionary allegories, *The Stormy Petrel* (*Burevestnik*) and *The Song of the Falcon* (*Pesnya o Sokole*). The most successful attempt by Gorky to write a real novel is *Foma Gordeyev*. In it the exotic way of life along the Volga is blended with the traditionally dreary daily life and interests of the merchant class in the city, realistically described. The main character is raised at times to heroic stature by his desperate rebellion against the hypocrisy of the *nouveaux riches* to which he belongs by birth. It is an attempt to revive, on a new background, the old theme of the 'guilty nobleman' fated to be a 'superfluous man'. (Instead of a young nobleman the hero is a merchant's son—a sign of the times.) Another novel *Mother* (*Mat'*) was considered by Lenin perfect as revolutionary propaganda. It was a blueprint for revolutionary activists, a didactic story which followed strictly the pattern of separating the 'good' from the 'bad' on the basis of revolutionary morality. Gorky's most remarkable works in the period which interests us are his semi-autobiographical *Childhood* (*Dyetstvo*) and *Among People* (*V Lyudyakh*). These together with his recollections of Tolstoy, are masterpieces of literary portraiture. As a playwright, he scored a tremendous success with *Lower Depths* (*Na Dnye*). It discussed the problem underlying Gorky's writings: the desire to throw off ugly reality, and the positive value of the escape into hope. Gorky's belief was that the duty of art was to depict a glorious future and the proud men who would make it possible. This was to be the origin of socialist realism.

In 1902 Gorky was appointed head of the publishing house *Znaniye* (Knowledge). There he fulfilled his urge to teach and direct young writers. The trend of *Znaniye* was to criticise the present and encourage action for a better social future through revolution. Many writers of this group achieved fame after 1917. Some of those who met with early success abandoned the group. To these belongs Leonid Andreyev, who for a while joined the symbolists, wrote psuedo-symbolist plays and sensational stories, became immensely popular, and is now remembered mainly for his pessimism. Another one is Alexander Ivanovich Kuprin whose stories, even when they stress the ugliness of life, as does *The Duel* (*Poyedinok*), express a longing for higher ideals. *The Duel* made him extremely popular because it exposed the cruelty and meaningless conventions of army life in peace-time: it was published in 1904 when pacifism was supported by the radicals. He saw the dangers of industrialisation, and represented the factory as an all-devouring god in *Molokh*. And in *The Garnet Bracelet* (*Granatovy braslet*) he performed the difficult task of telling a sentimental story without affectation.

Ivan Alexeyevich Bunin (1870–1953), the first Russian writer to obtain the Nobel Prize, was also connected with *Znaniye*. He has a place of honour in the literature of indictment because he described with pitiless lucidity and in beautiful language the moral and physical agony of the rural gentry and rich peasantry. But I believe that his stories without social implications will live longer, because in them he caught and expressed fugitive impressions that are, above all, human: *The Well of Days* (*U istoka dney*) and *The Antonovka Apples* (*Antonovskiye yabloki*) —of which Gorky wrote disapprovingly that they were 'not democratic'—and stories written after he emigrated.[23]

Bunin's masterpiece is *The Man from San Francisco* (*Gospodin iz San-Frantsisko*) which combines in a tense construction the plot—death at the moment of worldly success—and the grandiose symbolic background of nature, for which that death has no meaning. The story is told in beautiful language which shifts without effort from objective narrative to lyrical description. Bunin never accepted the symbolists' axiom that language has to suggest rather than inform. Compared to their style, his poetry is considered 'cold'. Yet it is possible that the unambiguous style of Bunin, who used all the accumulated wealth of the Russian language in his prose, will remain the best example of the craftsmanship of this period. Future generations might well be unable to appreciate the experiments, allusions, and literary devices of other great writers. A. Tvardovsky in his introduction to the Soviet edition of Bunin's works calls him the last classic Russian writer.[24]

Anton Pavlovich Chekhov (1860–1904), who died in the full maturity of his talent, stands by himself. He is the best proof of the demise of the old realism, though at first glance he seemed to continue it. Chekhov wrote stories about negligent officials and members of the intelligentsia who were 'superfluous men'; he ridiculed daily life deprived of any higher interest; he exposed the superficiality, selfishness and lack of faith of men and women. All these topics had been used before: coming from his pen they seemed different. He is full of understanding and pity. There can be no verdict of 'guilty' if we are shown events as the accused saw them. A masterpiece of the genre is *The Princess* (Knyaginya), in which Chekhov first tells us all the sins of the selfish princess as the honest doctor sees them, and then unfolds the thoughts of the princess, who is deeply hurt because she feels no guilt. He achieved fame at first because he made people laugh. But he can be lyrical, as in *The Steppe* (*Step'*); he can stress the importance of spiritual life and simple faith as in *The Student* and *Easter Eve* (*Student, V svyatuyu noch*); or, as in *The Duel* (*Duel'*), he can describe that seemingly impossible thing, the regeneration of a 'superfluous man', redeeming himself through drab daily work. His plays, which he called comedies, are produced as dramas with social significance. Yet it is not the proletarian who suffers from poverty and frustration in Chekhov's plays, it is the impoverished, hapless 'gentleman' and intellectual. To many he is just a writer of amusing stories about human failings, to others a deeply pessimistic psychologist. To others again, he is a first-rate satirist of a decaying society. Such critics consider each individual case in his stories as representative of an entire social group. *Ward No 6* and *The Man in a Shell* (*Palata No 6, Chelovyek v futlyare*) are interpreted in this way. D. Tschizewskij regards him as an impressionist.[25]

Chekhov, like Bunin, did not join the decadent or symbolist schools, but, unlike Bunin, he did see their importance in renewing literature. His *Seagull* (*Chaika*) written in 1896, discusses the problem.

As Mirsky said, he did not form a school: no one could write like Chekhov, and the secret of his art has yet to be discovered.

In order to exist, literature requires certain material conditions: paper, and the means to publish.

This was foreseen by Lenin. In 1905 he wrote: 'Literature must become imbued with the party spirit. . . . Away with non-partisan writers!' In 1948, A. Fadeyev, Secretary of the Union of Soviet Writers, called these words the 'utterances of a genius'.[26] They explain Gorky's attempts in 1907 and again in 1913 to stop the production of a play based on Dostoyevsky's novel *The Possessed*. He argued that it was 'socially harmful'. One of the first decrees (28 October 1917) of the Soviet administration ordered the closure of certain bourgeois newspapers. A week later Lenin declared: 'We said that we would close the bourgeois newspapers if we ever came to power . . . To tolerate the existence of these newspapers would mean to cease being Socialists.' His opinion prevailed after a heated debate. The resolution read: 'To restore the so-called "freedom of the press", to return the printing works and paper to the capitalists would be an inadmissible act of surrender.'[27]

At the time privately-owned printing facilities and stocks of paper still existed. On 15 January 1918, therefore, a decree was issued creating the Revolutionary Tribunal on Publishing Business. 'All the crimes and transgressions against the people committed in the printing trade' were to come under the jurisdiction of this Tribunal.[28]

Everything that happened to Russian literature thereafter has its explanation in these principles, which still apply in the Soviet Union today.[29]

Russian schools

OSKAR ANWEILER

*The forces underlying the development
of Russian education in the nineteenth century
and the structure of the Russian educational system*

In the 'civilised' countries of Europe most people tended to
regard tsarist Russia, both culturally and educationally, as a
backward land. On the face of it, this assessment seems to have
been justified, for at the turn of the century only a quarter of the
Russian population could read and write and only four per cent
were attending school (as compared with seventeen per cent in
Germany and nineteen per cent in the USA) while in the whole
Russian empire, from the Vistula to Vladivostok, there were only
nine universities. The Russian peasant community, which accounted for more than four-fifths of the population, was generally
regarded as 'sombre and uncouth', and although Tolstoy, in his
novels and stories, did his best to dispel this image, he merely
succeeded in romanticising it. This 'western' attitude was strengthened by the numerous criticisms made by the Russians themselves—of the low educational standard and anti-educational bias
of the Russian people and of the ineffectualness of the government's education policy—which reflected the general dissatisfaction of the populace as a whole with the political and social
conditions obtaining at that time.

It is hardly surprising, therefore, that after the October revolution of 1917 the new rulers should have seized upon this gloomy
picture of the pre-revolutionary period and, after suitable refur-
bishing, used it as a general backcloth to offset their own achievements. The following passage, which is taken from a review of
the first forty years of Soviet education, is typical of this official
attitude: 'The bourgeois constitution, which promoted the interests of the estate owners, denied the workers of tsarist Russia

access to culture and knowledge. [And so] this people, many of whose representatives had made contributions to culture and scholarship at an international level, was allowed to vegetate in darkness and ignorance.'[1] The author of this survey then went on to suggest that it was not until the Soviets had come to power that education was extended to all classes of the population and that since they had been left virtually nothing to build on in 1917, improvements which had been effected in the Russian educational system and the rise in the general level of culture were due primarily to policies pursued by the new ruling party.

But if we are to make a fair assessment of the Russian educational system at the time of the Bolshevik take-over in 1917, it is not enough simply to compare the conditions obtaining in Russia immediately preceding the revolution with those found contemporaneously in other European countries. First we have to assess the pre-revolutionary period in Russia in the light of previous Russian developments. After all, a straightforward comparison between the number of school-children and students or the number of professional and industrial schools in Russia and elsewhere, tells us very little about the dynamics of Russian education or the direction in which it was moving. What we have to do, therefore, is enquire into the many factors, positive and negative, underlying the development of the Russian educational system, for it was these which gave it its specific character. And although this system was criticised by its opponents as hopelessly antiquated, to those who were more benevolently inclined it seemed to hold out hope of a gradual improvement. The period between 1905 and 1917 was particularly fertile and produced many new plans and ideas, all of which were concerned with the modernisation of the traditional educational system and which formed part of the general process of economic and political change that was so characteristic of the inter-revolutionary years.

The liberal historians of the Russian school—Milyukov, Gessen and Hans—have pointed out that the development of Russian education in the nineteenth century proceeded along two specific paths: on the one hand there was the official government policy, implemented through the state schools and varying considerably from one period to another, while on the other hand there was a growing tendency for the 'public' (*obshchestvennost*) and 'society' (*obshchestvo*) to organise their own independent educational institutions. Soviet historians have also stressed the *rivalry between the state system and the educational activities of society*, which they have attributed to class differences and have tried to correlate with the political revolutionary movement. In education—as in politics—these two almost completely independent lines of development vied with one another until in the end both were engulfed by the revolution. Looking back on these events, we today are able to distinguish a pattern which the protagonists in this contest of progressive forces were unable to discern. Thus, the gradual painstaking acquisition of greater political and social freedom created the necessary framework for a democratic community; the pressure exerted by the government forced the people to act on their own initiative, with the result that Russian schools gradually became social rather than authoritarian institutions. To put it in another way, the negative effects of autocratic rule were replaced by the possibility of positive cooperation between an 'enlightened' government and a society which had meanwhile acquired a sense of responsibility and initiative. During the brief era of Count Ignatyev, last but one of the tsarist Ministers of Education, it seemed that for the first time ever such cooperation was about to be achieved. But this new development, welcomed by many, was frustrated first by the war and then by the revolution. The Bolshevik coup, which resulted in the integration of all social forces in the service of a single idea and under the leadership of a single party, sapped the tension between state and society and destroyed all the vital forces—such as the numerous private educational schemes—which this had produced.

This relationship between state and society—which is not normally interpreted in such a positive light—was one of the principal factors in the development of Russian education in the nineteenth century. A second important factor, and one which underlines the special problems encountered in Russia during this period, was the cultural division of the Russian people into a numerically small upper class whose members had received a 'European' education, and the great mass of the population who were completely 'uneducated'. This development, which was the central feature of Russian cultural and intellectual life, had two principal causes, namely, the failure of the Greek Orthodox Church to play an effective part in popular education, and the preference for western culture evinced by the upper classes ever since the reign of Peter the Great. But although this long-standing schism still existed at the close of the nineteenth century, it was not nearly as marked as it had been previously. The 'Europeanisation' of Russia—which was lamented by the Slavophils but welcomed by pro-western elements—was accompanied by the *democratisation of education*, a process which was taking place in all European countries at that time but which, because of the special conditions obtaining in Russia, assumed a somewhat different form there from what it did in other parts of the continent. In Russia it was the intelligentsia who tried to bring 'enlightenment' to the people and not the government, which considered that any move towards democratisation constituted a threat to the tsarist autocracy.

These two *leit-motivs*—the interaction between government policy and social initiative and the gradual democratisation of education—were both manifested in the specific educational spheres which we now have to consider. Once Peter I had proposed that school attendance should be obligatory, responsibility for education in Russia rested with the tsars. In 1786 Catherine II introduced her first project for building new schools in all major cities, and in 1804 Alexander I established a system of standardised schools throughout the empire. Two years earlier, in 1802, an independent Ministry of Education (*ministerstvo narodnogo prosveshcheniya*) had been set up and this remained the highest—although not always the most influential—education authority in Russia right up to 1917. Due to the class structure of Russian society this Ministry was concerned primarily with the development of secondary schools and institutes of higher education which provided the state with its officials. Consequently, until quite late in the nineteenth century, elementary education was left to the parish clergy or the peasants themselves. Whether the Minister of Education was able to assert himself vis-à-vis his ministerial colleagues depended very much on his personal stature, his energy and his political outlook. Some ministers helped to shape government policy while others were simply loyal administrators who carried out orders handed down from above. Between 1802 and 1917 this second category predominated. The fact that there were no fewer than ten Ministers of Education during the last two decades of the tsarist régime reflects the permanent state of crisis in which the government found itself (prior to the revolution) in respect of its education policy.

Not all educational institutions came under the Ministry of Education. On the contrary, there was a surprisingly large number of different administrative bodies, a fact which tended to inhibit the development of Russian education in general but which also had a beneficial effect in individual cases. The most important of these unofficial bodies was the *Holy Synod*, the supreme organ of government of the Orthodox Church and controlled by a lay procurator, who represented the Tsar. The Synod was responsible for the ecclesiastical parish schools (*tserkovno-prikhodskiye shkoly*) which had been founded at the beginning of the nineteenth century to provide a rudimentary form of primary education and which became an important factor in the Russian educational system following the publication of the statute of 13 July 1884. From then onwards church schools entered into open competition with secular primary schools run by the Zemstvos. What was at stake in this struggle was ecclesiastical influence on the one hand and the principle of secular education on the other. Between 1884 and 1897 various attempts were made to bring the whole of Russian primary education under the control of the Holy Synod. The chief protagonist of the church schools was K. P. Pobedonostsev, the influential adviser of Alexander III and Nicholas II. Virtually the whole of Russian 'society', on the other hand, wanted a secular educational system so that, when this was introduced by the Provisional Government in 1917, it received general approval.

But, while responsibility for primary education rested with just two bodies, the Ministry and the Holy Synod, the administration of secondary, professional and craft schools was divided among a number of authorities. As well as the traditional classical and non-classical secondary schools under the Ministry of Education, there were classical secondary schools and institutes for girls founded under the patronage of Empress Maria, commercial schools administered by the Ministry of Trade and Industry, theological seminaries and diocesan institutes for girls run by the Holy Synod, and officers' training schools run by the Ministry of War. Professional and craft schools were administered by the particular ministries or authorities under whose auspices they had been founded. Finally, although all universities and a proportion of other higher education institutions came under the Ministry of Education, the great majority of technical colleges were controlled by other bodies. This administrative diversity, which was exceeded only by the diversity of the different types of schools existing in Russia, was not the result of a conscious policy decision but had come about in a rather spontaneous manner. However, although it was generally agreed that such diversity was undesirable in the long run, none of the attempts to tighten up school administration and bring it under a single body ever passed the planning stage.

The schools administered by the Zemstvos, which were the pride and hope of 'society', effectively prevented the state from acquiring absolute control of Russian education. In the absence of any equivalent public associations, the Zemstvos, which had been created by Alexander II in thirty-four provinces of European Russia in 1864 in order to promote local self-government, soon developed into centres of general social activity and were regarded by the liberal intelligentsia as the germ cells of a Russian parliamentary system. But even if one is not prepared to accept the idealistic picture of the Zemstvos drawn by so many liberal historians, it must certainly be conceded that, in the educational sphere at least, they played an extremely positive role. True, the schools administered by the Zemstvos were also subject to the general supervision of the Ministry of Education, but they enjoyed greater freedom than the state schools in the provinces without local autonomy, which came under the direct control of the Ministry. Teachers in the Zemstvo schools were appointed by the Zemstvos and not by the state and although their curricula had to be submitted to the state for approval, the teaching methods employed in these schools were generally considered to be progressive.

However, the development of Zemstvo education did not always run smoothly. The pioneer work of Baron N. A. Korf (1834–83) in the province of Yekaterinoslav suffered a reversal after the promulgation in 1874 of the new law for the administration of primary schools, which increased the powers vested in the state. Ten years later, in 1884, the new parish schools, built by the Orthodox Church with state backing, provided the Zemstvo schools with dangerous rivals. Because they found approval with the intelligentsia the Zemstvo schools appeared suspect in the eyes of the authorities, who regarded them as a breeding-ground of a freer, almost a democratic spirit. But since the state could not afford to pay for the upkeep of the Zemstvo schools, the government was obliged to abandon its plans for placing them under the direct control of the Ministry of Education. In fact, during the last decade before the revolution the Zemstvos spent nearly fifty per cent more on education than the Ministry in any given year and in 1908 they were asked by the government to accept responsibility for the implementation of compulsory education. Between them, the Zemstvo schools and the community schools run by the municipal Dumas (which, apart from those in the major cities, were inferior), represented the popular facet of Russian education, which received support from 'society'. By 1917 the Zemstvo ideology was so firmly established that it even influenced the Bolshevik education programme.

The foundations of the Russian educational system were based on the *primary schools* (*nachalnye narodnye shkoly*) of the provinces and the towns. But—to continue the metaphor—these foundations revealed so many cracks and weaknesses that the upper storeys of the educational structure were virtually left hovering in the air. The task with which Russian ministers of education were faced during the closing decades of tsarist rule, and which they eventually bequeathed to the Soviet régime, consisted of strengthening the foundations of the educational system and improving access between the lower and higher grades. In order to achieve this they had to do two things: introduce compulsory education and reform the secondary school system. By 1917 considerable progress had been made towards both these goals, which provided the Soviet régime with a firm basis for its educational programme.

'We may say without exaggeration that the Russian primary school was actually founded by the Russian public and not by the government.' This epigrammatic statement of Milyukov's accurately describes the process whereby the general upsurge of pedagogical thinking combined with the reforms of Alexander II to focus attention on the needs of primary education. The practical and literary activities of Pirogov, Ushinsky and Tolstoy— to mention only the three most important pedagogues of the 1860s—aroused the interest of both the government and the public in this almost totally neglected sphere. The first 'Regulations for Primary Schools', which appeared in 1864, placed the onus for providing popular education on the population itself, i.e., on the peasants and the newly-created Zemstvos. The principle of *compulsory education* was considered in discussions which preceded publication of these regulations but was finally rejected, partly for practical reasons and partly because it was felt that the people should not have education forced on them. This view was held by conservatives and liberals alike, although for very different reasons, for while the conservatives thought that education would be wasted on the peasants, the liberals did not want the state to gain absolute control of the educational system. The peasants themselves were also dubious about the prospect of compulsory school attendance and initially even the Zemstvo schools were made to suffer from their lack of trust.

As more and more primary schools were built (in 1880 there were 28,118, in 1896 68,358, in 1905 92,501 and in 1911 100,295 within the Russian empire) the new educational plans which had been evolved and which envisaged a general school attendance of at least three, and if possible four, years, gradually became a viable proposition. From the 1880s onwards the concept of 'obligatory instruction' (*obyazatelnoye obucheniye*) had been replaced by that of 'general instruction' (*vseobshcheye obucheniye*) because educationalists had come to realise that before school attendance could be made compulsory, they would first have to create the necessary basis for general school attendance. It was thanks chiefly to the former primary school inspector V. P. Vakhterov, who devoted himself to this problem both as a speaker and as a polemicist after his dismissal from the school service, that the concept of 'general instruction' was adopted as a slogan by the Zemstvos, the municipal Dumas and the teachers' associations. The committees for primary education (*komitety gramotnosti*), which had been formed in Moscow and St Petersburg in the middle of the nineteenth century, published numerous articles on this subject. As a result, accurate assessments of the empire's educational requirements were made, budgets were produced, and the school building programme was speeded up. In a number of particularly active areas (such as the provinces of Tver, Saratov and Vyatka) the principle of general school attendance was almost completely realised before the outbreak of the First World War. All this local activity came to a head in the bill providing for general primary school education throughout the empire which the Duma passed in 1908 and subsequently extended.

But the great increase in the number of primary schools in Russia should not blind us to the fact that the general standard of primary teaching was very low. Although a few of these primary schools, which provided a five- or six-year course, had two teachers, in the vast majority of schools there was only one teacher, who had to give a three or four-year course of instruction single-handed. It was not until 1912, when the four-year higher primary school (*vyssheye nachalnoye uchilishche*) was introduced, that primary school pupils were able to proceed, under certain conditions, to classical secondary schools. A high percentage of classical secondary school pupils left school prematurely and so failed to receive even a three-year course of instruction.

The standard of Russian primary schools depended to a considerable extent on the ability of the individual teachers who ran them. The average village school-teacher knew little or nothing of recent developments in the pedagogical world; it was rare enough for him to possess books of his own, let alone subscribe to a pedagogical magazine. Russian teachers also received different kinds of training, depending on whether they attended state, church or private training establishments, which naturally made for varying levels of competence. All in all there were over a dozen different kinds of teachers' training establishment, the most important of which were the seminaries for intending primary schoolteachers. By 1916 there were 189 of these. The higher primary schoolteachers were trained in teachers' training institutes (*uchitelskiye instituty*) of which 48 had been built by

1916. Preparatory courses were also held at a number of higher primary schools and secondary schools. The Zemstvos and various private educational associations also ran teachers' training courses, primarily for women. By 1916 there were 150 courses of this kind. Finally, graduates from theological seminaries, secondary schools and diocesan girls' schools were also entitled to work as primary school-teachers. No progress was made towards the standardisation of teachers' training in Russia until after the revolution.

We have already pointed to the fact that until the closing years of the tsarist régime there was virtually no connection between primary education and secondary education (*sredneye obrazovaniye*), which was provided in a variety of different establishments. In Russia, as in western Europe, there were historical reasons for this separate development, and it was this that gave the secondary schools their distinctive character. But from the beginning of the twentieth century onwards the Russian public began to demand a standardised system of secondary education that would be available to all classes of society. This demand, made with increasing urgency over the years, came not only from the opposition groups (both socialists and liberals) but also from establishment circles, for it appeared in official conferences on the *reform of the secondary school system*, which were instituted in 1899 and continued for several years. The central theme of these discussions—one that was also being debated in Germany at that time—was provided by the controversy between the advocates of classical and non-classical secondary education. Although this controversy was never as fierce in Russia as it was in Germany, where it developed into a major philosophical dispute, it none the less helped to draw public attention to the state education policy, which was heavily slanted in favour of the classical curriculum. The Russian preference for the *classical gymnasium*, modelled on the Prussian prototype, went back to the era of Nicholas I and was subsequently strengthened by Count Tolstoy's statute of 1871. Only grammar-school boys were allowed to enter university. And yet Latin and Greek never really took root in Russia. Despite the most determined efforts on the part of the authorities to promote these subjects, they always remained an alien product, and the hope entertained by the government that by introducing these ancient languages into the curriculum it would be possible to inculcate into the youth of the empire a sense of loyalty to the state, proved entirely vain. Long before the revolution classical languages had lost much of their appeal, even among university professors, and by 1914 Greek had been dropped from the curriculum of all but a few grammar schools situated in university towns. Consequently, when in 1918 the Bolsheviks placed a general ban on all ancient languages they were, in one sense, merely completing a development that had set in long before.

According to the statute of 1872, the non-classical secondary schools, which pupils attended for a seven-year period, were also intended to provide a general education. Originally, however, pupils who attended these schools merely qualified for admission to technical colleges and not to universities. Later, at the beginning of the twentieth century, the regulations governing university entrance were relaxed to enable pupils from non-classical secondary schools to enter the faculties of physics, mathematics and medicine at Russian universities. At the *gymnasiums for girls*, most of which were run as private establishments, the pupils also attended for a total period of seven years. On completing their studies they were entitled to attend the 'higher courses for women' which were organised in close collaboration with the universities and served as a substitute for the normal degree course, from which women were debarred. The newest type of secondary school was represented by *commercial schools (kommercheskiye uchilishcha)*, which came into prominence from the turn of the century onwards. But despite their vocational bias, these schools none the less provided an all-round education (with special emphasis on the natural sciences and modern languages). In fact, many were nearly the same as the non-classical secondary schools and had been designated as 'commercial' schools for purely tactical reasons.

Between 1900 and 1904 four separate commissions were set up to investigate the possibility of reforming the secondary school system. Although this produced no practical results of any consequence it was still a noteworthy development, for this was the first time ever that projects were discussed which advocated the *unification of secondary schools* and their integration with the primary schools. The draft proposals evolved by the commission set up in 1900 under the chairmanship of P. G. Vinogradov, then Professor of History in Moscow, provided for a standardised five-year secondary school (with voluntary classes in manual work) and a three-year upper grade which was to provide instruction in the natural sciences, classical languages, and history and literature. The recommendations of the commission set up by Minister Vannovsky in 1901 were even more radical. They envisaged a new type of secondary school in which the first three classes would cover the whole of the primary school curriculum. This would have bridged the gap between the classical and non-classical schools, and it would also have gone a long way towards integrating primary and secondary education for although the proposals would not have done away with private tutors or preparatory classes, they none the less constituted an abrupt departure from traditional practice. We see, therefore, that by the turn of the century the concept of a 'differentiated standard school' was well known in Russia, which no doubt aided both Ignatyev and the Provisional Government when they came to introduce their reforms.

Professional and technical training, which was first established under Peter the Great but which did not make any really significant progress until the second half of the nineteenth century, formed an important part of the Russian educational system. Its subsequent development reflected more clearly than anything else both the economic changes, which were turning Russia into a 'hotbed of capitalism' from the end of the nineteenth century onwards, and also the obstacles which were inhibiting this process. In 1888 the 'Fundamental Regulations for Industrial Schools' were published, based on the 'General Scheme for Industrial Training' worked out by Vyshnegradsky, an important engineer who later became Minister of Finance. These provided for three types of industrial school: secondary technical institutes, lower technical schools and craft schools. The aims of these different schools were determined by the categories of technical personnel evolved by Vyshnegradsky. Thus, the secondary institutes were intended to train technicians, such as assistant engineers, the lower technical schools foremen, and the craft schools skilled workers. But within the next decade, and before this scheme was able to produce any significant results, new schools for apprentices were founded; in 1895 lower craft schools were opened and in 1901 these were supplemented by craft classes, which were held in special departments attached to the municipal primary schools. Meanwhile, although the mass of industrial workers continued to receive their training in factories, only a few state-owned industrial enterprises ran apprenticeship courses. But the 'Russian system' of practical training in the 'mechanical arts', developed by the engineer D. K. Sovyetkin about 1870, received international recognition and was subsequently adopted by the Americans for their manual-training high schools.

The major obstacle to the speedy development of technical training in Russia, which would have been highly desirable in view of the growing industrialisation of the country, was the low level of general education. 'The illiteracy of the workers', we are told in a resolution passed by the Congress for Professional and Technical Training in 1895, 'constitutes the principal obstacle to the dissemination of technical knowledge and is also the main cause of unproductive work'. The kind of apprenticeship that was traditional in western Europe was unknown in Russia, and consequently the technical training available there prior to 1914 was quite inadequate for modern industrial purposes. Inevitably, this led to a situation in which there were far too many unskilled workers and far too few skilled and semi-skilled workers. In the last few years before the revolution this imbalance was redressed to some extent but it none the less continued to pose one of the major problems for Russia's economic development, even during the period of the Soviet five-year plans.

To complete the picture of the Russian educational system at the beginning of the twentieth century, we now have to concern ourselves, if only briefly, with two other areas, in which the intelligentsia were particularly active: kindergarten and adult education. Up to 1917 the state had little or nothing to do with either of these forms of education, which were organised in such a way as to render state intervention extremely difficult. As a result they were able to develop far more freely than would otherwise have been the case and we find, in fact, that the teachers engaged in pre-school and adult education were particularly receptive to modern pedagogical ideas. Not surprisingly, therefore, educational reforms carried out during the early years of the Soviet régime had their roots in these extra-mural spheres.

Although Froebel's conception of the kindergarten was known to Russian educationalists as early as the 1860s, it was not until the end of the nineteenth century that the general public became interested in *pre-school education*. This led to the formation of various associations for its promotion and the establishment of the first free public kindergartens. After the revolution of 1905 further Associations for the Protection of Poor and Neglected Children were formed in working-class areas of the major cities and the new industrial settlements. It was at about this time that the first plans for the systematic development of kindergarten education and its incorporation into the state educational system were evolved and submitted to the government. But like the various campaigns mounted in the Duma these proposals produced no practical results, for the Ministry of Education regarded kindergarten education as an extra-mural activity that could not be promoted by the state, which needed all its available resources for the promotion of compulsory education. Since the Zemstvos were also loth to undertake this task, pre-school education remained in the hands of private individuals and associations right up to 1917. But lack of state support was not the only reason for the inadequacy of the Russian kindergarten system. The whole concept of pre-school education was essentially alien to the Russian people, whose traditional pattern of life was based on the family and the neighbourhood. It was only in towns, where industrialisation was creating new living conditions, that the kindergarten system was able to make gradual progress. Even during the first decade of Soviet rule there were still very few kindergartens, especially in country districts.

Extra-mural education—the term used in Russia from 1910 onwards for adult education—was also organised on a private basis by the Russian intelligentsia. It was provided through Sunday and evening classes for adults, public libraries and reading-rooms, public centres and people's universities, printing-houses producing popular literature (the most important of which was the *Posrednik* (*Intermediary*) run by Gorbunov-Posadov) and numerous other educational facilities. The immediate object of this extra-mural education was to give peasants and industrial workers a basic grounding in reading, writing and arithmetic. This was to be followed by elementary instruction in geography, history and the natural sciences and by lessons in hygiene and personal conduct. Finally, it was intended to provide an introductory course in Russian literature. This ambitious project, which was designed to bring 'enlightenment' to the people, did not meet with the approval of the authorities, who kept Sunday and evening classes under close surveillance and even went so far as to prohibit them for temporary periods. But following the revolution of 1905, which gave a great boost to adult education, the government's restrictive measures became less and less effective, with the result that—to quote the Soviet educational historian Medynsky—'there was a great future for private initiative in the development of extra-mural education.'[2] The principles on which adult education was based prior to the revolution were formulated by the All-Russian Education Congress of 1913, which called for decentralisation, freedom for teachers to follow their own teaching methods, and a combination of private enterprise and support from local organs of self-government. The growth of adult education in the two decades prior to the revolution testifies, perhaps more than any other development of the period, to the desire of the Russian people for knowledge and to the selflessness of the Russian intelligentsia in providing it. And the conversion of adult education into political indoctrination after the Bolshevik revolution was a sad falsification of the original intentions.

*The effects of the 1905 Revolution and
the educational policy of the Duma*

The revolutionary disturbances of 1905 also had far-reaching effects on Russian education. The events of 'Bloody Sunday' (9 January 1905) produced their strongest repercussions in universities and colleges, where political demonstrations were staged which led to their closure. But numerous secondary schools also became involved in the wave of unrest. Many of the older pupils took part in strikes and demonstrations, founded pupils' associations and demanded greater freedom both in and out of school.

This development came to a head when the pupils joined forces with the workers and the intelligentsia in the general strike of October 1905, which forced the Tsar to grant the October Manifesto. As a result of these political activities lessons were disrupted for nearly three months. Of course not all these disturbances in Russian schools were politically motivated. Many of the schoolboy demonstrations were prompted by high spirits and a desire to obtain some relaxation of school discipline. But they were none the less symptomatic of the way in which the authority of the state education system had been undermined. The more radically-minded parents supported the pupils' demands, but the vast majority of parents were deeply disturbed by the intrusion of politics into school life. The pupils gained some initial successes by their revolutionary actions: school uniforms were abolished, parents were allowed to form consultative committees and individual schools were granted greater freedom in teaching matters. But these concessions, which were announced in November 1905, were partially withdrawn eighteen months later.

The year 1905 also signalled the entry of the Russian teaching profession into the political arena and saw the emergence of its trade union organisation. In April and May of 1905 various groups within the intelligentsia formed politically-oriented professional associations, which then joined together to found the Association of Associations (*Soyuz Soyuzov*). The teaching profession was no exception. Its more active members also set up an Association in the spring of that year known as the *All-Russian Teachers' Association (Vserossiisky Soyuz Uchitelyey i Deyatelyey po narodnomu Obrazovaniyu)*. At its first congress in June 1905 this association announced its future programme, in which it called upon its members to fight for a 'fundamental reorganisation of the Russian educational system on the basis of freedom, democratisation and decentralisation, which presupposes the implementation of the following measures:

(a) the integration of all types of schools so as to ensure continuity between the lower- and those higher-grade schools providing a general education;
(b) the introduction of general, free and compulsory primary education and free secondary and higher education;

(c) the abolition of compulsory religious instruction;

(d) legislation specifying that all schools must provide a general education and authorising each individual school to pursue its own teaching methods;

(e) free instruction for all non-Russian ethnic groups in all types of school in their mother tongue;

(f) the transfer of responsibility for the administration of public education to the organs of local self-government, whose members are elected in direct, general and secret elections based on the principle of universal suffrage, and to the social organisations of a national character.'

The *All-Russian Association of Secondary School Teachers* (*Vserossiisky Soyuz Uchitelyey i Deyatelyey sredney Shkoly*), which was founded in February 1906 and in which the majority group supported the Constitutional Democrats, also subscribed to the idea of 'democratic, free and autonomous education'. It defined freedom and autonomy as follows: 'What we mean by the freedom of a school is its freedom from bureaucratic and police interference, while what we understand by its autonomy is the nature of the internal relations between the teachers employed in the school. Thus, the internal affairs of the school are run by the collegiate body, which can be enlarged by co-option, which elects both the individual officials and the school management and which decides the order and composition of the curriculum.' By 'democratisation' the association understood the general and unrestricted availability of secondary school education, the extension of the secondary school system and the reduction of school fees (as a first step towards their complete abolition).

Although these were the two most important teachers' associations, many other all-Russian or local groups were formed at the time of the first Russian revolution in order to strengthen the trade union organisation and promote the pedagogical interests of the teaching profession. A further measure of activity prompted by the revolution was the great increase in the number of pedagogical periodicals. Between 1860 and 1917, 175 such periodicals were published in Russia and of these about 100 appeared after 1905. Although most teachers' associations were forced to disband in 1907, when the conservative reaction set in, many individual teachers remained as revolutionary as ever and in the years immediately preceding the First World War these progressively-minded pedagogues found a new platform for their ideas at the great *cultural and educational congresses* which were held at that time. The most important of these were the general Congress of Zemstvos on Education held in August 1911, the First All-Russian Congress for Family Education in the winter holidays of 1912–13, and the First All-Russian Education Congress in the winter holidays of 1913–14. The last of these three congresses, which was also the biggest, was attended by over 6,500 people, most of whom were primary schoolteachers. The agenda drawn up for the congresses, and the resolutions which they passed, reflect the urgent problems which beset Russian education prior to the revolution and show us the sort of changes which 'society' wanted to see brought about.

But although these educational congresses were an important facet of the pedagogical scene in Russia prior to 1917, from a practical point of view the real pivot of educational activity during the last decade of tsarist rule was the Imperial Duma, which had been created in 1906. In this field the Duma occupied a central position. As a product of the revolution it provided a platform for the opposition forces, who wanted to change the traditional system; but it also came to accept the responsibility which devolved on it as a national assembly and so actively collaborated with the government on the development of the state's educational policy. Although both the Third Duma (1907–12) and the Fourth (1912–17) had conservative majorities, in educational matters the Octobrists and the Constitutional Democrats usually formed a common front, which was powerful enough to ensure that a whole series of important measures got through the house. By and large the reactionary elements in the government were not to be found in the Ministry of Education but in the Imperial Council, to which all legislative proposals had to be submitted and which rejected or radically altered many of the Duma's bills.

The introduction of compulsory education, a measure which would have required very large subsidies from the state, was the major problem in the educational sphere with which the Duma had to contend. The solution proposed by the Duma majority envisaged comprehensive legislation which would unify Russian primary education and set a time-limit for the implementation of compulsory school attendance. The Council of Ministers and the government, on the other hand, preferred to deal with the problem on a more pragmatic basis, acting only in individual cases. As the weaker party the Duma had to content itself with getting additional clauses inserted in the government's proposals. At the same time it took any practical steps it could to improve the situation. Thus, while continuing from 1908 onwards to press for a comprehensive law to regulate the whole of the educational system, it also proposed a series of new laws which were designed to establish the principle of general education.

The fundamental law of 3 May 1908 vested the responsibility for the implementation of compulsory education in the organs of local self-government (the Zemstvos and the municipal Dumas) which were to receive a regular annual subsidy from the Ministry of Education provided they themselves were able to provide stipulated sums and would undertake to build sufficient schools for all 8- to 11-year-old children in their districts. The revenue set aside by the state for this project was increased from year to year and by 1913 amounted to 62.9 million roubles. By 1916 all but three of the 441 district Zemstvos and 494 of the 789 towns with local self-government had entered into such an agreement with the government and had begun to introduce compulsory education. In thirty-three towns, including all the major cities, and in fifteen districts, the requisite number of schools had been built by 1915. In the provinces which had no Zemstvo administration responsibility for the introduction of compulsory education rested with the Ministry of Education; there progress was much slower.

In 1911, after long years of discussion, the Duma Education Commission produced draft proposals for a *comprehensive education law,* which constituted a compromise between the more radical scheme evolved by the 'League for Education' and the moderate approach favoured by the Duma majority. In its draft the Commission recommended that within three years all primary schools, including parish schools run by the Holy Synod, should be placed under the control of the Zemstvos and the

municipal Dumas, who would administer them in accordance
with the guidelines laid down by the Ministry of Education. It
was further suggested that in areas occupied by non-Russian
ethnic groups schools should provide a four-year course in the
local language. But although this draft was by no means radical,
its main points were none the less rejected by the Imperial
Council: the special position occupied by the parish schools,
which were regarded by the conservatives as a stronghold of the
church and the monarchy, remained unaltered. The clause providing for language classes in their native tongue for non-Russian
children was also dropped, and the proposed integration of
primary and secondary schools was curtailed. In August 1916
these ideas were revived by Ignatyev and appeared in the draft
proposals which he then submitted to the Duma but which the
house was unable to debate before the revolution.

From a purely quantitative point of view the *improvement in
the Russian educational system* effected as a result of the laws
passed by the Duma between 1906 and 1917 was very marked.
No previous decade had produced a comparable advance. In just
four years—from January 1911 to 1 January 1915—the number
of primary schools in Russia rose from 100,295 to 123,754 and
the number of pupils from 6,180,510 to 7,788,453. It has been
estimated that by 1915 51% of all children between the ages of
8 and 11 (inclusive) were receiving primary school education. And
if we consider the general *spread of literacy* among the Russian
population at this time we find that there too, although much
remained to be done, considerable progress had been achieved.
According to the census of 1897, 21.1% of the population of the
Russian empire (excluding Finland) were able to read and
write. It has been estimated that by 1913 this figure had risen
to 28.4%, which means that if we exclude children under 8 years
of age, 38–39% of Russians were then literate. But this still
leaves an illiteracy rate of over 60%, and this, combined with
the fact that almost 50% of Russian school-children received no
formal education, constituted a heavy burden which was bequeathed to revolutionary Russia by the tsarist régime and which
cast its shadow over every attempt to 're-educate' the Russian
people during the first two decades of Soviet rule.

*The reforms proposed by Ignatyev on
the eve of the 1917 Revolution*

Despite the progressive approach to education adopted by the
Duma and the pedagogical reform movement promoted by
society, the tsarist government maintained an essentially conservative attitude. The three Russian Ministers of Education (with
the un-Russian names of Kaufman, Shvarts and Kasso) who succeeded one another in office following the 1905 revolution, were
all more or less opposed to reform. During Kasso's ministry
(1910–14), for example, all proposals for the reform of Russian
secondary schools that were debated in the Duma were vetoed
by the Minister, who never once addressed the assembly. It is
understandable, therefore, that his successor, Count Pavel Nikolayevich Ignatyev (1870–1926), who was appointed Minister of
Education in January 1915, should have created a minor sensa-
tion in the bureaucratic circles of St Petersburg,[3] for from the
very outset he tried to gain the confidence of the Duma and the
support of public opinion by taking part in meetings of Duma
committees, by encouraging private enterprise and by introducing entirely new working methods in his ministry. Although
Ignatyev held office for only two years, his ministry is of great
historical significance. He was the first Russian Minister of Education to make a serious attempt to persuade the government, the
Duma and the public to work together in order to modernise
Russian education and bridge the crucial gap between the conservative attitudes of the régime and the liberal and democratic
ideals of society.

As President of the Kiev Provincial Zemstvo (1904–6), as
Governor of Kiev (1907–8), and as head of a department in
the Ministry of Agriculture (1909–14) Ignatyev had become
acquainted with many different aspects of the Russian educational system. It was during this ten-year period that he became
convinced of the necessity for modernising Russian schools, and
the ideas which he evolved at that time and which formed the
basis of his ministerial activities represented a marked departure
from many of the policies pursued by his predecessors. We now
propose to enquire in greater detail into the origins and objectives
of his proposed reforms, which reflect not only the influx of

progressive educational ideas from abroad but also the development of the Russian state from a semi-feudal to a bourgeois-
democratic institution.

Ignatyev—and many other critics—considered the *principal
deficiency in Russian education* to be the 'scholastic, excessively
classical' character of grammar-school education, which simply
served to prepare pupils for university. 'But only a minority of
those leaving secondary school went on to university. The rest
were released into real life without being properly trained; they
were completely unprepared for any kind of employment which
might await them. Practical knowledge was regarded as inferior
knowledge.'[4] But Ignatyev considered that Russian primary
schools were also far too preoccupied with this false conception
of a general education because they too failed to consider the
sort of practical activity in which their pupils would subsequently
have to engage. Instead of teaching peasant children the sort of
things that would enable them to farm the land more profitably,
provincial primary schools turned out either village clerks or
'bookworms' and 'abstract thinkers', who left the countryside
for the towns where they swelled the ranks of the semi-intellectual
malcontents. Consequently, while he was still working for the
Ministry of Agriculture, Ignatyev set up classes in practical work
in the primary schools run by his department, an innovation that
encountered stiff opposition from the Duma, which was worried
about 'premature specialisation'.

Although Ignatyev's approach to education was based in the
first instance on his own practical experience he later found con-
firmation of his views in the theoretical writings of the American
philosopher and pedagogue John Dewey, which were sent to him
from the USA by a Russian emigrant. It was in Dewey's *School
and Society* that Ignatyev first encountered the theory that
'school must become a normal part of the child's environment so
that the book of life may be opened for him.' This and other
theories discovered in American pedagogical works gave Ignatyev
the 'greatest help and encouragement to carry on and to try to
cultivate the same ideas on Russian soil'.[5] It is not at all difficult
to show the affinity between Ignatyev's proposed reforms and
Dewey's pedagogical pragmatism. The Russian Minister's rejection of the classical curriculum as 'unproductive' and his advo-

cacy of subjects related to the modern economy, his preference for practical and vocational training and his approval of industrial schools were all prompted by Dewey's pedagogical ideas. It can be assumed that Ignatyev must also have been acquainted with the writings of Georg Kerschensteiner, the other great educational theorist of the period. Certainly he instructed his subordinates in the Ministry of Education to study the pedagogical reforms carried out in Europe and the USA. Moreover, a number of the phrases which he used in his own writings—for example, his insistence that children should be educated in such a way as to become 'useful members of society' and 'conscious citizens'— are distinctly reminiscent of Kerschensteiner.

The First World War, which showed up Russia's economic and administrative weaknesses, provided Ignatyev with further arguments in support of his project for changing the Russian educational system so that it would be better able to serve the needs of a modern industrial and agrarian state. Apart from the introduction of compulsory education, which Ignatyev insisted must be completed by 1925 at the latest, this project envisaged an integrated educational system built up around an improved type of secondary school and incorporating a large number of professional schools. In a report submitted to the Tsar on 12 April 1915 Ignatyev developed his *plan for a unified educational system*, which constituted a 'radical departure from the type of educational system in current use on the continent of Europe' and which made no secret of its affinity to the American system. Under Ignatyev's proposals pupils were to spend four years at a general primary school, four years at a higher primary school and four years at a secondary school. Universities and colleges were to be open to all pupils who successfully completed their secondary school course. But although the three types of school were to be inter-connected to enable suitable children to proceed from one to another, each different type would provide a complete education at its own level so that children leaving school at any stage would be adequately prepared either for vocational training or for work.

The Tsar approved Ignatyev's plan in principle and the Minister was then able to work out detailed proposals, taking account of any earlier reform plans while bearing in mind the need for realism. The commissions of experts which he set up quickly produced numerous recommendations for the reformation of the Russian school system, which were not fully implemented until after the overthrow of the monarchy, when they appeared in the reform measures introduced by the Provisional Government and, subsequently, the Soviet régime. But a number of reforms were drafted and partially implemented in 1915–1916.

The first of these concerned *primary schools*. It was suggested both by the commission of experts and by members of a specialist conference that children in village primary schools should be given instruction in nature study and the practical side of agriculture. Nature rambles, gardening and light agricultural work were suggested as suitable ways of establishing a meaningful rapport between the schools and rural life.

The second of these measures affected *secondary school education*, which was undoubtedly the most important aspect of the whole reform question. In April 1915 Ignatyev convened a special conference to discuss the reform of secondary schools, which was attended by Duma delegates with a particular interest in education and by well-known bourgeois pedagogues of liberal persuasion. After the conference had laid down the necessary guidelines, various commissions were set up to work out a new schools statute and new curricula. The requirements established for the new secondary school were formulated as follows: 'First, the school should be national; secondly, it should fulfil an independent function by providing a comprehensive education instead of concentrating on preparing pupils for universities; thirdly, it should provide tuition over a seven-year period; fourthly, it should consist of two grades, the first providing a three-year course of education, the second a four-year course.'[6] The first grade, incidentally, was to correspond to the first three years of the higher primary school. Pupils would be able to enter the new secondary school from the four-year primary school, the lowest class of the higher primary school or upon completion of their studies at the higher primary school. The second stage of the new secondary school could also be used independently to provide a four-year course of secondary education which would assume one of three forms: modern languages, classical-humanist or natural sciences. The old type of classical and non-classical secondary schools would of course cease to exist.

However, although there were to have been different types of secondary school, they would all have taught Russian, history and mathematics, so that the differentiation depended primarily on whether a particular school specialised in modern languages or the natural sciences. A novel feature was the introduction of physical education and laboratory work. But another of the commission's recommendations, to the effect that manual work should be introduced as an independent subject, was temporarily shelved. Ignatyev himself, incidentally, was very much in favour of this particular proposal for he considered the 'work principle' to be a valuable educational aid better suited than any other to 'prepare pupils for the tasks that life would impose on them.'[7]

The 'Regulations for Gymnasiums (secondary schools providing a general education)' which were drawn up in conjunction with the new time-tables and curricula, granted both the pedagogical school councils (teachers' councils) and the individual teacher a greater measure of independence. They also enabled parents and local authority representatives to participate to some extent in school management. The 'Regulations for Parents' Organisations' published shortly afterwards, gave considerable rights to the elected parents' committees. Before proceeding to full reform of the secondary school system the government first introduced a number of smaller measures by issuing individual decrees which dealt with specific aspects of school life. Thus, in 1915–16, the end-of-term and school-leaving examinations were abolished, partly on account of the war but partly with a view to replacing them by an entirely new kind of examination.

The third reform measure evolved in 1915–16 was concerned with the professional schools, in which Ignatyev took such a great interest. 'The welfare of Russia and her whole future,' he stated in a report addressed to the Council of Ministers, 'depend on the country's productive forces being increased. Rapid and powerful growth is inconceivable unless professional education is greatly expanded. If the enormous natural resources of our motherland are to be rationally and fully exploited, we shall need thousands of men and women with technical training.'[8] The Ministry of Education worked out draft proposals for the reform of professional and technical education, which were debated in 1915–16, together with similar reform proposals drawn up by the Ministry of Trade and Industry and the Ministry of Transport. All three ministries called for a considerable increase in the number of professional schools and insisted that these must adapt their curricula to meet the special requirements of the different professions. They also wanted the schools to maintain close contact with industrial concerns so that their pupils could obtain practical experience of factory work.

Ignatyev's proposals provided for a comprehensive system of professional training based on the future needs of Russian technology and industry. The simplest form of training was to be given at craft schools, which would be open to all pupils who had completed a four-year primary school course and who would be trained to become charge-hands. The second type of professional school, the craft institute, was designed to cater for pupils with six years' primary education who wished to become master-craftsmen. Next came the technical institutes, where pupils who had attended a higher primary school for a period of eight years would be able to train as engineers of various types. Finally, there were to be technical and professional colleges, which Ignatyev proposed to keep quite separate from the universities, as training-grounds for specialists and as centres for the dissemination of scientific and technological knowledge. In order to coordinate these different schemes a Council for Matters Relating to Professional Education in Russia was formed in February 1916, headed by Ignatyev. Although Ignatyev's dismissal and the outbreak of the revolution frustrated this attempt to establish an effective system of professional training, the pioneering work carried out in this sphere during the final phase of the tsarist period paved the way for the measures introduced by the Provisional Government. Thus, in respect of both professional and secondary education, the post-revolutionary régime was able to build on Ignatyev's ideas.

If we consider all that Ignatyev was able to accomplish during his two-year period of office, then we must agree with Sir Bernard Pares, the eminent British historian, who said that he was 'possibly the best Minister of Education that Russia had had.'[9] Even Soviet historians—who have inevitably drawn attention to the 'bourgeois character' of Ignatyev's education policy—have had to concede that his reform proposals were both progressive and beneficial. Ignatyev himself stated that it was the war which prevented him from realising his objectives. But he also pointed out that although the remarkable progress made by the educational reform movement prior to 1914 was slowed down during the first two years of hostilities, it was not seriously endangered until the end of 1916. Thus, on the eve of the revolution of February 1917, Russian education was undergoing *a process of renewal and expansion*, in which every endeavour was made to incorporate the ideas evolved by the latest pedagogical trends while taking full account of the new economic and social conditions that had developed during the modern era. True, there were still numerous survivals of a moribund past and considerable opposition in conservative circles both at court and among the bureaucracy. But in all essential respects the rigid framework of the old order had been left behind. The revolution of 1917 then removed the remaining barriers which had hampered the educational reformers. But it also shattered the whole structure of society and drew Russian schools into the whirlpool of political upheaval with all the consequences that this entailed.

This chapter, which is an abridged version of the first three sections of *Geschichte der Schule und Pädagogik in Russland vom Ende des Zarenreiches bis zum Beginn der Stalin-Ära* [*History of Russian Schools and Pedagogy from the end of the tsarist régime to the beginning of the Stalin era*, Berlin, 1964] appears by kind permission of the author and the Ost-Europa-Institut at the Berlin Free University. Only a selection of the original footnotes have been reproduced. (*Editor*)

Notes

Russian foreign policy 1880–1914

GEORGE KATKOV and MICHAEL FUTRELL

1 Boris Nolde *L'Alliance Franco-Russe* (Paris 1936), p 456.

2 ibid., p 575.

3 Even Alexander III, who in the mid-eighties did not conceal his contempt and dislike for the republican régime in France, seems to have been mollified after meeting French military leaders (General Appert and General Boisdeffre) who, without concealing their attachment to the principle of monarchy, found it possible to serve their country under a republican régime.

4 See a most readable and entertaining account of world reactions to Nicholas II's initiative in Barbara W. Tuchman's *The Proud Tower* (New York and London 1966), p 239ff.

5 See Malozemoff *Russian Far Eastern Policy 1881–1904* (Berkeley 1958); and the Soviet historian B. A. Romanov *Russia in Manchuria* translated by S. W. Jones and published for the American Council of Learned Societies by J. W. Edwards (Ann Arbor 1952).

6 Malozemoff, op. cit., p 114.

7 Prince Bülow quotes the letter in full without giving the exact date. See Bülow *Denkwürdigkeiten* vol II (Berlin 1931), pp 174–5.

8 'Bericht des Grafen Pourtalès vom 13.3.1913' in *Archiv des Auswärtigen Amtes. Russia 61* vol 121; English translation: Richard Pipes (ed.) *Revolutionary Russia* (Cambridge, Mass. 1968), p 65.

Constitutional law in Russia

LOTHAR SCHULTZ

1 L. Schultz *Russische Rechtsgeschichte: Von den Anfängen bis zur Gegenwart einschliesslich des Rechts der Sowjetunion* (Lahr 1951), p 168.

2 *Svod zakonov Rossiiskoy Imperii* (Collected Laws of the Russian Empire), vol I, part 1 (St Petersburg 1832).

3 N. M. Korkunov *Russkoye gosudarstvennoye pravo* (Russian Constitutional Law), vol 1 (St Petersburg 1893), pp 158–62.

4 M. F. Vladimirsky-Budanov *Obzor istorii russkogo prava* (Concise History of Russian Law) 6th edn. (St Petersburg 1909), p 240.

5 Korkunov, op. cit., pp 163–7.

6 J. Engelmann *The Constitutional Law of the Russian Empire* (Freiburg i Br. 1889), p 38.

7 R. Maurach *Der russische Reichsrat* (Berlin 1939), pp 64–5.

8 Schultz, op. cit., p 173.

9 Vladimirsky-Budanov, op. cit., p 264.

10 B. Meissner 'Die Verfassungsentwicklung Russlands' in B. Dennewitz (ed.) *Die Verfassungen der modernen Staaten*, vol. 1 (Hamburg 1947), pp 104–17.

11 N. M. Korkunov *Rasporyazheniye i zakon* (Decrees and Laws) (Moscow 1894), p 327.

12 E. Amburger *Geschichte der Behördenorganisation Russlands von Peter dem Grossen bis 1917* (Leyden 1966), pp 47–54.

13 S. G. Pushkaryev, *Rossiya v XIX veke 1801–1914* (Russia in the Nineteenth Century) (New York 1956), pp 233–7.

14 *Svod zakonov Rossiiskoy Imperii*, vol I (St Petersburg 1911), pp 1–22.

15 A. Palme *Die russische Verfassung* (Berlin 1910), p 85.

16 M. Weber 'Russlands Übergang zum Scheinkonstitutionalismus' in *Archiv für Sozialwissenschaft und Sozialpolitik*, vol XXIII 1906, Appendix pp 249ff; and 'Zur Lage der bürgerlichen Demokratie in Russland' in *Archiv für Sozialwissenschaft und Sozialpolitik*, vol XXII 1906, p 345ff.

17 See also V. Gitermann *Geschichte Russlands* vol III (Hamburg 1949), p 424; N. V. Riasanovsky *A History of Russia* (New York and London 1963), p 504; J. Haller *Die russische Gefahr im deutschen Hause* (Stuttgart 1917), p 46.

18 P. Miljukov *Russlands Zusammenbruch* vol I *Die Scheinverfassung von 1906* (Stuttgart 1925), p 2.

19 O. Hoetzsch *Russland: Eine Einführung auf Grund seiner Geschichte von 1904 bis 1912* (Berlin 1915), pp 176, 534.

20 W. Gribowski *Das Staatsrecht des Russischen Reiches* (Tübingen 1912), p 20.

21 *Svod zakonov Rossiiskoy Imperii*, vol I, part 1 (St Petersburg 1911), pp 48–51.

22 M. T. Florinsky *Russia: a History and an Interpretation* vol II (New York 1953), p 1206.

23 H. Seton-Watson *The Russian Empire 1801–1917* (Oxford 1967), p 480.

24 Gribowski, op. cit., pp 158–60; Korkunov, op. cit., pp 372–5.

25 R. P. Browder and A. F. Kerensky (eds.) *The Russian Provisional Government 1917* (Selected Documents) vol III (Stanford 1961), pp 1657–8.

26 A. von Freytagh-Loringhoven *Die Gesetzgebung der russischen Revolution* (Halle 1920), p 18.

27 'Vremennoye pravitel'stvo v Rossii v 1917 g.' (The Provisional Government in Russia 1917) (Dictionary entry appearing under 'Vremennoye') in *Bolshaya Sovetskaya Entsiklopediya* (Large Soviet Encyclopedia), 2nd edn. (Moscow 1952) vol XII, p 285.

28 R. P. Browder and A. F. Kerensky (eds.) op. cit., vol I, p 137.

29 G. Vernadsky, *A History of Russia*, 3rd edn. (London and New Haven

1951), pp 236–7; 'Istoriya Kommunisticheskoy Partii Sovetskogo Soyuza', vol II (Moscow 1966), p 681.

30 Browder and Kerensky, op. cit., vol I, p 210.

31 ibid., vol III, pp 454–61.

The role of the political parties

ERWIN OBERLÄNDER

1 Quotation taken from *Polny sbornik platform vsekh russkikh politicheskikh partii* (Complete Collection of the Programmes of all the Russian Political Parties) (St Petersburg 1906), pp 19–28.

2 P. Sorlin *The Soviet People and their Society: from 1917 to the Present* (London and New York 1969), p 29.

3 See *Polny sbornik platform vsekh russkikh politicheskikh partii* (St Petersburg 1906), pp 11–18. (There is a German translation in B. Meissner *Das Parteiprogramm der KPdSU von 1903 bis 1961* (Cologne 1962), pp 115–20.)

4 V. Lenin, 'Zamechaniya na pervy proyekt programmy Plekhanova' (Observations on Plekhanov's First Draft for a Party Programme) in *Polnoye sobraniye sochinenii* vol IV (Moscow 1960), p 201.

5 Quotation taken from P. P. Maslov, 'Narodnicheskiye partii' (The Narodnik Parties) in L. Martov, P. Maslov, A. Potresov (eds.) *Obshchestvennoye dvizheniye v Rossii v nachale XX-go veka* (The Social Movement in Russia at the beginning of the Twentieth Century), vol III (St Petersburg 1914), p 139. Volume III of this series still provides the most comprehensive account of the emergence of the Russian political parties and the part they played in the first two Dumas.

6 V. A. Maklakov, *Pervaya gosudarstvennaya duma: Vospominaniya sovremennika* (The First State Duma: Memoirs of a Contemporary) (Paris 1939), p 147.

7 (P. B. Struve) 'Ot redaktora' (By the Editor) in *Osvobozhdeniye*, No 1 (Stuttgart 28 June 1902), p 2.

8 An English translation of the whole of this resolution, including the minority report, can be found in S. Harcave *First Blood: The Russian Revolution of 1905* (New York 1964), pp 279–81. (London 1965).

9 *Polny sbornik platform vsekh russkikh politicheskikh partii* (St Petersburg 1906), pp 58–67.

10 ibid., pp 76–87.

11 ibid., pp 93–103.

12 ibid., p 127.

13 For a critical assessment of this phenomenon see H. Rogger 'Was There a Russian Fascism?: The Union of Russian People' in *The Journal of Modern History* vol 36, 1964, pp 398–415.

14 These figures have been taken from *Dumsky sbornik. Gosudarstvennaya duma pervago sozyva (27 aprelya – 8 iulya 1906 g)* (Duma Anthology:

The First Imperial Duma (27 April—8 July 1906)) (St Petersburg 1906), p 9.
15 M. Baring, *A Year in Russia* (London 1907), pp 192 and 193.
16 Quotation taken from *Dumsky sbornik* (op. cit.), pp 120–123.
17 B. Pares *Russia and Reform* (London 1907), p 546.
18 See W. B. Walsh, 'Political Parties in the Russian Dumas' in *The Journal of Modern History*, vol XXII 1950, pp 144–150.
19 These groupings are tabulated in detail in W. B. Walsh, ibid., p 148.
20 Quotation taken from M. Hellmann (ed.) *Die russische Revolution 1917: Von der Abdankung des Zaren bis zum Staatsstreich der Bolschewiki*, 2nd edn. (Munich 1969), p 79.
21 See Th. Riha, 'Miliukov and the Progressive Bloc in 1915; A Study in Last-Chance Politics' in *The Journal of Modern History* vol XXXII 1960, pp 16–24.
22 N. V. Svyatitsky, *Kogo russky narod izbral svoimi predstavitelyami?* (Whom did the Russian People Choose as its Representatives?) (Moscow 1918), pp 10–11. The quotation reproduced here was taken from O. H. Radkey *The Election to the Russian Constituent Assembly of 1917* (Cambridge, Mass. and London 1950).

Russia's economic development

KARL C. THALHEIM

1 This figure was taken from Wossidlo, 'Die Petersburger Industrie' in M. Sering (ed.) *Russlands Kultur und Volkswirtschaft* (Berlin and Leipzig 1913), p 214.
2 Jürgen Nötzold *Wirtschaftspolitische Alternativen der Entwicklung Russlands in der Ära Witte und Stolypin* (Berlin 1966), p 103.
3 R. Portal, 'Das Problem einer industriellen Revolution in Russland im 19 Jahrhundert' in *Forschungen zur osteuropäischen Geschichte*, vol I (Berlin 1954), p 206.
4 P. I. Lyashchenko, *History of the National Economy of Russia to the 1917 Revolution* translated from the Russian by L. M. Herman (New York 1949), pp 298–9.
5 For further examples of industrial developments in St Petersburg see Wossidlo, op. cit., pp 203–18. Wossidlo was the trade attaché at the German Consulate in St Petersburg at the time.
6 Lyashchenko, op. cit., p 486. (1 pood = 16.38 kg.)
7 Wherever possible in these statistical tables the figures given for 'Russia' are those for the whole of the Russian empire within its pre-1914 borders, which included the three Baltic provinces of Livonia, Estonia and Courland and the Congress Kingdom of Poland (Russian Poland), whose industrial output was above the Russian average. This is an important distinction because present-day Soviet statisticians tend to take the Soviet Union within its present borders as the basis of their

calculations. Consequently, when they compare the industrial development of tsarist and Soviet Russia in order to establish the growth rates for Soviet industry, the figures cited for the pre-revolutionary period are almost invariably too low. The truth of the matter is that both the Baltic provinces and Russian Poland were fully integrated into the Russian economy and most of their industrial goods were produced for the Russian market. There is, therefore, no good reason why these areas should be excluded from any assessment of the economic growth of *pre-revolutionary* Russia and the fact that they have been excluded, not only in the Soviet Union but also in the *West*, has unfortunately produced a widespread misconception as to the tempo and extent of Russia's economic development during that period. The only territory within the Russian empire that should be excluded is Finland, which was separated from the rest of Russia by a customs frontier and so did not form part of the Russian economy. However, this is not the only reason why the estimates prepared by Soviet statisticians of the growth rates of Soviet industry have been exaggerated. They have also consistently disregarded the traditional cottage industries, which played an important part in the production of consumer goods.

8 Figures taken from S. N. Prokopovicz *Russlands Volkswirtschaft unter den Sowjets* (Zurich and New York 1944), pp 173–4. Prokopovicz speaks of 'major industries', by which he presumably means 'factory-based industries'.

9 Nötzold, op. cit., p 20. The expansion of Russia's major cities (which was originally linked with the expansion of her industry) was none the less quite marked, as is evident from the following table which has been taken from Prokopovicz, op. cit., p 36:

No. of inhabitants (in thousands)	1897	1914
Moscow	1038.6	1762.7
St Petersburg	1264.9	2118.5
Kiev	247.7	520.5
Baku	111.9	232.2
Tashkent	155.7	271.9
Tiflis	159.6	307.3
Novo-Nikolayevsk (now Novosibirsk)	7.8	73.0

10 Sources: For 1887–97 Lyashchenko, op. cit., p 526; for 1908 *Archiv für Sozialwissenschaft und Sozialpolitik* vol 64 1930, p 570.

11 Lyashchenko, op. cit., pp 688 and 690. There are certain discrepancies between Lyashchenko's figures and those taken from other sources, for which there appears to be no logical explanation. Even if we assume that Lyashchenko based his calculations on the present-day borders of the USSR, this still does not explain the discrepancies. However, the general development is the same in either case.

12 Sering, op. cit., p 185.

13 W. Woytinsky *Die Welt in Zahlen* vol IV (Berlin 1926), pp 318–20.

14 ibid., p 89.

15 ibid., p 234.

16 Nötzold, op. cit., p 103.

17 Otto Hoetzsch *Russland* 2nd edn. (Berlin 1917), p 73.

18 Quotation taken from Hoetzsch, op. cit., p 76 (Hoetzsch does not give a source).

19 This question has been investigated by B. Ischchanian, who provides a considerable amount of interesting material in his book: *Die ausländischen Elemente in der russischen Volkswirtschaft: Geschichte, Ausbreitung, Berufsgruppierung, Interessen und ökonomisch-kulturelle Bedeutung der Ausländer in Russland* (Berlin 1913).

20 'Finanzblatt' 1897 No 17, p 263 (quotation taken from M. Tugan-Baranowsky *Geschichte der russischen Fabrik* (German edition, Berlin 1900), p 407).

21 Ischchanian op. cit., p 146.

22 ibid., p 162.

23 ibid., p 212.

24 Margaret Miller, *The Economic Development of Russia 1905–1914*, 2nd edn. (New York and London 1967), p 184.

25 In 1917 Finland had 3909 km of track.

26 Kurt Wiedenfeld 'Russlands Stellung in der Weltwirtschaft' in *Russlands Kultur und Volkswirtschaft* (op. cit.), p 253.

27 A. Sartorius von Waltershausen, *Die Entstehung der Weltwirtschaft* (Jena 1931), p 432. According to von Waltershausen the net registered tonnage of the Russian fleet (*without* Finland) in 1913 was 757,000 tons, of which 500,000 tons were accounted for by steamships and 257,000 tons by sailing vessels. (In 1916 the net registered tonnage of the Finnish fleet was 486,000 tons, a large part of which was made up of sail.) See also *Statistisches Jahrbuch für das Deutsche Reich* Jg. 41 1920, p 28.

28 Theodor D. Zotschew has analysed this situation in his *Die aussenwirtschaftlichen Verflechtungen der Sowjetunion* (Tübingen 1969). On p 4 of this book he says: 'Russia's foreign liabilities during the period preceding the October Revolution have been estimated at 5162 million gold roubles in the form of state and other loans and 2000 million gold roubles in the form of foreign investments in the Russian economy . . . The capital repayments and interest on these loans and investments—between 800 and 900 million gold roubles per annum—placed a very heavy burden on Russia's finances and, more especially, her balance of payments; approximately half this expenditure was incurred by the interest on state loans while the rest was needed to cover the interest and capital repayments on foreign investments.'

29 See also Emil Zweig *Die russische Handelspolitik seit 1877* (Leipzig 1906) and Valentin Wittschewsky *Russlands Handels-, Zoll- und Industriepolitik von Peter dem Grossen bis auf die Gegenwart* (Berlin 1905).

30 Margaret Miller, op. cit., p 61.

31 See Wiedenfeld, op. cit., pp 263–71.

32 See also Leo Jurowsky *Der russische Getreideexport, seine Entwicklung und Organisation* (Stuttgart and Berlin 1910).

33 There were considerable variations between the Russian and the German export figures. According to the Russian statisticians there was a

very large balance in Germany's favour. In actual fact, however, this balance was relatively small. In Russia all exports were listed under the countries to which they were shipped and since a considerable amount of Germany's imports of Russian wheat and petroleum came via Rotterdam or Antwerp, they were listed as Dutch or Belgian. For a more detailed analysis of this question see Wiedenfeld, op. cit., pp 265–7.

34 ibid., pp 251–2.

35 This calculation is based on the figures provided in the *Statistisches Jahrbuch für das Deutsche Reich* Jg. 45 1926, pp 96–7.

36 V. I. Lenin, 'Razvitiye kapitalizma v Rossii' in *Polnoye sobraniye sochinenii* vol III, p 601. Like later Soviet writers Lenin placed particular emphasis on the highly concentrated state of Russian industry. For reasons of space it has not been possible to deal with this question in the text.

37 Lyashchenko, op. cit., pp 673–4. In certain instances Lyashchenko fails to provide any evidence in support of his argument. For example, his assertion that the level of machine production in Russia was 'very rudimentary' appears to be completely unfounded. So too does his highly improbable suggestion that France's industrial production was two and a half times greater than Russia's in 1913.

38 Margaret Miller holds a similar view. In the 'Conclusion' of her book *The Economic Development of Russia 1905–1914* she writes: 'In view of Russia's almost unlimited natural wealth, there was no doubt that ultimately the railway net would pay, that ultimately the industries which were so costly to establish would yield handsome profits. But the process demanded a long period of peaceful development. Russia seemed to have entered upon such a period, after the disturbances of the Russo-Japanese War and the 1905 revolution had been overcome. And from that time up to 1914 progress was steady and remarkable in every sphere of economic activity. But the outbreak of the war cut short this progress before the synthesis between a modern economic system and a backward social and political structure was anywhere near completion.'

The agrarian problem

HARRY T. WILLETTS

1 See *Arkhiv Grafov Mordvinovykh* vol VIII (St Petersburg 1903), pp 436–7.

2 See his speech to the State Council 28 January 1861, quoted in *Zhurnaly i Memorii Obshchego Sobraniya Gosudarstvennogo Sovieta po Krestyanskomu Delu* (St Petersburg 1915).

3 N. A. Milyutin (1818–72), Deputy Minister of the Interior from 1859–1861, was the main co-ordinator of work in preparation for emancipation, and a staunch defender of peasant interests against exorbitant demands from the gentry.

4 The legislation is summarized with incomparable clarity in the article

'Krestyane' in vol XXXII of *Entsiklopedichesky Slovar'* edited by F. A. Brockhaus and I. A. Yefron (St. Petersburg 1895), pp 659–725.

5 1 *desyatin* = 2.69 acres.

6 See V. I. Anisimov, 'Nadely' in *Velikaya reforma. Russkoye obshchestvo i krestyansky vopros v proshlom i nastoyashchem* vol VI (Moscow 1911), pp 76–103; here pp 92–3.

7 A. E. Lositsky *Vykupnaya operatsiya* (St Petersburg 1906).

8 A. V. Peshekhonov 'Ekonomicheskoye polozheniye krestyan v poreformennoye vremya' in *Velikaya reforma* op. cit., pp 200–48; here p 214.

9 See G. T. Robinson *Rural Russia under the Old Régime* (New York 1949), ch VI.

10 Peshekhonov, op. cit., p 206.

11 P. I. Lyashchenko *Istoriya Narodnogo khozyaistva SSSR* vol II (Moscow 1952), p 278. These figures are for the quinquennium before the First World War when Russia's relative performance had greatly improved.

12 A. N. Engelgardt *Iz derevni. 11 pisem* 2nd edn (St Petersburg 1885).

13 His most important works on agrarian matters are *Zemlevladeniye i zemledeliye v Rossii i v drugikh yevropeiskikh stranakh* (St Petersburg 1876) and *Melkii zemelny kredit* (St Petersburg 1876).

14 See I. V. Chernyshev *Agrarno-krestyanskaya politika Rossii za 150 let* (Petrograd 1918), p 249.

15 In his report on the budget estimates for 1899. See Th. H. von Laue *Sergei Witte and the Industrialization of Russia* (New York 1963), p 176.

16 Chernyshev, op. cit., p 283.

17 S. Yu. Witte *Zapiska po krestyanskomu delu* (St Petersburg 1905), pp 157–8.

18 For Kutler's project see *Agrarny vopros* I. I. Petrunkevich and P. D. Dolgorukov (eds.) vol II (Moscow 1907).

19 In his speech in the Duma on 10 May 1907 Stolypin distinguished between 'qualitative expropriation' (for purposes of land improvement) and 'quantitative expropriation'.

20 See S. M. Dubrovsky *Stolypinskaya reforma* 3rd edn. (Moscow 1963) ch 4 (1st edn Leningrad 1925, 2nd edn Moscow 1930).

21 I. V. Chernyshev *Obshchina posle ukaza 9 noyabrya 1906 g.* part I (Moscow 1917).

22 A. A. Kaufman *Agrarny vopros v Rossii* 2nd edn (Moscow 1919), p 184.

23 V. I. Lenin 'Ob otsenke tekushchego momenta' in *Polnoye sobraniye sochinenii* vol XVII (Moscow 1961), p 275.

24 See note 20.

25 A. Solzhenitsyn *V kruge pervom* (London 1968), p 436.

The economic and cultural development of Siberia

NIKOLAUS POPPE

1 N. M. Yadrintsev *Sibir' kak koloniya v geograficheskom, etnograficheskom i istoricheskom otnoshenii* (The Geographical, Ethnographical

and Historical Aspects of Siberia as a Colony) 2nd edn (St Petersburg 1892), p 243.

2 P. W. Danckwortt *Sibirien und seine wirtschaftliche Zukunft* (Leipzig and Berlin 1921), p 1.

3 M. Vetoshkin *Ocherki po istorii bolshevistskikh organizatsii i revolyutsionnogo dvizheniya v Sibiri: 1898–1907* (Historical Sketches of the Bolshevik Organisations and the Revolutionary Movement in Siberia: 1898–1907) (Moscow 1953), p 3.

4 A. A. Mukhin 'Vliyaniye sibirskoy zheleznoy dorogi na sotsialno-ekonomicheskoye razvitiye Vostochnoy Sibiri: 1897–1917 gg' (The Influence of the Trans-Siberian Railway on the Social and Economic Development of Eastern Siberia) in *Voprosy istorii Sibiri i Dalnego Vostoka: Trudy konferentsii po istorii Sibiri i Dalnego Vostoka* (Novosibirsk 1961), p 111.

5 'Pereseleniye' (Emigration) in *Bolshaya sovetskaya entsiklopediya*, 2nd edn vol XXXII (Moscow 1955), p 455.

6 1 *desyatin* = 1.09 hectares = 2.69 acres.

7 *Istoriya Sibiri s drevneyshikh vremen do nashikh dney* (History of Siberia from Ancient Times to the Present) vol III (Leningrad 1968), p 180.

8 P. I. Petrov *Ustanovleniye sovetskoy vlasti v Yakutii* (The Establishment of Soviet Power in Yakutia) (Yakutsk 1957), pp 21–2.

9 Donald W. Treadgold *The Great Siberian Migration: Government and Peasant in Resettlement from Emancipation to the First World War* (Princeton 1957), p 34 (London 1958).

10 *Narody Sibiri* (The Peoples of Siberia) (Moscow and Leningrad 1956), p 9.

11 *Kolonizatsiya Sibiri v svyazi s obshchym pereselencheskim voprosom* (The Colonization of Siberia and the Question of Immigration) (publication of the Council of Ministers: St Petersburg 1900), pp 14 and 16.

12 V. P. Semenov-Tyan'-Shansky (ed.) *Rossiya: Polnoye geograficheskoye opisaniye nashego otyechestva* (Russia: Complete Geographical Description of our Motherland) vol XVI (St. Petersburg 1907), p 174.

13 Marc Raeff *Siberia and the Reforms of 1822* (Seattle 1956), p 44.

14 S. G. Svatikov *Rossiya i Sibir': K istorii sibirskogo oblastnichestva v XIX v.* (Russia and Siberia: On the History of Siberian Regionalism in the Nineteenth Century) (Prague 1930), pp 82–3.

15 A. N. de Koulomzine, *Le Transsibérien* (Translated from the Russian by Jules Legras, Paris 1904), pp 57–61 and 195–6.

16 Treadgold, op. cit., p 34.

17 Immigration Department of the Central Office for Agricultural Development (eds.) *Aziatskaya Rossiya: Izdaniye Pereselencheskago Upravleniya Glavnago Upravleniya Zemleustroystva i Zemledyeliya* (Asiatic Russia) vol I (St Petersburg 1914), p 81.

18 *Encyclopedia Americana* vol V (New York 1965), p 306.

19 Yu. Gagemeyster *Statisticheskoye obozreniye Sibiri* (Statistical Survey of Siberia) vol II (St Petersburg 1834), p 19.

20 'Rossiya' in *Entsiklopedichesky slovar'*, F. A. Brockhaus, I. A. Yefron, *Dopolnitelny*, Tom II, p XII.

21 Arved Schultz *Sibirien: Eine Landeskunde* (Breslau 1923), p 164.

22 'Rossiya' in op. cit.

23 S. Patkanov 'Geographie und Statistik der Tungusenstämme Sibiriens' in *Keleti Szemle: Revue Orientale* vol VI 1905, p 173; Schultz, op. cit.

24 *Kolonizatsiya Sibiri* op. cit., p 354.

25 V. E. Popov *Problemy ekonomiki Sibiri* (Problems of the Siberian Economy) (Moscow 1968), p 15.

26 *Aziatskaya Rossiya* (op. cit.) vol II, p 272. The figure in brackets is Rumyantsev's, which is quoted by Schultz, op. cit., p 174.

27 I. I. Serebrennikov *Sibirevedeniye* (Geography of Siberia) (Harbin 1920), p 136. The author gives 8,908,500 desyatins as the total area of the territory. But this figure includes Akmolinsk and Semipalatinsk which lie outside Siberia proper.

28 ibid., p 139.

29 Schultz, op. cit., p 194.

30 These figures have been taken from the following sources: Danckwortt, op. cit., p 99; Schultz, op. cit., p 177; *Entsiklopedichesky slovar' tovarish-chestva Bratyev Granat* vol XXXVIII, p 480; Serebrennikov, op. cit., p 145.

31 1 pood = 16.38 kg.

32 Serebrennikov, op. cit., p 156.

33 ibid., p 157.

34 E. L. Zubashev 'Fabrichno-zavodskaya i kustarnaya obrabatyvayush-chaya promyshlennost' Sibiri' (Manufacturing Industry and Cottage Industry in Siberia) in *Vol'naya Sibir'*, p 144.

35 P. M. Golovachev *Sibir'* (Moscow 1902), pp 162–3.

36 *Aziatskaya Rossiya* op. cit., vol II, p 440.

37 V. A. Stepynin, 'Vliyaniye pereselenii na razvitiye agrotekhniki v derevnye Yeniseyskoy gubernii v epokhu kapitalizma' (The Influence of Immigration on the Development of Agrarian Techniques on the Land in the Yenisei Province during the Capitalist Epoch) in *Voprosy istorii Sibiri*, op. cit., p 142.

38 See *Istoriya Sibiri*, op. cit., pp 366–423.

39 M. N. Gernet *Istoriya tsarskoy tyur'my* (History of the Tsarist Prison), vol IV (Moscow 1962), p 21.

40 Harry de Windt *Siberia As It is* (London 1892), pp 114, 199, 259, 318, 323, 444.

41 Vetoshkin, op. cit., p 227.

42 V. V. Ryabikov *Irkutsk—stolitsa revolyutsionnoy Sibiri* (Irkutsk: Capital of Revolutionary Siberia) (Irkutsk 1957), pp 195–6.

The 'nationalities question' in the last phase of tsardom

VIOLET CONOLLY

1 George Kennan 'The Breakdown of Tsarist Autocracy' in *Revolutionary Russia* Richard Pipes (ed.) (Cambridge, Mass. 1968), p 11.

2 Bernard Pares *The Fall of the Russian Monarchy: a study of the evidence* (London 1939), p 103 (New York 1939).

3 Quoted by G. A. Yevreinov *Natsionalnye voprosy na inorodcheskikh okrainakh Rossii* (St Petersburg 1908), p 24.

4 B. H. Sumner *Survey of Russian History* (London 1944), p 224.

5 R. Luxemburg *Die russische Revolution 1918* (Frankfurt 1963), p 64.

6 Quoted by W. E. D. Allen *The Ukraine: a History* (Cambridge 1940), p 251 (New York 1941).

7 ibid., p 255.

8 Michael T. Florinsky *Russia: a History and an Interpretation*, vol II (New York 1953), p 1425.

9 ibid., p 1424.

10 Quoted by Anatole G. Mazour *Finland between East and West* (Princeton and London 1956), p 30.

11 J. Oppenheim et al *Mémoire à consulter sur la Question Finlandaise* (Haarlem 1910).

12 Tancred Borenius *Field-Marshal Mannerheim* (London 1940) pp 60–1.

13 This deed *inter alia* ceded civil and criminal jurisdiction over their peasants and almost unrestricted freedom of action over their land, to the gentry, who could thus control their peasants in the most arbitrary manner. See Arnolds Spekke *A History of Latvia* (Stockholm 1951) pp 195–7.

14 Many Latvians and Estonians undoubtedly looked to Russia to free them from the harsh régime of their German masters. Thus, a moving petition signed by hundreds of Estonian peasants was presented to the 'august monarch' in the sixties, lamenting their 'heavy slavery' and 'miserable situation'. See *Russkaya Starina* December 1899, p 655.

15 See E. Seraphim *Grundriss der Baltischen Geschichte* (Reval 1908) pp 387–403, for a Baltic German account of these measures. According to Seraphim, Alexander III rejected the Baltic gentry's protest against this policy with the remark: 'The gentlemen have become accustomed to react to all government measures with protests. That shouldn't be.' Op. cit., p 391.

16 See Florinsky op. cit., p 916f.

17 P. I. Lyashchenko *Istoriya narodnogo khozyaistva SSSR* vol II (Moscow 1952), p 496.

18 K. K. Pahlen *Mission to Turkestan 1908–1909* (Oxford 1964).

19 This summary is based on the detailed study of the subject in Richard Pierce *Russian Central Asia 1867–1917* (Berkeley and Cambridge 1960).

20 1 *desyatin* = 2.69 acres.

21 See R. Vaidyanath *The Formation of the Soviet Central Asian Republics 1917–1936* (New Delhi 1967) p 46.

22 Educational statistics for Turkestan are very scrappy. These figures are quoted from *Aziatskaya Rossiya* vol I (St Petersburg 1914), p 25.

23 ibid., pp 270–2.

24 Vaidyanath op. cit., pp 70–4; S. M. Dimanshtein (ed.) *Revolutsiya i natsionalny vopros: Dokumenty po istorii natsional 'nogo voprosa v Rossii i SSSR v XX veke* vol III (Moscow 1930).

25 Eugene Schuyler *Turkistan: Notes of a Journey in Russian Turkistan, Kokand, Bukhara and Kuldja* (London 1966), p 220.

26 Quoted in *Istoriya narodov Uzbekistana* vol II (Tashkent 1947), p 265.

The Muslim revival in Russia

HANS BRÄKER

1 M. V. Vagabov 'Bolshe vnimaniya sovyetskomu islamovedeniyu' (More Consideration for Soviet Research into Islam) in *Voprosy filosofii* No 12, 1966, pp 172–5.

2 See Hans Bräker *Kommunismus und Islam: Religionsdiskussion und Islam in der Sowjetunion* (Tübingen 1969).

3 For an analysis of the general development of this reform movement see especially Hélène Carrère d'Encausse *Réforme et révolution chez les musulmans de l'Empire russe: Bukhara 1867–1924* (Paris 1966) and N. A. Khalfin, *Russia's Policy in Central Asia: 1857–1868* (London 1965).

4 Quotation taken from 'L'Islam en URSS après 1945' in *La Documentation Française* December 8 1953.

5 According to the *Statistichesky Yezhegodnik Rossii* (Russian Annual Statistical Records) (St Petersburg 1915), p 799 there were 24,582 official Muslim communities in Russia by 1 January 1914. This means that there had been an increase of some 260 in just two years.

6 For a more detailed account of the Wahhabite movement see R. Hartmann 'Die Wahhabiten' in *Zeitschrift der Deutschen Morgenländischen Gesellschaft*, vol LXXVIII 1924, pp 176–213.

7 A select bibliography of the most important writings of Marzhani and the other Muslim reformers mentioned in this section together with a list of critical works on the period is provided in A. Bennigsen and Ch. Quelquejay *Les Mouvements Nationaux chez les Musulmans de Russie: Le 'Sultangalievisme' au Tatarstan* (Paris 1960).

8 In point of fact, the real 'spiritual father' of the theological reform movement in Russia was the Tatar theologian Abu Nasr al Kursavi (1783–1814). As professor at the theological school in Bukhara, al Kursavi worked for the reform of scholastic Muslim theology, thus preparing the ground for Marzhani. He was accused of heresy by Emir Haidar of Bukhara and condemned to death but was able to escape and founded the important Tatar theological school in Kursa. There he was persecuted by the mufti, who accused him of godlessness. Al Kursavi then fled to Istanbul where he finally died.

9 For further information on Melikov-Zerdabi see A. Bennigsen and Ch. Quelquejay *Islam in the Soviet Union* (New York and London 1967), p 37 and p 239.

10 There is a detailed account of Kunanbayev (with a bibliography) in *Bolshaya Sovetskaya Entsiklopediya* 2nd edn., vol I (Moscow 1949), pp 6ff.

11 See Bennigsen and Quelquejay, *Islam in the Soviet Union* (op. cit.),

p 148. The authors give no source for their information but they specifically state that the traditional *Qadim* schools—which remained unaffected by the reforms—continued to exist in considerable numbers. Thus, by 1916 there were 7,290 Muslim primary schools with over 70,000 pupils and 375 Muslim theological schools with 9,600 pupils in the Province of Turkestan alone, which at that time had only 97 secular schools with less than 3,000 pupils.

12 For further information on Ibragimov see especially Galimzhan Ibragimov *Tatary v revolyutsii 1905 goda* (The Tatars in the 1905 Revolution) (Kazan 1926).

13 Gaspraly developed this view in two books: *Russkoye Musulmanstvo* (Russian Islam) (Simferopol 1881) and *Russkovostochnye soglasheniya* (Russo-Eastern Agreements) (Bakhchisaray 1896).

14 For summaries of the proceedings see Bennigsen and Quelquejay, *Les Mouvements Nationaux chez les Musulmans de Russie* (op. cit.), pp 57ff. To the best of my knowledge neither the minutes of the first two congresses nor the resolutions which they passed have been published. This was probably due to the fact that the really crucial sessions had to be held in secret since the Russian authorities had prohibited public discussions of political questions. The third congress was not subject to this restriction and both the minutes of this congress and its resolutions have been printed in a Russian translation in A. Arsharuni and R. M. Gabidullin *Ocherki panislamizma i pantyurkizma v Rossii* (Essays on Panislamism and Panturkism in Russia) (Moscow 1931), pp 114–22.

15 See Safarov's speech to the Xth Party Congress of the RKP (b) in *Desyaty syezd RKP (b). Mart 1921 goda. Stenografichesky otchet* (Moscow 1963), pp 189–201.

16 This is quite evident from the fact that Soviet researchers are now concerned not only with Islamic modernism in general, but also with specific modernistic currents within present-day Soviet Islam. See Yu. G. Petrash and R. M. Khamitova 'K kharakteristike protsessa modernizatsii sovremennogo islama v SSSR' (On the Characteristics of the Process of Modernization of Islam in the USSR) in *Voprosy Nauchnogo Ateizma* part II (Moscow 1966), pp 322–34.

Church, state and society
GERHARD SIMON

1 *Tserkov' v istorii Rossii (IX. v.—1917 g.). Kriticheskiye ocherki* (The Church in Russian History (from the 9th century to 1917): Critical Essays) (Moscow 1967), p 262; I. Smolitsch *Geschichte der russischen Kirche 1700–1917* vol I (Leyden 1964), p 700.

2 *Vsepoddanneyshy otchet Ober-prokurora Sv. Sinoda po vyedomstvu pravoslavnago ispovedaniya za 1903/4 gg.* (Most Humble Report of the

Director General of the Holy Synod concerning the Administrative Authority for the Orthodox Confession for the Years 1903/4) (St Petersburg 1909), Statistical Appendix; Smolitsch, op. cit., pp 705ff; P. Milyukov *Ocherki po istorii russkoy kultury* (Essays on the History of Russian Culture) vol II (Paris 1931) p 210.

3 G. Simon *K. P. Pobedonoscev und die Kirchenpolitik des Heiligen Sinod 1880 bis 1905* (Göttingen 1969), pp 139ff.

4 *Vsepoddanneyshy otchet* . . . (op. cit.); N. M. Nikolsky, *Istoriya russkoy tserkvi* (History of the Russian Church), 2nd edn (Moscow and Leningrad 1931), p 337.

5 J. S. Curtiss *Church and State in Russia: The Last Years of the Empire 1900–1917* (New York 1940), pp 211ff.; I. Smolitsch 'Der Konzilsvorbereitungsausschuss des Jahres 1906; Zur Vorgeschichte des Moskauer Landeskonzils 1917/18' in *Kirche im Osten*, VII, 1964, pp 59–64; I. V. Preobrazhensky (ed.) *Tserkovnaya reforma: Sbornik statey dukhovnoy i svetskoy pechati po voprosu o reforme* (Church Reform. Collection of Essays appearing in the Ecclesiastical and Secular Press on the Reform Question) (St Petersburg 1905).

6 V. I. Yasevich-Borodayevskaya *Borba za veru* (The Struggle for the Faith) (St Petersburg 1912) pp 421–96 (see particularly pp 427, 441–2).

7 The drafts presented by Antony and Witte were printed, together with Pobedonostsev's incensed reaction and Witte's reply to this reaction, in A. P., *Istoricheskaya perepiska o sudbakh pravoslavnoy tserkvi* (Historical Correspondence on the Fate of the Orthodox Church) (Moscow 1912).

8 The Synod's address to the Tsar and the Tsar's resolution were published in N. D. Kuznetsov *Preobrazovaniya v russkoy tserkvi* (Reforms in the Russian Church) (Moscow 1906), pp 59–61, 63.

9 The most important resolutions passed by the special committee were published in *Vsepoddanneyshy otchet* . . . *za 1905/07gg.* (op. cit.) (St Petersburg 1910) pp 53–64. See also Smolitsch, *Der Konzilsvorbereitungsausschuss* (op. cit.), pp 74-93.

10 See Curtiss, op. cit., pp 270–2. The quotation from the synodal resolution appears on p 271–2.

11 This sermon is reported verbatim in Nikon (Rklitsky) *Zhizneopisaniye blazhenneyshego Antoniya, mitropolita Kievskago i Galitskago* (Biography of Antony, Blessed Metropolitan of Kiev and Galicia), vol II (New York 1957) pp 174–7.

12 V. Sabler *O mirnoy borbe s sotsializmom* (On the Peaceful Dispute with Socialism), 2 vols, 2nd edn. (Sergiev Posad 1911); A. I. Baby 'Borba pravoslavnoy tserkvi s nauchnym sotsializmom v Moldavii v kontse XIX— nachale XX veka' (The Struggle Between the Orthodox Church and Scientific Socialism in Moldavia at the End of the Nineteenth and the Beginning of the Twentieth Century) in *Izvestiya Akademii Nauk Moldavskoy SSR: Seriya obshchestvennykh nauk 1/1968*, pp 20–30.

13 Relatively little research has been carried out so far into the attitude adopted by the church to socialism and 'Christian Socialism' (which is dealt with on a later page). In the west the subject has been treated by F. Haase *Russische Kirche und Sozialismus* (Leipzig and Berlin 1922) and

J. Chrysostomus 'Die russische Orthodoxie angesichts der zeitgenössischen
sozialen Strömungen am Vorabend der Revolution von 1917' in *Ostkirchliche Studien XVII* (1968), pp 297–314—while the most recent Soviet
statement on this theme is to be found in E. F. Grekulov *Tserkov', samoderzhaviye, narod* (*vtoraya polovina XIX—nachalo XX v.*) (Church,
Autocracy and People (From the Second Half of the Nineteenth to the
Beginning of the Twentieth Century)) (Moscow 1969), pp 93–101. W.
Kunze (Göttingen) is at present preparing a dissertation, which will deal
with the kind of problems broached in this present chapter.
14 Nikon (Rklitsky), op. cit., vol III, p 243.
15 I. P. Pokrovsky *Sotsializm s drevneyshikh vremen i khristianskoye
veroucheniye* (Socialism Since Earliest Times and the Christian Faith)
(Perm 1910), pp 20–7, 27–8.
16 Sabler, op. cit., vol I, p VII.
17 Pokrovsky, op. cit., p 14.
18 I. Galakhov *Sotsializm i khristianstvo* (Socialism and Christianity)
(Chernigov 1913).
19 Sabler, op. cit., vol II, p 39.
20 See P. Scheibert, 'Die Petersburger religiös-philosophischen Zusammenkünfte von 1902 und 1903' in *Jahrbücher für Geschichte Osteuropas N. F.
XII* (1964), pp 513–60. The quotations are from pp 526–8.
21 Quotation taken from *Tserkov v istorii Rossii* (op. cit.), p 255.
22 A Vvedensky *Tserkov' i gosudarstvo: Ocherk vzaimootnoshenii 1918–
1922* (Church and State: Brief Sketch of Their Mutual Relations) (Moscow
1923), pp 24–30; Curtiss op. cit., p 199; G. S. Petrov *Dumy i vpechatleniya*
(Thoughts and Impressions) (St Petersburg 1907), pp 9–13, 38–39; G. S.
Petrov *Tserkov' i obshchestvo* (Church and Society) (St Petersburg 1906),
pp 58ff.
23 Archimandrite Mikhail *Kak ya stal narodnym sotsialistom* (Moscow
1907), pp 1, 25.
24 N. Smirnov *Iz sovremennykh problem: khristianstvo i sotsializm* (From
Contemporary Problems: Christianity and Socialism) (Moscow 1908).
The quotations are from pp 193, 196, 202.
25 Quotation taken from Smolitsch *Geschichte* . . (op. cit.), p 324.
26 Vvedensky, op. cit., p 49.
27 A. A. Bogolepov 'Church Reforms in Russia: 1905–1918' in *St
Vladimir's Seminary Quarterly* X (1966), pp 44–66; Curtiss, op. cit., pp
14–44; J. Chrysostomus *Kirchengeschichte Russlands der neuesten Zeit*
vol I (Munich and Salzburg 1965), pp 67–112.
28 V. F. Milovidov *Staroobryadchestvo v proshlom i nastoyashchem*
(Old Believers Past and Present) (Moscow 1969) pp 61–76; J. Chrysostomus 'Die Lage der Altgläubigen vor dem ersten Weltkrieg' in
Ostkirchliche Studien XVIII (1969), pp 3–15.
29 A. I. Klibanov *Istoriya religioznogo sektanstva v Rossii* (*60 e gody
XIX v.—1917 g.*) (History of the Religious Sects in Russia (from the
1860s to 1917)) (Moscow 1965), p 264 Note 440 (Prokhanov quotations),
p 279 (Pavlov quotations).
30 Klibanov, op. cit., pp 225–79; A. Blane *The Relations Between the*

Protestant Sects and the State: 1900–1921 (Typewritten Ph D dissertation: Duke University, Durham, N. C. 1964), pp 48–67; L. N. Mitrokhin *Baptizm* (Moscow 1966), pp 64–70.

The outlook for philosophy and the fate of the Slavophil Utopia

HELMUT DAHM

1 Fr. Engels *Ludwig Feuerbach und der Ausgang der klassischen deutschen Philosophie* (Stuttgart 1888), p 16.

2 See also: M. Gershenzon *Istoriya molodoy Rossii* (History of Young Russia), 2nd edn (Moscow and St Petersburg 1923); E. Radlov *Ocherk istorii russkoy filosofii* (Outline History of Russian Philosophy), 2nd edn (St Petersburg 1920); G. Shpet *Ocherk razvitiya russkoy filosofii* (Outline of the Development of Russian Philosophy), part I (St Petersburg 1922); B. Yakovenko *Ocherki russkoy filosofii* (Outlines of Russian Philosophy) (Berlin 1922).

3 V. A. Malinin *Osnovnye problemy kritiki idealisticheskoy istorii russkoy filosofii* (Moscow 1963), p 135.

4 Yakovenko, op. cit., pp 5–6.

5 Malinin, op. cit., pp 93–4.

6 All quotations from Vladimir Solovyev have been taken from the collected works *Sobraniye sochinenii Vladimira Sergeyevicha Solovyeva: Pod redaktsiey i s primechaniyami S. M. Solovyeva i E. L. Radlova* 2nd edn. ten vols (St Petersburg 1911–14; photostat copy Brussels 1966). For amplification of the Solovyev interpretation in this article see H. Dahm *Vladimir Solov'ev und Max Scheler: Ein Betrag zur Geschichte der Phänomenologie* (1971).

7 See also Malinin, op. cit., p 137.

8 A. Galaktionov and P. Nikandrov *Istoriya russkoy filosofii* (Moscow 1961), pp 382, 387.

9 E. Radlov 'Biografichesky ocherk' (Biographical Sketch) in *Sobranie sochinenii Vl. Solovyeva* vol X, pp xxx, xxxv, xxvii.

10 V. V. Zenkovsky *Istoriya russkoy filosofii* (History of Russian Philosophy), vols I–II (Paris 1948–50); N. O. Lossky *History of Russian Philosophy* (London and New York 1951).

11 Wl. Szylkarski 'Translator's Postscript' in Wl. Szylkarski (ed.) *Deutsche Gesamtausgabe der Werke von Wladimir Solowjew* vol VII (Freiburg i. Br. 1953 et seq), pp 433–4.

12 Szylkarski 'Postscript to "Theoretical Philosophy"' ibid., pp 107, 110.

13 Joh. Hessen *Max Scheler. Eine kritische Einführung in seine Philosophie* (Essen 1948), p 51.

14 M. Scheler *Wesen und Formen der Sympathie* (This is the 5th edition of *Zur Phänomenologie der Sympathiegefühle* of 1913) (Frankfurt/Main 1948) p 136.

15 L. Müller *Solovyev und der Protestantismus* (Freiburg i. Br. 1951), p 120.

16 Zenkovsky op. cit., vol II, p 54; K. V. Mochulsky *Vladimir Solovyev Zhizn i uchenye* (Vl. Solovyev: Life and Teachings) 2nd edn (Paris 1951) p 234.

17 E. Ryshkov 'Smysl chelovecheskogo sushchestvovaniya po Vladimiru Solovyevu (The Meaning of Human Existence according to Vl. Solovyev) in *Nauka i religiya* No 10 (1968), p 92.

18 S. N. Bulgakov 'Predisloviye' in *Ot marksizma k idealizmu: Sbornik statey 1896–1903* (St Petersburg 1903), pp xi–xii; S. N. Bulgakov 'Chto daet sovremennomu soznaniyu filosofiya Vl. Solovyeva' (The Significance of the Philosophy of Vl. Solovyev for the Contemporary Mind) ibid., p 264.

19 S. N. Bulgakov *Tikhie dumy* (Quiet Thoughts) (Moscow 1918); S. N. Bulgakov *Svet nevecherny: Sozertsaniya i umozreniya* (Immortal Light: Views and Insights), (Moscow 1917).

20 Ye. N. Trubetskoy *Metafizicheskiye predpolozheniya poznaniya: Opyt preodoleniya Kanta i kantianstva* (Moscow 1917); Ye. N. Trubetskoy *Smysl zhizni* (Moscow 1918; 2nd edn Berlin 1922).

21 See Max Scheler *Der Formalismus in der Ethik und die materiale Wertethik* 2nd edn (Halle 1921), pp 389, 397–8, 408–12.

22 See *Russische Religionsphilosophen—Dokumente* (edited and translated by N. von Bubnoff, Heidelberg 1956), pp 9–20; V. V. Rozanov *Izbrannoye* (Selected Texts) (edited and with an introduction by Yu. P. Ivask, New York 1956), pp 7–59.

23 See P. Scheibert 'Die Petersburger religiös-philosophischen Zusammenkünfte von 1902 und 1903' in *Jahrbücher für Geschichte Osteuropas, N. F.*, XII (1964), pp 513–60.

24 N. P. Poltoratsky 'Sbornik "Iz glubiny" i ego znacheniye—Vstupitelnaya statya ko vtoromu izdaniyu' (The Anthology 'From the Depths' and its Significance—Introductory Article for the second edition) in *Iz glubiny: Sbornik statey o russkoy revolyutsii* (Paris 1967). The introductory article has been reprinted in *Zarubezhye V/1* (Munich 1969), pp 12–16.

25 *Vekhi: Sbornik statey o russkoy intelligentsii* (Signposts: Collection of Articles on the Russian Intelligentsia) (Moscow 1909) (3rd edn Frankfurt/Main 1967); see also Gisela Oberländer *Die Vechi-Diskussion 1909–1912* (Cologne 1965).

26 M. P. Stolypina-Bok *Vospominaniya o moem otse P. A. Stolypine* (Recollections of my Father P. A. Stolypin) (New York 1953), p 344.

27 Veliky Knyaz' Gavriil Konstantinovich *V Mramornom Dvortse: Iz khroniki nashey semyi* (In the Marble Palace: From the Chronicle of our Family) (New York 1955), pp 171–189.

28 H. Dahm *Meuterei auf den Knien: Die Krise des marxistischen Welt- und Menschenbildes* (Olten-Freiburg i Br. 1969), pp 34–49.

29 I. F. Balakina 'O tak nazyvayemom russkom ekzistentsializme' (On So-called Russian Existentialism) in *Vestnik Moskovskogo Universiteta*, Seriya VIII, No 6 (1963), pp 88–96; I. F. Balakina 'Religiozno-ekzistentsialistskiye iskaniya v Rossii nachala XX v.' (Religious-existentialist

Experiments in Russia at the Beginning of the 20th Century) in *Sovremenny ekzistentsializm: Kriticheskiye ocherki* (Contemporary Existentialism. Critical Essays) (Moscow 1966), pp 430–49.

Russian literature from 1890 to 1917
ELISABETH STENBOCK-FERMOR

1 A. Akhmatova 'Poema bez geroya' in *Sochineniya* vol II (Munich 1968), p 117.
2 D. S. Mirsky *A History of Russian Literature* (New York and London 1960), p 432.
3 N. A. Trifonov (ed.) *Russkaya Literatura XX veka. Dorevolyutsionny period* (Moscow 1962), p 4.
4 *Istoriya russkoy literatury* vol X (Moscow 1954), pp 607, 764.
5 *Istoriya russkoy literatury v trekh tomakh* vol III (Moscow 1964), pp 17, 731.
6 Quoted in *Istoriya russkoy literatury* vol X (Moscow 1954), pp 778, 786.
7 *Russkaya literatura kontsa XIX—nachala XX v.* (Moscow 1968), p 26.
8 D. Merezhkovsky 'O prichinakh upadka i o novykh techeniyakh sovremennoy russkoy literatury' in *Polnoye sobraniye sochinenii* vol XV (Moscow–St Petersburg 1912), pp 209–305.
9 M. Gorky *O literature* (Moscow 1961) pp 3–14.
10 Ya. Frid 'Sotsialistichesky realizm i sovremennaya dekadentskaya literatura' in *Problemy sotsialisticheskogo realizma* (Moscow 1948).
11 On V. Ivanov and other writers of this period, see F. Stepun *Mystische Weltschau* (Munich 1964).
12 G. Donchin *The Influence of French Symbolism on Russian Poetry* (The Hague 1958), p 43 (New York 1959).
13 A. Blok *Sochineniya v dvukh tomakh* vol I (Moscow 1955), pp 771–4.
14 S. Bonneau *L'Univers poétique d'Alexandre Blok* (Paris 1946) is one of the best books on Blok's art.
15 See L. I. Strakhovsky *Three Poets of Modern Russia* (Cambridge, Mass. and London 1949).
16 For details of the symbolist press see G. Donchin, op. cit.
17 See V. Markov *Manifesty i programmy russkikh futuristov* (Munich 1967) pp 50–1.
18 See V. Erlich *Russian Formalism* (The Hague 1955).
19 B. Pasternak 'Avtobiografichesky ocherk' in *Proza 1915–1968* (Ann Arbor 1961), pp 1–52.
20 K. Leontyev 'O romanakh L. N. Tolstogo' in *Russky Vestnik* no VI (1890), p 249.
21 P. F. Yakubovich *Stikhotvoreniya* (Leningrad 1960), pp 483–4.
22 M. Gorky, op. cit.
23 I. A. Bunin *Sobranie sochinenii v devyati tomakh* vol II (Moscow 1965), p 482.

24 Bunin, op. cit., vol I, p 48.
25 D. Tschiževskij 'Über die Stellung Čechovs innerhalb der russischen Literaturentwicklung' in *Anton Čechov: some essays* T. Eekman (ed.) (Leyden 1960), pp 293–310.
26 A. Fadeyev 'Zadachi literaturnoy teorii i kritiki' in *Problemy sotsialisticheskogo realizma* (Moscow 1948), pp 7–8. The Lenin quotation is in V. I. Lenin *Polnoye sobranie sochinenii* vol XII (Moscow 1960), p 100.
27 *Istoriya russkoy sovyetskoy literatury v chetyrekh tomakh* vol I (Moscow 1967), p 687.
28 ibid., p 689.
29 See Roman Jakobson 'Von einer Generation, die ihre Dichter vergeudet hat' in *Slavische Rundschau* vol II (1930), pp 481–95.

Russian schools

OSKAR ANWEILER

1 M. M. Deyneko, *40 let narodnogo obrazovaniya v SSSR* (Forty Years of Education in the USSR) (Moscow 1957), p 9.
2 Quotation taken from O. Kaydanova, *Ocherki po istorii narodnogo obrazovaniya v Rossii i SSSR na osnove lichnogo opyta i nablyudenii* (Essays on the History of Education in Russia and the USSR. Based on Personal Experience and Observations) (Berlin 1938), p 275.
3 See W. H. E. Johnson, *Russia's Educational Heritage* (New Brunswick 1950), p 193.
4 P. N. Ignatyev, D. M. Odinetz, P. J. Novgorodtsev, *Russian Schools and Universities in the World War* (New Haven 1929), pp xx, xxi.
5 ibid., p xxii.
6 *Materialy po reforme sredney shkoly: Primernya programmy i obyasnitelnya zapiski, izdannye po rasporyazheniyu G. Ministra Narodnago Prosveshcheniya* (Materials for Secondary School Reform: Model Syllabuses and Explanations, edited at the instigation of the Minister of Education) (St Petersburg 1915), p 4.
7 N. A. Konstantinov, *Ocherki po istorii sredney shkoly: Gimnazii i realnye uchilishcha s kontsa XIX v. do fevralskoy revolyutsii 1917 g.* (Essays on the History of the Secondary School: Classical and Non-classical Secondary Schools from the End of the Nineteenth Century to the February Revolution of 1917), 2nd enlarged and improved edition (Moscow 1956), p 176.
8 Quotation taken from F. F. Korolev, 'Iz istorii narodnogo obrazovaniya v Sovetskoy Rossii (Nizshiye i sredniye professionalnye shkoly i vyssheye obrazovaniye v 1917–1920 gg.)' (From the History of Education in Soviet Russia (Lower and Secondary Professional Schools and Higher Education 1917–1920)) in *Izvestiya Akademii Pedagogicheskikh Nauk RSFSR, Vypusk 102* (1959), p 13.
9 Bernard Pares, *The Fall of the Russian Monarchy* (New York 1939), p 411.

Select bibliography

This bibliography is restricted chiefly to works in western languages. Its object is to enable the reader to obtain further information on the subjects dealt with in this book.

FOREIGN POLICY
Horst Jablonowski 'Die Stellungnahme der russischen Parteien zur Aussenpolitik der Regierung von der russisch-englischen Verständigung bis zum Ersten Weltkriege' in *Forschungen zur osteuropäischen Geschichte* vol V (Berlin 1957), pp 60–92.
Peter Jakobs *Das Werden des französisch-russischen Zweibundes 1890–1894* (Wiesbaden 1968).
Barbara Jelavich *A Century of Russian Foreign Policy 1814–1914* (Philadelphia 1964).
Andrew Malozemoff *Russian Far Eastern Policy 1881–1904: with special emphasis on the causes of the Russo-Japanese War* (Berkeley 1958, Cambridge 1959).
Clarence J. Smith *The Russian Struggle for Power 1914–1917: a study of Russian foreign policy during the First World War* (New York 1956).
Russian Foreign Policy: Essays in Historical Perspective Ivo J. Lederer (ed.) (New Haven 1962).

CONSTITUTIONAL LAW
Wiatscheslaw Gribowski *Das Staatsrecht des Russischen Reiches* (Tübingen 1912).
Anton Palme *Die russische Verfassung* (Berlin 1910).
Thomas Riha 'Constitutional developments in Russia' in T. G. Stavrou (ed.) *Russia Under the Last Tsar* (Minneapolis 1969, pp 87–116, London 1969).
The Russian Provisional Government 1917 (Selected Documents) R. P. Browder and A. F. Kerensky (eds.) 3 vols, (Stanford 1961).
Lothar Schultz *Russische Rechtsgeschichte: von den Anfängen bis zur Gegenwart einschliesslich des Rechts der Sowjetunion* (Lahr 1951).
Jacob Walkin *The Rise of Democracy in Pre-Revolutionary Russia:*

Political and Social Institutions under the last three Czars (New York 1962, London 1963).

POLITICAL PARTIES

George Fischer *Russian Liberalism: from gentry to intelligentsia* (Cambridge, Mass. and London 1958).

Michael T. Florinsky *The End of the Russian Empire* (New York 1931, 2nd edn 1961).

Horst Jablonowski 'Die Russischen Rechtsparteien 1905–1917' in *Russlandstudien: Gedenkschrift für O. Hoetzsch* (Stuttgart 1957, pp 43–62).

Oliver H. Radkey *The Agrarian Foes of Bolshevism: Promise and Default of the Russian Socialist Revolutionaries, February to October 1917* (London and New York 1958).

Die Russische Revolution 1917: von der Abdankung des Zaren bis zum Staatsstreich der Bolschewiki (dtv-Dokumente No 227/228) Manfred Hellmann (ed.) (2nd edn Munich 1969).

Hans Rogger 'The Formation of the Russian Right 1900–1906' in *California Slavic Studies* vol. III, 1964, pp 66–94.

Leonard B. Schapiro *The Communist Party of the Soviet Union* (London and New York 1960).

The Transformation of Russian Society: aspects of social change since 1881 C. E. Black (ed.) (Cambridge, Mass. 1960, London 1961).

Donald W. Treadgold *Lenin and his Rivals: the struggle for Russia's future 1898–1906* (London and New York 1955).

ECONOMIC DEVELOPMENT

Theodore H. von Laue *Sergei Witte and the Industrialization of Russia* (New York 1964).

Margaret Miller *The Economic Development of Russia 1905–1914* (2nd edn 1926, reprinted New York and London 1967).

Jürgen Nötzold *Wirtschaftliche Alternativen der Entwicklung Russlands in der Ära Witte und Stolypin* (Berlin 1966).

Roger Portal 'Das Problem einer industriellen Revolution in Russland im 19. Jahrhundert' in *Forschungen zur osteuropäischen Geschichte vol I*, (Berlin 1954, pp 205–216).

Theodor D. Zotschew *Die aussenwirtschaftlichen Verflechtungen der Sowjetunion* (Tübingen 1969).

AGRARIAN QUESTIONS

Terence Emmons *The Russian Landed Gentry and the Peasant Emancipation of 1861* (Cambridge 1968).

Geroid T. Robinson *Rural Russia under the Old Régime* (New York 1932).

The Peasant in Nineteenth Century Russia Wayne S. Vucinich (ed.) (Stanford 1968).

SIBERIA

P. W. Danckwortt *Sibirien und seine wirtschaftliche Zukunft* (Leipzig and Berlin 1921).
A. N. de Koulomzine *Le Transsibérien* (translated from the Russian by J. Legras) (Paris 1904).
Marc Raeff *Siberia and the Reforms of 1822* (Seattle 1956).
Arved Schultz *Sibirien: Eine Landeskunde* (Breslau 1923).
Donald W. Treadgold *The Great Siberian Migration: government and peasant in resettlement from emancipation to the First World War* (Princeton 1957, London 1958).

NATIONALITIES

W. E. D. Allen *The Ukraine: a history* (Cambridge 1940, New York 1941).
S. Becker *Russia's Protectorates in Central Asia: Bukhara and Khiva 1865–1924* (Cambridge, Mass. and London 1968).
Die Bedeutung Polens für Russland (Cracow 1917).
Tancred Borenius *Field-Marshal Mannerheim* (London 1940).
Violet Conolly *Beyond the Urals* (London 1967)
Roman Dyboski *Poland* (London and New York 1933).
P. Fedenko *Ukraine* (Augsburg 1951).
Finnland Geschichte und Gegenwart (Helsinki 1961).
Michael T. Florinsky *Russia: a History and an Interpretation* (New York 1953).
Nicholas Hans *History of Russian Educational Policy 1701–1917* (London 1931, reprinted New York 1964).
Finland, Creation and Construction H. Kallas and S. Nickels (eds.) (London 1968).
S. Kot *Five Centuries of Polish Learning* (Oxford 1941).
W. Kolarz *Russia and her Colonies* (London 1952, New York 1953).
W. Lednicki *Life and Culture of Poland as Reflected in Polish Literature* (New York 1944, London 1948).
W. R. Mead *Finland* (London and New York 1968).
Clarence A. Manning *The Forgotten Republics* (New York 1952).
Anatole G. Mazour *Finland Between East and West* (Princeton and London 1956).
Boris Nolde *L'Empire Russe* (Paris 1953).
K. K. Pahlen *Mission to Turkestan: being the memoirs of Count K. K. Pahlen 1908–1909*, translated by N. J. Couriss (London 1964).
Bernard Pares *The Fall of the Russian Monarchy* (London and New York 1939).

Alexander G. Park *Bolshevism in Turkestan 1917–1927* (London and New York 1957).

R. A. Pierce *Russian Central Asia 1867–1917* (Berkeley 1960).

Richard Pipes *The Formation of the Soviet Union* (Cambridge, Mass. 1964).

The Cambridge History of Poland W. F. Reddaway (ed.) (Cambridge 1950).

E. Schuyler *Turkistan: notes of a journey in Russian Turkistan, Kokand and Kuldja 1876* (reprinted London and New York 1966).

E. Seraphim *Grundriss der baltischen Geschichte* (Reval 1908).

A. Spekke *A History of Latvia* (Stockholm 1951).

B. H. Sumner *Survey of Russian History* (London 1944, 2nd revised edn 1948).

R. Vaidyanath *The Formation of the Soviet Central Asian Republics: a study in Soviet nationalities policy 1917–1936* (New Delhi 1967).

A. Tyrkova-Williams *From Liberty to Brest-Litovsk: the first years of the Russian Revolution* (London 1919).

R. Wittram *Baltische Geschichte* (Munich 1954).

MUSLIM REVIVAL

A. Bennigsen and Ch. Quelquejay *Les Mouvements Nationaux chez les Musulmans de Russie: le 'Sultangaliévisme' au Tatarstan* (Paris 1960).

Hans Bräker *Kommunismus und Islam: Religionsdiskussion und Islam in der Sowjetunion* (Tübingen 1969).

Hélène Carrère d'Encausse *Réforme et Révolution chez les Musulmans de l'Empire russe: Bukhara 1867–1924* (Paris 1965).

Stefan Wurm *Turkic peoples of the USSR: Their Historical Background, Their Languages and the Development of Soviet Linguistic Policy* (London 1954).

ORTHODOX CHURCH

A. A. Bogolepov 'Church Reforms in Russia: 1905–1918' in *St Vladimir's Seminary Quarterly* vol X (1966, pp 12–66).

John S. Curtiss *Church and State in Russia: the last years of the Empire 1900–1917* (New York 1940).

Gerhard Simon *K. P. Pobedonoscev und die Kirchenpolitik des Heiligen Sinod 1880–1905* (Göttingen 1969).

Igor Smolitsch 'Der Konzilsvorbereitungsausschuss des Jahres 1906: Zur Vorgeschichte des Moskauer Landeskonzils von 1917/18' in *Kirche im Osten* vol VII (1964, pp 53–93).

Nicolas Zernov *The Russian Religious Renaissance of the 20th Century* (London 1963, New York 1964).

PHILOSOPHY

Helmut Dahm *Vladimir Solovyev und Max Scheler: ein Betrag zur Geschichte der Phänomenologie* (Munich 1970).

Monarchia Sancti Petri Leo Kobilinski-Ellis (ed.) (from the Major Works of Vl. Solovyev) (Mainz 1929).

N. O. Lossky *History of Russian Philosophy* (New York 1951, London 1952).

Russian Philosophy James M. Edie, James P. Scanlan, Mary-Barbara Zeldin (eds.) vols I–III (Chicago 1965).

Russische Religionsphilosophen (Documents) edited and translated by Nicolai von Bubnoff (Heidelberg 1956).

Wladimir Solovjeff *Ausgewählte Werke* (German translation by Harry Köhler) 3 vols, (Jena 1914–17); 4 vols, (Stuttgart 1921–2) (these two editions are not identical in all respects).

Deutsche Gesamtausgabe der Werke von Wladimir Solovjew W. Szylkarski, et al. (eds.) Freiburg i. Br. (Volumes published to date: VII (1953), III (1954), II (1957), VI (1965)).

V. V. Zenkovsky *A History of Russian Philosophy* (translated by G. L. Kline) 2 vols (London and New York 1953).

LITERATURE

Sophie Bonneau *L'univers poétique d'Alexandre Blok* (Paris 1946).

G. Donchin *The Influence of French Symbolism on Russian Poetry* (The Hague and New York 1958).

Viktor Erlich *Russian Formalism* (The Hague and New York 1955).

Johannes Holthusen *Studien zur Ästhetik und Poetik des russischen Symbolismus* (Göttingen 1957).

D. S. Mirsky *Geschichte der russischen Literatur* (Munich 1964).

English edition *A History of Russian Literature from the earliest times to the death of Dostoyevsky 1881* (London 1927, revised edition edited by Francis J. Whitfield London 1949, New York 1958).

R. Poggioli *The Poets of Russia* (Cambridge, Mass. and London 1960).

Adolf Stender-Petersen *Geschichte der russischen Literatur* vol II (Munich 1957).

Fedor Stepun *Mystische Weltschau* (Munich 1964).

RUSSIAN SCHOOLS

Patrick L. Alston *Education and the State in Tsarist Russia* (Stanford and London 1969).

Oskar Anweiler *Geschichte der Schule und Pädagogik in Russland* (Heidelberg 1964).

Leonhard Froese *Ideengeschichtliche Triebkräfte der russischen und sowjetischen Pädagogik* 2nd edn (Heidelberg 1963).

Nicholas Hans *History of Russian Educational Policy (1701–1917)* (London 1931, reprinted New York 1964).

Nicholas Hans *The Russian Tradition in Education* (London 1963, New York 1964).

William H. E. Johnson *Russia's Educational Heritage* (New Brunswick 1950).

The authors

OSKAR ANWEILER Dr phil, Professor of Pedagogics and Education at the Ruhr University, Bochum.

HANS BRÄKER Dr phil, Head of the Economic Research Department in the Bundesinstitut für ostwissenschaftliche und internationale Studien, Cologne.

VIOLET CONOLLY OBE, Dr Econ Sc, Former Head of the Soviet Section, Foreign Office Research Department, London.

HELMUT DAHM Dr phil, Head of the Philosophical Research Department in the Bundesinstitut für ostwissenschaftliche und internationale Studien, Cologne.

MICHAEL FUTRELL Ph D, Professor of Slavonic Studies, University of British Columbia, Vancouver.

GEORGE KATKOV Dr phil, Fellow of St. Antony's College, Oxford, and Lecturer in Soviet Institutions, University of Oxford.

ERWIN OBERLÄNDER Dr phil, Fellow of the Bundesinstitut für ostwissenschaftliche und internationale Studien, Cologne.

NIKOLAUS POPPE Dr phil, Dr phil h c, Professor for Oriental Languages at the Universities of Leningrad (1925–41) and Berlin (1943–5) and the University of Washington, Seattle (1949–69). Corresponding Member of the Academy of Sciences of the USSR (1934–43) and of the German Academy for Science and Literature from 1957.

LOTHAR SCHULTZ Dr jur, Dr phil, Professor for Eastern European Law at the University of Göttingen.

GERHARD SIMON Dr phil, Fellow of the Bundesinstitut für ostwissenschaftliche und internationale Studien, Cologne.

ELISABETH STENBOCK-FERMOR Ph D, Assistant Professor for Russian and Russian Literature at Stanford University (1959–66), now Head of the Russian Department in the Monterey Institute of Foreign Studies, California.

KARL C. THALHEIM Professor Emeritus for Economics and Head of the Department of Economics at the Osteuropa-Institut at the Free University, Berlin.

HARRY T. WILLETTS Fellow of St Antony's College, Oxford, and Lecturer in Russian History of the 18th and 19th Centuries at the University of Oxford.

Index

Abduh, Muhammad, 186
Abdul Hamid II, 196
Acmeism, 265–78
Agrarian problems, 85–6, 101, 111–37; consolidated holdings, 133–4; in first Duma, 128–31; proposals for reform, 49, 58, 63–4, 68, 73–4, 78; Soviet solution, 137; Stolypin's policy, 86, 99, 105, 131–137, 148
Ahmad Khan, Saiyid, 186
Akhmatova, Anna, 263, 273–6, 278; works: 275
Aladin, A. F., 68, 130
al-Afghani, 186, 192
Alekseyev, E. I., 27
Alexander I, 112, 152, 269; introduces ministerial system, 36–9; liberal attitude to Poland, 155–6, 172; school system of, 290
Alexander II, 161–2, 183; emancipation of serfs, 98, 113; reforms, 39, 41–4, 69, 294; death of, 12, 270
Alexander III, 12–19, 33, 52, 291; coronation of, 122; inaugurates Trans-Siberian railway, 143; russification policies, 152, 170–1
Alexander of Battenberg, Prince, 14, 15, 17
Alexandra Fedorovna, Tsarina, 75–6, 200, 223–4
Algeciras, conference on Morocco, 31
al-Ghazzali, 187

All-Russian Church Council, 227–8
All-Russian Education Congress, 301
All-Russian Soviet of Soldiers' and Workers' Deputies, 55
All-Russian Union of Muslims, 194–6
All-Russian Union of Peasants, 63
al-Marzhani, Shihabeddin, 186–189
Alsace-Lorraine, 12
Amir'Ali, Saiyid, 186
Amu Darya, 180
Amur district, 138
Andizhan, 180
Andreyev, Leonid, 284
Annensky, I. F., 276
Antony (Khrapovitsky), Archbishop, 214, 228
Antony (Vadkovsky), Metropolitan of St Petersburg, 208–9, 211–13, 218, 223, 230
Apollon, 274, 277–8
Appanage peasants, 114–15, 117–19
Arms limitation conference, 23
Arseny (Stadnitsky) Archbishop, 228
Askoldov, Sergey, 252, 255, 258
Assembly, right of, 51, 56, 72
Association of Associations, 70, 302
Austria-Hungary, 12–14, 17, 20, 23, 32, 97, 102
Azerbaijan, 188
Azeri press, 189

Badayev, A. E., 81
Bakhchisaray, 190, 194
Bakst, L. S., 277
Baku, 86, 103, 189, 194
Balakina, I. F., 261
Balkans, 12–14, 17, 20, 32
Ballets Russes, 277
Balmont, Konstantin, 267
Baltic Provinces, 90, 138, 153,
    200, 209; economic develop-
    ments, 173–4; independence
    achieved, 174; position of
    Germans in, 169–74; russifi-
    cation, 170–3
'Banquet' campaign, 69
Baptists, 229, 231–2, 235
Basmach movement, 185
Battenberg, *see* Alexander of
Baudelaire, Charles, 281
Bazarov-Rudnev, Vladimir, 254
Belinsky, V. G., 221, 264
Belokrinitsa Convention, 231,
    233
Bely, Andrey, 266, 270–2, 276;
    Petersburg, 271, 277; *The
    Silver Dove*, 271
Benois, A. N., 277
Berdyaev, Nikolay, 220, 248–9,
    251, 253–6, 258, 262; works,
    261
Berlin, 193; Congress of, 12;
    Treaty of, 13
Bethmann-Hollweg, Theobald
    von, 32
Bezobrazov, A. M., 25–6
Bigi, Musa, 187
Birilev, Admiral, 30
Bismarck, Herbert von, 15
Bismarck, Otto von, 11–12, 14,
    17–20, 33, 100
Björkö agreement, 29–31
Black Hundreds, 75, 215
Black Sea ports, 165
Black Sea Straits, 13, 17, 22
Bliokh (on war of the future),
    23
Blok, Alexander, 266, 270, 272–
    276; poems, 272–3, 275

Blumhardt, Christopher, 222
Bobrikov, N. I., 166–7
Bogolepov, N. P., 63
Bogrov, D. G. (revolutionary),
    257
Bolsheviks, 58–60, 65–7, 79–81,
    83, 153, 216; abolish free trade,
    151; ban ancient languages,
    297; revolution, 223, 279–80
Bolzano, B., 245
Bosnia and Herzegovina, 13
Boxer Rising, 21, 24
Brentano, Franz, 245
Brotherhood of St Cyril and St
    Methodius, 160–1
Bryusov, Valery, 266–70, 276;
    Let's be like the Sun!, 267
Bugayev, Boris Nikolayevich,
    see Bely, A.
Bugayev, Nikolay, 252
Bukhara, 174, 179, 187
Bulgakov, S. N., 220, 240, 247–8,
    251–3, 255, 258
Bulgaria, 13–14, 17
Bülow, Prince Bernhard von,
    29–30
Bulygin, A. G., 71
Bunge, N. Kh., 26
Bunin, Ivan, works, 284–5
Burlyuk, D. D., 279
Buryat Mongols, 139, 145

Camus, A., 266
Canada, 108, 145, 163
Caspian Sea, 174, 180, 182;
    pilots sent to Baltic, 168
Catherine II, 40, 112, 160, 183,
    290
Caucasia, 138, 182
Central Asia, *see* Turkestan
Chaadayev, Pyotr, 236
Charles XII of Sweden, 160
Chekhov, Anton, 264, 283;
    works, 285–6
Chelpanov, Georgy, 252
Chemical industry, 96
Chernov, Viktor, 62, 64, 83
Chernyshev, I. V., 134

Chernyshevsky, N. G., 113, 253, 264
Chicherin, Boris, 255
China, 21, 24–6; Eastern railway, 26, 29
Christianity: and Islam, 185–6, 192; and socialism, 216–23, 233, 262; 'true', 253–4
Church, *see* Orthodox Church
Coal, 87, 89, 102–3, 163
Committee of Ministers, 10, 27, 36–9, 126; conference on church matters, 208–11, 229–230
Communist Party, 195, 197, 279–80
Constitution, Russian (1832), 35–41, 50; (1906), 34–5, 37, 44–7, 51–2
Constitutional Democrats (Kadets), 53, 67–8, 70–3, 76–81, 83–4, 128–31, 194–6, 221, 232, 233, 303–4; programme of, 72
Cooperatives, 147, 217
Cossacks, 139, 159–60
Cotton production, 87, 89, 91, 94–5, 104, 178
Council of Ministers, 37, 44, 46, 48, 50–1, 167, 305, 311
Crimea, 138, 175, 182, 188, 190–1
Crimean War, 104, 113

Dalny, port of, 24, 29
Danckwortt, P. W., 139
Danilyevsky, N. Y., 237
Dardanelles, 22
Death penalty abolished, 58
Decadent school, 265–6, 281, 283
Decembrists, 269
Descartes, René, 242
Dewey, John, 308–9
De Windt, H., 150
Diaghilev, Sergey, 177
Dissident sects, 199; *see also* Protestant sects

Districts (*uyezdy*), 40, 57
Dmowski, Roman, 158–9
Dobrolyubov, N. A., 264
Donets basin, 102–3, 163
Dorpat (Yuryev) University, 171
Dostoyevsky, Fedor, 13, 23, 210, 268, 270–1, 279, 286
Dragomanov, Mikhail, 162
Dreikaiserbund, 11–16, 29
Dubrovin, A. I., 75
Dubrovsky, S. M., 136
Duma, Imperial: educational policy of, 303–6; first, 44, 48–49, 60, 67–8, 78; in First World War, 81–2; last days of (1917), 53, 82; political parties of, 76–84; Progressive Bloc Coalition formed (1915), 81–2; rights and duties, 48

Economic expansion programme, 85–110; financial help from abroad, 100–6
Education: adult ('extra-mural'), 299–301; compulsory, 293–4, 304–6, 309; craft schools, 291, 298–9, 312; democratisation of, 290, 303; higher, 72, 149, 155, 171, 189–90, 199, 287, 290, 292, 295–7, 300–1, 308–9; Islamic, 178–9, 186, 188, 191; kindergartens, 171, 300; Orthodox Church schools, 199–202, 291–3; primary, 156, 199, 201–2, 226, 290–1, 293–9, 305–6, 308–10; private schools, 171, 179, 288–9; professional and technical training, 298–9, 311–12; reforms by Ignatyev, 307–13; secular system introduced, Siberia, 148–9, 291; secondary, 156, 291, 293, 295–298, 301–3, 306, 308–11; standards before and after revolution, 287–8; suppression of native languages, 152, 154, 156, 162, 164, 171–2; teachers' associations, 302–4; teacher-

training, 295–6; theological colleges, 171, 187, 199, 207–8, 212–13, 296; universities, *see* higher education *above*
Elections, 42–3, 47–8, 57
Emergency, states of, 51–2, 56, 212
Emigration, 139–45
Engelgardt, A. N., 122
Engels, Friedrich, 236
Estonia, 169–74, 209
Ethnic minorities, *see* Nationalities question
Eulenburg, Philip von, 29
Existentialism, Russian, 261
Exports, 98, 107–8, 123, 146–7

Fadeyev, A. A., 286
Famine (1891–2), 125
Far East: railway building, 20, 26; Russian policy, 21, 24–8, 33, 69, 182
February Revolution, *see under* Revolutions
Fergana *oblast*, 174, 178–9
Fet, A. A., 270
Filosofov, D. V., 253
Finland, Finns, 72, 105, 152–3, 165–9, 306; annexed by Russia (1809), 165; in First World War, 168; Grand Duchy of, 165; independence achieved (1917), 169; Lutheran Church, 165, 200
First World War, 58, 67, 81, 110, 193, 235, 274, 309, 313; Poland and, 156, 158–9; Ukraine and, 164
Floquet, C., 17
Florensky, Pavel, 220, 252
Florinsky, M. T., 49, 74, 165
Fourier, C., 237
France, 12, 22, 98; relations with Russia, 11, 16–19, 30–1, 33
Franz Ferdinand, Archduke, assassination of, 32
Frank, S. L., 220, 252, 255–6, 258

Free Economic Society, 134
Freycinet, C., 17
Frid, Y. V., 266
Fritsen, P. M., 232
Froebel, Friedrich, 171, 300
From the Depths, 255, 258
Fundamental rights, list of, 47
Futurists, 273, 278–80

Gabunov-Posadov, 300
Galaktionov, Anatoly, 238
Galicia, 161–2, 164
Gapon, George, 218
Gaspraly, Izmail, 190–1, 193–4, 196
Gavriil Konstantinovich, Grand Duke, 257
General strike (1905), 71, 302
Germany, Germans, 102, 163, 235, 287; relations with France and Russia, 12–19, 29–33; *Ritterschaft* (Baltic Germans), 169–74; trade with Russia, 107–8
Gernet, M. N., 150
Gershenzon, Mikhail, 236–7, 255
Gertsenshtein, M. Y., 131
Gessen, I. V. (historian), 288
Geyer, Louis, 104
Giers, N. K., 13–19, 33
Gippius, Zinaida, 219, 251, 253, 267–8
Gitermann, V., 45
'God builders', 254
'Godseekers', 219, 253
Goehre, Paul, 222
Gogol, N. V., 162, 271
Gök Tepe, battle of, 175
Goldmining, 93, 95, 106, 147, 178
Gorchakov, A. M., 13, 14
Goremykin, Ivan, 76, 78–9, 82, 125, 127–8
Gorky, Maxim, 254, 264, 266; works, 282–4
Governors, provincial, 37, 40–1, 52, 57
Great Britain, 22, 30, 107
Gribovsky, V., 46

Gringmut, V. A., 75
Grot, Nikolay, 252
'Group of 32', 220–2
Gubernii (provinces), 39, 40
Guchkov, A. I., 73
Guild of Poets, 274
Gumilyov, N. S., 270, 274–6

Hague International Court of
    Justice, 23
Haller, J., 45
Hans, N., 288
Hegel, G. W. F., 236, 238, 249
Herzen, A. I., 113, 221
Hessen, Johannes, 246
Hoetzsch, Otto, 45, 100
Holy Synod, 36, 200–4; first
    Metropolitan of, 208, 210;
    role in education, 291–2; role
    of Director General, 203;
    under Sabler, 223–4
Hrushevsky, Michael, 163–4
Hughes, John, 103
Husserl, Edmund, 245, 259

Ibragimov, Abdul Rašid, 192–4,
    196
Ignatyev, Pavel, 122, 289, 298,
    306; educational reforms,
    307–13
Iliodor (Sergey Trufanov), 215
Ilyian, Ivan, 252
Imperial Council, 36–9, 44, 50,
    77, 304, 306
Imports, 98, 107, 147; duties on,
    100–1
India, Muslims of, 185–6, 193
Industrialisation, 86–104, 109–
    110, 136; comparisons (tables),
    92–5; growth rate (tables),
    88–91; proletariat emerges, 61
Intelligentsia: radical, 61–9,
    225; religious and philoso-
    phical trends of, 219–20, 254–
    256; Struve's condemnation
    of, 256
Ioann (Kartushin), Archbishop,
    233

Islam, *see* Muslims
Ivan III, 35
Ivanov, G. V., 276
Ivanov, V. I., 268–9, 275–6
Izvolsky, A. P., 33, 76

Jadids, 188, 191
Japan, 21, 24 (*see also* Russo-
    Japanese War)
Jews, 56, 163; anti-semitism, 75,
    154, 215
Judicial system, reorganisation
    of, 41, 43, 57–8

Kadets, *see* Constitutional
    Democrats
Kant, Immanuel, 239, 247, 251
Kaplan, F., 258
Kara, political prison at, 150
Karakum desert, 180
Karsavin, L. P., 252
Kartashev, A. V., 227
Kasso, L. A., 307
Katkov, M. N., 13, 15–18, 20
Kaufman, A. A., 134, 307
Kazakh Steppes, 174–7, 180,
    183, 189
Kazakhstan, 178
Kazan, 175, 179, 184, 186–7,
    189, 192, 260
Kemal Atatürk, 196
Kennan, George, 154
Kerensky, A. F., 54–5, 82, 227
Kerschensteiner, Georg, 309
Kharkov, 163
Khiva emirate, 174, 179
Khlebnikov, V., 279–80
Khmelnitsky, Hetman, 159
Khodasevich, 276
Khodsky, L. V., 119
Kholm (Chelm), 158, 209
Khomyakov, 248
Kiev, 80, 160–2, 164, 248, 253,
    257, 307; missionary confer-
    ence, 216
Kievskaya Starina, 161
Kireyevsky, I. V., 248
Kiselyev, P. D., 113

Klyuyev, 277
Knoop, Ludwig, 104
Kokand emirate, 174, 179
Kokovtsov, V. N., 126–7
Komura (Japanese Foreign
  Minister), 29
Korea, 21, 26–7
Korf, N. A., 292
Korkunov, N. M., 40
Kornilov, L. G., 54, 227
Korolenko, Vladimir, 125, 282
Kozlov, Alexey, 252
Krainy, Anton, 268
Krasnoyarsk, 147
Krivoshein, A. V., 135
Kruchenykh, A. E., 279
Kulish, P. A., 161
Kunanbayev, Abai, 190
Kuprin, Alexander, 282, 284
Kuropatkin, A. N., 23, 27, 125,
  181
Kushka, 180
Kutler, N. N., 127–8
Kuzmin, M. A., 274

Labour Group (*Trudovaya
  gruppa*), 67–8
Lamsdorf, V. N., 27–8, 30, 33
Land prices, 119–20
Landsdell, Dr, 150
Language, 152, 154, 156–7, 162,
  169
Lapshin, Ivan, 249, 252
Latvia, 169–74, 209
Laue, Theodore von, 99
Lavrov, Pyotr, 253
Lawrence, D. H., 266
Laws: 'Collected Laws and
  Decrees of the Government',
  39; 'Collected Laws of the
  Russian Empire' (1832), 34–6;
  'Consolidation of Principles of
  Religious Tolerance', 208,
  229–30, 234; development of
  constitutional law, 34; elec-
  toral laws, 47–9, 76, 79, 132,
  158, 221; fundamental laws
  (1832 and 1906), 34–6, 153,

167; on missionary work, 208;
  of provisional government
  (1917), 56–7
Leibniz, G. W. von, 252
Lenin, 7, 65, 134, 137, 232, 253,
  283, 286; attempted assassina-
  tion of, 258; coup d'état (1917),
  83; on 'Development of
  Capitalism in Russia', 108;
  recognises Finnish independ-
  ence, 169
Leontyev, Konstantin, 253, 281
Lermontov, 278
Lesevich, Vladimir, 252
Leskov, Nikolay, 281
Levitsky, V., 75
Libau, industries in, 174
Liberation Alliance, 69–71
Liberation Movement, 68–9
List, Friedrich, 100, 102, 107
Lithuania, 155, 157, 169;
  russification policies, 172–3
Lithuanian Corps, 155
Little Russia, *see* Ukraine
'Living Church' movement, 223
Lobanov-Rostovsky, Prince A. B.,
  24
Lodz, cotton trade of, 104
Lopatin, L. M., 242, 246, 252,
  255
Losev, Alexey, 259
Lositsky, A. E., 117–18, 134
Lossky, Nikolay, 245, 249, 252
Lukyanov, S. M., 223
Lunacharsky, Anatoly, 254
Lutheran Church, 169–71, 200,
  209
Luxemburg, Rosa, 158, 160
Lvov, G. E., 55, 82
Lvov, V. N., 226–7
Lyashchenko, P. I., 88, 109

Machinery: imports, 98, 107;
  production, 93, 96
Malinin, Viktor, 237–8
Malinovsky-Bogdanov, A. A.,
  253
Mamontov, S., 277

Manchuria, Russian occupation, 24, 27
Mandelshtam, Osip, 274–8
Manufacturing, 89–93, 96, 174; mechanisation of, 97, 102
Maria Fedorovna, Empress, 291
Martens, F. F., 168
Martov, L., 65, 66
Marx, Karl, 240, 247
Marxism in Russia, 61–2, 64–5, 216, 220, 238–9, 247, 253–4, 260; 'legal', 68, 248, 258; of Soviet period, 261–2
Marzhani, *see* al-Marzhani
Maslov, P. P., 136
Maximalists, 64, 72
Mayakovsky, Vladimir, 278–9
Mazayev, D. I., 231
Mazepa, Ivan, 160
Mechnikov, Ilya, 252
Medical services, 149, 180
Medynsky, E. N., 301
Melikov-Zerdabi, H. B., 189–90
Melnik, Joseph, 32
Mendeleyev, Dmitri, 253
Mendelssohn-Bartholdy, Ernst von, 31
Mennonites, 232
Mensheviks, 65–7, 79, 83
Merezhkovsky, Dmitri, 219, 251, 253, 265–9, 277; articles and novels, 268–9; famous lecture, 265, 267; founds review, 269
Meshchanstvo, 283
Michael Alexandrovich, Grand Duke, 53
Mihajlov, M., 261–2
Mikhail (Semyonov) Archimandrite, 221
Mikhailovsky, Nikolay, 253
Military expenditure, 104–5
Milyukov, P. N., 70–1, 78, 288, 294
Milyutin, N. A., 114, 159
Minerals and mining, 87–93, 102–3, 142, 147, 163
Ministries, 36, 39–40, 46
Minsky, N. M., 253

Mirsky, D., *see* Svyatopolk-Mirsky, D.
Mochulsky, K. V., 246
Moderate Progressive Party, 73
Mohrenheim, A. P., 17
Moldavians, 163
Monarchist Party, 75
Monarchy, overthrow of, 54, 82, 225, 235, 257
Mordvinov, 113
Morning Star, 77
Moscow, 83, 190, 231, 253, 258; political parties in, 71–3; rising (1905), 71; publications, 13, 247–8; university, 189, 248, 276
Mukhin, A. A., 139
Müller, Ludolf, 246
Muratov, P., 277
Muravyov, M. N. (Governor of Lithuania), 172
Muravyov, M. N. (Foreign Minister), 22, 24, 27
Muromtsev, S. A., 77
Muslims, 152–3, 175, 178–9, 181; attitude to Christianity, 185–186, 192, 209; cultural and educational reforms, 188–91; modernist movement, 183–7; political nationalism develops, 191–8; theological reforms, 186–8, 194; under Soviet rule, 182, 196–8

Narodniki (Friends of the People), 62, 64, 68, 109
Narva, 174
Nasiri, Abdul Qaiyum, 189–90
Nationalities question, 152–81; in Baltic states, 169–74; in Finland, 165–9; in Poland, 155–9; in the Steppes, 174–81; in Ukraine, 159–65
National Progressives, 81
Near East, reason for crises in, 192
Nekrasov, N. A., 273
Nelidov, A. I., 22

Neo-Kantian movement, 251–2
Nesmelov, Viktor, 260
Nesselrode, K. V., 14
Neumann, F., 222
New Path, The (Novy put), 253, 269, 277
Nicholas, Grand Duke, 159
Nicholas I, 155, 161 166, 170, 205; code of laws, 34; concern for serf problem, 112–13
Nicholas II, 7, 20–33, 47, 143, 152, 170, 200, 291; abdication of, 53, 82; in and after crisis of 1905, 70–1, 75–6; meeting with Kaiser, 30; support for arts, 277
Nietzsche, Friedrich, 237, 283
Nikandrov, Pyotr, 238
Nizhny–Novgorod fair, 88, 194
Nobel, Alfred, Ludwig and Robert, 103
Nobel Prize, 284
Nötzold, J., 100
Novgorodtsev, Pavel, 252, 255, 258
Novorossiisk Company, 103
Novosibirsk, 148
Nystad, treaty of, 169

Oblastniky, 138
Obruchev, N. N., 22
Obshchina system (peasant communes), 62–3, 115–16, 127
October Revolution, *see* Revolution (Oct. 1917)
Octobrists (Union of 17 October), 53–4, 71–4, 213, 233, 304; aims of, 74; numbers in Duma, 76, 79–80
Odessa, administration of, 41
Oglu, Rizaeddin Fakhreddin, 187
Oilfields, 86–7, 103, 178
Old Believers, 199, 209, 229–35
Omsk, 147–8
Onipko (Deputy), 68
Orenburg, 161, 175, 179–80, 194; Muslim Ecclesiastical

Assembly, 187–8, 193
Orthodox Church, 36, 56, 152–3, 158, 179, 185, 199–234, 253; in Baltic states, 170–3; decline in authority of, 224–5; demand for church council, 206, 210–212, 227–8; failure in education, 290; law on religious tolerance, 208–9; in Muslim territories, 192, 194; parochial clergy, 204–7, 213, 215, 220–1, 226; patriarchate restored, 228; privileges withdrawn, 56; radicalism and socialism in, 212–23; Revolution of 1905 and reform, 205–12; state subsidies, 199–200; statistics, 201, 209; subservience to tsar and state, 200–4, 209–10

Pacific Ocean, 28, 30
Pahlen, K. K., 175
Parents' Organisations, 311
Pares, Sir Bernard, 78, 312
Pasternak, Boris, 278, 280
Paul I, 269
Pavlov, I. P., 252
Pavlov, V. G., 231, 233
Peasants, 41–3, 61, 108, 121–8, 132; collectives, 101; communes, see *Obshchina;* electoral privileges, 48; improved conditions in Siberia, 145, 148; Land Bank, 120, 135; relations with gentry, 111–21
Peking, siege of, 24
Pereyaslav, treaty of, 159
Peter the Great, 38, 87, 111–12, 160, 169; and the Church, 201–3, 210; and western culture, 290; training schemes, 298
Petroleum, 86, 89, 91, 93, 95, 103
Petrov, Grigory, 221
Petrunkevich, I. I., 72
Phenomenology, 241–6, 248–50, 259

Philosophy, Russian, 236–62; anthology of (1901), 254–5; criticism of, as 'imitation', 237–8; metaphysical transcendentalism, 251–2; new religious, 247–62; philosophical anthropology, 260; positivism, 237, 255, 258

Pilsudski, J., 158–9

Pirogov, N. I., 294

Pitirim (Oknov), Metropolitan, 224

Plehve, V. K., 63, 69, 166

Plekhanov, Georgy, 65, 253

Pleske (Minister of Finance), 27

Pobedonostsev, K. P., 13, 22–3, 203, 209–10, 223, 234, 291

Pochayev monastery, 215

Poe, Edgar Allan, 267

Pokrovsky, I. P., 217

Poland, Poles, 49, 72, 90, 94–6, 102–4, 114, 169; Catholic Church in, 153, 156–8, 200; education in, 155–6; growth of industry, 157; Kingdom of, integrated, 155–6, 172; land reform (1864), 157; political parties, 158; risings (1830, 1863), 155–6, 161, 172; russification of, 155–9; Russia's attitude to, 152–4

Police, 40, 43, 51–2, 58

Political parties: emergence of, 60–76; in the Duma, 76–84

Poltava, battle of, 160

Poltoratsky, Nikolay, 255, 258

Popular Freedom Party, 71–2

Popular Socialists, 64, 83

Population, 85, 97, 119, 306

Populists, *see Narodniki*

Portal, Roger, 87

Port Arthur, 24, 27, 29

Portsmouth peace talks, 25, 29, 31

Posrednik, 300

Potemkin mutiny, 70

Pouralès, Friedrich von, 32

Press: censorship in Poland, 156;

freedom of, 47, 51, 56–7, 218, 286

Problems of Idealism, 255, 258

Progressive Bloc, 81–2

Progressive Economic Party, 73

Prokhanov, I. S., 232–3

Protestant sects, 209, 229–35

Protopopov, A. D., 82

Provincial administration, 39–43, 57

Provisional Government (1917), 54–9, 82–3, 159, 174; and the Church, 225–7; fall of, 58–9; introduces secular education, 291

Pskov (Pleskau), 171

Publishing Business, Revolutionary Tribunal on, 286

Pugachev rising, 112

Purishkevich, V. M., 75, 224

Pushkin, Alexander, 263, 271, 279

Putilov Works, 88

Radlov, E. L., 236–7, 240

Raiffeisen, F. W., 217

Railways, 20–1, 24–6, 87, 99, 100, 158; to Baltic ports, 173–174; nationalisation of, 105; in Turkestan, 180 (*see also* Trans-Siberian railway)

Rasputin, G. E., 75, 80–1, 215, 223–5

Rassvet ('The Dawn'), 232

Rayev, N. P., 225

Raznochintsy, 254

Realism, 280–6

Redemption payments, 108, 115–18, 122–3

Reinsurance Treaty, 14, 17–19, 22

Religious-philosophical thinkers, 219–20, 253–9

Religious tolerance proclaimed, 56, 208, 229–30

Remizov, A. M., 281

Renewal Movement, 223

Reval, 171, 173–4

Revisionists, German, 222
Revolution (1905), 62, 70–1, 193, 196, 206, 218, 220, 232–3; effects on education, 301–6
Revolution (February 1917), 34, 52–4, 82, 154, 164, 222, 232, 258, 313; welcomed by Church Synod, 225
Revolution (October 1917, Bolshevik), 54, 58, 151, 182–3, 195, 228, 258, 276, 288–9
Riasanovsky, N., 45
Riga, 170, 173–4
Ritterschaft, 169–74
Rodzyanko, M. V., 54
Roman Catholics, 152–3, 156–8, 172–3, 200, 209
Romanov dynasty: overthrow of, 225, 235; 300th anniversary celebrations, 257
Romanticism, 'revolutionary', 281–2
Rominten, 29, 31–2
Roosevelt, President Theodore, 28
Rostow, W. W., 110
Rozanov, V. V., 219, 253
Rubber industry, 92, 96
Rural communities, *see* Obshchina *and* Volosti
'Rural illuminations', 122
Rurik, 137
Russian Assembly, 74
Russo-Chinese Bank, 26
Russo-Japanese War, 25–30, 33, 69, 70, 110, 193, 277
Rutebeuf, 273
Ryabikov, V. V., 151
Ryshkov, Yevgeny, 247

Sabler, V. K., 216–17, 223–4
Saburov, P. A., 13
Safarov, G. V., 196–7
Saint-Simon, Claude de, 236
St Petersburg, 53, 73, 82, 165–6, 179, 194, 208–9, 224; administration of, 41; as background for literature, 271, 275; delegates' club, 68; industries, 88, 96; social movements, 218–22, 253; university, 187, 276; Winter Palace, 77, 218
St Petersburg Soviet of Workers' and Soldiers' Deputies, 53–5, 59, 82–3; arrest of, 71
Sakhalin, 29, 152
Samarin, A. D., 224
Samarkand, 180
Sazonov, S. D., 33
Scales, The (Vesy), 269, 277
Schaffhausen, 69
Scheibler, Karl, 104
Scheler, Max, 245–6, 250–1
Schelling, Friedrich Wilhelm, 236, 246
Scorpion publishers, 269
Sechenov, Ivan, 252
Semirechye, 176–7
Semirechensk, 196
Senate, Russian, 38–9
Serbia, 14, 32
Serfs: emancipation of, 41, 43, 98, 108, 111–19; resettle in Siberia, 141–2
Severyanin, Igor, 279
Shaposhnikov, 68
Shestov, L. I., 261–2
Shevchenko, Taras, 161
Shipov, D. N., 73
Shishkin, N. P., 22
Shpet, Gustav, 236–7, 259
Shuvalov, Pavel, 15, 17–19
Shuvalov, Pyotr, 15, 18
Shvarts, 307
Siberia: agriculture and farming, 106–7, 145–7, 151; coalfields, 87, 102; colonisation of, 86, 105–6, 124, 135, 139–46, 163; conquest of, 138; native tribes, 145; prisoners and exiles, 58, 138–9, 141, 149–50, 172; urban expansion, 147–8
Signposts, see Vekhi
Sipyagin (Minister of Interior), 63
Sirius, 275

Slavophil utopia, concept of, 259

Smirnov, Nikolay, 222

Social-Democrats (RSDRP), 53–5, 60–1, 67, 69, 76, 214, 216, 224, 254; journal founded, 232; London congress, 65; programme of, 65–6, 134–5; in 2nd and 3rd Dumas, 78–80

Socialist Revolutionaries, 53–5, 61–4, 67–8, 69, 76, 117, 221–2, 253; in Duma, 78–80, 83; first party congress, 63

Society for Promotion of Belles-lettres, 274

Society for Study of Poetic Language, 280

Sofia (review), 277

Sologub, Fedor, 267–8, 276

Solovyev, Vladimir, 219, 236–51, 253–5; literary influence of, 258, 261, 270–1; *ordo amoris* theory, 242, 249; philosophical theories, 239–48, 260; revolutionary significance of, 259; works, 241–2, 245, 250, 259–260, 266

Solzhenitsyn, A., 137

Soviet régime: attitude of Church to, 223; education programme, 293; effect on writers and publishers, 276, 286; proclamation to Muslims, 182; religious policy, 235

Sovyetkin, D. K., 299

Spanish-American war, 22

Speransky, M. M., 35–6, 114, 141

Spinoza, Baruch, 246

Stanislavsky, K. S., 273

Stankevich, Nikolay, 238

Steel production, 87, 89, 91–2, 95

Steppe Region, 174–81

Stepun, Fyodor, 252

Stepunin, V. A., 148

Stishinsky Commission, 126–7

Stoecker, A., 222

Stolypin, P. A., 71, 78–82; assassination of, 80, 136, 257; and Finland, 167–8; and Poland, 158; reforms of, 8, 86, 99–100, 105, 126, 131–7, 148, 257

Stolypina-Bok, Maria, 257

Strakhov, N. N., 237

Struve, Pyotr, 69, 220, 248, 252, 254–6, 258

Stundists, 229–30, 234

Stürmer, B. V., 82

Subjectivism and Individualism in Social Philosophy, 254–5

Sumner, B. H., 160

Svyatopolk-Mirsky, Prince D., 263, 268, 286

Svyatopolk-Mirsky, Prince, 69, 70

Sweden, 165, 169

Symbolism, 265–78, 285

Syr-Darya *oblast*, 179

Szylkarski, Wladimir, 245–6

Tashkent, 174–5, 180

Tatars, 154, 163, 183–4, 188, 191; literary language created, 189

Taxation, 42, 77, 100–1, 124; in Finland, 165; pressure on peasants, 108, 123; Siberian settlers, 141

Teachers' associations, 302–3, 311

Tenisheva, Princess, 277

Ternavtsev, V. A., 219, 251

Textiles, 87–9, 91, 94, 103–4, 174, 177–8

Theosophy, 239–40, 247–8, 259

Tiflis, 189, 194

Tikhon (Belavin), Metropolitan, 228

Tikhvinsky, Fyodor, 221

Timiryazev, K. A., 253

Titlinov, B. V., 223

Tolstoy, A. K., 270

Tolstoy, A. N., 276

Tolstoy, D. A., 296

Tolstoy, L. N., 125, 266, 268, 271, 279, 281–2, 294; *Anna Karenina*, 271, 281; *War and Peace*, 281

Tomsk, 148–50

Tošović, 261

Towns: administrative system, 41–3; industry, 90; population, 136–7, 147–8

Trans-Siberian railway, 26–7, 85, 105, 139–40, 142–4, 147, 150

Treadgold, D., 80

Trepov, D. F., 78, 127

Trubetskoy, Sergey, 248–9, 251, 255; works, 249

Trubetskoy, Yevgeny, 248, 251, 255, 258; works, 249–51

Trudoviki, 76, 79–80, 82, 128–131, 214, 221, 224

Tsar: abdication, 82; autocratic powers, 34–9, 47; power curtailed, 44–7, 51; relations with the Church, 200; status and prerogatives, 10, 36

Tschirsky, Count, 30

Tschizewskij, D., 286

Tsushima, naval battle of, 28

Tsvetayeva, Marina, 276

Tungus, 139, 145

Turkestan (Central Asia): communications, 180; cotton and gold, 178; Muslims of, 152–3, 186; revolt (1916), 176–7, 180; Russian conquest of, 174–82; Russian scientists in, 178–9; settlement of, 176–7, 181

Turkey, 12–13, 22, 192–3, 196

Tvardovsky, A. T., 285

Tyutchev, F. I., 270, 278

Ukraine (Little Russia): desire for home rule, 49, 162–4; nationalities question, 159–65; Protestant sects, 229

Union of Christian Politics, 220

Union of Democratic Orthodox Clergy and Laity, 222–3

Union of Freedom, Truth and Love of Peace, 232

Union of Municipalities, 81

Union of 17 October, *see* Octobrists

Union of the Russian People, 75, 213–15

Unions, professional, 63, 286

United States of America, 28, 30, 86–7, 102, 163, 287, 308–9

Ushinsky, K. D., 294

Uvarov, S. S., 74

Uzen Ada, 180

Vadkovsky, *see* Antony

Vaisite movement, 184

Vakhterov, V. P., 294

Valéry, Paul, 266

Valuyev, P. A., 161; Valuyev Commission, 122

Vannovsky, P. S., 298

Varnava (Nakropia), 224

Vasilchikov, Prince A. I., 124

Vekhi (signposts), 255–6, 258; *Vekhi* group, 219, 239

Verlaine, Paul, 266–7

Vernadsky, V. I., 252

Vetoshkin, M., 138

Village communities, *see* *Obshchina*

Vilna, 155–6, 172

Vinogradov, P. G., 298

Vladimir, Grand Duke, 15

Vladivostok, 143, 148

Volga district, 105, 117, 125, 182, 191, 194, 209

Voloshin, M. A., 275

Volosti (cantons), 40, 43, 57

Vostorgov, I. I., 216

Vvedensky, A. I., 223, 252

Vyborg, court of appeal, 168

Vysheslavtsev, B. P., 252

Vyshnegradsky, I. A., 11, 25–6, 99, 100, 123, 298

Wahhabis, 184, 187

War Industry Committees, 81

Warsaw, 156–7

Warsaw-Vienna railway, 158
Weber, Max, 44–5
Wheat, export of, 108, 146
Wichern, J. H., 222
Wiedenfeld, K., 108
Wilhelm I, 17–19
Wilhelm II, 19, 20, 22, 29–31
Windau, 174
Witte, Count S. Yu., 11, 22, 25–33, 71, 142; agrarian reform proposals, 123–8, 136; church reform, 208–10, 227; financial reforms, 27, 99–102; protectionist policies, 100–2, 106; role in Russia's foreign policy, 28–33; supports railway development, 142–3
Witte, Countess Mathilde, 31
Women, position of, 56, 166–7, 190
World of Art, 277

Yadrintsev, N. M., 138, 140, 142

Yakovenko, Boris, 236–7, 252
Yakubovich, P., 281
Yakuts, 140, 145
Yekaterinoslav, 292
Yeniseisk, 148
Yesenin, S. A., 277
Young Turks, 196
Yuzhakov, S. N., 259

Zadar University, 261
Zemgor, 81
Zemlya i Volya (Land and Freedom) organisation, 62
Zemsky Sobor (Land Assembly), 70, 75
Zemstvo system, 41–3, 57–8, 81, 202, 207, 304–5; nobles, 68–70, 72–4, 79, 121, 124–6; schools 292–4
Zenkovsky, Vasily, 245–6
Zhdanov, A. A., 264, 275
Zhitomir cathedral, 214
Znanie publishing house, 284